Politics, Law, and Comı

In a revisionist account of the history of Islamic political thought from the early to the late medieval period, this book focuses on the thought of Ibn Taymiyya, one of the most brilliant theologians of his day. The standard accounts of Sunni political history typically end with the classical period and thereby leave out Ibn Taymiyya's contribution. This original study demonstrates how his influence shed new light on the entire trajectory of Islamic political thought. Although he did not reject the Caliphate ideal, as is commonly believed, he nevertheless radically redefined it by turning it into a rational political institution intended to serve the community (umma). Through creative reinterpretation, he deployed the Qur'anic concept of fitra (divinely endowed human nature) to center the community of believers and its commonsense reading of revelation as the highest epistemic authority. In this way, he subverted the elitism that had become ensconced in classical theological, legal, and spiritual doctrines, and tried to revive the ethico-political, rather than strictly legal, dimension of Islam. In its reassessment of Ibn Taymiyya's work, this book marks a major departure from traditional interpretations of medieval Islamic thought.

Ovamir Anjum holds the Imam Khattab Endowed Chair of Islamic Studies in the Department of Philosophy at the University of Toledo.

Cambridge Studies in Islamic Civilization

Published titles are listed at the back of the book.

Politics, Law, and Community in Islamic Thought

The Taymiyyan Moment

OVAMIR ANJUM
University of Toledo

CAMBRIDGE
UNIVERSITY PRESS

CAMBRIDGE
UNIVERSITY PRESS

32 Avenue of the Americas, New York NY 10013-2473, USA

Cambridge University Press is part of the University of Cambridge.

It furthers the University's mission by disseminating knowledge in the pursuit of education, learning and research at the highest international levels of excellence.

www.cambridge.org
Information on this title: www.cambridge.org/9781107687110

First published 2012
First paperback edition 2014

A catalogue record for this publication is available from the British Library

Library of Congress Cataloguing in Publication data
Anjum, Ovamir, 1976–
Politics, law, and community in Islamic thought : the Taymiyyan moment / Ovamir Anjum.
p. cm. – (Cambridge studies in Islamic civilization)
Includes bibliographical references and index.
ISBN 978-1-107-01406-0 (hardback)
1. Islam and state – History. 2. Political science – Islamic Empire – History.
3. Ibn Taymiyah, Ahmad ibn ʿAbd al-Halim, 1263–1328 – Political and social views.
I. Title.
JC49.A755 2012
320.5′57–dc23 2011049110

ISBN 978-1-107-01406-0 Hardback
ISBN 978-1-107-68711-0 Paperback

Contents

PART II THE TAYMIYYAN INTERVENTION

Table

Preface

Gazing though my window across the Saad Zaghloul Square of Alexandria into the Mediterranean, I can hear chants of the Egyptian revolutionaries who now want to secure the gains of their proud and peaceful revolution of January 25, 2011. In this wildfire of revolutionary fervor that has spread through the Middle East and has caught the region by surprise, Islam is deeply relevant. This is not an "Islamic" revolution like that of Iran, as everyone across the board is insisting, yet, with the passing of days and weeks, questions surrounding of the role of Islam in the future of the Egyptian and the new Arab states generally seem to loom ever larger. The subject matter of this monograph – the relationship between politics, law, and reason in Islamic thought – even though it pertains to the medieval world, is brought to life for me continually as I meet with Egyptians of various stripes in the midst of the revolutionary fervor and see their unprecedented openness toward expression of political views. The classical Muslim figures whose thought is examined here are alive and well today in the sermons and writings of the ulama, preachers, and Islamists. Given the nature of the subject matter, it is only appropriate to attempt to bring it into conversation with the contemporary problems in Islamic political thought. In the following pages, I do so by raising the set of questions that I address in this monograph.

One problem is that of the role of the ulama in politics in Islamic history. The courageous and largely peaceful protests against the atrocious injustice and corruption of the ruling elite drew sympathy and admiration from even the most skeptical observers in the world. Yet, the negative response by the traditional Muslim scholarly elite, from the Grand Mufti of Egypt, Shaykh ʿAlī Jumʿa (Ali Gomaa), to the Syrian traditionalist icon,

Shaykh Muḥammad Saʿīd Ramaḍān al-Būṭī, and others to such protests, and at times even their support of the autocrats even in their last moments, has once again brought out the question that has puzzled Muslim thinkers and activists for more than a century of attempts at reform and nation building. On the one hand, a large number of Muslims continue to revere Islamic tradition and its authorities, the ulama. Yet, on the other hand, the same Muslim scholarly tradition seems to be out of touch with or utterly deny the need for political justice that the same Muslims so widely and desperately seek. No doubt, prominent ulama have long stood by, and at times even led such protest movements, and Islamic tradition has always possessed strands that reflect such concerns and have come to greater prominence in modern times. But it is difficult to deny the presence of arguably the predominant strand in Islamic scholarship since the onset of the classical period that has been characterized as quietist, apolitical, and compromising (in theory, not necessarily in personal conduct) toward usurpers of power. As far as scholastics and intellectuals are concerned, quietism is not an incomprehensible position, safer in the ideal world of pious discourse and intellectual coherence than in the real world of power and negotiation. A closer examination suggests, however, that the ulama neither embodied the romantic ideal of living a life above intrigues of power nor persistently lacked moral courage to criticize the rulers. What was lacking was not ulama's involvement with power, but any sustained effort to *theorize* power – that is, to articulate realistic conditions of political legitimacy and, relatedly, the willingness to share the authority to speak in God's name with the men of power. This was not because of any lack of conceptual resources in the foundational texts and early sacred history, but rather because of certain historical commitments of the Islamic discursive tradition.

Put differently, as the issue was raised in my conversations with many Arab interlocutors in the wake of many of the ulama's support of the status quo, my contention to them can be rephrased in this book as follows: It is not that the ulama who deny the significance of political justice are merely capitulating, or that they consistently believe that power is inherently corrupt, or that there is nothing wrong from their perspective with the political state of affairs, but that their response, whatever the immediate reasons, has its roots in an important, often the dominant – but far from the only – strand of Sunni tradition.

Another ubiquitous question on the mind of the modern observer of the Muslim world is that of the politicization of Islam. My investigation leads me to suggest that the right question, for a historian of premodern Islam anyway, is not how Islam became *politicized*, but how it came to be *depoliticized*. The phenomenon of depoliticization is far from a unique feature of Islamic tradition. A political historian of the West thus comments on a similar transformation in the Greco-Roman world:

> If we ask: what was the intellectual response to the primacy of power? The answer is that nowhere was the failure of political philosophy more effectively demonstrated than in its inability to account, in political terms, for this central fact in the political life of these centuries. Confronted with power, one impulse of political philosophy was to flee and seek refuge in a "golden age" located somewhere in the pre-political past.[1]

Comparable (and hence comprehensible) as I argue this phenomenon is, it cannot be fully explained by individual scholars' contributions or compromises, or any pathology essential to Islam. We must attend to the discursive traditions to which our individual authors contributed. Here, my inquiry is indebted to Talal Asad's notion of Islam as a discursive tradition. When addressing the question of compromise or any other fundamental transformation, I understand the working of traditions as being, to borrow an analogy from genetics, similar to how organisms pass down their traits; it is not the accidental loss of an organ or two that the offspring inherits, but rather genetic mutations. The genes of a tradition are its commitments and core arguments, and only when a "compromise" is made consistently and argued successfully through the core commitments of a tradition can it pass down and itself become a commitment. This analogy allows us to overcome the problem of the continuity of a tradition in time – like organisms, traditions continue through time without remaining perfectly identical to their ancestors. This analogy also commits us to the task of examining the discursive transformation rather than merely the isolated works or authors.

Then there is the question of the relationship of religion to state and politics in theory and (inevitably, given that we are dealing with a tradition) history. I address the question by deconstructing the concept of politics, mapping it onto the discourses and problems organically found in Islamic traditions. Enough scholars have expressed their dissatisfaction with the generalization that religion and politics have always been fused and inseparable in Islam (the problem here is with the categories

[1] Wolin, *Politics and Vision* (Princeton University Press, 2004), 83.

"religion" and "politics" even before we could ask about any fusion). Even the now more prevalent position that medieval Islamic societies really had become *secularized* because the ulama accepted the status quo such that they tended to Muslim community while the rulers drew their political wisdom and model of behavior from extra-Islamic sources does not entirely hold to scrutiny. The rulers did draw wisdom and inspiration and even legitimacy from extra-Islamic sources, and often their conduct showed no concern for Islamic ideals, but secularism is not merely worldliness or lack of piety any more than all concern for women's welfare can be branded feminism or labor justice communism. Secularism, instead, is an attempt to define and hence delimit "religion." And whereas "irreligion" and disbelief are far from absent in Islamic history, especially among the ruling and the intellectual elite, I find no evidence of a sustained discourse in medieval Islam, either by the ulama or the practitioners of statecraft, that rejects reference to Islam for legitimation and postulates an alternative. However, given that the claim is made essentially about the mainstream Sunni Muslim tradition, instead of undertaking the much more difficult task of arguing from absence, I examine the Sunni tradition and argue that rather than "secularism," what we find is a variety of complex and surprising attitudes toward the possibility of restraining political power. We find political pessimists, the dominant strand, who see no legitimate agency that could restrain power after it had become corrupt and turn their attention to developing a rich inner life that could weather the storms of political tyranny and struggles as God-sent trials. We also find, most remarkably in Ibn Taymiyya, political optimists who tried to articulate other possibilities. In neither case can we speak of either secularism or theocracy as being the traditional ideal.

The Arab Spring once again has brought to the fore questions about the calls for a Sharīʿa-bound state and the possibility of an Islamic political sphere. More specifically, the question is that of the institutional protection of political justice in Islamic tradition, articulated more frequently as that of the compatibility of Islam with democracy. I do not claim to offer an answer to that specific question, but to one that I think is logically prior to it. Importing democratic institutions is once again sounding like an attractive (or perhaps the only) option, but to Muslim intellectuals, if the new institutions and their conceptual framework are not genetically incorporated into Islamic discursive tradition, they run the risk of lasting only briefly like foreign implants into Muslim societies. The less than admirable record of the political success of experimentation with various Western models in Muslim countries shows that this risk is not negligible.

As attempts are made afresh to transplant or grow new institutions, a better understanding of the "genome" of Islamic tradition is advisable.

My project of trying to understand Islam and politics goes as far back in my intellectual life as I can think, but its first evidence can be found during my years at the University of Chicago as I struggled to understand the disparate claims of contemporary Islamist movements and what appeared to be decidedly confused modern scholarship on the subject. My interest took a definite form as a project in intellectual history as a result of my years at the University of Wisconsin-Madison. Formative in this process were conversations with my graduate advisor, Professor Michael Chamberlain. His guidance and uplifting critiques were unfailing motivations for me to think and rethink all my arguments during my graduate work. His focus on method rather than the content of my work allowed me just the right kind of freedom and imposed perhaps just the right discipline. Numerous enlightening and enjoyable conversations with Professor David Morgan helped me get a sense of the topography of Islamic history and historiography as we struggled through classical Persian texts. Both of them have given me the support and encouragement that have made this project possible.

Professor Sherman Jackson, then at the University of Michigan, Ann Arbor, was another source of formative inspiration both through his scholarship and his humanity. I remain particularly in debt of the numerous hours he spent with me, especially during the fall of 2006, as I drove back and forth between Madison and Ann Arbor, punctuating my eight-hour drive with a stop every now and then to jot down an idea or a question. We read legal and theological texts, debated them passionately, and reflected on their meanings in the context of the medieval as well as the modern world. These conversations allowed me to challenge, almost playfully, aspects of Islamic legal tradition, and to do so with the comfort of being constantly checked and challenged by a leading authority on the subject. That intellectual experimentation, received with extraordinary encouragement, has proved seminal for my ongoing thinking of the interaction of the political and the legal in Islam.

Other scholars whose suggestions and critiques have helped me greatly include William Courtenay and Johann Sommerville, working in medieval and early modern Western traditions, Asifa Quraishi, in Islamic law, Charles Cohen, in the early American Christianity, and Kamal Karpat, in Ottoman and Islamic history – all at the University of Wisconsin. Hassan Laidi and Mustafa A. Mustafa, both seasoned connoisseurs of

Arabic scholarship, classical and modern, respectively, have been long-time friends and mentors, with whom I have read too many Arabic texts and debated too many issues, from theology and law to social science and politics, to recall now. I appreciate their generosity in time and spirit. I am grateful to my students over the years, whose questions have invariably improved my thinking on the subject. Numerous teachers, friends, and students who have shaped my thinking on the subject, alas, remain unnamed here, and not because I am any less grateful to them. The many shortcomings in this work are only mine.

Lastly, I should acknowledge the debts that are formative for me and not just my work. My wife Sarah, whose love and encouragement never fails me, and my children Ibraheem, Rahma, Ahmad, and now Safa, who are the "coolness of my eyes and heart" – give me my best reasons to try and to care about the world around me. My parents' faith, love, and generosity, their belief in virtue and charity, their reverence for learning, and confidence in the worth of what I do, often without much evidence, have been my greatest assets. It is to them that I dedicate this work.

Conventions and Abbreviations

I have generally followed the *IJMES* (see bibliography for abbreviations) conventions for transliterating Arabic. However, for the sake of simplicity, I have generally dropped special characters from names that are commonly used. I have also generally omitted the ending "h" that represents *tā marbūṭa*; thus "Sunnah" appears as "Sunna." I have also dropped after the definitive article "al" before proper names that appear frequently after their first mention (thus, al-Ghazālī appears as Ghazālī) except to avoid confusion (thus, al-Shāfiʿī gets to keep "al" to distinguish him from the Shāfiʿīs, the adherents of his school). Furthermore, for commonly known Arabic words, I omit italicization and special characters, thus: Allah (not Allāh, except when transliterating) and ulama (not *ʿulamāʾ*).

Introduction

> Islamic law is the epitome of the Islamic spirit, the most typical manifestation of the Islamic way of life, the kernel of Islam itself. For the majority of Muslims, the law has always been and still is of much greater practical importance than the dogma.[1]

> The community of scholars and holy men were the ones who truly carried on the legacy of the Prophet.... In this tradition, the realm of Islamic authenticity lies within the soul of the individual and in the relations of individuals to each other within small communities. This is the Islam that sees holiness and religion as incompatible with state power. Politics are expected to be violent and corrupt .... This renunciation of political utopianism may help explain some cases of acquiescence to patrimonial regimes and the relative weakness of democratic or other secular utopian movements in the present-day Middle East.[2]

Two observations about Islamic civilization have been commonplace, shared by Western as well as, often, Muslim observers. The first is the success and predominance of law in Islam; Islam is seen as "nomocratic and nomocentric."[3] The second is the failure of Islamic politics or the Muslim political enterprise to enact coherent and stable political institutions and of Islamic normative political thought to provide realistic guidance

[1] J. Schacht, "Pre-Islamic Background and Early Development of Jurisprudence," *Formation of Islamic Law*, ed. W. Hallaq (Ashgate Publishing, 2004), 29.

[2] I. Lapidus, "The Golden Age: The Political Concepts of Islam," *The Annals of the American Academy of Political and Social Science* 524 (1992): 16–17.

[3] In George Makdisi's words, "In the realm of religion, everything must be legitimized through the schools of law. For Islam is nomocratic and nomocentric" (idem, "Ḥanbalī Islam," in M. Swartz (ed.), *Studies on Islam* [Oxford University Press, 1981], 264).

to governments or avert cycles of tyranny, violence, and rebellion.[4] This failure has been attributed, on the one hand, to the high-minded idealism of the ulama, for governments insufficiently legitimated in terms of the normative apparatus of the society remained prone to continual rebellions. On the other hand, the ulama have also been held responsible for expediently lowering criteria for legitimacy and justifying any usurper, which has encouraged military aspirants to power.[5] Some revisionists question the idea of the failure of medieval Islamic political institutions but concede that normative Islamic political thought has been too impractical, idealistic, or otherwise deficient.[6] Others argue that whereas Muslim political reality indeed belied Islamic ideals, the ulama had in fact adjusted to a secular reality while paying lip service to the early golden age. And whereas the politics failed, the law, "[a]s a moral force, and without the coercive tool of a state … stood supreme for over a millennium."[7]

Yet, Islam is perhaps unique among world's religions in that it began with a resounding "political" triumph that was fueled by not just the religious zeal but also the political genius of its vanguard.[8] The Prophet of Islam was seen by his followers as a role model in political wisdom and leadership as much as in matters of spiritual guidance, social relationships, and otherworldly asceticism. Traditional accounts of the Prophet and his companions portray them as political leaders, not jurists. A judge

[4] One scholar observes: "Western scholars have long pointed to political instability as a besetting weakness of the Islamic tradition. The usual line has been that Muslims did not think government religiously indifferent but rather expected it to follow clear religious guidelines; that actual governments have never found it possible to live entirely by these guidelines" (C. Melchert, review of *Religion and Politics under the Early Abbasids* by M. Q. Zaman, *ILS* 6.2 [1999]: 272).

[5] B. Lewis, *Islam in History*, 2nd ed. (Open Court Publishing, 2001), 314.

[6] A. Hess, "The Legend of Political Failure," *JNES* 44.1 (1985): 31.

[7] W. Hallaq, *Sharīʿa* (Cambridge University Press, 2009), 125.

[8] C. Robinson, "Prophecy and Holy Men in Islam," in *The Cult of Saints in Late Antiquity and the Middle Ages*, eds. J. Howard-Johnston and P. A. Hayward (Oxford University Press, 1999), writes, "Whatever role the Prophet played in the genesis of Islamic law, there can be no question that the earliest stages of the tradition charted his career not so much as a law maker, but as a reforming monotheist battling the polytheist of the Peninsula; thus recording his *maghāzī* ('raids') appears to have all but monopolized the writing of Prophetic biography until well into the eight century" (250). F. Donner, *Early Islamic Conquests* (Princeton University Press, 1981) argues the early Islamic conquests were well planned and executed, that they were part of a state policy wherein the state was run by a group that was able to achieve an "organizational breakthrough of proportions unparalleled in the history of Arabian society," and that "the conquests were truly an *Islamic* movement. For it was Islam – the set of religious beliefs preached by Muhammad, with its social and political ramifications – that ultimately sparked the whole integration process and hence was the ultimate cause of the conquests' success" (269).

in his community the Prophet certainly was – the final judge of all matters indeed[9] – but not one who was known to have invested much time in constructing a formal system of law.[10] Similarly, his successors, the "Rightly Guided" (*Rāshidūn*) Caliphs, were rulers, statesmen, and ascetics. Men of legal or theological speculation they were not. Following the way of God mattered to them eminently, the tradition has no qualms about that, but they did not care to systematize law.

However, during much of the classical or early medieval period (fourth–seventh/tenth–thirteenth century),[11] the ulama – the "heirs of prophets"[12] – were, first and foremost, jurists (*fuqahā'*), practitioners of a growing body of *fiqh*[13] and the sole guardians of the *Sharīʿa*.[14] They were not statesmen, political thinkers, military commanders, popular leaders, missionaries, or even primarily theologians or mystics: They were jurists,

[9] The Qur'an states: "Nay [O Prophet], by your Lord, they have no faith until they make you in all disputes between them the [final] judge, and find in their selves no resistance against your decisions, and submit fully" (4:65).

[10] My point is not, as Schacht thought, that "in the time of the Prophet, law as such fell outside of the sphere of religion, and as far as there were not religious or moral objections to specific transactions or modes of behavior, the technical aspects of the law were a matter of indifference to the Muslims" (idem., *An Introduction to Islamic Law* [Clarendon Press, 1962], 19). Given the fair number of qur'anic legal commandments, such a view cannot be sustained; my point is only about the relative significance of systemizing law.

[11] The term "medieval" has been used to designate the period following the decline of the High Abbasid Caliphate until the rise of the Ottoman Empire (fourth–tenth/tenth–sixteenth centuries). This period was interrupted by the Mongol onslaught in 656/1258; hence divided between the "early medieval" period, also called the "classical" period (fourth–seventh/tenth–thirteenth centuries) and the post-Mongol "late medieval" period (seventh–tenth/thirteenth–sixteenth centuries). This periodization resembles Marshall Hodgson's "high Middle Ages" and "late Middle Ages," although I do not endorse his judgment on the earlier period as being more creative or productive than the latter. M. Hodgson, *Rethinking World History*, ed. E. Burke III (Cambridge University Press, 1993), 178–81.

[12] This is a widely held concept that appears in a longer *ḥadīth* graded by traditional critics variously as *ṣaḥīḥ* (sound), *ḥasan* (acceptable), or *ḍaʿīf* (weak). See A. Wensinck, *Concordance*, IV:321.

[13] The term *fiqh* (literally, understanding) is variously translated into English as "jurisprudence," or "law," or "positive law" (as opposed to theoretical jurisprudence, which is called *uṣūl al-fiqh*). In early Islam, as in Q, 9:122, it seems to have referred to a practical and acquired understanding of the religion associated most immediately with practical knowledge, piety, and religious exhortation and admonition. Since the classical age, Johansen informs us, it has come to mean "a system of rules and methods whose authors consider it to be the normative interpretation of the revelation, the application of its principles and commands to the field of human acts. It classifies and sanctions human acts, gives ethical and legal guidance to the believers" (B. Johansen, *Contingency in a Sacred Law: Legal and Ethical Norms in the Muslim Fiqh* [Brill, 1998], 1).

[14] See Chapter 1.

concerned with standardizing and formalizing the law as their principal obligation. Islam had now become primarily encoded in the law that they interpreted.[15] Furthermore, in the mutually reinforcing spiritual and intellectual milieus, the dominant mode of medieval religiosity saw political engagement as corrupt and corrupting. In medieval spiritual discourses of the ulama and the Sufis, a frequent theme is advice against associating with the rulers. "The worst of the ulama are those who seek after the rulers, and the best of the rulers are those who seek after the ulama,"[16] goes a popular adage. This adage expresses the predominant ideal (albeit not reality) of the classical relationship between politics and piety more truly than the formal theories of government. This was the ideal of the pious fleeing the world, and rulers chasing after them for their blessing but, so long as they remained engaged in worldly politics, unable to attain it. The social historian Ira Lapidus puts this perhaps too starkly: "Despite the origins of Islam and its own teachings about the relationship between religious and political life, Islamic society has evolved in un-Islamic ways."[17]

Explaining this transformation in his study of the fourth/tenth- and fifth/eleventh-century Islamic societies, when the Abbasid Caliphate had become reduced to a mere symbol of continuity for the emerging Sunni community and actual power had fallen into the hands of military adventurers like the Buyids in Iraq, Roy Mottahedeh observes that "the weakness of government threw society back on its own resources."[18] Mottahedeh

[15] Many scholars have noted this near-complete legalization of Islam. R. Bulliet writes, "Law was now enshrined as the central concern of Muslim scholars from the very beginning. Although the law schools took shape well after the lifetimes of the Prophet, his immediate successors, and even the schools' namesakes, Islam now came to be considered almost synonymous with *Sharīʿa* (idem., "Islamic Reform or 'Big Crunch'?" *Harvard Middle East and Islamic Review* 8 [2009]: 10–11). Hallaq notes even more starkly that it was *jurists* and no one else, not even theologians or mystics, who were the sole carriers of Islamic legal authority and indeed "the custodians of Muslim societies" and "spiritual and practical guides of the *umma*" who controlled, in addition to the legal system, "the entire infra- and super- structures of legal education; they ran what we might term municipal affairs." Briefly, "[t]he legal profession, with the jurists at its head, was therefore at once a religious, moral, social, and legal force" (idem., "Juristic Authority vs. State Power: The Legal Crisis of Modern Islam," *Journal of Law and Religion* 19.2 [2003–4]: 246).

[16] *Iḥyāʾ*, 2:179–80. Notably, there is no category of nonoppressive rulers in this discourse; it is taken for granted that the rulers are oppressive and this-worldly.

[17] I. Lapidus, "The Separation of State and Religion in the Development of Early Islamic Society," *IJMES* 6.4 (1975): 364.

[18] R. Mottahedeh, *Loyalty and Leadership in an Early Islamic Society* (Princeton University Press, 1980), 39.

goes on to conclude that "[b]y disengaging itself from government and the moral burdens of government, and at the same time giving enormous power to government, Islamic society of the Buyid period freed itself to maintain a community of duties and obligations in levels of life below government." This community "took over many of the functions of government" while allowing its members to maintain "the fiction of a universal Islamic caliphate." The relationships and institutions that developed in this milieu proved resilient enough to "withstand repeated changes of central government." In fact, this adaptation to life without politics was so successful that this community "has never entirely disappeared."[19] While it brings to the fore the adaptive genius of classical Islamic society and the social and cultural processes by which collective life could go on without politics and its moral burdens, Mottahedeh's obituary of the "political" in Muslim societies is silent about the causes and mechanisms of this disengagement and sanguine about its consequences.

Legal historians too have noted versions of the same paradox. Through his study of the structure of rights and obligations in the classical Ḥanafī fiqh, Baber Johansen asks why it was that "Muslim scholars throughout Islamic history acknowledged the fact that, in order to survive, the Muslim community needed a strong military and political force whose prerogatives they described as absolute, while at the same time deploring the injustices of the rulers and declaring that being among the retinue of the sultan constitutes a religious blemish[.]"[20]

The traditional Sunni response to this bewilderment would have been that the ideal of Islam is rule by a righteous caliph who unites the entire Community, like the first four "Rightly Guided" Caliphs, and decides its affairs through *shūrā* (consultation). But after the caliphate has been lost and kings (*mulūk* or sultans) have come to power, the Community lives in a state of emergency, guided instead by the ulama, awaiting the return of the true caliphate. The ideal caliphate would now be theorized by the ulama and form the cornerstone of Islamic political thought.[21] To maintain order, however, one had to deal with the ruling sultans just as, in Ghazālī's words, one is forced, in the absence of wholesome food, to eat carrion in order to save life.[22]

[19] Ibid., 190.

[20] Johansen, *Contingency*, 189.

[21] In the words of E. I. J. Rosenthal, Islamic "[p]olitical thought at first centers around the caliphate and is, in fact, a theory of the caliphate, its origins and purpose" (*Political Thought in Medieval Islam* [Cambridge University Press, 1962], 3).

[22] *Iqtiṣād*, 130.

Modern observers, impatient with this premodern attitude of life-in-waiting and messianic hopes, complain of the dysfunctional, utopian nature of classical Muslim political models that neither reflects their own reality nor serves to guide the modern one.[23] Notwithstanding a broad brush, Malcolm Kerr's following statement is a fine example of the disenchanted evaluation of the caliphate ideal:

> The failure of the constitutional theory of the Caliphate to provide a sufficiently positive allocation of procedural sovereignty disqualified it from serving as a practical constitutional instrument. It can perhaps be better understood as an apologia for the cumulative historical record of the institution and a defense of Sunnite practice against Shīʿite criticism, than as a reliable expression of what its exponents actually believed was the structure of rights, duties, procedures, and functions that they could normally expect to be observed.[24]

And:

> As the doctrine of necessity came to be invoked on a massive scale, suspension of legal requirements and bowing to the inevitable was not a matter of prudence in exceptional circumstances, but a resigned admission of powerlessness, with no comfort save the thought that times of evil and misfortune were the will of God. And in place of the essentially civic function of the caliph as law-enforcing executive, emphasis was put on the fanciful spiritual aura of his office and the assumption that while the sultan had been delegated effective civil authority, the caliph retained his symbolic religious prestige.[25]

But these accounts, both the traditional apologia and its modern critique miss something important about the nature of medieval Muslim societies. Ideals and realities have a strange way of adjusting to each other, and Muslims indeed did not just live in a waiting room eating carrion. As this society learned to live without government, there emerged an entire panoply of sociolegal institutions that provided another ideal to live by. This was the ideal of the otherworldly ulama and the pious living a life bound by law innocent of power and its machinations. This was just an ideal, of course, or perhaps a soothing myth.[26] In reality, the ulama – by no means a monolithic or static group – historically often remained involved

[23] M. Kerr, *Islamic Reform* (University of California Press, 1966), 12–13.

[24] Ibid.

[25] Ibid., 26.

[26] It should be emphasized that my observation pertains a persistent, if not the dominant, classical *ideal*, not the reality. A glimpse of this ideal can be found in a tenth-/sixteenth-century compilation of sundry *ḥadīth* reports that circulated as early as the second/eighth and third/ninth centuries: Jalāl al-Dīn al-Suyūṭī (d. 911/1505), *Mā rawāhu al-asāṭīn fī ʿadm majīʾ ilā al-salāṭīn* (What the Masters have Narrated in Prohibition of Visiting Kings) (ed., Majdī Fatḥī al-Sayyid, Dār al-Ṣaḥāba li ʾl-Turāth, 1411/1991).

in power as resisters, critics, advisors, collaborators, or exploiters. The two ideals, nonetheless, coexisted; given the sheer sanctity of the first missionary ideal enshrined in the Qur'an, the Sunna and the founding history, which required active engagement with the world, the second ideal, which made bearable the medieval reality of the ubiquitous illegitimacy of power, remained ever reverent of the first, hence was rarely articulated. It persisted in pietistic tropes and romantic selectivity toward early history, while in fact ordering life such as to make the first ideal ever more impossible to imagine.[27] The legalistic and apolitical, if not antipolitical, tempo of classical Islam became inscribed in the cannons of law, theology, and spirituality that continued to animate much of Muslim traditional vision of life until the onset of the modern age. The spread of modernity in the Muslim world has challenged this attitude and revitalized and sharpened the tension between ideals and realities.

In this study, I investigate the complex interplay of the two ideals of political life in Islam: the explicit ideal of a unified and vibrant religio-political life under a righteous caliph, and the alternate ideal of religious and spiritual life innocent of politics. In particular, my interest is to shed light on the transformation that led to the disappearance of the "political sphere" in the classical period. I begin by delineating the conceptual domain of the "political" in Islamic history and trace the history of intellectual attitudes and often silent presumptions underpinning political life, focusing in particular on a moment when the political ideas and attitudes of classical Islam were thoroughly questioned. This moment is the intervention in Islamic history of the well-known, controversial, and prodigious Ibn Taymiyya (d. 728/1328)[28] who, I contend, attempted to revive aspects of the early ideal of Islam partly by reconciling the two ideals and partly by critiquing and rejecting some key classical developments. Contextualized in the larger trajectory of Islamic thought, Ibn Taymiyya's critique of the theological, legal, and political traditions of the classical age allows us to better understand

[27] Among the attempts to capture this duality of ideals, notable are Lapidus, "The Golden Age," and Kerr, *Islamic Reform*. Kerr describes this as a "pessimistic consciousness of the tension between ideal and actuality" that underlies "the Islamic tradition of social thought," which led the medieval ulama to elaborate "their conceptions of the ideal," leaving the actual society to "cope with actualities by evolving its own practical, but largely unacknowledged, psychological and social mechanisms" (1).

[28] Taqī al-Dīn Abū al-ʿAbbās Aḥmad b. ʿAbd al-Ḥalīm b. ʿAbd al-Salām b. Taymiyya al-Ḥarrānī, born in Ḥarrān (Iraq, present-day Turkey) in 661/1263, and died at the age of sixty-eight in 728/1263. He lived in the era of the Baḥri Mamluks in Damascus with long stays in Cairo during his adult life.

the nature and relationship of the two ideals and leads us to see Islamic political thought in a new light.

Standard accounts of Islamic political thought typically end with classical authors such as Ghazālī, whereas later thinkers are treated at best as insipid continuation of the essential doctrines that had already been articulated in the classical period. In particular, the conventional view of late medieval political thought in the Mamluk world has been quite dismal.[29] Marshall Hodgson, for instance, writes: "Unless future research discloses unsuspected highlights, we must feel that precisely in the Late Middle Ages politics became as irrelevant as they ever have been in any civilized society. Such a state of affairs is reflected by the political thought of the period, which apparently abandoned all hope of forming political life according to its norms."[30]

Ulrich Haarmann asserts even more directly the relative "paucity of political writing in Mamluk Egypt and Syria," particularly compared to post-Mongol Persia, where some Muslim thinkers postulated "the concentration of spiritual guidance and executive power in the one and single hand of the *imam-sultan*." Mamluk Egypt and Syria, he writes, were rather barren in political thought during this time, because, he reasons, "[t]he consciousness of having been spared the pagan yoke of the vile Mongol foe produced a sentiment of rigorous fealty to the traditional social and legal norms in their Arab and orthodox garb! – *thus one may well formulate the doctrine not only of Ibn Taymiyya, the great religious thinker of early Mamluk times, but of social and legal thought in the Mamluk period at large*."[31] The failure of the political thought of this period owed to

> [t]he retrograde orientation of Mamluk society [which] impeded the contemporary observers in perceiving the inevitable institutional changes. The *de facto* disappearance of the caliphate was not made the starting point for a new theory of government. The old fiction of al-Ghazzālī's time was dragged along .... The radical changes the Mamluk system of government introduced were kept out of systematic speculation, huge as the number of jurists in this very period was. This silence refers both to the nature of the Mamluk ruling caste (were there limits to their political, military and economic power?), and to the consequential

[29] For a comprehensive bibliography of Mamluk studies, which lacks any recent works on the political thought of the period, see http://www.lib.uchicago.edu/e/su/mideast/mamluk/ (accessed October 25, 2006.)

[30] Hodgson, *Rethinking*, 182–3.

[31] U. Haarmann, "Rather the Injustice of the Turks Than the Righteousness of the Arabs-Changing 'Ulama Attitudes Towards Mamlûk Rule in the Late Fifteenth Century," *SI* 68 (1988): 61–2 (emphasis added).

relationship between the Mamluk elite, the *nās*, and the local population, to whom they, the ulama, themselves belonged.[32]

To the contrary, I show in this study that the disappearance of the caliphate in the post-Mongol world was indeed made the starting point for what we may call a new theory of government, one that was made up of elements from the early political model as well as classical institutions. Indeed, despite the range and depth of his engagements and polemics, Ibn Taymiyya's reformist endeavors can be best understood as a *political* project, namely one fundamentally concerned with the revival of the political sphere in Islam that had vanished in the classical age. To anyone familiar with the staggering scope of Ibn Taymiyya's writings, most of which fall in the realms of scriptural hermeneutics, theology, and jurisprudence, this claim would appear to be unwarranted or exaggerated. Unless, that is, "political" is freed from its common usage as relating to self-interested and even hypocritical action and is restored to its pride of place as relating to the highest activity of envisioning and enabling the collective pursuit of the good of the community. The word "political," of course, is a modifier, applicable to a wide range of nouns: thought, practice, community, agency, and so on, all of which, when so modified, are straddled by a mode of reasoning. If one is to excavate Islamic history for political ideas, one must carefully understand that mode of reasoning.

I therefore explore Islamic political thought by examining a large array of writings, some already familiar to modern scholars, others not; some on political subjects, others not hitherto seen as relevant. This way of reading Islamic political thought, to reiterate, is based on two methodological contentions. Firstly, it questions and then remaps how the very category "political" has been constructed in the studies on the subject. Drawing on developments in recent political theory, I argue that the political domain of thinking in any thought-world is grounded in its fundamental commitments and often silent presuppositions. Modern scholars have often understood Islamic political thought through the study of classical treatises on the caliphate, but have largely ignored the theoretical underpinnings of political life in epistemology, theology, and legal theory. Political mode of thinking is like one piece of a complex, interlocked edifice; singling it out of its natural conceptual setting for analysis and comparing it with its look-alike in another tradition is bound to find it anomalous.

[32] Ibid., 62. Haarman refers to "the polarization between ulama and umara" (66) as being Ibn Taymiyya's social model, a conclusion directly opposed by many other recent studies, including the present one.

This is not to suggest that Islamic political thought cannot be examined outside of its original habitat, so to say, or by an adherent of another tradition; indeed, the recognition of these dependencies and sensibilities is likely to make for a more illuminating comparison and even judgment.

The task imposed by the first methodological orientation gives rise to the second: to examine and evaluate Islamic political thought as being part of Islamic discursive tradition – that is, by recognizing the centuries-long dialogues in which Islamic political writers consciously participated.[33] This study, therefore, is conceived not primarily as one of Ibn Taymiyya's political thought per se, but of conversations on political ideas in which he participated. A third way in which the present study departs from conventional studies on the subject is its emphasis on a conservative figure, a Ḥanbalī traditionalist[34] of the Mamluk period. Until recently, he had been seen as a literalist, anti-rationalist, and traditionalist (each of these amorphous terms is taken to imply each other);[35] at best, scarcely original,

[33] Both of these commitments are captured by the concept of "discursive tradition," which I discuss in O. Anjum, "Islam as a Discursive Tradition: Talal Asad and His Interlocutors," *Comparative Studies of South Asia, Africa and the Middle East* 27.3 (2007): 671–2.

[34] In the period before the *Miḥna*, I use the term "traditionalist" to mean what scholars have variously referred to as the "consensus-minded" community (R. Mottahedeh, *Loyalty and Leadership in an Early Islamic Society* [Princeton University Press, 1980], 19–20), or "proto-Sunnis" (M. Q. Zaman, *Religion and Politics under the Early Abbasids: The Emergence of the Proto-Sunni Elite* [Brill, 1997]), or what M. Watt refers to as "the moderate or center party in the general religious movement" (M. Watt, *Formative Period*, 100). At this stage, traditionalists are to be contrasted with the Muʿtazila, the Shīʿa, and the Khārijīs. Their characteristic but not strictly marked attitudes can be said to be as follows: (1) adherence to the Prophet's *sunna*, largely through *ḥadīth*, Medinan custom, or the practice of the first two or three pious generations; (2) emphasis on some kind of sanctity of the general community (*jamāʿa*) rather than radical claims of any kind; (3) their reverence for the memory of Abū Bakr and ʿUmar, the first two successors, because they best followed the *sunna* and the collective existence of the Community was properly organized in their reigns as a *jamāʿa*; hence the label *Ahl al-Sunna wa 'l-Jamāʿa* on which they settled sometime in the third/ninth century. The first appearance of the term *ahl al-sunna* is noted with Muḥammad b. Sīrīn (d. 110/729) (Zaman, 49). By their foes, they were labeled often as the *Ḥashwiyya* (the riffraff, the commoners). Even with the pejorative connotation, the basic denotation of the "larger community" is identifiable (Ibid., 54). After the *Miḥna* of Aḥmad b. Ḥanbal and the consolidation of Sunni orthodoxy, I use this term to refer to those Sunnis who rejected *kalām* and were known as *ahl al-ḥadīth* (the *ḥadīth* folks), and often identified with the Ḥanbalīs, although found in all legal schools. "Traditionalist" is not to be confused with "traditionist"; the latter refers to *ḥadīth* critics (*muḥaddithūn*) who were often but not always ideologically traditionalist.

[35] M. Fakhry, *A History of Islamic Philosophy*, 2nd ed. (Columbia University Press, 1983), 312–8, who calls Ibn Taymiyya's critique of philosophy "misology" whose seeds, he maintains, had been sown by Ghazālī (312); Ibn Taymiyya's work and of those influenced by him, like Ibn al-Qayyim, are further characterized as "antirationalist reaction to theology,

opposed to all that modern scholars find subtle and sublime, such as Sufism, reason, and philosophy. His influence was seen as limited to and best represented by Wahhabism.[36] The traditional Muslim informants, themselves sharply divided about Ibn Taymiyya, had been at least partly responsible for this image. The ideas and practices that he attacked and the scholarly establishment that underpinned them remained in vogue for centuries to come and did not receive his uncompromising censure passively. The last two centuries have seen an enormous rise in interest in Ibn Taymiyya among various Muslim reform movements, which is only beginning to reflect in Western scholarship in the last two decades or so. An early exception to this general neglect of Ibn Taymiyya was Henri Laoust, whose treatment of Ibn Taymiyya's social and political thought, comprehensive and insightful, was for the most part ignored for several decades.[37] The results of the new research have been surprising. Ibn Taymiyya's mastery of *falsafa* is now understood to have surpassed that of most Muslim theologians, emulating, in Yahya Michot's assessment, that of the great Ashʿarī-philosopher, Rāzī.[38] His approach toward Sufism is now appreciated as quite complex, reflective of deep appreciation of, if not involvement with, what he considered genuine Sufism of its early masters and critical primarily toward what he believed to be some

philosophy and mysticism"; Ibn Taymiyya's "inflexible" opposition to rationalism was complemented by "an insistence on the necessity of returning to the orthodox ways of the 'pious forebears,' or the first generation of Muslims" (318). George Makdisi, although he did not share the vehemence displayed by Fakhry, also characterized Ibn Taymiyya in his early writings as belonging to the camp of "anti-rationalist traditionalism" that opposed "rationalist Ashʿarism." G. Makdisi, "Ashʿari and the Ashʿarīs in Islamic Religious History," *SI* 17 (1962): 37–80. In a later article (1975), he seems to have completely changed his view of Ibn Taymiyya (G. Makdisi, "Ḥanbalī Islam," 256–62.)

[36] Representing the common wisdom, Rosenthal states that Ibn Taymiyya's "views found little favour in his own day unexpectedly bore more fruit after his death in the reformist theology of Muhammad b. 'Abd al-Wahhab (d. 1787)." (Ibid.) In contrast, Fakhry notes in dismay that the eighth/fourteenth century was the Ḥanbalī century because of Ibn Taymiyya's influence.

[37] H. Laoust, *Essai sur les doctrines sociales et politique de Taki-D-Din Ahmad b. Taymiya* (Imprimerie de l'Institute Francais D'Archeologie Oriental, 1939). On the neglect of Laoust's work until the last quarter of the twentieth century, see Maksidi, "Ḥanbalī Islam."

[38] See Y. Michot, "A Mamlūk Theologian's Commentary on Ibn Sīnā' s *Risāla Aḍḥawiyya:* Being a Translation of a Part of the *Dar' al-Taʿāruḍ* of Ibn Taymiyya, With Introduction, Annotation, and Appendices," *JIS* 14 (2003): 149–203 (Part I) and 309–63 (Part II), 157, for his philosophical acumen and nuanced critique of Ibn Sīnā and *kalām* scholars alike, and Hallaq, *Ibn Taymiyya Against the Greek Logicians* (Oxford University Press, 1993), for an argument for his pioneering synthesis of nominalist and empiricist epistemology, as well as his deconstruction of Greek logic.

later accretions.[39] His influence in the centuries intervening his own time and the modern period seems to have been continuing and significant, but despite some worthy studies, a thorough investigation of the matter remains a desideratum.[40] His jurisprudential reforms have had crucial influence on a range of reformers in the Muslim world ranging from the Mogul to the Ottoman Empires.[41] His influence, however, far exceeds what would be expected from this patchy and slow recovery of his influences on various traditional disciplines; it is no exaggeration to say that there is scarcely a Muslim reformer since the eighteenth century who has not related to and drawn on Ibn Taymiyya's legacy in one way or another. The historical record from the Mamluk period shows that Ibn Taymiyya was not just another scholar; his knowledge, ascetic piety, and activism astounded friends and foes – both of which he made many – and turned him into a phenomenon with whom anyone who discoursed on religion had to contend. As the ninth-/fifteenth-century Cairean historian Maqrīzī notes, since the rise of the Ashʿarī school, the next major event in Sunni Islam was its critique by Ibn Taymiyya, who "championed the school of the salaf and did his utmost to refute the Ashʿarī school," and as a result, "people were divided into two groups":

> A group that followed him, relied upon his views, acted in accordance with his opinions, held him as Shaykh al-Islām and the most prominent preserver of the Islamic *umma*. The other group declared him to be a heretic, a deviant,

[39] See G. Makdisi, "Ibn Taymīya: A Sūfi of the Qādiriya Order," *The American Journal of Arabic Studies* 1(1973): 118–29, who proposes that Ibn Taymiyya was a certified Sufi; T. Michel, "Ibn Taymiyya's *Sharḥ* on the *Futūḥ al-Ghayb* of ʿAbd al-Qādir al-Jīlānī," *Hamdard Islamicus* 4.2 (1981): 3–12, who presents a more complex view; O. Anjum, "Sufism without Mysticism? Ibn Qayyim al-Jawziyya's Objectives in *Madārij al-Sālikin*," in *A Scholar in the Shadow: Essays in Legal and Theological Thought of Ibn Qayyim al-Jawziyya*, eds. C. Bori and L. Holtzman (Oriente Moderno, 2010), 113–39, where I evaluate claims of Ibn Taymiyya's relationship to Sufism based on his and his disciple Ibn al-Qayyim's writings and argue that neither he nor his student ever embraced the title "Sufi"; they were deeply sympathetic to Sufism while also remaining skeptical of not only popular practices and philosophical mysticism, but the epistemological basis of mystical Sufism, attempting to recover what I call nonmystical Sufism of the early period.

[40] Cf. K. al-Rouayheb, "From Ibn Ḥajar al-Haythamī (d. 1566) to Khayr al-Dīn al-Ālūsī (d. 1899): Changing Views of Ibn Taymiyya among Non-Ḥanbalī Sunni Scholars," in *Ibn Taymiyya and His Times*, eds. Rapoport and Ahmed.

[41] O. Arabi, "Contract Stipulations (*Shurūṭ*) in Islamic Law: The Ottoman Majalla and Ibn Taymiyya," *IJMES* 30.1 (1998): 9–50, for the influence of his liberal opinions on the issue of contracts on the Ottoman legal practice; K. A. Nizami, "The Impact of Ibn Taimiyya on South Asia," *JIS* 1(1990): 129–49, for his influence on the Muslim governance and reform in South Asia.

rebuked him for affirming divine attributes, and censured him over his juristic opinions ... in some of which they claimed he opposed the consensus of the Muslims (*ijmāʿ*).[42]

Although an investigation of Ibn Taymiyya's thought is significant in its own right, it is primarily of interest here because it epitomizes a moment of extraordinary clarity, internal criticism, and the fundamental questioning and resettlement of long-standing debates in Islamic thought. Ibn Taymiyya's commitment to the early tradition of the preclassical age – the way of the predecessors (*salaf*) – along with his iconoclastic questioning of most of the subsequent developments of that tradition on its own terms, makes his critique all the more valuable for our purpose. Indeed, it is this groundedness in early Islamic tradition that explains his enormous continuing influence in the subsequent Islamic history since his own times.[43] My purpose in this study, however, is not only to point out why Ibn Taymiyya's legacy has been found useful by later reformers, but also to show that the full import of his thought has rarely been appreciated even by his ardent followers. And while his expositions of the scriptural tradition, along with his reformist zeal and activism, have found many followers, his most intellectually fruitful contributions – which, I argue, lay in epistemological and political domains – have remained untapped. Unlike Ibn Khaldūn, who has been increasingly recovered in modern scholarship, Ibn Taymiyya's comparable creative genius[44] has been veiled in the cloud of his reputation as an ultraconservative traditionalist and his association with various contemporary forms of Islam. An investigation of these ideas helps us see not only his thought, but the entire trajectory of Islamic political thought in new light and is deeply relevant to the political and religious discourse in the contemporary Muslim world.

[42] Taqī al-Dīn al-Maqrīzī (d. 1364/1442), *Khiṭaṭ Maqrīziyya* (Dār al-Ṭabāʿa al-Miṣriyya, n.d.), 2:358–9.

[43] Along with Ghazālī, Ibn Taymiyya is frequently cited as the one of the two most influential premodern scholars of Islamic history. The name of this fourteenth-century thinker appears in the official report on the 9/11 tragedy as somehow having fathered ideas that led to it. Yahya Michot has recently shown, through a careful analysis of a half a dozen modern Muslim ideologues, how Ibn Taymiyya's ideas have been misappropriated because of his enormous influence and moral authority (idem., *Muslims under Non-Muslim Rule: Ibn Taymiyya* [Interface Publications, 2006]).

[44] For a systematic analysis of the two thinkers' similar epistemological contentions, see Abū Yaʿrib al-Marzūqī, *Iṣlāḥ al-ʿaql fī' l-falsafa al-ʿarabiyya min wāqiʿiyya Arasṭū wa Aflāṭūn ilā ismiyya Ibn Taymiyya wa Ibn Khaldūn* (Reform of Reason in Arabic Philosophy from Aristotle and Plato's Realism to Ibn Taymiyya and Ibn Khaldūn's Nominalism) (Markaz al-Dirāsa al-Waḥda al-ʿArabiyya, 1994).

WHERE TO LOOK FOR ISLAMIC POLITICAL THOUGHT?

On the methodological level, I take issue with the available literature on Islamic political thought on its presumptions about the very nature of political thought and on the grounds on which Islamic political ideas have been explained and evaluated.

To begin with, the use of the word "political" with respect to the caliphate discourse must be seen as merely conventional, for it is not the good of the *polis* but of the Muslim Community – the *umma* – that the contributors to that discourse contemplated. We cannot easily brush aside differences between *polis* and *umma*, between, on the one hand, a territorially defined community that seeks the good life in this-worldly pursuits of material prosperity and intellectual enlightenment and, on the other, an ideologically defined community (with territorial unity mostly taken for granted) that seeks the ultimate good in the eternal afterlife and sees this life as only a means; between a community that sees itself and its god(s) all bound by the same brooding verdicts of fate, or laws of nature, and a community that believes in an omnipotent, personal God.[45] It would be tempting to invoke Leo Strauss's dichotomy between Athens and Jerusalem, but Mecca's identity with Jerusalem on the issue of political thought cannot be taken for granted.

One influential strand of Western scholarship does indeed see Mecca as an extension of Jerusalem, and hence argues that political thought remained an unnatural implant into the body of Islam.[46] Political philosophy, most Western historians and philosophers readily inform us, was born in Athens, and Athenian intellectual soil was essential to it: To have proper political thinking, one must believe in laws of nature independent of any deity, laws that bind gods as much as they enslave humans. How can human thought capture any order in the social world if it is at the mercy of unpredictable and unbound forces? The Hebrews and other non-Westerners did not have a concept of politics or liberty to begin with and perhaps cannot so long as they remain true to their traditions.[47]

[45] One renowned historian writes that politics emerges in Athens for the Greek concept of "an impersonal and inexorable Fate, brooding over and ultimately controlling both god and men" created a resemblance between laws of nature and laws of polis in their minds (W. McNeill, *The Rise of the West: A History of the Human Community* [University of Chicago Press, 1963], 214–5).

[46] P. Crone, *God's Rule* (Columbia University Press, 2004), 6. For the argument that Islam was based on a Jewish messianic movement, see P. Crone and M. Cook, *Hagarism* (Cambridge University Press, 1977).

[47] G. Mosca, *A Short History of Political Philosophy* (Crowell, 1972), 11.

Recent studies of Western political history have helped shed this essentialist understanding of political thought. Sheldon Wolin, a seminal figure in contemporary political philosophy, argues that the subject matter of political philosophy in various cultures that are included as part of the Western heritage over the last two and a half millennia has been stable and has recurrently included concerns such as "the power relationships between ruler and ruled, the nature of authority, the problems posed by social conflict, the status of certain goals or purposes as objectives of political action, and the character of political knowledge."[48] These concerns seem common enough to ail any large community. But Wolin is insistent that not all thinking about the aforementioned problems can be called "political." It was Plato's "achievement ... to point out that in order to think in a truly political way, one had to consider society as a systematic whole."[49] He goes on to write: "The etymological meaning of political had been 'concerning the *polis,*' while in terms of political philosophy it had related to *the knowledge and actions that would help or harm the community*."[50] Referring to Plato's myth of the Age of Kronos, Wolin sums up the Athenian charge against Jerusalem: "The political order took shape and identity only when the divine governance had been relaxed. 'When God was Shepherd there were no political constitutions'."[51]

The relaxation of divine government need not be taken to mean removal of any supernal ideals, for even Plato's politics was supremely concerned with such ideals. Although the social order was separable from the natural order in the sense that men's political actions seemed to have predictable consequences, the best political order, to Plato, was one that conformed to the idea of the natural order. True politics was an art, a "soul-craft," by which statesmen molded the political society in order to attain the highest good for all – a kind of voluntary return of the

48 Ibid., 5.

49 S. Wolin, *Politics and Vision* (Princeton University Press, 2004), 5. Political thought emerged, Wolin states, in Greece in stages. In the first step, nature was deemed as something comprehensible to reason rather than dependent on whims of gods – something governed by laws. In the next step, perhaps with Socrates or the Sophists or even earlier, the social world was thought of as being distinct from the natural world – one that was manipulable for good or evil ends. Plato is said to have been the first to view political society as a system of interrelated functions, "conceptualizing political institutions, procedures, and activities as a system dependent upon the performance of specified functions or tasks" (Ibid., 31).

50 Ibid., 65 (emphasis added).

51 Ibid., 32.

community and, through it, the individual to divine perfection. Wolin thus states his own concept of political thought through Plato: "Plato understood *political* philosophy to mean knowledge pertaining to the good life at the public level and *political* ruling to be the right management of the public affairs of the community."[52]

Politics is inherently a multivalent word and could refer to political philosophy, science, or self-interested calculation. Political philosophy in its idealistic form is the *art* of purposeful management of public affairs based on the ultimate knowledge of the unchanging essences of political objects. Political science is best represented in Aristotle's sense of political knowledge as an empirical science of systematic observation of political life.[53] These two are distinct from the usual sense of *politics* as self-interested struggle for competitive advantage, which inevitably goes on in all societies or groups.[54] No developed human community is free of self-interested political negotiation and intrigue, but not all reflect systematically on political philosophy or science. The fundamental elements that make proper political thought and action possible can be summed up, from the foregoing discussion, as follows: (1) the conception of the collectivity as an interconnected system – namely, a *political community* – one of whose features is that it is a community that competes for limited resources, and hence is often associated with a bounded territory; (2) a normative vision of collective life and the capacity of human *reason* to discern it; and (3) a positive account of human *agency* to manage that system in service of the given vision. Put differently, some or all of the members that share interest in the available resources are assumed to possess the reason to recognize the collective good and the agency to attain it.

The language or logic employed in conceptualizing these factors may be theological and that does not need to reduce the political character of a discourse; indeed, where one looks for political thought in a given thought-world depends on its fundamental commitments. Plato envisioned politics as an art; for Aquinas, it formed part of a Christian cosmology; the Hegelian vision emphasized progression of the state in

[52] Wolin, 39 (emphasis in original).

[53] For a discussion of the distinction between Plato's metaphysical political thought and Aristotle's relative empiricism and realism, see J. Murphy, *Political Theory: A Conceptual Analysis* (Dorsey Press, 1968), 9–11. Its lack of the noble idealism and imaginative possibilities that characterize Plato's views is seen as the downside of Aristotelian realism (Ibid., 12).

[54] Wolin, 39.

history; Hobbes utilized the newly discovered metaphors of science, in particular physics; and, finally, in modern times, political vision has frequently been colored by economic models.[55] In an Islamic context, theology and religious law are the natural places to look for direct or indirect debates about political concepts. And although Islamicists have certainly done so, the relationship between theology and political thought has been deemed at best accidental.[56]

Furthermore, the conceptual conditions that make political thought and action possible are often collective attitudes of a civilization, which may be long-standing but not necessarily part of its timeless essence. This caution has been given particular attention by Wolin, who sees the "political" as a noble but elusive ideal that cannot be taken for granted. It declines in an intellectual milieu where any of the aforementioned conditions declines; when, for instance, the sense of belonging to a political community deteriorates, as in the wake of the expansion of the Roman Empire when "political association" was replaced by "primacy of power" and Athenian political philosophy gave way to despair, individualism, or even cosmopolitanism that dissipated civic responsibility and belonging.[57] The political sphere might also wilt when human agency is undermined or negated, be it due to religious fatalism, scientific determinism, or the dominance of large unaccountable business corporations in a globalizing world.[58]

This unpacking of the category "political" has thus alerted us that it is not the divide between the Semitic and the Greek mind or religion, but the availability of certain conceptual elements and conditions on which

[55] Wolin, 19–20.

[56] Perhaps the most detailed work on the political content of early Islamic thought is Josef van Ess's, who nonetheless shares this attitude (*Theologie und Gesellschaft im 2. und 3. Jahrhundert Hidschra* [de Gruyter, 1991–7], 1–6); see also a summary of the relevant volume (i.e., IV) of this work in his "Political Ideas in Early Islamic Religious Thought," *British Journal of Middle East Studies* 28.2 (2001): 151–64, where he writes, "In early Islam [political] ideas were produced in a way slightly different from our own, but the scientific bogus around them was not less annoying than nowadays.... Most of [the available] sources are 'theological' in character: Ḥadīth and theology proper, i.e., *'ilm al-kalām*" (151).

[57] Wolin, 82; 85–6. Not only were Cynicism and Epicureanism such antipolitical philosophies, but even Stoicism, with its noble ideals of "equality, freedom and human dignity," was no exception, for its "commitment was towards a society which lay outside of politics" (Ibid., 73).

[58] E.g., Hobbes's scientific model of politics evaded politics by preferring "contented, and 'lusty' citizens"; Utilitarians like James Mill and economists like Adam Smith similarly assured us that "we may often fulfill all the rules of justice by sitting and doing nothing" (Ibid., 250–1; 378–83).

the possibility of politics depends.[59] These concepts, namely community (*umma*), reason (*ʿaql*), and agency (*qudra*) – each of which constituted veritable problematiques in early Islamic discourse itself – have the merit of being not only internal to Islamic discourse, but also general and basic enough to allow us to understand Islamic discursive tradition on its own terms without imposing unfit categories while also allowing for insightful comparison. Properly identifying these concepts or their equivalents in Islamic tradition helps avoid essentializing Islam's attitude toward politics and prompts us to look in the right places. Although the traditional discourse on the caliphate remains a key element in Islamic political thought, in itself it does not sufficiently capture the conceptual elements highlighted in the foregoing. The approach outlined here requires us to turn to discourses that surrounded and produced the caliphate discourse, such as Islamic theology (*kalām*), legal theory (*uṣūl al-fiqh*), and law (*fiqh*), and to investigate doctrines and attitudes toward human agency, reason, and community before turning to aggregate concepts conventionally related to governance such as politics (*siyāsa*), power (*mulk*), and caliphate (*khilāfa*).

Explaining Islamic Political Thought

Having explored the conditions under which we can meaningfully speak of Islamic political thought, my second critique of the available literature concerns the way political programs of premodern Muslim thinkers have been explained or evaluated. It is not sufficient to explain the failure or success of political programs in terms of merely intention or context of the thinkers and thus to either dismiss them as being irrelevant for serious political analysis or to apologetically defend so as to exempt them from being examined for the cogency or moral and political implications of

[59] This is a "minimalist" definition of politics, of course, and does not include the notion of politics as secular negotiation of interest groups as it developed in modern European societies (B. Crick, *In Defense of Politics*, 4th ed. [Chicago: University of Chicago Press, 1993], 17–18). In its secular-liberal form, such a definition of politics would require separating the notion of truth or reason from legitimate, normative politics and governance and would not be appropriate for premodern (Islamic or other) societies where both truth and reason were grounded in religion. An element of negotiation within the limits of the accepted vision of the good, however, is inherent in any politics. The scope of my inquiry excludes the important problem of religious minorities (both Muslim and other) that inhabited the Muslim lands, for there existed other, more fundamental problems that shaped the very possibility of political thinking, which can be better examined if the problem of minorities is shelved for the time being.

their ideas. But most classics of Western political literature have shared these characteristics: Hobbes's *Leviathan* responded to the civil disorder of his day, whereas John Locke's *Two Treatises of Government* is used as a textbook example of both rationalization and polemic.[60] The trajectory of English political thought would be insufficiently understood without examining either of these giants, even though the former's prescription, as we have noted, would eliminate proper politics. We may identify three dimensions of analyzing a body of political thought: its immediate sociopolitical context, its location within the discursive tradition of which it is a part, and its posture toward the conceptual elements that constitute political life. Only an analysis that accounts for each of these can illuminate the particular ways in which a given thinker privileges certain aspects of his or her tradition over others, prioritizes ethical goods, and intends to make a difference. Thus, to explain Māwardī's work as an attempt to justify and protect the Abbasid caliph against the Buyid warlords and Ghazālī's attempt as intended to bolster the caliph's symbolic authority against the Fatimids in Egypt[61] is to merely give their sociopolitical context, which says nothing about the political insights, implications, coherence, and vision of these works. This further suggests that the most common attempts at explaining Muslim political thought as being apologia for one political event or a natural response to another are no explanations at all.

Furthermore, political thought or its evaluation cannot be disconnected from its underlying moral vision. This means that Gibb' s indignation (overstated, perhaps) toward what appears to him to be Māwardī's unprincipled legitimization of usurpers is a more appropriate response – because at least it takes him seriously – than Patricia Crone's casual dismissal that by justifying an usurper, Māwardī did what most theorists in history have done,[62] or Khaled Abou El Fadl's explanation that Māwardī was simply employing a "legal fiction," thus "doing what was, by training and habit, dictated by [his] legal culture; that is resolving conflict and maintaining order."[63] Regardless of whether any of these is an accurate description of Māwardī's project, it is insufficient to explain away jurists' propositions that might, for instance, lead to unfeasible or oppressive political arrangements as a consequence of their being jurists. Abou El

60 Wolin, 25.
61 See Chapter 2.
62 Crone, *God's Rule*, 233.
63 Rosenthal, 30–1; K. Abou El Fadl, *Rebellion and Violence in Islamic Law* (Cambridge University Press, 2001), 9n6.

Fadl has contended that the Muslim jurists' pronouncements on the duty of obedience to those in power ought not to be treated "as if they are a genre of political thought or theory."[64] But one does not need to be a card-carrying member of a political philosophy club or state retinue for his or her thought to be politically significant enough to influence a tradition or its immediate context, and thus be deserving of political critique. Rejecting the view of political theory as an idealized activity, which once occurred in ahistorical Athens, scholars such as Wolin, Quentin Skinner, and others have shown that most thinkers whose ideas have made political impact and shaped political imaginations beyond their immediate contexts have thought and written within historical contexts, often to advance specific ends, and in various disciplines, idioms or languages. Any idea or act that protests or supports a public order or a collective vision of life acquires political significance.[65] This means that the political ideas that ought to be the primary object of the investigation of Islamic political history are not of those who formally declared themselves to be doing political philosophy (as only a handful of Hellenized Muslim philosophers did), but those ideas that animated actual struggles over power, authority and legitimacy. Furthermore, any authoritative theory or decision concerning public order, inasmuch as it presupposes a particular political and moral vision, bears a corresponding level of responsibility. And no group in classical Islamic societies carried the authority that the Muslim jurists did; they not only spoke in the name of God, but often claimed the exclusive authority to do so.

Political versus Legal Mode of Reasoning

My contention that in medieval Islam law trumped politics depends on the premise that the two activities can be distinguished despite their admittedly intermeshed and interdependent existence in real life. A philosophically neat distinction between the two fields, even if possible, is not

[64] Abou El Fadl, 8; Rosenthal, 31.

[65] For the same reason that I consider Abou El Fadl's explanation insufficient, modern intellectual historians are skeptical even of the category of discourse called "political theory." Quentin Skinner champions the view that "the characteristic activity of political theorists is that of legitimizing or challenging existing institutions and beliefs" and goes on to suggest, in his latest writings, that if this is granted – and he argues that it should be – then "the notion of a distinct 'history of political theory' begins to melt into air" (Q. Skinner, "Surveying the Foundations: A Retrospect and Reassessment," in *Rethinking the Foundations of Modern Political Thought*, eds. A. Brett and J. Tully [Cambridge University Press, 2006], 244).

relevant to the present endeavor so long as a workable distinction can be maintained within my subject matter.[66] I proceed in the following to first outline such a distinction between two ideal types and then place that distinction in the context of Islamic history as well as modern scholarship.

Legal and political modes of reasoning can be seen as located on a continuum, both being ways of settling disputes and keeping order in public life, but law does so by invoking rules or precedence, politics by negotiating conflicts of interest under particular circumstances. Law seeks authority by tying itself to the authority of precedence or higher writ, whereas politics does so by satisfying the sense of justice and interests of the parties involved. Politics by its very nature requires the settling of human disputes and the redistribution of resources in ways that cannot be found in timeless recipes or codes of conduct; it is unabashedly the domain of contingencies, compromises, and settling of particular interests. To use a modern metaphor from computer science, law is analogous to the "software" of a computer program, whereas politics to the "run-time" operation by a human user.

Because political negotiation is a conflict-ridden and unpredictable process, there have been attempts throughout history to find ways to eliminate politics, disabling the role of negotiation and statecraft. The need for political thought, virtue, and institutions may be denied in the name of the free-market model of selfish citizens as being sufficiently self-regulating, or an elite bureau of ideologues distributing resources according to a higher ideology, or an all-encompassing divine law whose spokesmen, being above politics, claim omnicompetence. Against such attempts, political theorists widely agree that political reason cannot be codified or contained in legal codes or prefabricated formulae. The conservative philosopher Michael Oakeshott captures this in his endorsement of the idea of "political tradition" against what he calls "political rationalism," whereas Wolin supports the same idea when he imagines politics as an art or a craft, privileging the idea of political knowledge as "tacit knowledge" against what he labels "methodism."[67] In the words of

[66] The two domains, of course, are not independent and their points of commonalities and interactions are numerous. The typical interaction between law and politics has been that the rulers (politics) often created or used law in order to gain legitimacy (W. Ullmann, *A History of Political Thought: The Middle Ages* [Penguin Books, 1970]). In modern times, this interaction has many more dimensions.

[67] M. Oakshott, *Rationalism in Politics* (Basic Books Publishing, 1962), 128–9; Wolin, "Political Theory as a Vocation," *American Political Science Review* 63.4 (1969): 1062–82.

the critical legal theorist Roberto Unger: "The practice of politics calls for prudence, the perception of particulars and the making of choices about particulars. But prudence can never be overtaken by a metaphysic that remains committed to the language of the universal."[68]

Yet, political negotiation requires rules of engagement and some minimally shared goals in the form of laws or mediating cultural and social institutions without which, relying solely on calculation of particular interests, it is likely to result in arbitrariness and tyranny. Thus, in well-balanced complex societies, politics and law can be better seen as distinct but complementary and mutually dependent rather than conflicting modes of public thought. The challenge of political theorization is to bind political craft and practice to some shared vision and standards of normative conduct – that is, to the spirit of law when the words of law run out or fail to suffice.

Turning to the Islamic context, the intellectual historian of Islam must ask how, to what extent, and why Islamic tradition became "nomocratic and nomocentric"; in what ways were law and politics related; to what extent it is legitimate to represent traditional bodies of *fiqh* through modern concepts of law and medieval Islamic views on governance through modern political theories; and what is gained and lost in such representation. It is most logical to address these questions in the reverse order. Let us consider what happens when the ideal types of law and politics as universal categories are applied to Islamic tradition. The existing scholarship on Islamic political thought that is also attentive to the methodological problems of political theory is quite scarce, a reflection perhaps of the bias of Islamic tradition itself; the present study must therefore venture into a terra incognita. In the realm of legal scholarship, however, a number of studies have deployed Western notions of the nature of law to explore the boundaries between law and the state in Islamic tradition.

Baber Johansen has pursued Schacht's contention that public aspects of *fiqh* (i.e., other than ritual worship) be understood as a sum total of individual rights rather than deontological norms that presuppose the interior world of the believers to be comprehensible; in other words, aspects of *fiqh* could be modeled after a secular legal system familiar to Western scholars.[69] Khaled Abou El Fadl's aforementioned study of the Islamic law of rebellion is perhaps the most insistent attempt to understand *fiqh* as a jurisprudential system whose claim to divine origin is incidental to

[68] R. M. Unger, *Knowledge and Politics* (The Free Press, 1984), 293–4.
[69] Johansen, *Contingency*, 62; Schacht, *Introduction*, 208–9.

its workings. Deploying extensively Alan Watson's work on the nature of law, he asserts that, like any law, *fiqh* is "molded by a corporate identity" and legal culture, possessing even "its own domains of truth."[70] He adds, however, as if compelled by the logic of his first argument that "juridical discourses are only a part of the reality of Islam."[71] This specialized and limited status of Muslim jurists for him places them above political analysis (as noted earlier) and explains, among other things, jurists' acceptance of usurpers so long as they could restore law and order (naturally, at the expense of justice and other goods).[72] He explains, for instance, that the dominant trend among Muslim jurists by the classical period was to depoliticize the discourse on rebels with the consequence that the state and the rebels were treated as neutral categories, regardless of their legitimacy.[73] Put differently, the legitimacy of a government and whether it grounded its actions in the normative apparatus of the society were of no consequence to the jurists. But this is hard to explain away as the professional detachment of the jurists, for the ulama (whom Abou El Fadl identifies in a one-dimensional way as "jurists" and thus attempts to settle the debate by this very choice of words) were also the "heirs of prophets," the conscience of the society, who claimed ubiquitously to speak exclusively in God's name with omnicompetence.[74] If we take the ulama's claim to omnicompetence (both the authority to judge every matter and being the only voice to judge every matter) as a theoretical as well as a social reality, then modern secular legal models need to be abandoned or fundamentally rethought to incorporate the authority and hence responsibility of the Islamic jurists as God's spokespersons.[75] Alternatively, if we grant the limitedness of the role of the jurists, then we need to look for how limits to their authority were articulated and what other group or domain of thought and activity were authorized to balance their normative authority. In either case, further investigation is call for.

[70] Abou El Fadl, 322.
[71] Ibid., 21.
[72] Ibid., 28–9.
[73] Ibid., 330.
[74] For instance, the fifth-/eleventh-century Shāfiʿī scholar al-Khaṭīb al-Baghdādī unremarkably appropriates for scholars the highest possible accolades: They are "God's caliphs in his earth, his proof upon his servants, whom God has deemed sufficient so that there is no need for any more prophets" (R. al-Sayyid, *Al-Jamāʿa wa 'l-mujtamaʿ wa 'l-dawla* [Dār al-Kitāb al-ʿArabī, 1997], 37–8).
[75] In the sense that the modern legal profession cannot claim to be the only moral voice in the society, and, to take the American case, is formally independent of politics (as a different branch of government) but also subservient to it (for the sovereignty belongs to the people and represented through politics).

An excellent and perhaps the only modern study to explore attempts by medieval legal theorists to demarcate the line dividing the authorities of jurists and rulers is Sherman Jackson's study of the late medieval Egyptian Mālikī jurist Shihāb al-Dīn al-Qarāfī (d 684/1285). Jackson too employs Watson's notion of law but, because his is a study precisely of the limits of law, does so in a more limited (and hence more successful) fashion than Abou El Fadl. He explains the central and much debated notion of classical Islamic law, *taqlīd* (following of another jurists' authority), versus *ijtihād* (independent reasoning) through Watson's concept of "legal scaffolding" – the jurists' way to solve new problems by adapting and tweaking existing precedent rather than solving each problem afresh. This mode of legal reasoning, which he takes to be the essence of all law resulting from its need for consistency and authority, leads nonetheless to a system of "horrendous complexity" increasingly distant from the needs of the society and difficult to reform.[76] Jackson thus counters the common misconception of *taqlīd* as being peculiar to Islamic law and the source of its intransigence and rigidity and, as is often held, responsible for the Muslim decline. Yet, as Abou El Fadl notes in agreement with Watson, law is essentially conservative and resistant to change,[77] indeed, in Watson's words, "legal change is frequently the result of efforts of non-lawyers or of lawyers outside the tradition."[78] Jackson comes to a similar conclusion: "Legal systems are only a part of the civilizations to which they belong, and, as such, are affected by any number of non-legal advantages and disadvantages conferred by the carrier civilization."[79]

Thus, any legal system that seals itself from external influence and claims to stay within the walls of its formal legal logic is likely to either be outdated or stifle its adherents. This recognition of something other than law saves Jackson and Abou El Fadl from the kind of cynicism that characterizes the approach of another able scholar of Islamic law. Wael Hallaq believes that the *Sharīʿa* is simply unsalvageable in the face of modernity, in particular the modern nation-state. Such central elements

[76] Jackson, *Islamic Law*, 97–9; Watson, *Nature of Law*, 95.

[77] Watson's contentions that law is fundamentally concerned with order, is averse to change, and works through "legal scaffolding" or "baby-steps" rather than what might be the needed adjustments have been found particularly applicable to Islamic law by scholars like Abou El Fadl and Jackson. See A. Watson, *Nature of Law* (Edinburgh University Press, 1977), 43.

[78] Alan Watson, *Evolution of Law*, qtd. in Abou El Fadl, 111.

[79] Ibid., 101.

of the nation-state as legal centralization and codification as well as key elements of modernity are incompatible with the *Sharīʿa*.[80]

Hallaq's conclusion falls out of the structural problem I have just outlined, and his rigorous conclusion throws the dilemma of modeling Islamic law as secular law into sharpest relief. That is, Hallaq, like Schacht, Johansen, and Abou El Fadl, models Islamic law after Western secular legal models for all practical purposes, but goes beyond them perhaps in seeing it as a self-contained system or mode of reasoning that embodies all of Islamic normativity. It is noteworthy that Schacht had not shared Hallaq's pessimism about the future of Islamic law vis-à-vis modernity precisely because his hypothesis of the origins of Islamic law in foreign sources had denied the rootedness of Islamic law in its professed scriptural sources (the Qur'an and the Prophetic *ḥadīth*), believing that if it could develop out of custom and borrowing once, it could do so again. Our modern knowledge of the origins of Islamic law, not the least because of Hallaq's own contributions, cannot sustain such a simplistic belief.[81] Hallaq therefore finds himself in a bind with respect to Islamic law: It is a self-contained system whose scriptural origins, especially after the development of the rigorous oversight of an overdeveloped tradition, ensure that it simply cannot produce anything radically new or adapt to modernity without losing its essence. He concludes, therefore, that Islamic law is doomed. But Hallaq is only mostly hopeless; after detailing the enormous odds against it, he gives one rather uphill way for "a revival of Islamic law" in the modern world:

> The solution for the Sunnite countries, therefore, is for the *new* Muslim state to incorporate the religious intelligentsia into its ranks. The custody of Islamic law, history has shown, must reside with a learned hierarchy largely dissociated from political power: the independence of law from the concerns of politics is as much an Islamic phenomenon as it is American or European .... The state ... must financially sustain religious institutions, especially sharīʿa colleges; it must install the religious hierarchy in the respective social and political hierarchy so as to sense and reflect concerns on all levels ... none of this can be attained without a genuinely Islamic polity.[82]

80 W. Hallaq, "Can the Sharīʿa be Restored?" in *Islamic Law and the Challenge of Modernity*, eds. Y. Haddad and B. Stowasser (Altamira Press, 2004), 22.

81 For a recent review of scholarship on the subject, see H. Motzki, *The Origins of Islamic Jurisprudence: Meccan Fiqh before the Classical Schools*, trans. Marion H. Katz (Brill, 2002).

82 Hallaq, "Can the Sharīʿa," 47.

The main problem with this proposal thus stated is its political unfeasibility: What interest (read: political reason) would rulers and other groups in society have to leave their fate in the hands of the few experts of law? Curiously, however, this proposal calls upon a meta-legal – indeed *political* – mechanism (the determined policy of a legitimate state) as the only way to salvage Islamic law in the modern world. Societies can, of course, engage in collective projects and pursue shared visions, and the dynamic negotiation and envisioning of such projects is the domain of politics. Hallaq wishes to assign to the future Muslim politics the indispensable role that he believes Islamic law in history mostly did without. But did it?

I argue in what ensues that it did not. By this I do not mean to make the banal claim that political interests influenced Islamic law, but that within the core of Islamic tradition there existed veritable tendencies that theorized a positive role for political life and action and saw law as only one of Islam's many complementary manifestations. This was the strand most forcefully represented by Ibn Taymiyya. On the other end of the spectrum were those jurists whose vision of Islam came quite close to the aforementioned legalistic image. In the following chapters I offer an investigation of this tension between law and politics, its theoretical underpinnings and consequences.

IBN TAYMIYYA'S POLITICAL THOUGHT

To understand Ibn Taymiyya's political thought, scholars have examined his treatises such as *al-Siyāsa al-sharʿiyya* and *al-Ḥisba*, and occasionally a larger polemical work, *Minhāj al-sunna*. But the method I have advocated in the foregoing requires turning to Ibn Taymiyya's magnum opus, *Darʾ taʿāruḍ*, which presents his key epistemological and philosophical contentions and hence is central to the present study. It has not so far been critically studied, let alone related to his political thought.

It is a testament to both Henri Laoust's astute scholarship and the difficulty of the challenges involved in supplanting it that, while numerous bits and pieces of his interpretation of Ibn Taymiyya have been revised, his work is still not entirely obsolete. Most influential interpreters of Islamic political thought, ranging from Gibb, Lambton, Rosenthal, Lapidus, Watt, and Crone to most recently Baber Johansen, have reproduced with remarkable faithfulness Laoust's reading (as well as misreading) of Ibn Taymiyya.

Laoust had rightly observed Ibn Taymiyya's emphasis on the harmonization of reason and revelation, although without connecting it to its full sociopolitical implications or seeing its implications against the backdrop of *kalām* and *falsafa*. Laoust had also noted that Ibn Taymiyya appears acutely aware of the defects of contemporary political, social, and religious life and that his reforming zeal extended not only to theology, but also to day-to-day administration of the Muslim state, which he tried to bring into line with the ideal demands of the *Sharīʿa*. He thought that although Ibn Taymiyya was opposed to the Mamluk state as it developed in his day, he seems to have accepted its structure because to him the *amīrs* and the ulama remained the two most important groups, and it is these that supported the "military dictatorship" on which the state was erected. Rosenthal built on Laoust's as well as Goldziher's conclusions about Ibn Taymiyya and observed, based on his reading of *al-Siyāsa al-sharʿīyya*, that Ibn Taymiyya's shift of focus from the caliphate to the Community and the *Sharīʿa* was distinctive and remarkable.[83] Rosenthal recognized that Ibn Taymiyya

tried to escape from the vicious circle in which Ibn Jamāʿa and his predecessors were caught, by concentrating on the *Sharīʿa* and its application to the life of the community with the religious fervour and reforming zeal characteristic of Ḥanbalism at that time. In attitude, approach and treatment he stands in marked contrast to the other jurists. The title of his treatise must be understood as his programme: *Siyāsa sharʿiya*; it implies that he is concerned in the first place with the role of the divinely revealed law. While acknowledging the necessity of 'political' authority he recognizes the *de facto* power of the ruler of the day and the necessity of obedience to authority in the interests of the *Sharīʿa* and for the benefit of the community.[84]

Despite the paucity of his sources, Rosenthal's distillation of the basic program of Ibn Taymiyya's *al-Siyāsa al-sharʿiyya* is not entirely off the mark:

It is clear from this attitude that the center of gravity has shifted from the *khilāfa* and the *khalīfa* to the community, whose life must be regulated by the divine law. At the same time he pleads for close co-operation between the imam – the necessary authority – and the community. He accepts the state as it is and is entirely interested in just government on that basis, whether the imam is legal or illegal as far as his assumption of power and authority is concerned, in fact even if he enjoys neither and is a mere figurehead. Hence Ibn Taymiya stresses insistently the religious duties of all Muslims, rulers and subjects alike. This is tinged with

83 Rosenthal, 246.

84 Ibid., 52.

a certain *political realism*, since he is concerned with the maintenance and good order of the political framework so all Muslims may attain the bliss of the world to come.[85]

These commentators perceptively felt the difference between Ibn Taymiyya's political vision and the classical legacy, which led Laoust and others to ascribe to Ibn Taymiyya an outright rejection of the caliphate theory.

Among the significant studies that have appeared during the last three decades, one is Qamaruddin Khan's, who cogently rejects Laoust's suggestion that the motive behind Ibn Taymiyya's disregard for the classical theory of caliphate had been his proclivity toward Khārijism.[86] Nonetheless, vested in seeking Ibn Taymiyya as an ally in undermining the traditional caliphate theory, Khan too ends up endorsing Laoust's thesis that Ibn Taymiyya had rejected the caliphate theory.[87] Mona Hassan's recent article carefully presents the case against Laoust's contention that Ibn Taymiyya demolished the classical caliphate theory, highlighting the mainstream Sunni orthodox inspiration of most of Ibn Taymiyya's positions. For instance, Laoust suggested that Ibn Taymiyya takes the plurality of *imams* for granted, thus implicitly denying the conventional thesis of the need for the unity of caliphate. Hassan shows that Ibn Taymiyya's *Minhāj al-sunna*, which formed the basis of Laoust's interpretation, clearly establishes the opposite.[88] In *Minhāj*, Ibn Taymiyya explicitly details all the traditional Sunni *ḥadīth* on the issue of what constitutes a "proper caliph," endorsing the "Qurayshī lineage, the possible methods of his ascension to the caliphate, and guidelines for proper electoral procedures."[89] On the whole, for Hassan, apart from emphasis on the responsibility of the people to improve their own condition, maintain political order through qualified obedience, and especially "the Muslim community's duty to offer sincere advice (*naṣīhah*) to those placed in authority over them," there is little that sets Ibn Taymiyya's political thought apart from the rest of the Sunni tradition.[90] Hassan's study seeks

[85] Ibid.

[86] Laoust, *Essai*, 282; Q. Khan, *Political Thought of Ibn Taymiyya* (Adam Publishers, 1992), 42. Khan argued that the Khārijīs constituted no threat at the time with which Ibn Taymiyya would care to seek conciliation, and in fact, Ibn Taymiyya harshly condemned their extremism.

[87] Khan, 38–9.

[88] M. Hassan, "Modern Interpretations and Misinterpretations of a Medieval Scholar: Apprehending the Political Thought of Ibn Taymiyyah" in *Ibn Taymiyya and His Times*, eds. Y. Rapoport and S. Ahmed, 340–3.

[89] Ibid., 343.

[90] Ibid., 346.

to establish Ibn Taymiyya's contribution as nothing more than a continuation of the age-old caliphate tradition, now set against the background of the Mongol onslaught. He engaged, she writes, "in a process similar to the one that Sunni jurists had been preoccupied with for centuries – namely, how to comprehend the historical position of the caliphate from a sound Islamic legal perspective."[91] Despite Hassan's welcome correctives, I show in this study that the "nothing new" position is untenable. For one, it was never the jurists *qua* jurists who composed this discourse; it was the ulama as theologians. The only study that seems to have recognized this fact, albeit not its significance, is that of Kūnākātā.[92] Dealing extensively with both kinds of text – those that Hassan has used to present her case as well as those of practical political import that Laoust and others had used – Kūnākātā reaches yet another conclusion, namely that Ibn Taymiyya endorsed the caliphate but rejected its normative status for the future generation. An assessment of these contradictory views, possible only after understanding Ibn Taymiyya's conceptual universe, is offered in Chapter 7.

An important dimension in understanding Muslim political thought, as Charles Butterworth has suggested, is "in terms of the tension between prudence and legitimacy, that is to say, the tension between a philosophical understanding of politics and a strictly legalistic one."[93] He further noted that

> those who pursued the legalistic path stressed the need to understand and to implement the Divine Law as it was set forth in the Quran and the traditions of the Prophet, whereas those who praised prudence sought to understand politics as a craft and an art and how one skilled in it could rule well. [The legalistic group] further denied that anything could be gained by investigating the way thinkers not aware of the Islamic revelation had attempted to explain political life

[91] Ibid., 343.

[92] Kūnākātā starts off with the presumption that the caliphate theory belongs in jurisprudence. Rather than taking it for granted, however, he surveys an impressive amount of jurisprudential literature consisting of dozens of traditional manuals from all the four Sunni legal schools produced over a thousand years and comes to the conclusion that it is *kalām* and not jurisprudential discourse that had produced and determined the shape of the caliphate theory. Only after it had been more or less settled around the fifth/eleventh century at the hands of Juwaynī and Ghazālī that the jurisprudential manuals of most schools came to include a brief chapter on the subject stating its conclusions. The more practically minded Ḥanafī jurists in the east still resisted including a chapter on a fiction that had no practical implication (Ḥ. Kūnākātā, *al-Naẓariyya al-siyāsiyya 'ind Ibn Taymiyya* [Dār al-Akhillā', 1994], 17, 19–20).

[93] C. Butterworth, "Prudence versus Legitimacy: The Persistent Theme in Islamic Political Thought," in *Islamic Resurgence in the Arab World*, ed. A. E. H. Dessouki [Proeger, 1982], 84–5.

and its requirements. Thus, to speak of this group as proponents of legitimacy or as legalistic is simply to heed their own efforts to implement the Divine Law.[94]

Butterworth then proceeds to name the champions of the "legalistic" path: Juwaynī, Ghazalī, and Ibn Taymiyya. In lumping Ibn Taymiyya with the rest, and in failing to distinguish between theology and jurisprudence, I think, he falters.

If my construal of Ibn Taymiyya's contribution is correct, the generalization that all the ulama had been primarily concerned with legitimacy in terms of formal requirements of the *Sharīʿa*, whereas it was only the (Aristotelian) Muslim philosophers who concerned themselves with prudence, is also untenable. I argue that Ibn Taymiyya does not belong in either this legalistic list, or the list of Hellenized philosophers who advocated prudence inspired by Greek political wisdom, or, for that matter, in the long line of scribes and bureaucrats who built on Persian and Greek wisdom in their own peculiar way. Rather, Ibn Taymiyya forged a new genre altogether: *al-siyāsa al-sharʿiyya* – Islamic politics – which drew in an unprecedented way (this contention I make in Chapter 7) on the early Islamic model and scriptural resources to furnish a feasible model of substantive legitimacy (as opposed to legalistic or formal legitimacy) to both the rulers and their political activity on the basis of the *Sharīʿa*, and also provided *Sharīʿa*-based political advice and norms to such a political authority. Despite his remarkably straightforward use of Islamic "raw material" to offer political guidance, Ibn Taymiyya's political thought was *sui generis*.[95] The phrase *al-siyāsa al-sharʿiyya*, despite its stunning simplicity, was unheard of, if not oxymoronic, during the classical age.

Baber Johansen's is the most recent and involved development of the line of scholarship on Ibn Taymiyya's political contribution that began in Laoust.[96] Johansen concludes that Ibn Taymiyya was essentially interested in bolstering the Mamluk state and curtailing the authority of his fellow ulama in exchange for the supremacy of the *Sharīʿa* not only as

[94] Ibid.

[95] Ibn Taymiyya's way of approaching the revelational texts (*nuṣūṣ*) on sociopolitical matters is new (that is, distinct from classical formulations) and rational (that is, commonsensical rather than dictated by other, hidden premises of the discourse). None of the classical works on the caliphate ever mention these scriptural texts for this purpose, nor do any of the juristic manuals that reproduced the formal conditions of the caliphate (Kūnākātā, 83–4).

[96] B. Johansen, "A Perfect Law in an Imperfect Society," in *The Law Applied: Contextualizing the Islamic Sharīʿa*, eds. P. Bearman, W. Heinrichs, and B. Weiss (I. B. Tauris, 2008) and Johansen, "Signs as Evidence: The Doctrine of Ibn Taymiyya and Ibn Qayyim al-Jawziyya (d. 1351) on Proof," *ILS* 9.2 (2002).

law but as a font of political norms as well. To this end, he endorsed commonsense justice and order and opposed classical juristic formalism. However, Johansen takes for granted Laoust's erroneous conclusion about Ibn Taymiyya's rejection of the caliphate, and thus fails to comprehend the full complexity of Ibn Taymiyya's political thought. Furthermore, in seeking an explanation for what appears to be Ibn Taymiyya's notable departure from the classical doctrines, Johansen limits himself to Ibn Taymiyya's immediate sociopolitical context and ignores the theological and intellectual problems that had been central to Islamic political thought and that really motivated Ibn Taymiyya's writings. Sensing, nonetheless, that this explanation is unpersuasive, Johansen acknowledges that we are unable to understand these developments in the legal doctrine "unless we have a better knowledge of the epistemology that underlies the reasoning of jurists like Ibn Taymiyya."[97] In the present study, I take this invitation to be my point of departure.

THE CONTOURS

The present study has two interdependent objectives. The first is to trace the transformation of Islamic discursive tradition from the early to the classical period. To this end, I investigate the theological-political polemics of the period and identify the particular ways in which this transformation was crystallized, explained, normalized, and passed on, allowing its settlements and attitudes to be reproduced over and over through the centuries. The interpretation of early Islamic political thought poses several methodological challenges. One is faced with the task of having to interpret sparsely contextualized sources that were written after the conflict had already long been in existence and the terms of the debate already fixed. Beside the problem of authenticity and historicity, the hermeneutics are daunting, as these sources are naturally silent about shared premises and presuppositions that had been evident to them but are barely so to us. The scholarship on the political thought of the first centuries of Islam thus has been largely speculative in nature and quite divided on its attitude toward the sources and hence on its conclusions. A reconstruction and revision based on a synthesis of recent research are undertaken in the first section (Chapters 1–3) of this study.

[97] Johansen, "Signs," 193.

The second objective is the investigation of the particular moment in history when the classical tradition was most thoroughly questioned and subjected to a "total critique" from within by Ibn Taymiyya. This vantage point offers particular insights, for discursive transformations and adjustments are subtle arguments carried out in (at times deliberately) specialized language, extended over long periods of time, requiring at times centuries for their central commitments to be fully articulated and sharpened. The most poignant conceptual questions of the age are often addressed by thinkers in oblique ways, perhaps because the stakes in broaching them are high, and in settling them in the "wrong" ways even higher.[98] Thus there are ways in which adherents of a tradition see and speak to each other more clearly and in a language more authentic than to us. Furthermore, the richness of the historical sources available in the medieval period (in particular the Syro-Egyptian Mamluk world) allows us to see our thinkers, their texts, and contexts with clarity that outdoes anything in any earlier period. The second section (Chapters 4–7) of this study substantiates my contention that Ibn Taymiyya's life and work allow us a unique window into the intellectual world of not only late medieval, but also early and classical Islam.

The prevalent accounts of Islamic political thought (Chapter 1) share one common premise, that early Islamic thought (roughly, the first three centuries) had a profound, if not determinative, influence on the political thought and practice of the classical world (the next three centuries). Attempts are made to determine the essential character of early Islamic political thought – a daunting task given the scarcity and treacherousness of the sources of the period. Classical political thought is then seen as either a reflection and continuation or pathological reversal of early political thought. This story of Islamic political thought is often deemed finished and sealed with the end of the classical period – that is, with the "first six centuries of Islam." Finally, the task then becomes one of assigning the real blame for this pathology, and depending on how early Islam is seen (Gibb, et al.: too good of an ideal to sustain; Lapidus, Crone et al.: stillborn, doomed to failure from the get-go; etc.), classical political thought is then seen as a failure to sustain the early ideal or as bound to fail because of it.

Certainly, the lines of influence between early and classical thought are too thick to dismiss. Early Islam bequeathed to the classical world its

[98] A. K. Reinhart, *Before Revelation: The Boundaries of Muslim Moral Thought* (SUNY Press, 1995), 5.

moral world, language of discourse, religious doctrines, political conditions, a blossoming legal tradition, and most of all, the powerful memory of a golden age, which classical Muslims, on the whole, neither wished nor managed to transcend (Chapter 2). Nor do I wish to challenge the thesis of failure; one could complain about the intractability of measures of success and point out the adaptive genius of Islamic societies, as well as the many anachronisms involved in assigning the blame. Idealist critics are likely, nonetheless, to point to the glaring chasm between the political ideal of Islam and its historical reality, whereas the more ruthless may thwart such apologies by pointing to centuries of rule by foreign slaves, regicides, constant political instability, eruptions of violence, and most of all the conscious political cynicism of medieval Muslim observers themselves. However, given that no civilization (and I understand the difficulties of using the construct of "civilization" too precisely) is free of such failures for long stretches of time, it is best to move on, as most scholars have, to different, perhaps smaller but more meaningful questions.

The issue I do take with the generalizations I have presented is whether we can better understand the so-called ideal, or what I prefer to call, following Sheldon Wolin, vision of early Islamic political thought. The last wave of master narratives on Islamic political thought were produced in the 1970s, and they have since provided the paradigms for decades of extremely productive research on the subject as well as, in the nature of things, crippling limits. The same research has produced sufficient exceptions and correctives to the paradigmatic narratives to warrant the search for a more precise paradigm. What follows is an attempt to articulate one. My main contention in Chapter 1 is that the early Islamic political thought did not hold to a single monolithic vision, but was rather a struggle between distinct political visions of Islam, as it was between ideals and reality. As I set the stage to offer a new explanation of Islamic political thought and the continued tension between its various visions, one key conclusion that emerges is that given the multiplicity of political visions in early Islam, classical political thought cannot be seen in a simple relation to it. Classical political thought, in other words, has its own explaining to do. In the classical age, starting in the fourth/tenth century, as the early doctrinal diversity (chaos?) became more disciplined (yet by no means eliminated) through the consolidation of sects and doctrines, Sunni thinkers – being the object of my focus – made choices based on their intellectual commitments that were limited but not forced onto them by early Islamic heritage (Chapter 3). Yet, understanding early Islamic thought and its language is indispensible – that is, necessary without being sufficient – in understanding, as J. G. A. Pocock would put it, the redeployment of that language in the political thought of the classical era.[99]

Although classical Islamic thought was a lot more consolidated, finished, and hence dogmatic in its contentions as well as persuasive power than early Islamic political discourse, a similar relationship can be postulated between classical and postclassical (late medieval: the next three centuries, from the mid-seventh/thirteenth to the tenth/sixteenth) thought. That is, postclassical thinkers too could make choices, albeit much less freely. The concepts and sensibilities that came to maturity in the classical period and became imbricated in political, theological, and legal traditions, as well as social and legal institutions, continued to shape political imagination through many a transformation and upheaval, and thus reproduce familiar institutions throughout the premodern Muslim lands.

There was one door still ajar for reopening the classical consolidation. The postclassical medieval thinkers now had inherited two eras of religious and political thought, and they consciously recognized this distinction as the era of the *salaf* (predecessors) and that of the *khalaf* (those who succeeded).[100] If one could argue that the classical consolidation or its dominant streaks had failed to properly interpret the early tradition or picked the wrong models to follow from it, one could still make a very powerful yet fully traditional case for rethinking, reform, and innovation. This was precisely Ibn Taymiyya's point of departure (Chapter 4–7).

[99] Quoted in Skinner, "Surveying," 240.

[100] *EI*², s.v. "al-Salaf wa'l-Khalaf" (E. Chaumont).

PART I

THE CLASSICAL LEGACY

I

A Tale of Two Visions: Sharīʿa and Siyāsa in Early Islam

The objective of this chapter is to give an account of the unfolding of key events and concepts that have defined Islamic political discourse since its inception and provided the context for the political thought of the classical period.

Let us consider some of the more influential accounts that address the transformation of early Islamic political vitality into the classical society's flight from political life. Among the more perceptive of the earlier modern scholars of the subject was H. A. R. Gibb, who concluded that it was "[t]he nemesis of the over-rapid conquests of the Arabs – and the political tragedy of Islam ... that the Islamic ideology never found its proper and articulated expression in the political institutions of the Islamic states."[1] The caliphate, rather than "becoming a truly Muslim institution, standing in proper relation to all the other institutions derived from the principles of the Islamic ideology," turned into a hierarchical, autocratic institution, in particular under the Abbasid "cult of the Sassanid tradition."[2] The jurists too, he held, ultimately failed to resist the imperial imposition and have resorted ever since to legitimizing brute force and maintaining the status quo. The formal Sunni political theory, rather than capturing "the inner principle" of the Islamic political ideal, was "only the rationalization of the history of the community ... and all the imposing fabric of interpretation of the sources is merely the *post eventum* justification of the precedents which have been ratified by *ijmāʿ*."[3]

[1] Gibb, *Studies on the Civilization of Islam* (Princeton University Press, 1982; originally published in 1939), 44–5.
[2] Ibid., 45.
[3] Ibid., 162.

Fazlur Rahman, driven by modernist and reformist concerns, similarly blamed the incompetence of the ulama: "But if the Muslims had really looked into the Qur'an, the solution was there. The solution that the Qur'an gives to [the problem of government] is *shūrā*, which means deciding affairs through mutual consultation and discussion [rather than Sassanid-style despotism]."[4] Rather than elaborate and insist on the political model that was laid out in the Qur'an, Rahman believed that Muslim political thought seems to have rationalized the existing state of affairs during any given demise of the Abbasid power era.[5]

After the demise of the Abbasid power, actual statecraft came to be unreservedly guided by the vision of Persian statesmen like Niẓām al-Mulk (d. 485/1092).[6] This influential Saljuq vizier, argued A. K. S. Lambton as she developed Gibb's line of inquiry, devised a political theory that unsuccessfully attempted to synthesize Islamic and Persian elements. Ultimately, "[b]y restating the old Persian tradition of monarchy, with its independent ethical standards based on force and opportunism, he reaffirmed the duality between the ruling and the religious institutions."[7]

Yet merely the presence of the Sassanid heritage does not explain why and how Islamic tradition came to be dominated by it over and against its own vision. The account of the ulama as passive recipients of Persian influence against the evident qur'anic spirit demands explanation. One such explanation was offered by Ira Lapidus, who boldly turned the account given by Gibb, Rahman, and others on its head. According to Lapidus, the Persian influence was simply a by-product of the vacuum left by an "inherently flawed" structure of authority in early Islam; the fault

[4] F. Rahman, "The Principle of Shura and the Role of the Ummah in Islam," in M. Ahmad (ed.), *State Politics and Islam* (American Trust Publications, 1986).

[5] This appears to be a serious charge, given that the jurists' entire claim of legitimacy rested on their loyalty to the Islamic scriptures, namely the Qur'ān and the teachings of the Prophet, the Sunna. However, the Muslim tradition's negligence toward the Qur'an (as well as reason) was a frequent criticism Rahman systematically elaborated in many of his writings, especially in his posthumous publication, *Revival and Reform in Islam* (Oneworld Publications, 2000). Incidentally, Rahman considered Ibn Taymiyya to have been an exception to this attitude – his last mentioned work is full of admiration for and lengthy quotations from Ibn Taymiyya – which indicates that Rahman might have changed his mind about his earlier sweeping critiques of the tradition.

[6] Ḥasan b. ʿAlī of Ṭūs, known as Khwāja Niẓām al-Mulk – perhaps the most celebrated vizier in Islamic history, known for his decisive mark on Saljuq administration – was in some ways a "shadow ruler" of the Saljuq Empire, whose *Siyāsat-nameh* (*The Book of Politics*), also known as *Siyar al-mulūk* (*Lives of Kings*), is the most influential treatise in the genre of Islamic "mirrors for princes."

[7] Ibid., 64.

lay with the Islamic ideal, not the ulama. The absolute caliphal religio-political authority on the one hand and the availability of the Qur'an to all believers on the other made caliphal authority unsustainable and the early polity inherently unstable. He writes:

> The Caliphal version of Islamic civilization was inherently flawed. While Caliphs were considered the heirs of the Prophet's religious authority as well as his political leadership, they did not inherit Muḥammad's prophethood. The Quran, the revealed book, stood apart from the Caliphs, and was available to every believer. At the core of their executive and symbolic primacy there was a void, for the Caliphs did not have the authority from which Muslim religious conceptions and practices were derived.[8]

Thus on the one hand, the medieval ulama needed to pay lip service to the absolutist and utopian ideal of the golden age of Islam that had sought the union of religion and politics, and on the other, they needed to adjust to the de facto separation of religion and politics. A similar account of early Islamic political thought has been postulated by the German scholar Tilman Nagel.[9] Lapidus maintains that Khurāsānī Arabs, like Aḥmad b. Ḥanbal (d. 241/855), whose ancestors had supported the Abbasid revolution, were disappointed by the Abbasids and were "the first to question the religious authority of the Caliphate, which marked the onset of a new type of political thinking in Muslim societies – *one that is best understood as secularization.*"[10] These third-/ninth-century Baghdadi movements prompted the infamous Miḥna (lit., "inquisition") of traditionalists like Ibn Ḥanbal. As the Khurāsānī pietists came out victorious in the Miḥna, wrenching religious authority from the caliphate, the vacuum that was created by the recession of caliphal absolutism was filled by the new expectation of brute political rationality in which power was justified in itself. The caliphate declined soon thereafter in its political power as well, giving way to military patronage states. The norms of this new "power state" were expressed in the readily available Persian political heritage, according to which the ruler was ipso facto the shadow of God on earth "independent of religion."[11] Yet the sultan of this secular paradigm both upheld order and served as a moral example to his

[8] I. Lapidus, *A History of Islamic Societies* (Cambridge University Press, 2002), 81.

[9] T. Nagel, *Rechtleitung und Kalifat*, 1975, 63 ff. Lapidus's suggestion of secularization is also found in Nagel's reference to Juwayni in *Die Festung des Glaubens: Triumph und Scheitern des islamischen Rationalismus im 11. Jahrhundert* (C. H. Beck, 1988).

[10] Lapidus, "Separation," 384 (emphasis added).

[11] Lapidus, "Golden Age," 17.

subjects, and thus the government "served a religious purpose apart from Islam and apart from the spokesmen of the religious establishment":[12]

> Governments in Islamic lands were henceforth secular regimes – Sultanates – in theory authorized by the Caliphs, but actually legitimized by the need for public order. Henceforth, Muslim states were fully differentiated political bodies without any *intrinsic religious character*, though they were officially loyal to Islam and committed to its defense.[13]

Not only did the new sultanate lack any "intrinsic religious character," but the ulama's idealistic theories too paid only lip service to the early golden-age ideals; they were in fact making room for a secular reality:

> The practical tradition of separation of state and religion also generated a socio-political theory. Muslim political theorists, such as al-Bāqillānī, al-Māwardī, and Ibn Taymiyya, devised a theory of the caliphate that symbolized the ideal existence of the unified *umma*, while at the same time allowing for historical actualities. The conclusion of their theorization was that *the state was not a direct expression of Islam but a secular institution whose duty it was to uphold Islam.* The community of scholars and holy men were the ones who truly carried on the legacy of the Prophet.[14]

Lapidus's bold conclusions prompt more questions. What exactly does it mean for the state to be "a direct expression of Islam" and have an "intrinsic religious character"? If the medieval state upheld Islamic law and defended its Community, in what ways was it secular? How could such a modern concept as "secularization" be mapped onto the history and language of Islamic tradition? Subsequent research on the subject has shown that all the major pieces of Lapidus's account, including his interpretation of authority in early Islam, the nature of the classical caliphate discourse, and the Miḥna itself, are untenable in their detail. His account of the traditionalist movement in Baghdad and its culmination in the Miḥna stood on the claim that the challenge had been initiated by the emerging Khurāsānī traditionalist elements, which has been laid to rest by John Nawas's empirical research showing that the inquisition targeted not just the Khurāsānis or even just the *ḥadīth* scholars, but a wide range of *ḥadīth* and *fiqh* scholars from various ethnic backgrounds and regions.[15]

[12] Ibid., 17.
[13] Lapidus, "Separation," 364 (emphasis added).
[14] Lapidus, "Golden Age," 16–17 (emphasis added).
[15] J. Nawas, "The Mihna of 218 A.H./833 A.D. Revisited: An Empirical Study," *JAOS* 116.4 (1996): 708.

In another study, Nawas established that the challenge was initiated by the caliphate, not the newly emergent scholars.[16]

To characterize the medieval state as secular requires defining the original nonsecular vision against which the secular medieval state is to be measured. Lapidus characterizes the early caliphal authority as "unique and absolute" such that "[n]o other person possessed religious or administrative authority in the *umma* as a whole, except in so far as he served as the Caliph's delegate." Using a language reminiscent of the church publicists of thirteenth- and fourteenth-century Europe, who considered the ecclesia to be embodied in the person of the pope,[17] Lapidus states that the "Caliph personified Islam – the one element of identity common to the tribal factions that made up the community. The Caliph was the very person of the *umma*." In fact, he goes on to aver that this characterization of the early caliphate "seems to be beyond dispute." [18] Against this backdrop, medieval polities that otherwise upheld religious law and were legitimated by their defense of the Islamic community seemed, naturally enough, less religious and hence secular.

Lapidus's "inherent flaw" thesis presumes both early caliphal absolutism and the availability of the Qur'an to the believers, yet he neither provides evidence for the first claim nor examines the qur'anic political ideas or their reception to give a satisfactory account of how they supported or obstructed caliphal authority. The most serious flaw in Lapidus's account is logical: If the availability of the Qur'an to the early believing community thwarted the absolutist claims of the caliphs, on what ground did this absolutism stand to begin with? We are perhaps to understand that any religious community that answers to a transcendent power is inherently unstable or flawed politically because the demands of its religious teachings (whose source is transcendent, and not delegated to an earthly authority, perhaps like the church) would naturally conflict with its political organization. Yet this surely is the challenge of any religious community, and one with an egalitarian and antipriestly impulse like the early Muslim community must face its

[16] J. Nawas, "A Re-examination of Three Current Explanations for Al-Ma'mun's Introduction of the Mihna," *IJMES* 26 (1994): 629.

[17] M. Wilks, *The Problem of Sovereignty in the Later Middle Ages: The Papal Monarchy with Augustinus Triumphus and the Publicists* (Cambridge University Press, 1963), particularly 30–31, 34.

[18] Lapidus, "Separation," 364.

particular version of that inescapable challenge; to posit an inherent flaw on this basis appears to be a bit hasty.[19]

The other influential account of Islamic political history appears in Patricia Crone and Martin Hinds's *God's Caliph*, which aspires to establish the thesis not only of caliphal absolutism but of an even greater claim by the early caliphs to infallible authority bordering that of the Prophet. Acknowledging that the title "*khalīfat Allāh*" (God's caliph) had been limited in its usage (hence the difficulty of documentation), they insist that God's direct vicegerency was the official and widely acknowledged meaning of the caliphate in the Umayyad period. Furthermore, it has been so throughout Islamic history until modern times, and although we cannot confirm it for the first twelve years of the reign of Abū Bakr and ʿUmar, it is likely to have been the same, for "it seems a little strained to propose that its meaning changed during the twelve years from 632 to 644 and remained stable for thirteen centuries thereafter."[20] Crone's other monographs complete and reiterate an account of early Islamic political thought that can be outlined as follows: The early caliphs, including the Umayyads (41–132/661–750), saw themselves as God's caliphs rather than successors of the Prophet Muḥammad ("caliph," or *khalīfa*, could mean deputy or successor), and hence claimed absolute religio-political authority. This may be explained, as Crone and Cook do in *Hagarism*, as Islam's having been a Jewish heretical messianic movement that therefore inherited the political pathology of the Jewish people, who believed themselves to be ruled directly by God and lacked any vision of statehood. When introduced into a stateless, tribal Arab society, the absolutism of God's rule, which assumed a new imperial aura in the vast new empire, clashed with the antistate, tribal Arab spirit. With the consolidation of a priestly class that had held to the tribal vision in the Umayyad century, the caliphs" claim to being God's caliphs increasingly came to be disputed. This priestly class, later triumphant as the ulama, possibly fabricated the entire tradition and history that came to form the basis of Islam and, in theory, deprived the caliphs of any religious function. With the rise of the Abbasids, the tribal basis of Islam vanished, and the ulama, who had espoused the tribal vision, rejected the religious authority of the

[19] For instance, if one cursorily considers the broad outlines of liberal democracy, a political system doctrinally free of any metaphysical values, in which decisions are to be made through rational negotiation based on some shared ground (which itself has been impossible to define and unceasingly debated), one might well judge such a political arrangement to be entirely fantastical and "inherently flawed."

[20] P. Crone and M. Hinds, *God's Caliph* (Cambridge University Press, 1986), 19; 4–6.

Abbasid state. This they achieved by codifying, freezing, and controlling the Sunna – the way of the early caliphs and the Prophet – which had earlier been a "living," growing, and amorphous tradition of norms (without the Prophet's conduct being particularly normative) in whose creation the caliphs had participated as much as, if not more than, the Prophet.[21] By the Abbasid period, the ulama's control over the Sunna was so strong that caliphal attempts to create a legitimating ideology were bound to fail. The caliph al-Ma'mūn naively tried to reassert the claims of the early caliphs, but he was too late by a century. The Abbasid state was soon overtaken by slave soldiers and disintegrated. The divorce of religion and politics, or society and the state, was thus finalized. "Intellectually, it is the very totality of the distinction between the exponents of the state and religion that explains why the relationship between the two could come to be seen even by the medieval Muslims as a symbiosis: once the divorce was finalized, there was nothing to obstruct an improvement in the relationship between the divorcees."[22]

Numerous scholars have relied on this seemingly well-documented thesis. Aziz al-Azmeh, for instance, reiterates Crone and Hinds's view generally, chastises its critics, and insists that the term "God's caliph" was "in constant and ubiquitous use." Conceding, unlike them, that whereas the earliest use of the term *khalīfa* simply designated "the fact of succession to the position of command occupied by the Prophet," he insists that "this conception was very rapidly supplemented – or perhaps superseded – by more sublime associations."[23] Azmeh goes on to note that "[t]he notion of God's caliphate is congruous with the Shīʿī notion of the imāmate officially adopted at a later date." So far so good, but the difficulty arises in Azmeh's generalization: "This doctrine of political authority was never absent from the theory and practice of the Sunni caliphate, although it was never formalized in legal and religious doctrines of public authority."[24] Other recent studies have reiterated similar conclusions.[25]

21 Ibid., 90–91.

22 P. Crone, *Slaves on Horses: The Evolution of the Islamic Polity* (Cambridge University Press, 1980), 85–88.

23 A. Al-Azmeh, *Muslim Kingship* (I. B. Tauris, 1997), 74. Based on a misunderstanding, al-Azmeh places in ʿUmar's reign a coin known to have been minted in ʿAbd al-Malik's and hence thinks that the title "God's caliph" was employed as early as the reign of the second caliph (A. Shahin, "Arabian Political Thought in the Great Century of Change" (PhD Dissertation, University of Chicago, 2009), 407).

24 Al-Azmeh, 76.

25 For instance, A. Marsham, *Rituals of Islamic Monarchy* (Edinburgh University Press, 2009), which focuses on an extremely narrow genre of documents comprising oaths of

Methodologically, Crone and Hinds had based their account on a radical skepticism that refused even minimal reliability of the entire Islamic historical corpus including the Qur'an, except for the fragmentary evidence the authors deemed salvageable. As such, it is built on the interpretation of sparse and disparate pieces of evidence, and its central claims have failed to inspire confidence even among other skeptical historians.[26] Careful studies of the very sources these scholars have relied on have discredited key segments of this account. Uri Rubin, for instance, has pointed out critical errors and omissions in Crone and Hinds's reading of the letter by the Umayyad caliph, Walīd II (r. 125–6/743–4), which they present as the critical piece of evidence for their claim that in the Umayyad worldview "the Islamic era does not begin with Muḥammad but rather with the caliphs who ruled after him."[27] They write, "Al-Walīd here sketches out a salvation history divided into two eras, one of prophets and another of caliphs." Muḥammad, in their interpretation of Walīd's letter, "represented the culmination of prophethood and on his death the era of the prophets came to an end." Hence:

> What is so striking about this letter is that caliphs are in no way subordinated to prophets (let alone to the Prophet.) Prophets and caliphs alike are seen as God's agents, and both dutifully carry out the tasks assigned to them, the former by delivering messages and the latter by putting them into effect. The caliphs are the legatees of prophets in the sense that they administer something established by them, but they do not owe their authority to them (let alone to Muḥammad on his own). Their authority comes directly from God.[28]

They base this conclusion on a key passage of the letter, which they translate in full in an appendix.[29] Rubin, in his study of the idea of prophetic

succession primarily from the late Marwānid period and interprets such documents to represent Islamic political thought. Because he methodically avoids the use of narrative, juristic, or theological sources that might have given him another perspective, his conclusion is unsurprisingly "ruler-centered." What follows can be seen as an argument against such an approach.

26 Even generally skeptical scholars in the field have found Crone and Hinds' approach wanting, pointing out that their impressive collective of data is "ineffectual" in itself because of the complexity of the meanings the phrase had and the varieties of ways in which it has been used in Islamic political imagination. In offering a radically revisionist account of the entire early Islamic history, these authors have adopted "not only some of the methods of Biblical criticism ... [but also] some of the Biblical critics' conclusions" (F. Donner, *Narratives of Islamic Origins*, The Darwin Press, 1998), 29. According to another scholar, the radical revisionist trend is on the whole discredited and has "little affected the scholarly consensus." Nonetheless, "its distrust of early literary sources jostled" all of those who work in the classical period (Melchert, review of Zaman, 273).

27 Crone and Hinds, 89.

28 Ibid., 27.

29 Ibid.,118–9.

inheritance as depicted in the Qur'an, contends that "[t]he English translation of this passage in Crone and Hinds" *God's Caliph* is erroneous and misses the idea of successive authority that is being conveyed here. Due to this error, Crone and Hinds believe to find in the letter support to their supposition that the Umayyads did not see themselves as Muḥammad's heirs, only as God's deputies."[30] Rubin shows that the correct reading of the letter shows that the Umayyad caliphs are God's deputies "in the sense that they are guardians of God's religion, but they only gained this status thanks to the fact that God chose to make them Muḥammad's legatees."[31]

Umayyad poetry also endorses Rubin's reading. Regarding the work of the Umayyad court poet Farazdaq (d. 112/730), Crone and Hinds write that "though Muḥammad is now clearly invoked to legitimate the caliphate, it is to God on the one hand and 'Uthmān on the other that the caliphs are directly indebted for their authority."[32] Rubin shows this conclusion to be untenable as well, for Farazdaq repeatedly describes Umayyads elsewhere as having inherited the legacy of "our chosen prophet," and in fact eulogizes the caliphs preceding 'Uthmān, tracing the ultimate earthly authority of the Umayyad caliphate not in 'Uthmān, but in Muḥammad.[33] In Rubin's view, Farazdaq's poetry reflected the authentic Umayyad self-image for it was what the Umayyads wanted to hear about themselves (although one still has to account for poetic exaggeration and political rhetoric). In several verses documented by Rubin, Farazdaq made it a point to describe the Umayyads as being heirs to the Prophet's particular relics, such as his sword, his pulpit, and the ring that had inscribed on it "Muḥammad [is] the Messenger of God." Hence what could be more appropriate, asks Rubin, than the title *khalīfat rasūl Allāh*, "the successor of the Messenger of God," for those who claim the mission of

30 U. Rubin, "Prophets and Caliphs: The Biblical Foundations of the Umayyad Authority," in H. Berg (ed.), *Method and Theory in the Study of Islamic Origins* (Brill, 2003), 91. Rubin shows persuasively that the sentence "wa kāna bayna-hum wa-bayna man maḍā min al-umami wa-khalā min al-qurūni qarnan fa-qarnan," deemed incomprehensible by Crone and Hinds (118–9), establishes that the religion of Islam has been passed down the line of prophets until Prophet Muḥammad, from whom the caliphs inherit the task of preserving and passing on the message, and it is due to their role in the preservation of the Prophet's message (both in theory and especially in practice, through governance and *jihād*) that these caliphs must be obeyed (92–3). "The caliphs, like Muḥammad, are meant to secure the endurance of the revived religion that had been preached by all the prophets, and therefore everyone must obey them, while God himself will punish anyone who rejects them" (90).

31 Rubin, 93.

32 Crone and Hinds, 31.

33 Rubin, 93–4, 97.

the Messenger of God, symbolically through relics and in reality through their leadership of the *umma* as well as *jihād*.[34]

Farazdaq, in fact, helps explain another key issue: namely, the alleged distinction between the title "God's caliph" and the "caliph of the Messenger of God," on which Crone and Hinds have based their entire panoply of interpretation. In one poem addressed to Walīd II, Farazdaq says that this caliph fought the infidels with the sword with which Muḥammad had fought his enemies at Badr.[35] It is interesting that elsewhere, in praising the military achievements of Yazīd II and other Umayyads, Farazdaq uses the same symbolic "sword of Muḥammad" interchangeably with the "sword of prophethood" and the "sword of God."[36] Thus Rubin, like other scholars who have been skeptical of this thesis,[37] effectively establishes that the authors of *God's Caliph* have made too much of that title. He concludes, "Thus it becomes clear yet again that God and Muḥammad are complementary components of the idea behind the title "God's caliph.' A caliph of this kind is one who has inherited from the Prophet Muḥammad the mission of protecting God's religion."[38] Rubin's critique of the "God's caliph" thesis and his reading of the sources is further corroborated by Aram A. Shahin's extensive comparative study of a vast range of nondiscursive evidence from pre- and early Islamic history. He examines the political titulature of all existing empires of Eurasia as well as inscriptions, coins, and papyri to determine the meanings of key political terms (like *khalīfa*) and concepts (dynastic succession and norms of rule and legitimation), thus organizing invaluable "hard" data on the context of the early caliphate. He concludes that Islamic political thought and practice marked a significant break with Eurasian imperial and royal traditions. The title of choice for Arabian

[34] Ibid.

[35] Ibid., 95.

[36] Ibid., 95–6. This is hardly different from how today ordinary Muslim preachers describe their missionary work interchangeably as "the work of the Prophet," "the work of the Companions," and "the work of God."

[37] One scholar, for instance, writes, "The title of *khalīfat Allāh* does imply divine legitimation, a divine sanction or source for whatever power the ruler exercises, without, in itself, identifying the nature of that power or the extent of its jurisdiction" (M. Morony, review of *God's Caliph*, *JNES* 48.2 [1989]: 135). Another scholar points out that the Sudanese president Numayri, when he inclined toward implementing certain Islamic measures in 1983 and abjured his secular beginnings, called himself "Allah's representative on earth" – without the slightest implication that he inhered the Prophetic or absolute religious authority (A. Rippin, review of *God's Caliph*, *SOAS* 51.2 [1988]: 328).

[38] Ibid., 96.

sovereigns for nearly a thousand years prior to the coming of Islam had been m.l.k (the most common form of this root being *malik*, "king"), a title that, along with its equivalents in the neighboring empires, was rejected and even disparaged by early Muslims.[39] Contrary to the contention of Crone et al., the use of the title *khalīfa* (let alone *khalīfat Allāh*) was quite late and far from widespread. The title most commonly attested for all the early caliphs starting with ʿUmar – certainly attested for ʿUthmān – and ever since is *amīr al-mu'minīn* (the chief of the believers), not *khalīfa* in any of its forms.[40] The first appearance of the title *khalīfat Allāh* does not occur until the second half of the first/seventh century, and it cannot be attested to have been used by ʿUthmān or ʿAlī.[41] It first appears in the reign of Muʿāwiya, but only in rare literary sources and never in official documents. The next appearance is in the reign of ʿAbd al-Malik, another Umayyad whose reign, like Muʿāwiya's, followed a civil war.[42] The inscription "n.ṣ.r Allāh, amīr al-mu'minīn, kh.l.f.t Allāh" appears on coins minted early on in ʿAbd al-Malik's reign, and was apparently removed after the counter-caliphate of Ibn al-Zubayr had been subdued; "*khalīfat Allāh*" is a disputed – though most plausible – reading of the last phrase.[43] In more than one thousand preserved verses of more than one hundred Khārijī poets, the term "*khalīfa*" appears only once, and "*khalīfat Allāh*" never makes an appearance.[44] Furthermore, the meaning of the term *khalīfa*, even when it does appear, is unlikely to have been as suggested by Crone and Hinds. Based on extensive investigation of the etymology of the Semitic root kh.l.f and its widespread

[39] Shahin argues, on the basis of a broad comparison of the practice of emergent dynasties in Eurasia, that the early Muslim state was exceptional in that it refused to adopt the title "king" and borrowed regional titles from neighboring regions (Shahin, 387).

[40] Shahin, 554. One Chinese literary source describing a Muslim envoy dated from ʿUthman's reign (31/651) refers to their emperor with a term that could only be a rendering of "amīr al-mu'minīn." Ibid., 550–4.

[41] Shahin, 465–70, rejects the lone source (Ḥassān b. Thābit) that uses the title for ʿUthmān as having been written in the reign of Muʿāwiya.

[42] Shahin, 554. Shahin speculates that Muʿāwiya's supporters felt the need for an added title possibly because of the need for added legitimacy to make up for the civil war against Ali, the counterclaims of Alids, and his attempt to install his son as his successor. Furthermore, he notes, "[t]he title is almost exclusively found in the poetry associated with Umayyad sovereigns, usually in panegyrics" (461). The next time this title is employed is with ʿAbd al-Malik b. Marwān, who also had survived a civil war – this time a powerful challenge to the Umayyad rule by Ibn al-Zubayr – and was in greater need to bolster authority and compensate. This is the first appearance on coins (555).

[43] Ibid., 407.

[44] Ibid., 461.

use in pre-Islamic times in personal names in various languages across the entire Near East,[45] Shahin concludes that "[s]cholars are unanimous on the meaning of the names that are based on the root kh.l.f: it is not "replacement or substitute *of* a god," but rather "replacement or substitute (of a deceased person) *by* a god.'"[46] This reading is strengthened by the fact that toward the beginning of the seventh century AD, the Roman emperors in Constantinople added a new title to their already impressive titulature that meant "crowned by God."[47]

Having presented sufficient evidence against the claim of the absolutism of religio-political authority of the early caliphs implied in the title *God's Caliph*, I now briefly point to the scholarship on the alleged "divorce" between the ulama and the state in the Abbasid period that is crucial to Crone's as well as Lapidus's account. The most direct challenge is M. Q. Zaman's study, which demonstrates the "deep involvement of the early Abbasids in the religious life of the times":

> [T]hat the early Abbasid caliphs (except al-Ma'mūn) enjoyed or claimed any religious authority over and above the 'ulamā' is not as evident ... as it seems to be to the authors of *God's Caliph*; that the caliph's participation in religious matters was effectively terminated with the failure of the *Miḥna*, as is argued, *inter alia*, by Lapidus, is a view which seems to require considerable revision, so does Nagel's view that the proto-Sunni 'ulamā' were irrevocably hostile to the Abbasids until the failure of the *Miḥna*.[48]

Nor, argues Zaman, was the view of the early Abbasids like Hārūn al-Rashīd on the religious authority of the caliphate very different from that of the ulama themselves.[49] To further assess the different views of the relationship between the ulama and the caliphs in the Abbasid period, we must first establish a plausible narrative of the earlier history, a task to which I now turn.

WHAT HAPPENED? A TALE OF TWO VISIONS

The following account of the political evolution of the early Muslim community is based on a source-critical and minimalist method in that

[45] He examines documents from the various ancient dialects of Arabic, including Safaitic (Old North Arabian dialect), Nabataean, Thamudic, Lihyanic, South Arabian, and as transliterations in Greek or Latin inscriptions in Greater Syria, to arrive at his conclusion (Shahin, 566–618).

[46] Ibid., 617–8; emphasis in the original.

[47] Ibid., 627.

[48] Zaman, 11.

[49] Ibid.

it relies on our best historical sources of the period, starting with the Qur'an, whose origins are placed by increasing accumulation of recent studies nearly definitively in the lifetime of the Prophet Muḥammad and its codification within fifteen years after his death at the latest. These developments require that historians of early Islam return to the qur'anic text – after the lapse of a few decades introduced by the ultra-skeptical turn in the 1970s – to reconstruct early Islamic thought and society with greater confidence.[50] Our approach to the *ḥadīth* corpus, on the other hand, needs to be much more cautious, for even as recent scholarship is unveiling the sophisticated workings of traditional Muslim criticism, our knowledge needs to improve much further before we can treat it with greater confidence. Yet it cannot be dismissed wholesale; and, for our purpose, the widespread appearance of *ḥadīth* reports serves as an indication of the concerns of Muslims, at least at the time such reports can be reasonably established to have become widespread.[51]

[50] For the recent historical evidence dating the Qur'an to the seventh century, possibly as early as within the life of the Prophet Muhammad, see B. Sadeghi and U. Bergmann, "The Codex of a Companion of the Prophet and the Qur'ān of the Prophet," *Arabica* 57 (2010): 343–436. Sadeghi provides latest and most definitive arguments based on radioactive carbon dating, which places the particular Qur'anic codex with high probability to within fifteen years of the Prophet's death (348). For a review of theories of John Wansbrough (1977) and others about later origins of the Qur'an, which have been now mostly discredited, see A. Rippin (ed.), *The Blackwell Companion to the Qur'an* (Blackwell Publishing, 2006), in particular the article by Angelika Neuwirth, "Structure and the Emergence of Community." Neuwirth notes, even without the benefit of Sadeghi's aforementioned research, that "evidence of old Qur'an codices as well as new philological and historical studies have provided strong arguments in favor of the Qur'an's emergence from an Arabian environment and of an early date of the Qur'anic redaction" (141). Also, for an even earlier view, E. Whelan, "Forgotten Witness: Evidence for the Early Codification of the Qur'an," *JAOS* 118.1 (1998): 1–14.

[51] The historical confidence we can have in any report that is not multiply transmitted (*mutawātir*) does not approach anywhere near what we have in the Qur'an. Furthermore, the potential or real mutual contradictions in the *ḥadīth* material have historically rendered its use open to diverse interpretations that require serious caution. My account, therefore, is not dependent on this "raw material," but employs it only to determine general trends. Religious authenticity (i.e., truthfulness) and hence significance of the report, which is the primary concern for traditional *ḥadīth* critics, is not relevant to our analysis, except inasmuch as that traditional criticism provides invaluable and often trustworthy data on the history, narration, versions of, and disputes around a report, which, combined with content analysis, allows us to make inferences about its contemporary conceptual milieu. I do not take the fact that a report speaks to contemporary political events to mean necessarily that it is fabricated, nor does its appearance in authentic collections sufficient to furnish certainty that it represent the Prophet' s words. This approach is not new even to Muslim tradition, and Muslim theorists (both legal and theological) have held this view. The *ahl al-ḥadīth*, on the other hand, have generally insisted that such

The Community-Centered Vision of the Qur'an

Islam, as noted earlier, began as a politically vibrant religion. The closest companions of the Prophet of Islam, the tradition has it, were men and women of exceptional other-worldly piety as well as worldly talent and organizational skill. This pietistic yet activist milieu is well reflected in the Qur'an. Before addressing the key political concepts of the Qur'an, some reflection on the nature of the qur'anic injunctions and in what sense they can be considered political is in order. The Qur'an called its prescription to humankind Sharīʿa, which seems to mean in the few places it appears in the Qur'an not so much a body of law, as it has ubiquitously come to mean today, but God's open and clear way as opposed to the vain desires of those ignorant of divine revelation.[52] The qur'anic statements covered the entire range of human activity. Some expressed metaphysical truths; others were general exhortations to universal values such as justice, benevolence, piety, and equality that we label ethical and moral; and yet others were specific and had meaning only in the context of the Prophet's career. Finally, there were others regarding routine rituals (*ʿibādāt*) or dealings (*muʿāmalāt*) that formed the basis of believers" lives; only this last type formed the subject of law or jurisprudence proper. What concerns us here are those that were fundamental to the constitution and collective existence of the community of believers, the *umma*.[53] Such verses assigned to this community its purpose and mission:

reports may, if supported by context and corroborated by other reports, furnish certitude. See J. Brown, *Ḥadīth* (Oneworld, 2009), 104; A. Zysow, "Economy of Certainty" (PhD Dissertation, Harvard University, 1984), 141–7.

[52] Q, 45:18, 5:48. The *totality of Islam* was referred to in the Qur'an in a number of ways, such as (1) *dīn*, which seems to mean the generic term for "way of life" or "religion," which could be true or false; (2) *islām*, which is the name for the true *dīn* (3:19: "the [true] *dīn* before God is *islām*"; 3:85), and (3) Sharīʿa. More commonly, especially in the *ḥadīth* corpus, it is referred to simply as (iv) "*al-amr*" (the matter or the affair). The term Sharīʿa (Q, 45:18; in a different grammatical form, 5:48), primarily means God's prescribed way for a given community. One interpretation has been that Sharīʿa refers to a body of laws as opposed to creed or ethics, whereas *dīn* refers to the creed (Ibn Saʿd, *Ṭabaqāt*, 1: 345, 355). Since, at the latest, the medieval period, Sharīʿa has come to fulfill the need for a term to refer to the totality of the normative aspects of Islam as preached by the Prophet Muḥammad and that is inclusive of creedal, ethical, legal, and any other domain of life. Both senses are widely employed today, although when used in its limited sense, often another functional equivalent such as Islam or *dīn* is used to refer to the totality of normativity. I will use the term Sharīʿa in its all-encompassing meaning.

[53] Riḍwān al-Sayyid has made insightful and original contributions to our understanding of the emergence of this concept. See idem, *al-Umma wa 'l-jamāʿa wa 'l-sulṭā* (Bayrūt: Dār Iqra', 1986), in particular, 43–9. For our purpose, the concept of *umma* is of interest

Thus we have made you a community of the golden mean (*ummatan wasaṭan*), that you be witnesses unto people and the Messenger witness unto you... (2:143)

And,

You are the best community ever brought forth to humankind, you command what is right, forbid what is evil, and believe in God. (3:110)

These are not merely legal commands, but constitutional, for they found the community and the context in which all the legal commands were to acquire meaning and direction; they define the very purpose and the mission of the new community. In this sense, they speak to Islam's earthly mission. This vision, inasmuch as it gives agency, responsibility, and a set of goals to the entire community, and not merely a set of rules to the individual, can be called political, not merely legal or spiritual. This vision must, therefore, be the starting point for any understanding of early Islamic political thought.

The most striking feature of this vision is that it addresses the *umma*, the community of believers, all at once and without distinction. The ethic of the Qur'an is on the whole egalitarian[54] and activist,[55] enhanced by its Arab tribal milieu and reflected in the early Islamic society.[56] Furthermore, the unyielding monotheism of the Qur'an, coupled with its insistence on rational piety that required obeying none but God and his Prophet, encouraged questioning authority and using one's own reason instead of following tradition or other men's judgment.[57]

after its formative phase when it acquired the stable meaning of the entire Muslim Community.

[54] For a discussion of the "strikingly egalitarian" nature of early Islamic society and their Qur'anic inspiration, "accentuated ... by its conjunction with ... Arab tribalism," see L. Marlow, *Hierarchy and Egalitarianism in Islamic Thought* (Cambridge University Press, 2002), 1–6; esp. 4.

[55] E.g., Q, 13:11.

[56] The egalitarianism of early Islamic society along with the Qur'anic concept of piety historically materialized in the form of excellence (in faith and devotion; *faḍīla*) and precedence (in embracing Islam; *sābiqa*) as being the foremost requirements for leadership (A. Afsaruddin, *Excellence and Precedence: Medieval Islamic Discourse on Legitimate Leadership* [Brill, 2002]); idem, "The Excellences of the Qur'an: Textual Sacrality and the Organization of Early Islamic Society," *JAOS* 122.1 (2002): 18. To take one instance, 'Umar is told by one of his governors that he left Ibn Abzā, a *mawlā* (a slave or freedman) in charge of Mecca behind him because "he is a reciter of the Book of God the Exalted," to which the *amīr al-mu'minīn* exclaimed, "God raises some by this Qur'an and diminishes other by it" (ibid.).

[57] The blind following of one's forefathers or customs is scorned frequently in the Qur'an, for instance, 21:53, 26:74, 43:22, 43:23, and evidence (*sulṭān*) for claims frequently demanded, as in 7:71, 10:68.

Ulu 'l-amr

The natural problem that arose from the passing of the prophetic mission to the entire community of believers[58] is that of organization within the community. There are surprisingly few verses that allow for hierarchy or structure within the community, and only a couple that are explicit. One states: "O you who believe! Obey God, and obey the Messenger, and those charged with authority among you. If you differ in anything among yourselves, refer it to God and His Messenger..." (4:59). Thus sandwiched between the exhortations to obey God and his Prophet is the command to obey "those charged with authority among you" – *ulu 'l-amr minkum* – which, both in the qur'anic discursive context and its early Muslim reception, referred to leaders of expeditions or delegations rather than experts of legal or religious knowledge, and hence pointed to primarily a political rather than epistemological organization.[59] The verse does not indicate how this authority is to be acquired, but it does indicate the need for discipline and obedience (an understandable concern in a community not accustomed to state control), but also the limits of that obedience (i.e., only inasmuch as such obedience does not entail contradicting God and the Messenger). The suggestion that the leaders are "from among you" and not a superior breed corroborates the general qur'anic spirit of egalitarianism.

There is at least one other verse that advised returning confusing questions in matters of public concern to "those charged with authority" so that "those who could investigate that matter could know the judgment regarding it."[60] Once again, the ethos is political, and the authorities and investigators implied are more likely to be experienced leaders and strategists than trained jurists. What's more, the wording permits that

[58] The analogy of the *umma*'s mission to that of the Prophet's is clear: "so that you [all] be witnesses unto humankind and the Messenger a witness unto you ..." (2:143).

[59] The exegetical history of this term is revealing: According to the more traditionally sound reports attributed to the chief exegete of the first generation, 'Abd Allāh b. 'Abbās (d. *ca.* 68/688 or 70/690), this phrase primarily referred to the leaders of missions and delegations that the Prophet dispatched out of Medina. Ṭabarī, *Jāmiʿ al-bayān fī ta'wīl al-qur'ān*, 24 vol. (Mu'assasa al-Risāla, 2000), 8:495f., lists six reports that take *ulu 'l-amr* to mean leaders or rulers and then a dozen that take it to mean scholars. Ultimately, Ṭabarī concludes that the first opinion is the correct one on the basis of three general *ḥadīth* reports that require obeying the ruler. For the historical evolution of the two meanings of this phrase, see Sayyid, *Jamāʿa*, 37–8.

[60] "When there comes to them some matter touching (public) safety or fear, they divulge it. Had they only referred it to the Messenger and those in authority among them, those seeking its meaning (*yastanbiṭūnahū*) would have found it out for them" (Q, 4:83).

the "authorities" (*ulu 'l-amr*) and "investigators" not necessarily be the same person. This also reinforces the early exegetical reports that take the authorities implied in both verses to be political leaders who may happen to be, or else must seek the advice of, experts on matters of strategy or scriptural interpretation.

Shūrā

Besides the concept of the religio-political community, that is, *umma*, which must obey authorities from within itself as long as they obey the Qur'an and the Prophet, another key qur'anic concept is *shūrā*, or consultation.[61] Although not exclusively a political concept, it does seem to have had primarily normative political connotations as being the way the believers in positions of authority ought to make collective decisions.[62] The concept needed little elaboration, for in this case the Qur'an simply reinforced a pre-Islamic Arab tribal trait. The Prophet practiced *shūrā* (i.e., consulted) with his companions in collective decision making. In one of the two verses where it appears, the Qur'an commands and approves of the Prophet's act of seeking consultation and of acquiescing to the majority on a decision that went against his own better judgment, thus suggesting the practice of *shūrā* as a virtue in principle and not merely an expedient tactic to consolidate loyalty.[63] The logic of the Prophet's *shūrā* is strengthened by the fact, amply evident in the Qur'an as well as *ḥadīth*, that not all decisions even of the Prophet were considered divinely ordained in a direct sense nor his authority deemed absolute; that his followers appreciated that he made judgment calls or strategic decisions that the Qur'an at times corrected and criticized; and that his followers were aware of the distinction between divine command and his opinion.[64] However, the

[61] Western scholars' attitude toward *shūrā* has been largely dismissive of its political significance and is often limited to a discussion of ʿUmar's nomination of six candidates, one of whom was to be elected by *shūrā* (for instance, *EI*[2], s.v. "Shūrā" [C. E. Bosworth]).

[62] Q, 42:38 and 3:159. See also, Sayyid, *Jamāʿa*, 35 ff. and idem, *al-Umma*, 78–83.

[63] Traditional reports about the Prophet that occasioned the main *shūrā* verse (3:159) suggest that it addressed a case when the Prophet and the senior Companions disagreed with the majority and the Prophet obliged. Ṭabarī, *Jāmiʿ al-bayān*, 7:343–5; there is disagreement on whether the Prophet himself was commanded to seek *shūrā* for its own sake or only to win over his followers' hearts. Ṭabarī himself opts for the latter, arguing that the Prophet needed no advice because God could inform him of any matter. In any case, the implication for anyone after the Prophet is clear.

[64] For the Qur'an's censure of the Prophet's actions, see 8:68; 33:37; 66:1; 80:1–5. In an amusing anecdote, a freed slave girl is asked by the Prophet to consider returning to her former husband, upon which she inquires whether he is commanding her or merely suggesting; she then rejects the suggestion. See *Sunan Ibn Mājah*, "K. al-Ṭalāq," no. 2065, JK.

Qur'an also established the uniqueness of the Prophet's authority, later articulated in the concept of the Prophet's protection from error (*ʿiṣma*), and warned his followers of the necessity to submit to the Prophet in an absolute sense, bestowing prima facie probity to any judgment of the Prophet not explicitly revoked.[65]

The occasion of the succession of the Prophet and the accession of Abū Bakr is shrouded in controversy, yet despite their divergence, these accounts establish at the minimum that the first successors (caliphs) of the Prophet did not have the final and revelation-backed authority of the Prophet; rather, they served as first among equals. This was natural enough, for institutionalization of charisma takes time, and if the successors did not inherit the Prophet's authority and if the appointment of the caliph was contested, which all sources agree it was, the authority of the first caliph must have been quite precarious. The caliph did, however, quickly come to serve as the main reference point for political, legal, and theological issues, particularly in the face of the threats apostasy wars posed to the nascent Medinan state. This state of affairs is better understood as the lack of differentiation or definition of various functions and authorities of the new caliph, natural in a nascent community lacking developed political heritage, rather than the absoluteness of the authority of the caliph.

The Qur'an and most likely the Prophet himself having been silent on the subject,[66] it was the conduct and decisions of Abū Bakr that helped define the role of the Prophet's successor to a large degree. The first defining moment was Abū Bakr's purported deployment of the Qur'anic verse in the wake of the Prophet's demise, which reminded the believers that the mission of Islam was not concluded with the life of the Prophet.[67] Abū Bakr's decisiveness against the so-called apostate tribes settled another fundamental question for centuries to come, if not forever.[68] The question ultimately was whether allegiance to the Medinan state,

[65] Q, 4:65. On different views of the Prophet's *ʿiṣma* in Islamic tradition, see S. Ahmed, "Ibn Taymiyya and the Satanic Verses," *SI* 87 (1998): 67–124.

[66] Whether the Prophet explicitly chose a successor is a major point of disagreement: the majority opinion among the Sunnis remains that he did not, and among the Imāmī Shīʿa, that he did. For an early Zaydī Shīʿī opinion that he did not, see later.

[67] Q, 3:144: "Muhammad is no more than an apostle: many were the apostles that passed away before him. If he died or were slain, will ye then Turn back on your heels? If any did turn back on his heels, not the least harm will he do to Allah. But Allah will swiftly reward those who (serve Him) with gratitude."

[68] A. al-ʿAskar, *Al-Yamāma in the Early Islamic Era* (Garnett Publishing, 2002), who explains that many had not embraced Islam to begin with.

the expression of the political unity of the *umma*, was part and parcel of being Muslim;[69] Abū Bakr's answer was a decisive yes – although the implications of this affirmation remained ambiguous.[70] A third intervention by the first caliph, equally significant but less appreciated, was his explication of the role of the caliph in his inauguration speech: "I have been given charge over you while I am not the best of you. If I do well, support me, and if I err, straighten me ... obey me so long as I obey Allah and His Messenger – but if I disobey Allah and His Messenger, you have no obligation to obey me."[71] This attitude of Abū Bakr responded to a central question about the nature of the office of Prophet' s successor, namely, whether or not that office carried with it any inherently divine authority that gave an infallible character to its occupier. What's more, the guardian of the Community, on this view, had a guardian: the Community itself.

The Medinan state under the first successors of the Prophet loosely embraced the principle of *shūrā*, which had had clear limits in the life of the Prophet; however, those limits now had to expand significantly. All issues, whether devotional or practical, that did not have a clear answer in the Qur'an or Prophet's teachings could now be the object of *shūrā*. Yet no systematic attempt appears to have been made to include non-senior members of the Community or, for that matter, to exclude them. Rather, there seems to be a lack of concern for institutionalization by men who perhaps could not imagine how "religiously" posterity would look at their commissions as well as omissions.

The second caliph, ʿUmar, is seen in many reports as emphasizing the necessity of *shūrā* for the legitimate leadership of the Community. One report has ʿUmar say, "Whoever calls to his own rule or that of someone else without consultation (*mashwara*) with the Muslims must be

[69] F. Donner, "The Formation of the Islamic State," *JAOS* 106.2 (1986): 283–96, writes, "The idea of indivisibility of political authority seem to go back to the earliest experiences of the Islamic state and to the earliest chapter in Islamic history" (295). Despite the difficulty in practice of sustaining this idea of a unified state as a necessary expression of Islam in the face of the political frustrations of the ensuing centuries, Muslims, both Sunnī and Shīʿa, on the whole have maintained it in different forms.

[70] The Shīʿa came to consider political order under the right religious authority (*imām*) a part of creed, whereas the Sunnis consider the caliphate an obligation (i.e., to be attained if possible). See Chapter 2.

[71] Ibn Qutayba al-Dīnwarī (d. 276 AH), *Al-Imāma wa 'l-siyāsa* (Dār al-Kutub al-ʿIlmiyya, 1418/1997), 19 (the attribution of this book to Ibn Qutayba is disputed); Sayyid, *Jamāʿa*, 102. For a slightly different version, see F. Donner (trans.), *The History of al-Ṭabarī*, vol. X (SUNY Press, 1993), 11. For a discussion of another version of this speech as reported by al-Jāḥiẓ, see Afsaruddin, *Excellence*, 148–50.

executed."[72] In one widespread report, 'Umar describes the election of Abū Bakr as accidental or unpremeditated (*falta*) and strongly warns against pledging allegiance to a new caliph without the *shūrā* of the generality of Muslims.[73] Yet this particular speech of 'Umar creates a few difficulties. For instance, the majority of the Helpers and senior members of the Immigrants reportedly participated in Abū Bakr's election, which means that 'Umar's critique was directed at the unplanned and unannounced nature of Abū Bakr's election, and his view of *shūrā* would then seem to be that the generality of Muslims must be informed of the consultation, if not invited to participate in it. The other difficulty in this account is that 'Umar's own election had involved even less *shūrā* than Abū Bakr's, unless we assume that the lack of *shūrā* in that case was mitigated by the fact that he was appointed or at least nominated by the reigning caliph. In some reports, 'Umar considers options for his succession and even considers nominating no one, as the Prophet had done. Other reports have 'Umar nominating (or appointing) someone, as Abū Bakr had done in choosing him.[74] One way to resolve this contradiction, if we accept both sets of traditions as sound, is to assume that 'Umar considered Abū Bakr's choice of him as nomination rather than appointment, which was then put to *shūrā* and ratified.[75]

'Umar's practice also provides a clear example of the significance of *shūrā* for the early caliphs. In one instance, when deciding the fate of the conquered lands of Iraq, 'Umar's opinion was strongly against dividing such vast lands among the conquering army, as had been the practice of his predecessors. Yet he could not impose his opinion and hence called for *shūrā* first the leading Immigrants and then, when a decision could not be reached, he further included in the process ten important personages from the Helpers. After a long debate, which according to some reports continued for three days, 'Umar found a qur'anic verse to settle the argument, and only then could the council be convinced.[76]

[72] 'Abd al-Razzaq al-Ṣan'ānī, *al-Muṣannaf*, 11 vols. (al-Maktab al-Islāmī, 1403), 5:445.

[73] The report has it: "No one should deceive himself by saying that Abū Bakr's *bay'a* was an accident [*falta*] and worked out well. It indeed was so but God saved [us from] its evil... If someone pledges allegiance to a man without consultation with the generality of Muslims, then the man pledging and the one being pledged must be executed" (Ṣan'ānī, *al-Muṣannaf*, 5:445). The same report appears in Ibn Hishām (d. 183/799), *Sīrat al-nabī*, 5 vols., ed. Majdī Fatḥī al-Sayyid (Dār al-Ṣaḥāba li'l-Turāth, 1416/1995), 4:365, par. 2097; Bukhārī, "K. al-Muḥāribīn," no. 6918.

[74] Ibn Sa'd, *Ṭabaqāt*, 3:353.

[75] This, at least, seems to be the view of Ibn Taymiyya; see Chapter 7.

[76] Abū Yūsuf, *K. al-Kharāj* (al-Maktaba al-Salafiyya, 1382), 25–6.

The theme of *shūrā* is also evident in accounts of ʿAlī's accession to the caliphal office. When his supporters wished to pledge allegiance to him as the next caliph, "ʿAlī said at the occasion of his accession to the caliphate, "My *bayʿah* [pledge] cannot be clandestine, nor can it take place without the agreement of Muslims.... [Despite the threat against him] he refused for it to take place except in the main mosque. Thus, the Immigrants and the Helpers proceeded to give their pledge, followed by the [generality of the] people."[77] Similarly, at the occasion of the arbitration between ʿAlī and Muʿāwiya, the arbiters reportedly agreed to suspend their respective claimants and leave the matter of caliphate to *shūrā* (*jaʿl al-amr shūrā*), or, in another reported wording, to let the Community decide which of the two it preferred for the position. The matter, however, came to naught as Muʿāwiya's representative famously backed out.[78]

Despite the recurrent indications of its significance, however, *shūrā* remained an expansive concept akin to prudence, diplomacy, and consensus building, not a precise political institution. Yet the political potency of this concept was such that it defined the political struggles of the first century and a half of Islam, giving rise, or at least providing ammunition, to numerous rebellions against rulers who were seen as having fallen short in their practice of *shūrā*; this continued until the concept itself evolved away from its egalitarian and destabilizing implications. It is this potency of *shūrā* that has led modern scholars such as Fazlur Rahman to read modern concepts seamlessly into the Qur'an, thus representing a widespread modernist tendency: "To carry on their collective business (government), the Qur'an asks [Muslims] to institute *shūrā* (a consultative council or assembly), where the will of the people can be expressed by representation. *Shūrā* was a pre-Islamic democratic Arab institution which the Qur'an established."[79]

Furthermore, as argued earlier, there is evidence that early Muslims consciously understood their way of ruling to be distinct from and superior to kingship (*mulk*) precisely on account of *shūrā*. According to a report by Ibn Saʿd (168–230/784–845) of the statement of the pro-ʿAlid Companion Abū Mūsa al-Ashʿarī (d. ca. 42–52/662–72) during the reign of Muʿāwiya, the major difference between the two is that "Leadership (*imra*) is that which is carried out collectively [or attained through collective opinion], while kingship (*mulk*) is that

[77] Ṭab., 4:427.
[78] Ṭab., 3:112–3.
[79] F. Rahman, *Major Themes of the Qur'an* (Bibliotheca Islamica, 1989), 43.

which dominates by the sword."[80] One *ḥadīth* has it, "The caliphate in my Community (*umma*) is thirty years, then [it will become] kingship after that." After this statement of the Prophet, the tradition reports a dialog between the reporting Companion and the Successor (*tābiʿī*) who narrated it. The upshot of the dialog, which seems to have taken place in the early Umayyad period, was that the Umayyad claim to be the caliphs is false, for they are in fact "kings from among the worst of them!"[81]

Finally, early Islamic thought seems aware of the rational aspect of the job of ruling; it was not, in other words, assumed to be "God's rule." The issue of human agency was posed quite starkly by the Khārijī militants who asserted that "the *ḥukm* [rule/judgment] is for none but God" – an assertion based on a qur'ānic verse[82] that some of them took to mean that no human agency was therefore needed. ʿAlī is reported in both Shīʿī and Sunni collections to have responded: "The rule is for God, indeed, but on earth there are rulers. People cannot do without a chief [*amīr*] – be he [in his person] pious or impious – who gathers the scattered affairs and unites them, distributes the revenues, fights the enemy [*yujāhid al-ʿaduww*] ... so that the pious may be at peace and saved from the impious."[83] This statement, far from considering the caliphate God's hand, limits its functions to four: internal peace and security, distribution of revenues and resources, defense against external enemies, and dispensation of justice. It notably lacks any specifically religious function of the state unless *jihād* is considered strictly religious.[84] This is not to say it precludes any ritual significance for the Muslim ruler altogether, but it certainly seems to contradict any suggestion that without a caliph, religious life would be relegated to illegitimacy or ineffectuality. The justifications proposed are rational rather than of creedal or ritual import, and notably absent is the need for an infallible leader to guide the community in religious matters.

[80] Ibn Saʿd, *al-Ṭabaqāt al-Kubra* (Dār Bayrūt, 1957), 4:113; Sayyid, *Jamāʿa*, 118.

[81] *Musnad Aḥmad*, 5:220, qtd. in Sayyid, *Jamāʿa*, 118.

[82] Based on a qur'anic phrase repeated at least thrice – 6:57, 12:40, 12:67 – and many more times in different wording.

[83] The Shīʿī source for this quote being: al-Sharīf al-Riḍā, *Nahj al-balāgha*, ed. Muḥammad ʿAbduh (Dār al-Ḥadīth, 2004), 67; Ibn Abī 'l-Ḥadīd, *Sharḥ nahj al-balāgha*, qtd. in Sayyid, *Jamāʿa*, 28. A similar report is found in Ṣanʿānī, *al-Muṣannaf*, 10:149. For a thorough analysis of Ṣanʿānī's *Muṣannaf*, which dates it on the basis of content-cum-source analysis to, at the latest, the last quarter of the first/seventh century, see Motzki, *Origins*.

[84] Sayyid, *Jamāʿa*, 49.

Siyāsa

The political concepts attending early Islam presented so far, including the "*umma*," which inherits the prophetic mission and whose affairs are managed by "authorities from within it" through "consultation," – represent a conscious break from the Israelite tradition in the sense that God's spokesmen now no longer ruled directly.[85] This break is not unremarkable, for in most ways continuity with the Israelite tradition was the rule. The Qur'an referred to the Israelites frequently as an earlier community of Muslims from whose examples, both good and bad, Muslims were to learn. Yet despite this sense of similarity and continuity, there is evidence in early Islam of the recognition of a categorical difference between Islamic and Israelite attitudes toward political power, for the Muslim Prophet had been the last one, and the caliphs after him were neither divinely chosen nor guided in a direct sense. This belief is expressed in the following *ḥadīth* report: "The Israelites used to be led by prophets [*kānat banū isrā'īl tasūsuhum al-anbiyā'*]; whenever a prophet died, another followed him. But after me, there is no prophet, but there will be many deputies [*khulafā'*]."[86] The root "s.w.s" used in this report to refer to the Israelite prophet's management and leadership of his people also provides the Arabic word for politics, *siyāsa*. This *ḥadīth* report, which circulated at the latest during the late first/seventh century, (and there is little reason to doubt its attribution to the Prophet), can be credited with the first use of the root "s.w.s" in this sense in Islamic sources. Originally derived from an ancient word that referred to the training and administration of horses, it has generally been used to mean ruling through making policies and administering them.[87] The end of *siyāsa* by prophets entails a future in which it will be the *ulu 'l-amr minkum* – members of the *umma* with no divine claim – who will be responsible for the leadership of the *umma*.

[85] Cf. Sayyid, *Jamā'a*, 117.

[86] This *ḥadīth* is graded authentic by traditional critics, although it is reported through an *āḥād* chain. It was narrated by Ahmad in his *Musnad*, *Bukhārī* (K. al-Anbiyā') and *Muslim* (K. al-Imāra). Ahmad's chain is "Aḥmad b. Ḥanbal – Muḥammad b. Ja'far – Shu'ba – Furāt al-Qazzāz – Abū Ḥāzim (d. ca. 100/718) – Abū Hurayra." Another chain in *Musnad Abī 'Awāna* is "Furāt's son – Furāt – Abū Ḥāzim – Abū Hurayra" (*Musnad Abi 'Awāna*, 4:410). The chains merge at Furāt b. 'Abd Allāh al-Qazzāz, who flourished in Kūfa during the late first and early second century AH.

[87] The Arabic verb *sāsa* etymologically relates to attending or caring for horses. B. Lewis, "Translation from Arabic," *Proceedings of the American Philosophical Society* 124.1 (1980): 41–7, 44.

Although conceptually *siyāsa* – understood as the ruler's wise management of men and groups and the rational weighing of options in the service of the polity's goals – aptly describes the way of ruling of the early caliphs, the first use of the term *siyāsa* that I have come across is by the first Umayyads during the mid-first century. According to one report, Ziyād [b. Abīh] (d. 53/673) said:

> The Chief of the Believers [Muʿāwiya (d. 61/680)] did not object to any of my policies (*siyāsa*) except once, [when] I employed a man who collected too much tax [and embezzled?], and fearing that I would chastise him, he fled to the Chief of the Believers, who wrote to him that such conduct is tantamount to lack of respect for the one before me [in authority over you, namely, Ziyād], and he wrote to me, "It is not proper for me or you to apply the same policy [*nasūsu al-nāsa siyāsatan wāḥida*], to either be soft towards all, which would encourage them to feel lax in sin, or to be harsh towards them all, which would cause their ruin. Rather, you should deal with them in a harsh and strict manner while I shall deal with them kindly and mercifully."[88]

This early usage of *siyāsa*[89] seems to connote, at this point, ruling prudently and politically and does not have any sense of being in contradiction with the normative way of Islam, *dīn*, or Sharīʿa.

It may strike one as odd that while recounting qur'anic political concepts I have not so far introduced the concept of *khilāfa*. This is in part because the term *khalīfa* as used in the Qur'an does not seem to have any relation to the internal political organization of the Muslim Community. Wadād al-Qāḍī enumerates its various meanings during the Umayyad period[90] and concludes that no attempt seems to have been made by the

[88] Ibn Abī Shayba (d. 235), *Muṣannaf*, 6:187, the *isnād* being: "ʿAbd Allāh b. al-Numayr –Mujālid – Shaʿbi (d. 103/721)."

[89] Cf. Schacht's assertion that *siyāsa* was a later Abbasid development: "The discretionary power of the sovereign which enables [the ruler], in theory, to apply and to complete the sacred law, and, in practice, to regulate by virtually independent legislation matters of police, taxation, and criminal justice, all of which had escaped the control of the *qāḍi* in early ʿAbbasid times, was later called *siyāsa*" (Schacht, *Introduction*, 54).

[90] W. al-Qāḍī, "The Term "Khalīfa" in Early Exegetical Literature," *Die Welt Des Islams* 28.1 (1988): 392–411. She observes that the root "kh-l-f" appears nine times in the Qur'an, often in the context of God making someone *khalīfa* of the earth or on the earth, and her survey of the exegetical literature of the Umayyad period shows that the root was ascribed five meanings: (1) to succeed, (2) to replace someone temporarily as a deputy, (3) to replace permanently someone who has perished, (4) to inhabit or cultivate, and (5) to rule (as in 2:251, referring to God's making of David a successor on the earth) (398–404). The first three of these convey the sense that the basic meaning of the term is for someone to succeed another, and the question is whether this succession is temporary or permanent; the last two are merely contextual elaborations, for to inhabit and

Umayyad-period exegetes to employ the term in order to ground the Umayyad authority in the Qur'an; that trend caught on among the ulama only in the Abbasid period (note that on Crone and Hinds's view, one would expect the opposite).[91] Furthermore, that the Umayyads had some divine right to rule and be obeyed as God's caliphs was "a claim made by Walīd II in 125/742 *for the first time in Umayyad history*, in the testament in which he appointed his two sons as his consecutive successors to the caliphate."[92] Walīd II's use of the "Adam verse" (2:30) to refer to himself, al-Qāḍī notes, does not seem to have impressed the contemporary exegetes, inept as that reference in itself had been, for that particular verse clearly referred to the entirety of humankind and not the ruler as being the "*khalīfa*"; it made no reference to anyone being "God's *khalīfa*, and finally, forewarned of this *khalīfa*'s proclivity to "cause corruption and spill blood."[93] We may therefore conclude that the qur'anic usage of the term *khalīfa* was not the chief reason why it came to refer to the ruler of the Muslims. Rather, it was most likely applied early on to those who literally "succeeded the Prophet." As such, it offered no definitive theological advantage.[94] Even when the phrase "God's caliph" was used, as noted earlier, it did not connote too much more than "the caliph of God's Prophet."

The early Islamic political vision presented here has the following characteristics: (1) It places the *umma*, the community of all the believers, as the recipient of the Prophet's mission to humankind; one qur'anic term to refer to this mission is *al-ʿahd*, keeping of God's covenant.[95] (2) It requires

cultivate or rule the earth is related to this root because in either case the idea is to take the place of others who did so before. She concludes that in the Qur'an the term does not carry primarily political connotation, and the early exegetes did not give it the political meaning of ruling. The meaning (5) is specific to David. The exegetes were mostly puzzled by the "Adam verse," in which *khalīfa* referred to humankind as a whole, and it was not clear whom Adam or his progeny were supposed to succeed or replace.

91 Ibid., 406–7.

92 Ibid., 410 (emphasis added).

93 Walīd II attempts to conflate the general sense of deputyship (*khilāfa*) of the entire humankind on earth, as stated in the Qur'an in reference to the story of creation (Q 2:30 ff), with the specific sense of the deputyship (of God or the Prophet) as a political office, such as attributed to David in the Qur'an (Q 7:129; 24:55; 38:26).

94 The *ḥadīth* reports, in contrast, mention the Prophet's successors as *khulafāʾ* (sg. *khalīfa*), but despite their internal differences, they do not cast the caliphs, with the exception of the first two, three, or four, in particularly positive light and frequently advise tolerating their oppression (Sayyid, *Jamāʿa*, 89).

95 The Qur'an frequently mentions "the covenant" with reference to the Israelite prophets (2:40), but all earlier communities who received a prophet in effect had a covenant that they often failed to keep (7:102). The Muslims constituted the new community that

rendering qualified obedience to authorities from among themselves. (3) It requires *shūrā*, the practice of participation and consultation in collective affairs, and (4) by corollary, considers the Community's collective affairs in need of rational human management. Finally, another corollary of the Community's inheritance of the mission and God's covenant is that (5) this vision considers the caliph answerable to those he rules, the Community. I will name this the Community-centered vision of Islam, that is, a vision of ordering authority and responsibility of Islam's mission (i.e., commanding right, forbidding wrong, upholding faith) in such a way that the entirety of the Community, rather than a ruler, particular institution, or lineage, stands atop the hierarchy of legitimation. This Community, of course, is ruled by a successor of the Prophet but one who does not inherit the infallible authority of the Prophet. The ruler is given that authority to dispense with the worldly aspect of office of the Prophet through his election and appointment by the Community. Only the ruler who can fulfill the onerous responsibility of shepherding the *umma* in accordance with the Qur'an and the way of the Prophet while also consulting with it can be called the true successor (*khalīfa*) of the Prophet; those who fail to do so are caliphs only in name.

The Community-centered vision of Islam was not merely an ideal expressed in the Qur'an, but was inherent to the qur'anic doctrinal structure. It responds to the key question of early Islam: How could a ruler who enjoys no infallibility, as the Prophet did, take his place in guiding both the political and religious life of the community? This perhaps unarticulated yet ineluctable question seems to have been an underlying theme in much of the political turmoil of the early centuries. We have shown the implausibility of the answer proposed by Crone and Hinds: that the Prophet's infallibility continued with the successors of the Prophet. A more plausible answer has been proposed by Tilman Nagel, who suggested that although the Prophetic authority did discontinue after his demise, an *Ersatzinstitutionen* (surrogate) was found in the devotion to the Sunna (thus keeping the Prophet virtually alive) or the imamate (ascribing functional infallibility to a living person, possibly the ruler).[96] Insightful as this recognition is, it fails to recognize the most obvious

received the covenant of God after the Israelites and are warned against violating it (3:76–7; 13:20; 16:91). The substance of the covenant encompasses all of religion but specifically comprises observing strict monotheism and bearing witness to all humankind, as described in the aforementioned "constitutional" verses.

[96] Cited in Zaman, 8.

candidate to inherit the Prophetic "mission," "charisma," or covenant (*al-ʿahd*): the Community.

FROM KHILĀFA TO MULK, OR NEGOTIATING SHŪRĀ AND JAMĀʿA

The Community-centered vision of early Islam, when brought to bear on real political life, comprised two parts. The role and responsibility that went along with "being the best community" necessitated the tasks of learning, teaching, and elaborating the divine message, critiquing the Community's observance of it, and enjoining righteousness and forbidding wrong *within* the Community so that it may live up to its ideals. This first part was inward-looking and, without the dogma of the infallibility or religious supremacy of any one authority or institution and with emphasis on *shūrā* and mutual advice, it (this first part) necessitated a distributed authority. There may be, after all, many members of the Community who are more pious and knowledgeable than the caliph. The second part concerned the mission to the rest of humankind, which during the Umayyad era primarily meant the unity of the Community and *jihād* at the frontiers. This part necessitated a central caliphal authority. The two aspects of this vision are far from disjunctive or mutually contradictory, but a source of tension, which scholars like Lapidus have noted perhaps in too exaggerated a form, does seem to exist. How could the two aspects of this mission coexist?

Inasmuch as this vision remained dependent on the piety and integrity of those in authority rather than enshrined in robust institutions, its inherent tension could readily yield another vision in which the ruler became the center and the Community's rights were left to the mercy of the ruler's pious scruple. The effects of what Gibb has called the over-rapid expansion of Islam, already visible during the third and fourth caliphs' reign, led during Muʿāwiya's reign to a readjustment in the modus operandi and vision of the caliph's office. The transfer of the caliphate to Damascus is described in idealist sources as the transformation of caliphate to kingship. Perhaps to add decisiveness, Muʿāwiya is made to say, "I am the first of kings" and, some traditions add, "and the last of caliphs."[97] This change was registered by early Muslims as the loss of *shūrā*, which remained the most important weapon in the armor of the

[97] Ibn Kathīr, *Bidāya*, 8:144.

critics of the Umayyads. Some even saw it as the end of caliphate itself and as the advent of worldly kingship (*mulk*) in Islam. The *ḥadīth* reports on the subject express inevitability as well as censure of kingship,[98] and the general religious opinion of the period suggests that the Umayyads were excluded from the honor roll of the *Rāshidūn* (Rightly Guided ones) chiefly because of their abandoning of *shūrā* (consultation).[99]

The Umayyads could lay claim to many redeeming qualities, the most important of which was their ability to hold together an increasingly volatile empire. Later hostile accounts portray Muʿāwiya as a villain and a cowardly usurper, whereas Sunni accounts range from a grudging acceptance of his political wisdom while emphasizing the worldly character of his rule to a more reverent acceptance of his place among the Companions. During his own time, it appears that he was accepted, perhaps grudgingly, by most for his ability to bring peace – the year of his accession being known as the "year of union" (*ʿām al-jamāʿa*), and the ensuing twenty years confirmed his talent in diplomacy and maintaining peace.[100] In ideological warfare, which they ultimately lost, the Umayyads emphasized their leadership of *jihād*, Islamic grounds for the supremacy of the Quraysh, the culpability of the senior Companions in Medina in abandoning ʿUthmān, which nullified their right to *shūrā*, and finally, pure and simple will of God that had favored the Umayyads.[101] Even as it dismayed the idealists, many could appreciate the advantages of Umayyad rule,

[98] For a list and analysis of such *ḥadīth* reports, see Sayyid, *Jamāʿa*, 61–121, esp. 117–9.

[99] For Ḥasan al-Baṣrī's famous list of Muʿāwiya's four deadly sins, among them lack of *shūrā*, see Ṭab., 3:232; Ibn Kathīr, *Bidāya*, 8:139.

[100] For an overview of the political history of the Umayyad period, see Hugh Kennedy, *The Prophet and the Age of the Caliphs* (Pearson Education Ltd., 1986); in particular, on Muʿāwiya's reign, 82–4. For an excellent recent survey of historical depictions of Muʿāwiya, see Khaled Keshk, *The Historian's Muʿāwiya: The Depiction of Muʿāwiya in the Early Islamic Sources* (VDM Verlag Dr. Müller, 2008). Many modern scholars like H. A. R. Gibb, J. Wellhausen, H. Lammens, and E. L. Peterson, following Ibn Khaldūn, see Muʿāwiya's successful adoption of existing Arab tribal systems adjusted according to the available imperial models for ruling a vast empire as being more practical than the older model of pious but vulnerable caliphate. W. Madelung, however, sees him as a cowardly usurper. Both sets of historians ultimately choose which accounts they see as credible, although it seems that the view of the former set of scholars who see him in a moderate light as a shrewd politician is more persuasive (Keshk, 3). Also Sayyid, *Jamāʿa*, 39.

[101] On Muʿāwiya's justification of his rule by underscoring the superiority of Quraysh, see Ṭab., 1:2909; Sayyid, *Umma*, 128; that the Quraysh were the noblest of the Arabs is an idea put forth against the Helper's candidacy by Abū Bakr and ʿUmar as well (Sanʿānī, *Muṣannaf*, 5:423; Bukhari, 8:211). For Muʿāwiya's insistence on the Quraysh's eternal right to caliphate, see Bukhārī, "K. al-Manāqib," no. 3540; Sayyid, *Umma*, 129–130.

thus according it what one scholar has called "pragmatic legitimacy."[102] The Umayyads' success in restoring the unity (*jamā'a*) of the umma was thus the single most effective justification that they used to trump the calls for *shūrā*.[103] It was perhaps in order to bolster this pragmatic justification of their rule that, in Khalid Blankenship's words, they turned the early Islamic state into a "*jihād* state," although this measure seems to have met only temporary success and possibly led to their unpopularity and ultimate demise.[104] In fact, the Umayyad strategy of perpetual *jihād* failed to harness religious sentiment from the get-go; Medinan jurists, for instance, remained critical of the *jihād* claims of the Umayyads.[105] Over time, this complex balance of justifications and calculations increasingly leaned against the Umayyads, and they ran dangerously low not only on ideological but also pragmatic legitimacy.

Of the many Umayyad-period critics and rebels who called for *shūrā*,[106] the most successful was 'Abd Allāh b. al-Zubayr, another member of the Qurayshī elite and a young companion of the Prophet.[107]

[102] Sayyid notes a distinction among Muslims of the first century AH between foundational legitimacy (*al-shar'iyya al-ta'sīsiyya*) and pragmatic legitimacy (*al-shar'iyya al-maṣāliḥ*; I prefer to distinguish the two as *formal* versus *substantive* bases of legitimacy) (idem, *Jamā'a*,120).

[103] Sayyid, *al-Umma*, 132–4.

[104] For the argument that the Umayyads' foreign policy of continuous *jihād* ultimately destroyed them, not the internal conflicts, see K. Blankinship, *The End of the Jihad State: The Reign of Hisham Ibn Abd Al-Mālik and the Collapse of the Umayyads* (SUNY Press, 1994).

[105] Sayyid points out that the Medinan jurists, for instance, resented the Umayyad claims of religious authority and did not consider their *jihād* as sufficient justification for their claims – they, accordingly, did not consider expansionist *jihād* as an obligation on Muslims. The Syrian jurists, on the other hand, who were more sympathetic (albeit never slavish) to the Umayyads obviously, saw *jihād* as an obligation and a sufficient reason to support the less than ideal rulers (Sayyid, *Jamā'a*, 32). See also R. Mottahedeh and R. al-Sayyid, "The Idea of Jihad in Islam before the Crusades," in A. E. Laiou and R. Mottahedeh (eds.), *The Crusades from the Perspective of Byzantium and the Muslim World* (Dumbarton Oaks, 2001).

[106] *EI*^{2}, s.v. "Shūrā," where Bosworth suggests that *shūrā* as a principle of election seems to have been especially attractive during the Umayyad period for zealots, rebels, and dissidents. He points out 'Umar II, al-Ḥārith b. Surayj, Yazīd III, and the Khārijīs as having particularly underscored *shūrā*. Of more than a dozen significant revolts against the Umayyads, all the major ones were fueled by *shūrā* slogans. See Ḥ. 'Aṭwān, *Malāmiḥ min al-shūrā fī al-'aṣr al-umawiyy* (Beirut: Dār al-Jīl, 1991); Abou El Fadl, 70–4; Kennedy, *Prophet*, 101, 114–5.

[107] For the role of *shūrā* in the most threatening rebellion, by 'Abdullāh b. al-Zubayr, who set up a counter-caliphate in Mecca for several years, see Sayyid, *Jamā'a*, 37; idem, *al-Umma*, 132. Scholars, traditional as well as modern, have been sharply divided on whether Ibn al-Zubayr's revolt was tribally motivated self-aggrandizement or a genuine

Purportedly awaiting proper *shūrā*, he did not declare himself caliph until the death of Yazīd, but rather installed himself in Mecca as a "refugee of God's House." Until then, and unlike the dynastic appointment of Yazīd, his call had been that Muslims ought to choose their ruler by *shūrā*, which attracted to his cause non-Qurayshī Arabs, in particular the Khawārij, but also non-Arab new Muslims, the *mawālī*. Whether his call to *shūrā* meant that non-Qurayshīs at least in theory could be candidates is unclear. Given the uncompromising Khawārij position that the Quraysh had no exclusive right to the caliphate, it is likely that Ibn al-Zubayr preached that position or perhaps equivocated to that effect. When Yazīd died, Ibn al-Zubayr declared himself caliph without *shūrā* from all the groups, which led to the secession of the Khārijīs and others from his group.[108] There are other reports of slightly pro-Umayyad tenor that relate that both Yazīd b. Muʿāwiya and ʿAbd al-Malik b. Marwān (d. 86/705) agreed to *shūrā* in their negotiation with Ibn al-Zubayr, and in fact it was Ibn al-Zubayr who resisted *shūrā*.[109] Regardless of the accuracy of these reports, what is noteworthy is that *shūrā* is brandished as the main legitimating factor by all parties, including the Umayyad apologists.

Outside of the Qurayshī elite and the emerging scholarly elite, the appeal of *shūrā* was wider, and non-Qurayshīs and even non-Arabs were possible candidates. I will label this the radical *shūrā* position. The most prominent among those who rejected the Qurayshī stipulation on the caliphate were the Khārijīs,[110] whose fanaticism was also responsible perhaps more than any other factor in making *shūrā* unattractive if not threatening to the Muslim Community at large. The early *kalām* partisans also advocated this position. Ghaylān of Damascus, a Murji'ī of Qadarī tenor, held that not only is non-Qurayshī caliphate valid, but also that

call to reform and *shūrā*. For the divided Muslim opinion, see Abou El Fadl, 70n38; for Gibb' s largely negative view, *EI*², s.v., "ʿAbd Allāh b. al-Zubayr."

108 Balādhurī, *Anṣāb*, 4:2:17, 4:2:58; Ṭab., 5:494; *Ta'rīkh Khalīfa b. Khayyāṭ*, 1:323.

109 The report about Yazīd b. Muʿāwiya comes from al-Madā'inī (d. *ca.* 228/843) in Balādhurī, *Anṣāb al-ashrāf*, 4:2:16. Other reports have ʿAbd al-Malik b. Marwān concede during the revolt of ʿAbd Allāh b. al-Zubayr that the caliph is to be decided by *shūrā bayn al-quraysh*, that is, the consultation of Muslims about a candidate from the Quraysh. In one report, ʿAbd Allāh b. ʿUmar calls to *shūrā* ʿAbd Allāh b. al-Zubayr and ʿAbd al-Malik b. Marwān, and it is Ibn al-Zubayr who rejects this proposal (Balādhurī, *Anṣāb*, 5:195, 5:338; al-Kāmil, 4:326; ʿAtwān, *Malāmiḥ*, 192).

110 *Milal*, 1:124. Followers of Shabīb b. Yazīd al-Shaybānī considered the caliphate of a woman to be valid; Shabīb's mother, Ghazālā, was even declared an *imām* at one time (Ṭab., 5:63; Ibn al-Athīr, *al-Kāmil*, 3:326).

any claim of caliphate without the consensus of Muslims is invalid.[111] The Murji'a of Jabrī tenor, like al-Ḥārith b. Surayj al-Tamīmī (d. 128/746), who rebelled against the Umayyads in Khurāsān in 116/734, and Jahm b. Ṣafwān, his secretary, also made *shūrā* one of their rallying cries.[112] Ḍirār b. ʿAmr in fact preferred a non-Qurayshī so it would be easy to remove him from power if he acted unjustly.[113]

Apart from these many voices that came to be set aside as heretical by later Muslim history (their radicalism in *shūrā* may have played a part in settling their heterodoxy), the only Umayyad who were remembered positively by posterity were those who held to some kind of *shūrā* position. (We may surmise that too much or too little *shūrā* got one into trouble with posterity.) Notable among these are Muʿāwiya II, ʿUmar II, and Yazīd III.

Muʿāwiya II, the son of Yazīd b. Muʿāwiya, is reported to have acceded to the caliphate for only a few months during the rebellion of Ibn al-Zubayr, mysteriously given it up, and then died under suspicious circumstances. One story of Muʿāwiya II's renunciation of caliphate, rejected as spurious by modern scholars without much comment or justification,[114] has him criticize his own family's repressive tactics, praise the ʿAlids, and, more importantly, give up the caliphate before a gathering of the generality of Muslims, asking them to "choose a caliph from among them." We have no way to ascertain this anecdote, but regardless, the general message of the anecdote, which is neutral in tone and shows Muʿāwiya II as being both pious and weak, conveys that leaving the generality of the *umma* to choose a caliph from among themselves was the pious and right thing to do.[115]

The most important case is that of ʿUmar b. ʿAbd al-ʿAzīz or ʿUmar II (d. 101/719), whose impact on Islamic history cannot be overstated. He

[111] *Milal*, 1:143. Shahrastānī writes that Ghaylān combined three unorthodox doctrines: free will (*qadar*), Murji'ism, and Khārijism. On the later construction of Ghaylān's image in historiography, see Steven Judd, "Ghaylān al-Dimashqī: the Isolation of a Heretic in Islamic Historiography," *IJMES* 31.2 (1999): 161–84.

[112] *EI*², s.v. "Al-Ḥārith b. Surayj". Al-Ḥārith's passionate opposition to the Umayyad injustice led him to join the non-Muslim Turkish army in Central Asia against the armies of Hishām. He issued a manifesto urging that the governor of Khurāsān be chosen by *shūrā*. Jahm b. Safwān was to later earn dubious fame as the arch-heretic of Islam. See also *EI*², s.v. "al-Jahm b. Ṣafwān."

[113] *Milal*, 2:91.

[114] *EI*², s.v. "Muʿāwiya II" (Bosworth).

[115] ʿAṭwān, *Malāmiḥ*, 206. The report is mildly anti-Umayyad, but cannot be easily dismissed as ʿAlid or Abbasid propaganda, for it leaves the matter to all Muslims.

stands out in Islamic tradition for having righted all that had gone wrong in the Umayyad practice since the *Rashidūn* caliphs, thus earning the honorary title "the Fifth Rightly Guided caliph" and becoming the yardstick against which all the vices of the Umayyads could be measured.[116] His accomplishments in a brief period extending a little more than two years showed in fact that the early caliphal model of piety was, although rarely attained, not impossible. There is little reason to doubt the general outline of the account of ʿUmar II's life and reforms, which, even if exaggerated, depicts how the second-/eighth-century ulama, when these accounts were reduced to writing, saw their political predicament.[117] Among his most remarkable acts, according to some accounts, after being bequeathed the caliphate was to give it up, as the ideal Muslim caliph should have, instead leaving the matter to the *shūrā* of the Muslims. One version of his inaugural sermon reported by a fourth-/tenth-century biographer has it: "O people, I have been burdened with this task without my opinion or desire, or consultation with the Muslims. I hereby set you free of my allegiance that is around your necks. You are free to choose for yourself."[118] In another report of the same event, he announced in his first sermon that his acceptance of the office is contingent on the *shūrā* of Muslims from other cities confirming his election.[119] Following his "revival" of *shūrā*, an act of crucial but mostly symbolic import, he addressed the more palpable issue of the attitude toward the treasury and fiscal structure: It was the generality of Muslims, not the caliph's family, that owned the wealth in

[116] The first to bestow this title on ʿUmar II was reportedly Sufyān al-Thawrī. Suyūṭī, *Tarīkh al-khulafā'*, 201. This notion of ʿUmar being the fifth Rightly Guided caliph, incidentally, is not present in his earlier biographies; see the next footnote.

[117] Our main source on ʿUmar II is a work by a student of Mālik (Mālik was a child of less than ten years when ʿUmar II ruled) and a contemporary of al-Shāfiʿī, ʿAbd Allāh b. ʿAbd al-Ḥakam (d. 214/829), *Sīrat ʿUmar b. ʿAbd al-ʿAzīz*, ed., Aḥmad ʿUbayd (ʿĀlam al-Kutub, 1984). For a recent study of the author, see J. E. Brockopp, *Early Mālikī Law: Ibn ʿAbd al-Ḥakam and His Major Compendium of Jurisprudence* (Brill, 2000); for comments on his biography of ʿUmar II, see p. 62. Next to Ibn ʿAbd al-Ḥakam in significance and detail is another third-century account by Ibn Saʿd in his *Ṭabaqāt*, 5:330–408. The most comprehensive modern sources are W. Barthold, "Caliph ʿUmar II and the Conflicting Reports on His Personality," *Islamic Quarterly* 15.2/3 (1971): 69–95 and Ṣ A al-ʿAlī, *ʿUmar b. ʿAbd al-ʿAzīz*, 2nd ed. (Sharika al-Maṭbūʿāt li'l-Tawzīʿ wa-l-Nashr, 2002).

[118] Abū Bakr al-Ājurrī (d. 360), *Akhbār Abī Ḥafṣ ʿUmar b. ʿAbd al-ʿAzīz* (Mu'assasat al-Risāla, 1980), 56.

[119] Al-Suyūṭī, *Tarīkh al-Khulafā'*, ed. Muḥammad M. ʿAbd al-Ḥamīd (Maṭb aʿa al-Saʿāda, 1952), 200; al-Dhahabī, *Siyar aʿlām al-nubalā'*, 5:126. Ṭabarī's version is similar; it mentions ʿUmar II's dislike for the office, but does not mention his inaugural sermon (Ṭab., 4:60).

the treasury.[120] One of the most persistent themes in all accounts of ʿUmar II is his extremely meticulous personal piety and asceticism, which could not have been more distinct from the imperial decadence the Umayyads increasingly symbolized. Other major moves by ʿUmar II addressed particular but more urgent grievances. He recalled the armies engaged in expensive and futile warfare at the borders, citing the sanctity of the blood of Muslim soldiers. He also reversed policies against the new converts, saying famously that "Muḥammad was sent as a prophet, not a tax-collector or circumciser."[121] He wrote letters to emperors inviting them to Islam and engaging in religious polemics.[122] Other sources of grievance against the Umayyads such as official invective against the ʿAlids were stopped.

Indeed, ʿUmar II's opinion on *shūrā* may have dangerously neared the viewpoint of the staunchest enemy of the Umayyads, the Khārijīs. The Khārijīs, after being defeated in their rebellion by the caliph's military, were invited by him for a debate. Apparently after being satisfied in other respects, they asked him, "Tell us about Yazīd. Why do you acknowledge him to be your successor as Caliph?" When ʿUmar excused himself by saying that this was the will of his predecessor that he must fulfill, the Khārijīs responded, "Suppose you were administering some property that belonged to someone else and you then entrusted it to someone who was unreliable. Do you think that you would have conveyed the trust to its owner?" Apparently silenced, ʿUmar II said, "Give me time," thrice.[123] "When they left him," the report goes on, "the Banū Marwān feared that he would deprive them of what they have [the caliphate] as well as their wealth and renounce Yazīd, so they had him poisoned. He lived not even three days after the two men had departed."[124] If true, this report is another confirmation of the prevalence of the view that ultimately only the community had the right to elect its ruler, and that although championed by the Khārijīs, it was not exclusive to them.[125] Ṭabarī's

[120] Ibn ʿAbd al-Ḥakam, *Sīrat ʿUmar*, 45 (on ʿUmar II's attitude toward the treasury), 149 (reports of his asceticism), 118 (his patronage of the scholars); Suyūṭī, *Tarīkh*, 201; Dhahabī, *Siyar*, 5:126. For a modern critical assessment of ʿUmar's financial policy, see H. A. R. Gibb, "The Fiscal Rescript of "Umar II," *Arabica* 2 (1955): 1–16.

[121] Crone and Hinds, *God's Caliph*, 79; Ṭab., 4:64 (which mentions only "circumciser").

[122] A. Jeffery, "Ghevond's Text between the Correspondence between ʿUmar II and Leo III," *The Harvard Theological Review* 37.4 (1944): 269–332.

[123] Another reading could be, "Give me three days."

[124] Ṭab., 4:62.

[125] Although we cannot ascertain the authenticity of this report, it is consistent with what we know of all the parties involved. The poisoning of ʿUmar II was discounted by Wellhausen but supported by Crone and Hinds, *God's Caliph*, 76–7.

account indicates that despite all the hyperbole surrounding ʿUmar II's status reaching messianic heights in his own lifetime, the reality on the ground and the inertia of the Umayyad practice and of his subordinates did not allow his revolutionary policies to succeed, and he was forced to reverse many of them in his very lifetime.[126] Nonetheless, ʿUmar II was neither naïve nor remembered merely for his piety; his impact on the legal and political formation in the subsequent Islamic history has been quite significant,[127] and to that we will presently return.

The Ruler-Centered Vision

Already in the policies of Muʿāwiya and his emphasis on the Quraysh's ownership of the historical project of Islam, we can notice a shift in emphasis from the Community to the caliph. After the second civil war (the rebellion of Ibn al-Zubayr), beginning with the consolidation of the Marwānids in power and their noticeable lack of precedence (*sābiqa*) and excellence (*faḍīla*) in Islam, the imperial trappings of the office of the caliph became more pronounced, as did his distance from the community. The brief intervention of ʿUmar II shows that egalitarian and Community-centered ideals were still recoverable. His failure, however, shows that this was far from easy. A different picture of the caliph's role and authority is presented by the epistle of the short-lived caliph Walīd II discussed earlier, which originated toward the end of the Marwānid period. It begins unremarkably then goes on to state that now begins the era of God's caliphs who lead the *umma*:

> Then God deputed His caliphs over the path of His prophethood – when He took back His Prophet and sealed His revelation with him – for the implementation of His decree [*ḥukm*], the establishment of His normative practice [Sunna] and restrictive statutes (*ḥudūd*), and for the observance of His ordinances [*farā'iḍ*] and His rights, supporting Islam, consolidating by which it is rendered firm … keeping [people] away from His forbidden things, providing for equity [*ʿadl*] among His servants and putting His lands to right.[128]

Having established the implausibility of Crone and Hinds' view that Walīd II was claiming near-prophetic authority as "God's caliph," we are faced with the task of explaining the view of authority underlying

[126] Ṭab., 4:62f.
[127] For a study of ʿUmar II's religious and legal opinions, see H. Q. Murad, "Ethico-Religious Ideas of ʿUmar II," (PhD Dissertation, McGill University, 1981).
[128] Ibid., 94; Crone and Hinds, *God's Caliph*, 120.

Walīd II's political hyperbole, unusual in its braggadocio even among the Marwānids.[129] Walīd II does not reject the centrality of the Prophet or claim infallible divine authority, except perhaps by the implication of his political rhetoric (but what is political rhetoric if not such insinuation?). If understood figuratively, his claims on the whole are not a startling departure from the caliphal role as the shepherd of the *umma* except in its singular emphasis on the caliph's role, which was not absent in the Community-centered accounts but had been balanced by the elective and corrective role ascribed to the Community. In this new vision, we find subjects of the caliph as passive recipients of his guidance and discipline. Their obligation is to obey God and hence the caliph appointed by God, whose job it is to establish God's Sharīʿa – obedience to the caliph is tantamount to obedience of God. This is underscored by Walīd II's claim of being the guardian-recipient (*walī*) of God's covenant (*al-ʿahd*). In the Qur'an, this symbolic covenant has been made with the entire believing Community, but Walīd conflates it with the covenant of succession (*wilāyat al-ʿahd*), thus conferring upon his appointment of his two sons as his heirs an aura of sanctity and religious urgency.[130] The view of Islamic authority and mission outlined here is what I will call the ruler-centered vision of Islam.[131]

That Walīd II's vision was seen as outlandish even among the Marwānids is further supported by the fact that he was executed in less than a year in a rebellion led by his cousin, Yazīd III, a rebellion in which central prominence was given to the issue of *shūrā* with the *umma*. Yazīd III's inaugural sermon chastises Walīd II as "the violator of sacred things on a scale not perpetrated by either a Muslim or an unbeliever." Parts of the letter as translated by Crone and Hinds are reproduced here:

> [When Walīd's ill-conduct transgressed all limits] I went to him with the expectation that he would mend his ways and apologise to God and *to the Muslims*, disavowing his behaviour and the acts of disobedience to God which he had dared to commit, seeking from God the completion of that which I had in mind by way of setting straight the pillar of the religion and holding to that which is pleasing among its [His?] people.[132]

[129] al-Qāḍī, "The term "'Khalīfa,'" 410. Riḍwān al-Sayyid also observes that these claims of Walīd II were far removed from reality as well as the generally accepted limits of the theoretical powers of the caliph; they constitute the most extreme claim even in the Marwānid tradition (Sayyid, *Jamāʿa*, 96).

[130] Crone and Hinds, *God's Caliph*, 123–4; Sayyid, *Jamāʿa*, 96.

[131] The idea of two potentially conflicting visions in Islam had been intimated but not systematically developed in al-Sayyid, *Jamāʿa*, 61–121.

[132] Crone and Hinds, *God's Caliph*, 127, emphasis added.

The letter then mentions a delegation that its author had sent to his recalcitrant cousin:

They called upon him to set up a shūrā in which the Muslims [Balādhurī's version has it: the wise and the pious among the Muslims] might consider for themselves whom to invest [with authority] from among those they agreed on; but the enemy of God did not agree to that. So, in ignorance of God, he hastened to attack them, but found God is mighty and wise.... So God killed him for his evil behaviour and those of his agnates too who were with him, forming his vile retinue. They did not reach ten [in number], and the rest of those who were with him accepted the truth to which they were called.... [I hasten to tell you this so] you may praise God and give thanks to Him. You are now in a prime position, since your rulers are from among your best men and equity is spread out for you, nothing being done contrary to it among you....

Listen to and obey me and whoever I may depute to succeed me from *those upon whom the community agrees*. You have the same undertaking for me: I shall act among you in accordance with the command of God and the *sunna* of His Prophet, and *I shall follow the way of the best of those who have gone before you*. We ask God, our Lord and Master, for the best of His granting of success and the best of His decree. (emphasis added)[133]

The tone of Yazīd III in his opening speech is the exact opposite of his dethroned cousin's. Not only does he abjure the caliphate-centered view of his cousin, but in fact makes clearly Community-centered claims, surpassing even ʿUmar II in his expression of humility and the limitedness of his jurisdiction. The emphasis on consultation with the Muslims (*shūrā*) in election as well as in ruling is unmistakable. For whereas ʿUmar II had reserved for himself as the caliph the right to give religious and judicial verdicts in the absence of the verdict of the Qur'an or Sunna, Yazīd seems willing to give up even that right in favor of obedience to the Prophetic Sunna.[134]

The foregoing analysis establishes that the properly contextualized reading of the very sources Crone and Hinds had used to project a straightforward "God's caliph" vision of the Umayyads is suggestive of a picture that is much more complex; there is a tension between two

[133] Reported by al-Ṭabarī on the authority of al-Madā'inī; translated in Crone and Hinds, *God's Caliph*, 126–8.

[134] Scholars disagree on the sincerity of Yazīd III's claims; Shaban holds that he was a genuine reformer in the spirit of ʿUmar II, whereas Wellhausen thinks that he was an adventurer seeking popularity (Kennedy, *Prophet*, 113). There is a curious report about Yazid III claiming imperial descent from all the great emperors of the world (C. E. Bosworth, "The Heritage of Rulership in Early Islamic Iran and the Search for Dynastic Connections with the Past," *Iranian Studies* 11.1 [1978]: 7–34, 12). If correct, this would corroborate Wellhausen's view.

visions in which the Community-centered vision is often the prevalent one even among the Marwānid caliphs.

Yet we cannot deny the increasing appeal and influence of the ruler-centered vision, with the increasing fragmentation of the Community and centralization of the caliphate in the late-Umayyad and early-Abbasid era. Despite the militantly egalitarian heritage of Arabia endorsed by Islam, also irresistible must have been the imperial heritage of all the contemporary or recent empires in the Near East and indeed the entirety of Eurasia: This heritage was emphatically ruler-centered, with a descending view of political authority that deemed the emperor in one way or another an (if not *the*) expression of divine will and conduit of divine favor. In this view, the ruler is appointed by God and the community plays no role in electing him or in holding him accountable. This view of government, which seems to have emerged in the later Marwānid period, survives and reappears subsequently in different versions. In this period, the ruler-centered vision seems to have stood on two mutually reinforcing pillars: the ideological pillar of the inheritance of the prophets, in particular the Prophet Muḥammad and the continuous line of caliphs after him, and the practical justification by the fact of being in power.

In essence, this view is not very different from that of medieval Muslim sultans and the state-centered writers who viewed kingship as a token of God's approval and support. This sultan-centered view differs from the caliph-centered version in that the focus is shifted from Islamic ideology to the fact of power. That is, it lacked the caliphate's sense of having inherited the mission of Islam, and hence in its articulations the idiom of the Qur'an and the Sunna is comparatively mitigated or absent, and the second justification, the fact of power in itself, assumes the central role. In a way not unfamiliar to the ancient Near East, and which was brought to Islam in particular through the Sassanid tradition, sanctity and divine favor invariably accrue to those in power; power is justification in itself. Yet in reality, this vision is an ideal type, expressed in court literature and eulogies but taken to its logical limits only by the haughty odd-balls among the sultans, like the Marwānid Walīd II or the Abbasid Ma'mūn among the caliphs. In reality, sultans in medieval Islam could be quite aware of their limits and dependence on the socioreligious elite – the ulama and the Sufis – for spiritual blessing, social status, and real influence. Another factor that set caliphate-centered pretensions apart from sultans' claims in the medieval period is the well-formed socioreligious corporate status of the ulama and to some extent the Sufis, a post-Umayyad development that severely limited the religious claims of ruler in the medieval period.

The ideological component of the earlier caliph-centered vision, now shorn of power, was claimed by the Shīʿa of various stripes. In this third garb, the ruler-centered vision was reversed in its relationship to power. The fact of power that had been the chief justification for the ruler-centered vision since the Marwānids lost all value and the focus shifted entirely to the *imām*'s inheritance of the Prophet's charisma through a sacred bloodline. The *imām* in this vision is the sacred personage regardless of any temporal power, but with exclusive religious authority and divine right to all power.

THE RISE OF THE SUNNA-CENTERED VARIANT

The foregoing account of roughly the first century and a half of Islam establishes that two visions of authority in Islam struggled for dominance. The ideals of qur'anic egalitarianism resonated with Arabian tribal meritocracy and upheld the community as the primary recipient of the prophetic mission and authority, and exigencies of an expansive Near Eastern empire militated in the direction of increasing stratification and accumulation of power at the center. Neither ideal could vanquish the other. The ruler-centered view had the decisive advantage of being practical and of evident interest to the wielders of power, whereas the Community-centered view had the ideological edge; however, without robust institutions, it could only remain an ideal that could spark rebellions but not underpin stable rule.

The nature of the conflict between the two can be brought out through the lens of an able critic of the Community-centered vision: al-Qāsim b. Ibrahīm (169–246/785–826) was a Zaydī of Muʿtazilī leaning, a fifth generation descendant of ʿAlī, and a contemporary of Aḥmad b. Ḥanbal.[135] In his works we find one of the earliest-developed articulations of the theory of imāmate. He wrote polemics against the Rāfiḍīs (non-Zaydī Shīʿa)[136] and various other opponents such as the Murji'a, the

[135] For the most recent work on his political writings, see Binyamin Abrahamov, "al-Qāsim b. Ibrahīm's Theory of the Imamate," *Arabica* 34 (1987): 80–105. Al-Qāsim believed that the Prophet named Abū Bakr as his successor according to the command of God, but after him the legitimate *imām* should be appointed on the basis of his relationship to the Prophet; although he does not reject the caliphate of ʿUmar (ibid., 83).

[136] Al-Qāsim applies this term pejoratively sometimes to all the non-Zaydī Shīʿa, at others times to those who deserted Zayd b. ʿAlī in his rebellion. The term later came to be

Qadarīs (i.e., Jabrīs),[137] the Nawāṣib (anti-ʿAlids), the Khārijīs (in particular their doctrine of election of the *imām*), and most of all, the Ḥashwiyya (a pejorative for the traditionalists).[138] Whereas the early Zaydī school of Kūfa had held that an *imām* should be elected through *shūrā*, late second-century Zaydīs, like al-Qāsim, came to strongly denounce this position.[139] Yet the primary functions of the *imām* that al-Qāsim enumerates are rational, similar to what we observed in ʿAlī's comment earlier, rather than of constitutional significance for religion (unlike, that is, the later Imāmī doctrine).[140] The *imām* has the role of a father toward a young child: He is a guide to teach the people proper restrictions and punish those who disobey; without these functions they would perish.[141] He does go on to add religious functions to the ruler's job, such as the need for an *imām* in collective prayers, distribution of *zakāt*, and leadership of the annual pilgrimage, but he does not explain why such an *imām* needs to be divinely chosen. Perhaps to compensate for the frailty of this argument, he turns up rhetorical heat, insisting that the imamate is the greatest of obligations (*afraḍ al-farā'iḍ*). He makes an attempt to prove the obligation of imāmate through the *khilāfa* verses, but given the little help they provide, he shifts the emphasis to the general verse of *ulu'l amr minkum* (4:59), which he deems the best available proof. Yet because the verse gives little help in identifying these authorities, to address the problem of how the *imām* is to be chosen and why that *imām* must be of the family of the Prophet, he turns to rational arguments, urging that the *imām* must have nearness (*qarāba*) to the Prophet in addition to perfection of wisdom (*ḥikma*) and piety (*taqwa*).[142] Abrahamov concludes that al-Qāsim

applied to all non-Zaydī Shīʿa as they were seen as "refusing" (*yarfuḍūn*) the caliphates of Abū Bakr and ʿUmar. He severely chides the Rāfiḍā for: (1) their doctrine of *waṣiyya* (an *imām* necessarily appoints his successor, as the Prophet appointed ʿAlī) – al-Qāsim believes that the Prophet appointed Abū Bakr; (2) their anthropomorphism; (3) their equation of *imāms* with prophets (in claiming their infallibility); (4) their doctrine of *taqiyya* (dissimulation of true beliefs for the reason of safety); and finally (5) the impious conduct of their *imāms* (Abrahamov, 94n70). For sources on the Rāfiḍa, see Zaman, 42.

137 Himself being a Qadarī in the sense of adhering to the Muʿtazilī doctrine of free will, Qāsim applies the term to the proponents of predestination, who are more commonly known as the Jabriyya.

138 Abrahamov, 82n6.

139 Ibid., 83–4.

140 Ibid., 85.

141 Ibid., 86.

142 The closest qur'anic argument he finds is that in the Qur'an, the prophets' descendents are also blessed with prophecy or kingship. Yet none of this nears evidence for his critical claim, which he therefore proceeds to make on rational grounds.

"opposes the right of the community to choose (*'ikhtiyār*) an imam. Only the most excellent man is the legitimate imam. There is no imamate of one-who-is-known-to-be-excelled-by-others (*mafḍūl*)." He goes on to list many reasons why finding the best man is more feasible and correct than going by the choice of the people. The ultimate reason is this: "It is God who chooses the imām not people."[143]

The forcefulness of his argument gives us a sense of the seriousness of opposition. In a *kalām*-style polemic, he argues: The question is who chooses the *imām*, the common people (*al-ʿawāmm*) or the elite (*al-khawāṣṣ*). If the entire community chooses, then the choosing is unachievable, "since members of the community are scattered all over the world and their number is not fixed because of births and deaths." If the choice is with the elite, then how could they be identified, and who will decide that they are worthy as electors?[144] In another work, al-Qāsim goes on to repeat the argument against *shūrā*: Even though the *shūrā* of people from all over the regions could be imagined, it would lead to every group claiming an *imām* from within itself, thus leading to civil war.[145] The primary target of this argument could not have been the mainstream traditionalists (proto-Sunnis), for by the late second century they had already limited the *shūrā* to choosing a candidate from the Quraysh. Rather, the target seems to have been the radical *shūrā* position, which must have been widespread enough to merit such detailed and repeated rebuttals.

Al-Qāsim's polemic brings out the strengths and weaknesses of both competing visions. The ruler-centered vision had little to justify itself in the Qur'an or early history, whereas the unfeasibility of the Community-centered vision was increasingly evident. It is in the context of this predicament, which was becoming clearer already since the many failed rebellions in the Marwānid period (such as Ibn al-Zubayr's and then Ibn al-Ashʿath's), that the need for an alternative vision of political authority must have been felt.

The first major milestone in the emergence of this alternative vision of authority perhaps is the career of ʿUmar II. His attempts at *shūrā* and fiscal reform and his attitude toward non-Arabs and non-Muslims – all of which reflect his association with the traditionalist circles of Medina

143 Ibid., 89.
144 Ibid., 91.
145 Ibid., 91–2.

in which he was raised[146] – and, even more importantly, the eventual frustration of these attempts, highlight the dilemma that faced the traditionalists. In trying to put into practice the ideals of the pious tradition of Medina that he had been taught, ʿUmar II raised the private scholarly enterprise to a whole new level by commissioning and legitimizing the collection of traditions (*sunan*; sing., *sunna*) of the Prophet and the early caliphs, thus rendering state practice an object of private scholarly circles' legal discourse. Already in the Community-centered program of ʿUmar II, we see a dual emphasis, on the Sunna of the Prophet and the pious caliphs (the sacred past) on the one hand and "the way of the believers" on the other. This attitude is reflected in the following statement of ʿUmar II:

> The Prophet and the holders of authority [*wulāt al-amr*] after him established traditions [*sunan*]. To adhere to them means to conform to the book of God, perfecting one's obedience to Him, and strengthening his religion.... Whoever seeks guidance from them will be guided, and whoever seeks success through them will be successful. And whoever contravenes them "follows a path other than that of the believers" [*yattabiʿ ghayra sabīl al-muʾminīn* (Q, 4:115)], God will turn him over to what he has turned to.[147]

In this construction of authority, one pull is toward the accumulated normative authority of the sacred past, and the other is toward a divine guarantee of the overall rectitude of the way of the living Community of the believers. This second dimension is more clearly formulated somewhat later as the doctrine of the infallibility of the *ijmāʿ* of the believers, and it is no surprise that in proving its authority, Shāfiʿī employed the same verse that ʿUmar II had to ground the collective rectitude of the believers.[148] The two, the sacred Sunna and the living "path of the believers," may or may not be in conflict. To understand the relationship ʿUmar II and his likes might have envisaged between the two, let us

146 Al-ʿAlī, 93f., evaluates traditional and modern sources and establishes that whereas ʿUmar II may or may not have been born in Medina (Ibn ʿAbd al-Ḥakam reports that he was), he was raised in Medina and had significant contact with the well-known "seven jurists of Medina" as well as other scholars. *Cf.* Barthold, 71, who casts doubt on this in too cursory a fashion.

147 Ibn ʿAbd al-Ḥakam, *Sīrat ʿUmar*, 40. Another sermon has it: "I am not a judge but an executor, not an innovator but a follower. None should be followed in disobedience to God. I am not the best of you, but a man from among you, who bears a burden heavier than any of you" (ibid.). For a discussion of these sermons of ʿUmar II, see Sayyid, *Jamāʿa*, 97–8. For Mālik's use of it, see A. Shamsy, "Rethinking *Taqlīd* in the Early Shāfiʿī School," *JAOS* 128.1 (2008): 3.

148 Zysow, 208.

examine the attitude toward authority among the scholars of Medina, ʿUmar's alma mater. This is evident in the career of the great Medinan traditionist al-Zuhrī (ca. 51–124/671–742), the first systematic historian of the great events of the Prophet' s life (*sīra*), in whose works the central concerns were "the development of the *Umma*, as well as the *Sunna* (living traditions) of Medina." His accounts "generally show the community (*Umma*) in the right" and underscore the doctrine of election of the ruler by the Community (rather than designation). Despite Zuhrī's association with the Umayyad caliphs, his history is not biased toward them and shows ʿAlī in the right against Muʿāwiya.[149] Zuhrī's star student, Mālik, the towering traditionalist-jurist who is said to have absorbed and faithfully preserved the tradition of Medinan learning,[150] reflected the same Community-centered concerns as well as the dual themes of Community and Sunna. He frequently invoked the aforementioned declaration of ʿUmar II. In a recent study Ahmed El Shamsy observes that Mālik's concept of custom (*ʿamal*), which came to play a key and distinctive role in the formation of the Mālikī school, was not simply a device to preserve the Sunna of the Prophet,[151] but rather was an indication of the "multilayered and composite nature" of Mālik's legal theory, which Shamsy likens to Schacht's concept of the "living Sunna" of the first century and a half. This dynamic doctrine afforded a large measure of discretion to political authorities (*wulāt al-amr*, by which Mālik means judges, governors, scholars, as well as caliphs).[152] On the one hand, he appears to have embraced a largely egalitarian and Community-centered vision of Islam, emphasizing equality of all Muslims,[153] and even condoning if not actually supporting rebellion against the illegitimate or unjust ruler.[154] On the other hand, the role of the state in the Medinan jurisprudence Mālik

[149] A. A. Dūrī, "Al-Zuhri: A Study in the Beginning of History Writing in Islam," *BSOAS* 19.1 (1957): 9–10.

[150] For Mālik's relationship with the seven jurists of Medina who flourished in the latter half of the first/seventh century, see Abd-Allāh, "Mālik's Concept of *ʿAmal* in the Light of Mālikī Legal Theory" (PhD Dissertation, University of Chicago, 1978), 62–8.

[151] See also Yasin Dutton, *The Origins of Islamic Law: The Qur'an, the Muwatta' and Madinan Amal* (Routledge, 2002), who argues otherwise.

[152] Shamsy, "Rethinking *Taqlīd*," 3. For Mālik's use of *wulāt al-amr*, see Abd-Allāh, "Mālik's Concept," 428–30.

[153] Mālik, for instance, strongly rejects the notion that the *mawālī* women were inferior to and should not be allowed to marry Arab men, as had been argued by the Irāqī jurists under the doctrine of *kafāʾa* (compatibility), and recalls a strong statement on the equality of all Muslims by ʿUmar b. al-Khaṭṭāb (Abd-Allāh, "Mālik's Concept," 42–3).

[154] Abou El Fadl, 76; Zaman, 148–9; A. al-Dumayjī, *Al-Imāma al-ʿuẓmā ʿind ahl al-sunna wa 'l-jamāʿa* (Dār Ṭība, 1404), 534–6.

represents is quite positive, and the state is given a large measure of discretionary authority.[155]

Mālik's critical attitude toward the state is not in contradiction to his acceptance of the role of state's discretion in the Community's life; rather, it is a natural result of it. It was precisely because government mattered in the normative life of the Community and the judgments of its officials carried normative weight that it needed to be just and legitimate. Therefore, engagement, critique, and even rebellion were proper attitudes toward the state: It was a reflection of a Community-centered view in which the ruler must be legitimate and in some way accountable. Mālik's Community-centered attitude toward the state was not odd, but was actually shared by the variety of scholars who partook in rebellions that called for *shūrā* and reform. The rebellion in southern Iraq of Ibn al-Ashʿath (d. 85/704), himself motivated perhaps by tribal or status concerns, had attracted a wide range of pious luminaries from among the Successors (the generation following the Prophet' s companions), and even included the Companion Anas b. Mālik[156] and most likely the well-known al-Ḥasan al-Baṣrī.[157] Similarly, the rebellion of al-Nafs al-Zakiyya against the Abbasids a little more than a decade after the Abbasid accession to the caliphate was similarly widely supported by those who had no particular Shīʿī leanings. Given how the later Sunni position came to unconditionally proscribe rebellion, it is remarkable how many of the great "proto-Sunni" authorities of the late first and early second centuries

[155] For instance, Mālik gives the ruler the right to conclude a girl's marriage if her guardian disallowed it for invalid reasons such as race of the man, and gives the state the ownership of mines rather than allowing the discoverers' descendents to inherit them (Abd-Allāh, "Mālik's Concept," 43, 62).

[156] These included: The Meccan authority on *ḥadīth* and *fiqh*, ʿAṭā b. Abī Rabāḥ (*ca.* 114/732), whose lectures Abū Ḥanīfa is reported to have attended (*EI*[2], s.v. "ʿAṭā b. Abī Rabāḥ"); the exegete Mujāhid b. Jabr al-Makkī (d. ca. 100–4/718–22); the Kūfan Successor Saʿīd b. Jubayr (d. 95/714; a disciple of Ibn ʿAbbās and Ibn ʿUmar, executed by al-Ḥajjāj for rebellion); the *muḥaddith* al-Shaʿbī (d. 103/721), the Qadarī Maʿbad al-Juhanī (executed by Ḥajjāj in 83/703; on him see *EI*[2], s.v., "Maʿbad b. ʿAbd Allāh"), Ibn Abī Layla (the father), Ḍarr b. al-Ḥamdānī (d. 82/701), and the Companion Anas b. Mālik (d. 93/712) (Abou El Fadl, 70–1). For a comprehensive study on this rebellion, see Riḍwān al-Sayyid's dissertation as: R. Sayed, *Die Revolte des Ibn al-Ashʿatth und die Koranleser* (Freiburg i.Br. 1977).

[157] Whether al-Ḥasan al-Baṣrī took part in the rebellion is debated, and although modern scholarship largely accepts that al-Ḥasan was not involved even while opposing the Umayyads, a recent study persuasively argues otherwise; his participation may also explain why he spent the rest of his life hiding from the ruthless governor al-Ḥajjāj. See S. A. Mourad, *Early Islam between Myth and History: Al-Ḥasan al-Baṣrī (d. 110H/728CE) and the Formation of His Legacy in Classical Islamic Scholarship* (Brill, 2006), 34–40.

partook in or supported such rebellions. Among the supporters of al-Nafs al-Zakiyya were Abū Ḥanīfa, Mālik b. Anas (other chief *ḥadīth* scholars of the time) the Murji'a, the Qadarīs, and the Muʿtazila; indeed, it was claimed, not without some exaggeration, that "none from amongst the *fuqahā'* stayed back," and "the *aṣḥāb al-ḥadīth* all rebelled together with him [sc. Ibrāhīm in Basra, Muḥammad al-Nafs al-Zakiyya's brother]."[158] Al-Shāfiʿī also ran afoul of the authorities a few times and was even suspected of conspiring to rebel against Hārūn al-Rashīd on account of his Alid sympathies.[159] The motives for such widespread dissatisfaction with the rulers remain a mystery. Zaman suggests a list of possible motives: (1) doubts about the legitimacy of the Abbasids; (2) dissatisfaction with the conduct of the caliph or his governors; (3) a romantic sense that the pristine purity of "the early days of the *umma*" might be restored;[160] and finally, (iv) the belief that al-Nafs al-Zakiyya might be the promised *mahdī*.[161] As in the rebellion of Ibn al-Ashʿath, it is evident that different groups coalesced in such rebellions for widely different reasons. Furthermore, there is a common thread of grievances and associated attitudes of doubts about – or outright rejection of – the legitimacy of the caliphs on the grounds of deficiency in *shūrā* and requisite piety, which have often been passed over in silence or dubbed as one parochial tendency or another by modern scholars.

Abū Ḥanīfa's also appears to have been a principled Community-centered stance against the legitimacy of caliphs who had usurped the office without *shūrā* and ruled without observing proper limits. A critical study of Abū Ḥanīfa's political thought is long overdue, but from what we can gather, his refusal to accept judgeship, his (cautious) support of

[158] For a discussion of reports of the authorities who took part in al-Nafs al-Zakiyya's revolt, see Zaman, 73–5: "[T]he ʿAlid revolt of 145/762 was remarkable not only for the backing of many scholars, but also for the diversity of those scholars' backgrounds: jurists, *aṣḥāb al-ḥadīth*, Muriji'a, Qadarīs and Muʿtazila, and scholars and holy people with no precise or determinable orientation could all come together to endorse the revolt in Mednia and Basra" (77).

[159] Abou El Fadl, 83n111.

[160] Mālik reports about his teacher Ibn Hurmuz (d. 117/735), a prominent Medinan *muḥaddith* of Persian extraction, among whose students were other teachers of Mālik, including such luminaries as al-Zuhrī: "I would go to see Ibn Hurmuz, and he would command his slave girl to bolt the door and to lower the curtain. Then he would reminisce about the early days of the umma and weep until his beard was wet. When later he rebelled with Muḥammad, someone said to him, 'By God, there is no fight left in you!' 'I am aware of that,' he replied, 'yet some ignorant fellow may see me and follow my example'" (Ṭab., 4:448–9; Zaman, 75).

[161] Zaman, 75.

rebellions, his doctrine of the invalidity of the rule of a *fāsiq* (an openly impious person), and his emphasis on the sanctity and salvational significance of the great majority of Muslims, *al-sawād al-aʿẓam*,[162] all strengthen the gist of the reports that have him state valiantly to the Abbasid Manṣūr, "The *khilāfa* is only by the agreement of the believers and their consultation."[163] Ibn Abī Dhi'b, a Medinan Qadarī ascetic and onetime judge who, like Mālik and Abū Ḥanīfa, had been involved or implicated in the revolt of al-Nafs al-Zakiyya, is depicted as having been particularly fearless in telling off the caliph for his neglect of *shūrā* and usurping the caliphate.[164]

The terms of negotiation between the caliphate and the traditionalist community, evolving as they had always been in a rapidly changing political milieu, underwent a significant change resulting from the rupture in the continuity and prestige of the caliphate caused by the bloody Abbasid takeover. This political rupture contrasted sharply with the continuously growing authority of the ulama, the keepers of the Sunna. Increasingly involved in systematizing legal precedents, collecting traditions of the Prophet and the early predecessors, and establishing scholarly networks, these circles were on their way to a corporate identity as scholars.

For the Abbasids, seeking alliance with the emerging class of scholars was simply good politics, if not a necessity. Unlike the Umayyads, whose claim to rule had rested primarily on their ability to unite the community and assert continuity with the tribal past, the Abbasids had come to power riding on messianic religious slogans of Shīʿī provenance, and needed to distance themselves from their extremist base and embrace a

[162] *EI*[3], s.v. "Abū Ḥanīfa." Schacht considered Abū Ḥanīfa's rejection of judgeship a "bibliographical legend" (ibid.), but other than hypercriticism in order to prove his larger thesis of the generally misleading character of Islamic historical sources, there seems to be little basis for this rejection. Abū Ḥanīfa consistently appears to be critical of the Umayyad as well as the Abbasid state on grounds that were very similar to those of rebels like Ibn al-Zubayr and in particular al-Ḥārith b. Surayj. His sympathy for al-Ḥārith, the rebel in the name of *shūrā* and justice who even joined with the non-Muslim army against the Umayyads, is attested by the fact that he complied to write a letter of introduction for al-Ḥārith when the latter sought an amnesty from the pro-*shūrā* caliph, Yazīd III. He was also sympathetic to the cause of the Alids such as Zayd b. ʿAlī (d. 122/740), and was acquainted with the leading Alid critics of the Umayyads, although he was not committed to Shīʿism. Along with a large number of other scholars, he also supported the revolt of al-Nafs al-Zakiyya against the Abbasids (Zaman, 73). For his doctrine about the invalidity of the rule of an impious caliph, see A. A. Mawdūdī, *Khilāfat-o-mulūkiyat* (Maktaba-e-Islāmī Publishers, 2001), 233, quoting al-Jaṣṣāṣ and al-Sarakhṣī.

[163] Al-Kardarī, *Manāqib al-Imām al-Aʿẓam* (Dā'irat al-Maʿārif, 1321), 16. The details of such encounters do not inspire confidence, but the basic positions do.

[164] Ibid.; Zaman, 74, 150.

religious aura in accordance with the beliefs of the moderate majority.[165] Building on their predecessors' imperial momentum and institutions and replacing Arab tribal alliances with their Khurāsānī base, the Abbasids introduced changes that were on the whole expedient rather than principled in nature.

On the ulama's side, the benefits of this alliance were not decisive. To those religious groups who had harbored Community-centered hopes, the Abbasids were more than a disappointment, for they only increased the distance between the ruler and the ruled, in a social as well as intellectual sense, far beyond the Umayyads.[166] Thanks to their Shīʿī rhetoric and incredible success in propaganda, the Abbasids turned the religious discourse of the time away from *shūrā* and any role of the *umma*, and toward the question of which part of the clan of the Prophet, the Abbasids or the Hāshimites, had the greater right to inherit the caliphate.[167] However, the emergent ulama also had reasons to acquiesce that had less to do with any merit of the Abbasids; in particular, after the failure of al-Nafs al-Zakiyya's revolt, exhaustion with futile violence and their new status allowing them to negotiate more favorably with the caliphate may have been some of the reasons why they found it useful to shy away from political activism.

Political quietism or neutralism had been one of the positions of the piety-minded as early as the ʿAlī-Muʿāwiya conflict; the Abbasid era only furnished further reasons for it to become predominant. An example of this trend is the Syrian jurist and master Arabic prose writer al-Awzāʿī (d. 157/774), who, embraced later by Sunni traditionalists as an impeccable authority on par with Mālik and Abū Ḥanīfa, served in the administration

[165] For an account of the essentially Shīʿī inspiration of the Abbasid movement's slogans, but a fluctuating relationship between the Abbasid caliphs and the Shīʿa, see Zaman, 33–48.

[166] In the pithy words of one observer, Abū Bakr al-ʿAyyāsh, who said to the Abbasids upon being asked to compare them with the Umayyads, "You are better in prayers, they were more beneficial to people" (quoted in Sayyid, *Jamāʿa*, 121).

[167] "[W]hatever the precise circumstances of Abū al-Abbās's accession in 749–50 the idea of *shūrā* in the sense of the formal choice of a leader through a consultative assembly of the Muslim quickly disappeared, to be replaced by patrimonial and dynastic notions of succession with the 'Prophet' s family'" (Marsham, *Rituals*, 187). Also, Sayyid, *Jamāʿa*, 42–3, argues that although there had emerged in the main cities of Islam during the early-second-century civil associations that emphasized the sanctity and role of the generality of the *umma*, or *al-sawād al-aʿẓam* and *shūrā*, "such civil associations had not sufficiently consolidated and established by the time of the rise of the Abbasid call and then the state, both of which accentuated the religious character of the ruler of the believers, as they relied on their being *ahl al-bayt* (from the Prophet's clan)."

of both the Umayyads and the Abbasids while courageously criticizing their errors in the language of the Sunna of the Prophet. One recent study has argued that he espoused a quietist view in which caliphs' wrongs were to be suffered and corrected through advice but never through rebellion, for only God could hold the caliph accountable.[168] Awzāʿī presented an early version of the doctrine that was to be embraced by the conservative faction of emerging Sunni orthodoxy, a view that was being fashioned out of the increasingly available "raw" material of *ḥadīth*, which could have been employed to support a number of political attitudes.[169] This view was essentially a variant of the Community-centered vision, in which the meanings of the Community and its rectitude were being rethought. The waywardness of large sections of the Community called into question its sanctity, prompting the pious to rethink the plethora of scriptural references to the centrality of the Community. The response was to freeze the "way of the believers" in the Sunna of the Prophet and the words and deeds of the pious generations of believers. Thus, there are many traditions that promise salvation to the *jamāʿa* (the congregation of believers) or *al-sawād al-aʿẓam* (the great blackness, meaning the majority of Muslims); but these end anticlimactically when some authority explains that the *jamāʿa* does not really mean the Muslim community at large, but some specific individuals, such as Abū Bakr and ʿUmar or a certain Abū Ḥamza al-Sukrī.[170]

Just as the ruler-centered vision was reconfigured in the course of the second/eighth and third/ninth centuries, so was the Community-centered vision. As the Community could no longer be maintained as a united

[168] A. Alajmi, *Political Legitimacy in Early Islam: Al-Awzāʿī Interactions with the Umayyad and Abbasid States* (VDM Verlag Dr. Müller, 2009), 169. Alajmi's study brings a fresh and needed perspective to the field, applying Harald Motzki's critical *isnād-cum-matn* criticism to bear on politically relevant traditions. However, his argument that al-Awzāʿī held a descending view of authority is *ex silentio*; that al-Awzāʿī interacted with and clearly tolerated both the Umayyads and the Abbasid caliphs and opposed rebellions against them does not seem sufficient to establish this position.

[169] For a recounting of pro- and antiactivism traditions, see Abou El Fadl, 112–31.

[170] Al-Shāṭibī, *al-Iʿtiṣām*, ed. Maḥmūd Ṭ. Ḥalbī (Dār al-Maʿrifa, 1420/2000), 515–21, collects various opinion on the meaning of the *jamāʿa* that is meant by the "saved sect" in a famous *ḥadīth*. He categorizes the answers given by authorities over the centuries in five categories: (1) *al-sawād al-aʿẓam* (the vast majority), (2) the (Sunni) ulama of the Community, (3) the Companions of the Prophet, (4) the Community when it agrees on an issue, and (5) the Community when it agrees on a leader. An interesting response, attributed to ʿAbd Allāh b. al-Mubārak (d. 181/797), is that the *jamāʿa* means "Abū Bakr and ʿUmar," and when told that they had long passed away, he said, "Abū Ḥamza al-Sukrī" (518). The idea being that given widespread corruption, the "saved group" could be limited to one man about whose rectitude one is certain.

political body, the theoretical part of its job was transferred to the sacred Sunna, and the living part to a minority in every generation who embodied the Sunna. This shift is particularly noticeable as we move from Abū Ḥanīfa to his disciples. Abū Yūsuf (d. 182/798), Abū Ḥanīfa's ablest associate-disciple, accepted, like his other Ḥanafī colleagues, the Abbasid appointment to judgeship; he later became the chief judge in the reign of Harūn al-Rashīd (r. 170–93/786–809). One of Aḥmad b. Ḥanbal's authorities in *ḥadīth*, Abū Yūsuf's association with the caliphate, whose legitimacy had been questionable to many in the preceding generation of scholars, did not injure his scholarly credentials. He built a seminal alliance between his school and the Abbasid Empire and made important concessions to the caliphate's claims. In his *K. al-Kharāj* he conceded that "God ... has appointed the rulers to be caliphs[171] upon His earth, and has granted them the light of wisdom which illuminates the confused affairs of their subjects and makes clear to them the rights and duties about which they are in doubt."[172] Yet the role of the caliph's guidance in this view is primarily to execute the Sunna of the Prophet and the pious predecessors, rather than to legislate on his own or to rule with a free hand: "The wisdom of the rulers is manifested in applying the prescribed punishments [*ḥudūd*] and in restoring established and proven rights to the owners thereof, by absolute and clear orders. For this purpose, the revival of the study of the ways [*sunan*] which the pious men of old [*salaf*] have established as precedents is of chief importance."[173]

Abū Yūsuf had no difficulty granting the right of policy making (*siyāsa*) to the caliphs in the name of God's religion so long as the limits of God's words as understood by the early authorities (*salaf*) were respected. This view is distinct from both the Community- and the ruler-centered views that we have come across. The caliph is not the ultimate authority with the Community reduced to his unquestioning obedience, nor is the Community's role in electing or restraining the caliph taken to heart. Neither Awzāʿī nor Abū Yūsuf makes any mention of *shūrā* in a political

[171] Lambton's translation incorrectly adds "His" before "caliphs," thus incorrectly suggesting that Abū Yūsuf considered the rulers to be God's caliphs. The rendering is correct in Crone and Hinds, 82.

[172] Lambton, *State and Government in Medieval Islam: An Introduction to the Study of Islamic Political Theory: The Jurists* (Oxford University Press, 1981), 56; Crone and Hinds, 82n160.

[173] Ibid. I have modified the translation slightly for clarity and given the Arabic original as well. For Abū Yūsuf, these *salaf* include, as his repertoire of authorities of the traditions throughout the treatise shows, not only the Rightly Guided caliphs but also the private scholars, such as Abū Ḥanīfa.

sense. Rather, the final authority is invested in the great models of the past. The stern, pietistic, principled, yet measured tone of Abū Yūsuf's *K. al-Kharāj* does not smack of opportunism. It was rather the principles themselves that had evolved.

In contrast, the legal implications of the ruler-centered vision of the second century had been best articulated a generation earlier by Ibn al-Muqaffaʿ.[174] His theory of Islamic jurisprudence reflects a moderate and rational caliphate-centered vision and takes into account a new threat to this vision. This threat was no longer constituted by the Community-centered rebels and *shūrā*-inspired naysayers, but the Sunna-centered vision constituted by the regionally specific legal systems of private scholars that had been steadily growing, as had been their authority to define the Sunna. Joseph Lowry observes in a recent study that Ibn al-Muqaffaʿ attempted to secure the authority of the caliph by drawing "a careful and deliberate distinction between a sphere of law that is settled and unproblematic and a sphere of law that requires interpretation."[175] Although acknowledging the indisputable authority of the settled and unproblematic sphere of law based on the Qur'an and the general Sunna, Ibn al-Muqaffaʿ grounded the *legitimacy* of the caliph in his adherence to this unproblematic sphere but claimed for the caliph all the interpretive *authority*.[176]

Abū Yūsuf and Awzāʿī would have agreed with Ibn al-Muqaffaʿ's grounding of caliphal legitimacy in the agreed-upon aspects of the Sharīʿa. They would not, however, agree to surrendering all the interpretive authority to the sole discretion of the caliph. Abū Yūsuf's gives large discretionary leeway (*siyāsa*) to the caliph and considers obedience to the caliph part of obedience to God, so long as that obedience did not contradict the agreed upon sphere of the Sharīʿa. However, beyond *siyāsa*, Abū Yūsuf demanded that the caliph follow the Sunna of the Prophet and the early righteous caliphs, including the Umayyad ʿUmar II. This effectively meant following the scholars of the *salaf*, including jurists like Abū Ḥanīfa, who had preserved and systematized this Sunna. The key difference between the two systems lay in their view of authority: The

[174] Ibn al-Muqaffaʿ's moderating inclinations can be appreciated from his worry about the extremism of many in their Khurāsānī troops who believed that the caliph could move mountains and reverse the direction of prayer. J. Lowry, "The First Islamic Legal Theory: Ibn al-Muqaffaʿ on Interpretation, Authority, and the Structure of the Law," *JAOS* 128.1 (2008): 29–30.

[175] Lowry, 25.

[176] Ibid., 33 (emphasis added).

caliph to Abū Yūsuf or Awzāʿī had no inherent, infallible, or even superior authority to interpret the sacred texts, and hence the only authority lay in the knowledge of the Sunna and, to pro-opinion jurists like Abū Yūsuf, in mastering Qur'an-based legal argument to defend one's positions. In contrast, Ibn al-Muqaffaʿ's caliph, although not infallible, was the highest interpretive authority. Thus, the dispute between the two visions really concerned the middle region between the indisputable aspects of the Sharīʿa on the one hand and the discretionary *siyāsa* on the other, and the line between the two was not clearly established yet by either.

The argument for Sunna by the likes of Abū Yūsuf was ill-served by the intense internal rivalry among the emerging groups of jurists. There were the pro-opinion Iraqi circles of Kūfa and Basra and the protradition circles of Medina, Syria, and Egypt (the tradition could be either based on *ḥadīth* reports or, in case of Medinan jurists like Mālik, the continued customary practice *ʿamal* of the Prophet' s city).[177] It is in the context of the threat of the centralizing policies of the Abbasids and the intractable diversity and parochialism of regional schools that al-Shāfiʿī attempted to create a harmonious jurisprudence by disciplining the seemingly arbitrary use of tradition by the Medinans and the unbridled use of opinion by the Iraqis. A rigorous legal theory tightly bound to scriptural authority was the best way for the private jurists to close ranks against the caliphate's encroachment. Yet Crone and Hinds put the matter too starkly: "Having been deprived of the authority to institute new *sunan*, the Abbasid caliphs also found that the past which they were supposed to imitate consisted of narrowly defined rules, not of vague ancestral practice compatible with any interpretation which they might wish to put on it. In practice, their hands had thus been tied."[178] This statement presupposes that the Umayyads had held near-total authority over an entirely amorphous tradition, a premise that ignores the presence of the Qur'an and its Community-centered view as well as the fact that the Umayyads' relations with the private scholars were of a nature not entirely distinct from that of the Abbasids.[179] Yet this statement correctly suggests that the

[177] See Abd-Allāh, "Mālik's Concept," 76f. for Mālik's attitude toward *ḥadīth* versus custom, Shamsy, "Rethinking Taqlīd," for Shāfiʿī's critique of it; idem, "From Tradition to Law: The Origins and Early Development of the Shāfiʿī School of Law in Ninth Century Egypt" (PhD Dissertation, Harvard University, 2009), for the conflict between Iraqi and traditionist approaches.

[178] Crone and Hinds, 91.

[179] See comments on al-Zuhrī earlier, for instance. There are many reports in the Umayyad period of a close relationship between learned individuals and the rulers. For one account, see Sayyid, *Jamāʿa*, 108–16.

Abbasids had less freedom than the Umayyads, and that the organization, development, growth, and consolidation of Sunna had something to do with it. The greater Umayyad freedom was not because they had wielded unrestrained religious authority, but rather because of the infancy of all the processes, which in their developed form provided a more sophisticated and workable legal system to the Abbasids while also limiting their freedom in dealing with religious norms.

Zaman has persuasively argued that in the Abbasid period, the caliphs participated with scholars in the derivation of norms and shared their vision of authority. No separation of "religion" and "politics" ever took place, the *Miḥna* instituted by Ma'mūn was an exception rather than the rule, and despite some tensions under such circumstances, the earmark of the relationship between the ulama and the caliphs (or later, sultans) was cooperation by the ulama, patronage of the rulers, and sharing of political and religious authority. This symbiotic relationship, as well as the threat of repression by the rulers, generally goaded the ulama into political quietism.[180] Khaled Abou El Fadl argues that Zaman may have overstated the case, for this cooperation still did not mean that the caliphs wielded superior legal authority. Sunni legal literature never cites the decisions of caliphs or their governors or judges as authoritative, with the obvious exception of those agreed upon by the Sunni community as the *Rāshidūn* (Rightly Guided). Indeed, it is elaboration of juristic doctrine within schools, not the judgments of the caliphs or their governors that ever constituted valid precedent in Islamic law.[181] Abou El Fadl thus accepts in a qualified way Crone and Hinds' thesis that "the caliph was merely executor of the law chosen by the community," and that this movement against the absolute caliphate authority had commenced earlier, al-Shāfiʿī's being "simply nails in the caliphal coffin."[182] Yet quickly moving on to his own point, which is to underscore that "the jurists became the representatives of the divine law," Abou El Fadl misses the ambiguity in Crone and Hinds formulation: Was it the Community or the Sunna that was used to oppose the caliphal authority? How and when did the Community become identical with the Sunna? Because Crone and Hinds insist on a singular "God's caliph" view of political authority in early Islam, the idea of the Community could be dismissed as a cover by traditionalists like al-Shāfiʿī for their invention of the Sunna and

[180] Zaman, 49, 76–8, 81–2, 98.
[181] Abou El Fadl, 94–5.
[182] Crone and Hinds, 93; quoted in Abou El Fadl, 93.

resistance to caliphal authority, and hence one can speak of the Sunna and the Community without distinction. Abou El Fadl does not pause at this conflation, perhaps because to him – interested in legal theory rather than history – Islamic jurisprudence is a timeless category (at one point, he calls even the Prophet' s Companion Anas b. Mālik a "jurist").[183]

Yet al-Shāfiʿī's contribution was the formulation of an ongoing transformation, not invention, of the tradition. He and the emergent juristic culture were transforming the original Community-centered view of political authority into a Sunna-centered variant in order to resist caliphal centralization and imperialization. Sunna in its basic form needed little defending, but the legal edifice the traditionalists were erecting – *fiqh* – did. Because the Qur'an did not explicitly endorse its authority (that is, there was no equivalent of "Petrine commission" for juristic enterprise in Islam like there is asserted for the church in Catholic doctrine), concepts grounded in the mission and infallibility of the *umma* in theory were deployed to ground this new enterprise.

A key characteristic of the emerging jurisprudence was its omnicompetence (it addressed every domain of life and thinking).[184] N. J. Coulson aptly sums up the consequences of this development of *fiqh*:

> The first 150 years of Islam were characterized by an almost untrammeled freedom of juristic reasoning in the solution of problems not specifically regulated by divine revelation … in these early days law had a distinctly dual basis. It was a compound of the two separate spheres of the *divine ordinance* and the *human decision*. But this pragmatic attitude soon fell victim to the increasing sophistication of theological and philosophical inquiry. Among the growing body of scholars whose deliberations were attempting to explain the essence of their faith arose a group who took their stand on the principle

[183] See, for instance, Abou El Fadl, 58n110. This designation might have been fine if he were using "jurist" to simply mean something like "learned persons in Islam," but he in fact frequently invokes theories of technical juristic culture derived from Western literature, thus adding a layer of anachronism throughout his otherwise excellent study.

[184] "Jurisprudence (*fiqh*) not only regulates in meticulous detail the ritual practices of the faith and matters which could be classified as medical hygiene or social etiquette – legal treatises, indeed, invariably deal with these topics first; it is also a composite science of law and morality, whose exponents (*fuqaha'*, sing. *faqih*) are the guardians of the Islamic conscience" N. J. Coulson, *A History of Islamic Law* (The University Press, 1964), 83. Johansen writes, "In the sense of a normative system concerned with human acts," *fiqh* at least since the second/eighth century onward has provided "the judiciary with the standards for judgments which are legitimate" on both religious ethics as well as juristic methodology. As judges (*qāḍīs*) and jurisconsults (*muftīs*), the role of the *fiqh* scholars "is not restricted to the production of legal rules to be applied by the courts: they lead debates on ethical as well as legal obligations[,] and their norms address not only the courts but also the religious conscience of the Muslims" (Johansen, *Contingency*, 3).

that *every aspect of human behaviour must of necessity be regulated by the divine will. In their philosophy of law, the legal sovereignty of God was all-embracing.*[185]

To hone Coulson's observation a bit, that every aspect of human behavior is within God's province in some way is immediately obvious from the Qur'an, but that was not significant for the ulama's purpose until joined by the premise that it must be regulated by the juristic enterprise whose job it was to derive every legal judgment and every rule as directly as possible from the words of revelation. Furthermore, al-Shāfiʿī's goal was to tie law to scriptural texts as tightly as possible in order to restrain the unending subjectivity of regional approaches; he was unwilling to allow teleological reasoning based on general goals or common sense, like the Ḥanafī *istiḥsān*, or potentially inconsistent and inscrutable sources like Mālik's "custom of Medina." Every human act was to be governed by a scriptural text or a linguistic or analogical extension derived therefrom. This task came to require highly technical experts who were not merely scriptural exegetes or generally learned or pious men. Certainly being a qur'anic exegete was of little help; being a *ḥadīth* expert was relatively more useful given the vast expanse of particular rulings in *ḥadīth*. Ultimately, however, no one could compete with the jurists who employed qur'anic and *ḥadīth* texts and ultimately created a body of law and legal reasoning.

The Miḥna

The intellectual efforts of system-building traditionalists like al-Shāfiʿī (whose initial impact is a matter of some controversy)[186] were not, as Crone and Hinds have written, "nails into the caliphal coffin," for the struggle was not yet over. Unless we wish to read history deterministically, it is possible to imagine that things might have turned out quite differently if a few Abbasids had turned out like ʿUmar II at this juncture; the ulama would have been only too happy to serve. The fact that it was al-Shāfiʿī whose Sunna-centered approach (and not that of any of his intellectual rivals among the jurists who had been less Sunna-centered)

[185] N. J. Coulson, *Conflicts and Tensions in Islamic Jurisprudence* (University of Chicago Press, 1969), 4. (emphasis added)

[186] Hallaq, "Was al-Shafiʿi the Master Architect of Islamic Jurisprudence?" *IJMES* 25 (1993): 587–605, questions the role of al-Shāfiʿī; Shamsy, "From Tradition to Law," esp. 167–79, reestablishes it.

won out was not a foregone eventuality, and one important factor that helped decide the future was the inquisition and heroic triumph of Ibn Ḥanbal.[187] Over the next two centuries, as the Abbasids lost both symbolic and political power, the juristic enterprise continued to flower and developed into various legal traditions (*madhhabs*) whose grip on Islamic normativity was irrevocably consolidated.

The Miḥna began as an unprecedented bid by the brilliant, learned, and ambitious caliph al-Ma'mūn (r. 198–218/813–33) to add total religious and symbolic authority to his political dominion and perhaps to end the growing ambiguity and tension in religious authority caused by the increasing consolidation of the traditionalists. Recent studies have further added to the evidence that it was the caliph and not the ulama who had invented something entirely new. The reasons could lie, according to one study, in the Abbasids' generally and in particular Ma'mūn's extraordinary messianic inclinations.[188] In addition, Ma'mūn's contact with the imperial Sassanid heritage (with its ideals of religion and state as twins, and absolutism of the imperial power),[189] the Shīʿī ideas (he seems to have harbored plans to assume the role of the Shīʿī *imām*), and Hellenistic philosophy all seem to have added both to the elitism and intellectual depth of the young ambitious prince.[190] This background firmly rooted him in belief in absolute and unified rule and hence aversion to the simple, xenophobic faith of the traditionalists as well as the masses (*ṭughām*) that followed them.

[187] The inquisition, Miḥna, of Aḥmad b. Ḥanbal and other traditionalist authorities instituted by the Abbasid caliph al-Ma'mūn and carried forth by his successors, al-Muʿtaṣim, al-Wāthiq, and al-Mutawakkil, lasted for fifteen years (218–34/833–48), after which the caliph Mutawakkil converted to the position of Aḥmad b. Ḥanbal. Some recent studies on the subject are: Christopher Melchert, *Aḥmad ibn Ḥanbal* (Oneworld, 2006); N. Hurvitz, "Who is the Accused? The Interrogation of Aḥmad Ibn Ḥanbal," *Al-Qanṭara* 22 (2001): 359–73, which sees the Miḥna as a culmination of the struggle between the *mutakallimūn* and *muḥaddithūn*, which also provides an up-to-date bibliography on the subject.

[188] See H. Yücesoy, *Messianic Beliefs and Imperial Politics in Medieval Islam: The 'Abbāsid Caliphate in the Early Ninth Century* (University of South Carolina, 2009), 116–35, for Ma'mūn's messianic claims; in particular, 131–2 for some of his questioning of previous interpretations such as Crone and Hinds' as well as Zaman's.

[189] Brought up in a Persian foster family of the Barmakids viziers, he imbibed Persian statecraft, in particular the *Testament of Ardshir* with its Machiavellian absolutism, as his ideal (Cooperson, 29–33).

[190] This interpretation is supported generally in M. Cooperson, *Al Ma'mun* (Oneworld, 2005); T. El-Hibri, "The Reign of the Abbasid Caliph al-Ma'mun (811–833): The Quest for Power and the Crisis of Legitimacy" (PhD Dissertation, Columbia University, 1994).

As for traditionalists, the dual nature of their rising authority are aptly captured by the title they ultimately adopted, *Ahl al-Sunna wa'l-Jamāʿa*, that is, the group representing Sunna and the united Community, as well as the name their opponents gave them, the *nābita*, a new, popular, and dangerous social force.[191] What was new was not the doctrines they espoused, but the new vision of authority (which was deadly effective against the caliphal claims) in which the final say beyond God's word lay not in the ruler (as the later Umayyads, the Shīʿa, and now the Abbasids had claimed) or in the Community (the seemingly unfeasible original ideal), but in the Sunna (in its "raw" form as *ḥadīth* or systematized form as *fiqh*), an idea which empowered but also ultimately froze the will of the Community.

Aḥmad b. Ḥanbal did not just represent the traditionalists; he became synonymous with Sunni Islam. It is also clear that he did not seek to restore the Community-centered vision of Islam. His predecessors may have rebelled against the state in the name of the *umma* or justice; he had no interest in political activism:[192] He challenged not the political aggrandizement of the caliph but only the claim of his being the *imām al-huda* (the ultimate religious authority), *al-mahdī* (the guided one), or *al-mujaddid* (the renewer of faith).[193] He only contended that the caliph could not claim privileged access to normative authority of Islam above and beyond the tradition of discourse that the Community, represented by its scholars of tradition and law, had come to embrace.

Rather than a triumph, the Miḥna is better understood as sealing the deal on a trade-off. It reaffirmed the traditionalists' surrendering to the caliphate the Community's political "rights" that the many early rebellions had aimed to restore. The loss appears serious until one considers what had been won in return. The post-Miḥna acceptance, even by the caliphate, of the status of the Muslim *jamāʿa* (a united and organized form body of the *umma*) as the site of infallibility and charisma meant that the ulama, the representatives of the Community and of its

[191] W. al-Qāḍī, "The Earliest 'Nābita' and the Paradigmatic 'Nawābit,'" *SI* 78 (1993): 27–61.

[192] "Ibn Ḥanbal's doctrine," observes Michael Cook, "is a deeply apolitical one" and emerged as a result of "the adaptation of an activist heritage to a civilian society for which political quietism was an increasingly relevant position" (Cook, *Commanding*, 106). He "stood in unhesitating obedience to the ruler, except in disobedience to God. Yet it was obedience without a shadow of warmth or a hint of a smile" (Ibid., 111–13). Although his Ḥanbalī followers did engage in social activism, that was, Cook thinks, largely in opposition to the founder's quietist and apolitical legacy.

[193] Yücesoy, 88, 140.

fount of normativity, the Sunna, became the true leaders of Islam, whose obedience in a general sense became a religious obligation. It is in this politico-theological context that we can appreciate the true significance of the doctrine of *ijmāʿ* (consensus), which remains notoriously elusive in the context of legal theory (because consensus never seems to obtain in practice).[194] In the words of al-Sayyid:

> It was the *umma* and its congregation [*jamāʿa*] that remained sacrosanct, the object of God's deputyship [*khilāfa*], and that remained the fundamental and highest source of legitimacy, granting anything else subsidiary legitimacy to the extent that it remained within its purview. Thus the caliphate dissolved a long time ago while the *umma* and its charisma (its consensus, and its infallibility!) stayed. Thus the *umma* in Islam has been the fundamental source of legitimacy [*sharʿiyya*]. All other sources of legitimacy, including the caliphate, have been subsidiary and contingent upon it.[195]

This picture of the Community's historical centrality tells only half the story, the theory rather than the practice. The Community, of course, is a theoretical construct, an idealization, which loses significance if not expressed in political institutions. It is politics that creates institutions (and constitutions), and law works with and within them. If the Community were to have an active role, it would have been through politics, not legal doctrine (this, I think, explains the elusiveness of *ijmāʿ* as a legal doctrine). The consequences of giving up the Community's claims amounted to the loss of normative agency in the political realm. For the Sunnis, there simply was no alternative route to political legitimacy, and the consequences became evident in the ensuing centuries.

[194] This is not to deny the significance of this concept in legal theory. According to A. Zysow, "Economy of Uncertainty," 199 ff., esp. 211, in the Ḥanafi *fiqh*, "the chief function of *ijmāʿ*, its *raison d'être*, is to confirm the results of legal procedures, analogy, interpretation, and the acceptance of unit-traditions which are not in themselves certain." See also 200f. for Shāfiʿī reservations about consensus, 223 and 237–9 for Ḥanbalī views.

[195] Sayyid, *Jamāʿa*, 57–8.

2

The Political Thought of the Classical Period

> In spite of [the turmoil caused by the First Crusade] there is no hint of any threat to Islam or Islamic territory from the non-Muslim world in al-Ghazālī's works: it would seem that the universal aims of Islam had been forgotten in the face of problems which had been raised by the fragmentation of the Islamic world.[1]

About the same time as the central caliphate was drawing near its end, a distinctly Islamic society and culture was reaching its prime. This society and its institutions proved remarkably adaptable and capable of weathering the ensuing centuries of frequent military invasions and political instability. The new military and bureaucratic elites drew from Turkish and Persian stock, and these traditions now furnished the political culture and institutions of the medieval Islamic world while Islam's religious law and tradition grew under the watch of the ulama. Furthermore, in contrast with the early caliphs who had ruled over a non-Muslim majority, the lands of Islam were now inhabited by a clear majority of Muslims.[2]

The decline of the Abbasids during the fourth/tenth century, who were already suffering from the de facto independence of a number of provincial elites, gave way to a number of dynasties of Shīʿī provenance, inaugurating what has been called "the Shīʿite century," with the Fāṭimids in North Africa and Egypt, Ḥamdānids in Syria, Zaydīs in Yemen, and the Buyids (345–446/945–1055) in Iraq and Persia, including Baghdad,

[1] Lambton, *State*, 109.
[2] R. Bulliet, *Islam: the View from the Edge* (New York: Columbia University Press, 1994).

the very house of the Sunni caliphate.[3] Throughout the classical period, Baghdad remained the center of key developments in law, political thought, statecraft, and the caliphate discourse. The Persian-Shīʿī Buyids ruled over it for a century, leaving the Sunni Abbasid caliph in place nonetheless. In 446/1055, the eastern and central Islamic lands were conquered by Turkic Sunni invaders, the Saljuqs, whose central power fragmented quickly but lasted for centuries afterward as petty warring principalities, occasionally growing into more ambitious kingdoms.

These military patronage states were characterized by an unbridgeable gap, not between religion and politics, but between the ruler and the ruled. The two often spoke different languages and possessed different cultural and social sensibilities, although the powerful sociolegal culture of Muslim societies was often successful in incorporating the ruling elite to an extent. What could rarely be imagined was a political community that elected its rulers or held them systematically accountable. Yet the lingering ideal of the early caliphate was strong enough to allow an alternative imagination, however vague and romanticized, of the basis of political legitimacy, and often precluded among the ulama total acceptance of the military rule as the norm. Thus, an almost planned political illegitimacy, which occasionally stooped to outright despotism, seems to have become the lot of Muslim societies of the long medieval period.

When the Sunni Saljuqs acceded to power, having vanquished the Shīʿī Buyids (it is unlikely that either were particularly committed to their respective religious identities or rites), and further acquired a pragmatic kind of Islamic justification for their rule by defeating the Byzantines at Manzikert in 463/1071, the Sunni ulama could no longer afford to ignore this new presence as mere usurpers. The religious integration of the Saljuqs was helped further along by the shrewd Niẓām al-Mulk, who introduced a new institution, the *madrasa*, and established a network of these religious schools that primarily taught Sunni jurisprudence. The *madrasa* mediated between the rulers, who used their political and economic advantage to endow them and thus insert themselves into the sociocultural fabric of the cities, and the ulama, many of whom taught at the *madrasas*, received stipends, and vied with each other for

[3] See C. E. Bosworth, *Islamic Dynasties* (Edinburgh: Clark Constable Ltd., 1980). For a detailed treatment of the ulama and the institutions in the Buyid period, see J. J. Donohue, *The Buwayhid dynasty in Iraq 334 H./945 to 403 H./1012: Shaping Institutions for the Future* (Leiden, Boston: Brill, 2003).

positions.[4] Although there always remained the naysayers among the ulama, who resisted employment with and subservience to the rulers, on the whole the fifth/eleventh century saw the emergence of a new type of relationship between the two, in which many of the ulama served as "regular members of courtly circles, frequently employed on diplomatic missions and other state business." The Saljuqs and their successor states (in particular, Zengids and Ayyubids) provided "livelihood and power to thousands of scholars and students, thus entrenching religious knowledge as a career, a well-marked ladder of advancement involving teaching, preaching and the judiciary."[5]

SIYĀSA AND FIQH

Three distinct bodies of literature can be identified in the classical period that treated politics from different vantage points. The ulama began to theorize the ideal caliphate (at about the same time, ironically, as the central caliphate was losing its actual power) in treatises of theological polemics directed in particular against the Shīʿī theological and political threat. The most prominent treatises on the subject were authored in Baghdad sunder the Buyids and then the Saljūqs. Yet there had been two other growing bodies of literature that more closely guided the practical life of the two types of the elite of the classical period: the *fiqh* – the legal discourse of the ulama, who were the social elite par excellence – and statecraft literature, in particular, "mirrors for princes," which addressed the rulers.

Jurisprudence (*fiqh*) is a natural place to look to understand how classical ulama dealt with power in reality. Until the consolidation of *fiqh* in the third/ninth century, the caliphal governors had dispensed justice based on custom and scripture, whereas the real development and systematization of Islamic law was taking place in private circles of scholars in centers like Iraq and Medina. As noted in the previous chapter, the relationship between *siyāsa* and *fiqh* (and between the rulers and the ulama) was far too supple at this point to allow for a clear-cut distinction, and hence the suggestion by Schacht that the political (*siyāsa*) at this time stood apart

[4] M. Chamberlain, "Military Patronage States and the Political Economy of the Frontier, 1000–1250," in *A Companion to the History of the Middle East*, ed. Youssef M. Choueiri (Wiley-Blackwell, 2008), 135–53; idem, *Knowledge and Social Practice in Medieval Damascus, 1190–1350* (Cambridge University Press, 1994), 27–68.

[5] T. Khalidi, *Arabic Historical Thought in the Classical Period* (Cambridge University Press, 1994), 191–2.

from the "ideal system of the *Sharīʿa*" is anachronistic. It assumes that the Sharīʿa had already become identical to these private jurists' teachings, thus the actual practices of Umayyad governors and judges could be only surreptitiously imported into their ideal system. With the decline of the Abbasid power and ensuing political fragmentation, the ulama acquired greater religious authority vis-à-vis the rulers, becoming organized in legal communities (*madhhabs*) networked across the Muslim lands, which served as professional schools or guilds of law-providing guidance and identity to their followers.[6] The attitudes of the various groups of ulama toward the military rulers remained varied and ambivalent, consisting of dependence and acceptance on the one hand and criticism and rejection on the other. This ambivalence was reflected in their jurisprudence. In Abou El Fadl's words, the relationship between the ulama and the rulers was not "a dogmatic one-sided relationship." Rather, it was a "reciprocal and dialectical process of accommodation and resistance" that changed with the sociopolitical context.[7] Yet the jurists were not merely or transparently responsive to sociopolitical changes in an either positive (as in response to the needs of the society or demands of justice) or negative sense (as in capitulation), for, like any legal tradition, theirs too imposed its demands and commitments, its constraints and logic.[8]

Besides the irony of the ulama both legitimizing usurpation and implicitly encouraging rebellion, scholars have noted yet another irony in the ulama's doctrines. On the one hand they demanded absolute obedience to the ruler,[9] yet on the other they were committed to a legalistic view of authority; they denied the rulers any authority except as executors of the law. Baber Johansen's study of Ḥanafī *fiqh* examines this paradox. Following Schacht, he posits that the Ḥanafī jurists conceived of society as consisting of proprietors and *fiqh* as the sum total of individual rights.[10] They defined two types of rights (*ḥuqūq*), those of God's servants

[6] G. Makdisi, "The Guilds of Law in Medieval Legal History," *Zeitschrift fur Geschischte der Arabisch-Islamischen Wissenschaften Band* 1(1984): 233–52; C. Melchert, *The Formation of the Sunni Schools of Law, 9th-10th Centuries C.E.* (Brill, 1997).

[7] Abou El Fadl, 102.

[8] Ibid., 23–31, 102, 110f.

[9] Thus Lambton, *State*, 20: "The *Sharīʿa*, which had absolute authority, preceded the state and was its law. The individual could therefore have no rights against the state but merely the right to expect that the leader of the community, the caliph, would act in conformity with the law.... Later jurists were to demand absolute obedience to the caliph as a religious obligation defined in terms of the *Sharīʿa* and justified by the Qur'anic obligation."

[10] Johansen, *Contingency*, 62; see earlier.

(*ʿibād* or *ādamiyyūn*) and those of God. The precarious balance of individuals' rights, the classical Ḥanafī jurists held, could "only be fulfilled by a Muslim state." "The Islamic state is considered to be the trustee and the executor of the 'claims of God,' of the *ḥuqūq Allāh*, or to use the synonymous expression, the *ḥuquq al-sharʿ*, the claims of the law." The Ḥanafī jurists "all agree in interpreting the *ḥaqq Allāh* as representing the public interest (*maṣāliḥ al-ʿāmma*), or the interest of all Muslims (*kāffat al-muslimīn*)."[11] In this view, "the public sphere is the realm of the absolute, the realm of God, as represented by the ruler."[12] Whereas in theory, Johansen argues, these jurists considered a government indispensable, in reality they did not leave any legitimate space for it, the reason being that Ḥanafī law "is based on the rights of the individual and gets into difficulties whenever it tries to reconcile these rights with the public interest." Thus, the classical jurists leaned toward the individual "by protecting the rights of the individual" against the state, and by accepting that the "state must inevitably transcend the sphere of competence which the lawyers are willing to grant it" – thus effectively rendering the state either ineffective or illegitimate.[13] Yet this insight still does not help us understand why classical jurists engaged in such oddly contradictory attitudes toward state and politics. Johansen's answer suffers from the same limitation as Abou El Fadl's to our earlier question by attributing the attitude of jurists toward political authority to juristic culture or formal legal constructions. Although features of Islamic juristic culture remain indispensable guides in understanding the jurists' doctrines, we need to dig deeper to understand the constraints that shaped the legal doctrine itself.

STATECRAFT AND THE ULAMA

Aside from jurisprudence, there had grown in the Islamic world statecraft and political advice literature written by men in power or their observers, secretaries, and scribes. Men like ʿAbd al-Ḥamīd b. Yaḥyā (d. 132/750), scribe to the last Umayyad caliph, Ibn al-Muqaffaʿ (d. 139/759), whose caliphate-centered view we have already encountered and who was

[11] Ibid., 210.
[12] Ibid., 212–13.
[13] Ibid., 217. Corresponding to this theoretical prejudice, Johansen observes, the Ḥanafī law is well-developed in the area of the "rights of humans" (*ḥuquq al-ādamiyyīn*). In the domain of the "rights" or "claims" of God, only worship is a well-developed area; "penal law and fiscal law are rough drafts" compared to these, and "administrative law is virtually non-existent in the law books" (216).

scribe to an Umayyad and then an Abbasid personage, Qudāma b. Jaʿfar (d. 337/948),[14] a late-Abbasid state official and scholar, as well as others had already created a distinctly statist or imperial view of politics that drew on Sassanid and Hellenist political heritage. This view was not necessarily secular, but its starting point was the survival of the state and the ruling elite, not religious doctrines or vision. The political ideas, notes Lambton, "found in administrative handbooks and mirrors for princes hold a position midway between the theory of the jurists on the one hand and that of the philosophers on the other."[15] The Muslim philosophers (*falāsifa*) assigned purely instrumental value to religion and were committed to Greek wisdom on society, politics, and metaphysics as inherited in its Near Eastern Neoplatonist form. The Persianate statecraft literature and the Neoplatonist philosophers were in agreement in one crucial respect, namely, their vision of agency in political life and their exclusive focus on the person of the ruler. They "located the effective agent of political community in the ruler whose task it was to govern society by enforcing its laws, punishing its rebellious members and training himself in the various virtues and norms of conduct."[16]

Siyāsa as a Friend

The ulama also contributed to practical statecraft, first through legal manuals (various compositions along the lines of Abū Yūsuf's *K. al-Kharāj*) and, with the rise of the military patronage states, in their capacity as officials and judges, in the idiom of Persian statecraft tradition. Abū Yūsuf had recommended to the caliph the righteous predecessors' ways of ruling in strictly Islamic idiom, but the classical ulama had to deal with a different audience, rulers who on the whole had no appreciation of or attachment to the constructions of Sunni *fiqh*. Yet the ulama's contribution to statecraft literature did not mean that their main body of thought (*fiqh*) systematically theorized power in Islamic terms. They never bridged the gap between the private juristic enterprise of *fiqh* and the realities of power.

[14] For a comprehensive recent treatment of this figure, see P. Heck, *The Construction of Knowledge in Islamic Civilization: Qudāma b. Jaʿfar and his Kitāb al-Kharāj wa ṣināʿat al-kitāba* (Brill, 2002).

[15] A. K. S. Lambton, "Islamic Political Thought," in J. Schacht and C. E. Bosworth (ed.), *The Legacy of Islam* (Oxford University Press, 1979), 416.

[16] Heck, 195.

In order to understand this relationship between Sharīʿa and politics, I begin with a text that has been called "one of the clearest statements of the problematic relationship between *siyāsa* and *Sharīʿa*."[17] This was, according to Tarif Khalidi, the influential mirror *Sirāj al-Mulūk* (*Guiding Sun for Kings*), by the sixth-/twelfth-century Māliki jurist, *ḥadīth* scholar, and well-known ascetic, Abū Bakr Muḥammad b. al-Walīd al-Ṭurṭūshī (b. 451/1059; d. 520/1126):

With a wealth of historical examples, Ṭurṭūshī had stated in clear terms the case for a secular state, one based upon an orderly routine of government and working to maintain public peace and stability. A state well ordained and firmly ruled, no matter what the religion or its ruler, was infinitely preferable to one ruled piously but incompetently. In adopting this approach, Ṭurṭūshī was bypassing a long tradition of political thought represented by thinkers like al-Māwardī and Abū Yaʿlā.[18]

Khalidi further qualifies this characterization of Ṭurṭūshī's thought in a footnote:

In calling Ṭurṭūshī's thought "secular", I must emphasize that he was writing very much within the Islamic tradition, especially the *Adab*-history tradition. Nevertheless, the Qur'an was for him "the mine of *siyāsāt*" while the ethics he advocated, largely of Sufi inspiration, e.g., mercy in the ruler and patience in the subjects, all presume total obedience to the ruler, just or unjust. Uppermost in his mind is state preservation and not the integrity of the ruler nor his relationship to *Sharīʿa*, as in political thought of the *sharʿī* tradition.[19]

Let us examine the case Khalidi has built for this conclusion. Khalidi quotes an illuminating passage in Ṭurṭūshī's *Sirāj* in which he writes about the relationship between *siyāsa* and legal ordinances (*aḥkām*). He writes:

When I examined the histories of ancient nations … and the policies (*siyāsāt*) they instituted for governing states as well as the laws they adhered to for the protection of their religions, I found these to be of two kinds: legal ordinances (*aḥkām*) and state policies. The ordinances, which included what they took to be licit and illicit and the laws governing such things as commerce, marriage, divorce, and so forth … were all such as they had agreed upon by convention or mentality, there being no rational proof for any of them nor any commandment about them from God … nor were these nations following any prophet. The ordinances had simply been issued by the priests of fire-temples and guardians of idols.… It would therefore not be impossible for anyone to enact such ordinances on his own

[17] Ibid., 193.
[18] Ibid., 195.
[19] Ibid., 195n31.

initiative.... But as regards the policies they instituted to uphold and defend these ordinances ... here they followed the path of justice, sound policy, consensus and equity in obedience to these ordinances, as also in their conduct of war, protection of high ways and preservation of wealth.... In all these matters, they pursued a laudable path, none of which was contrary to reason if only the principles and basics had been sound or compelling. In their admirable pursuit of means to protect their corrupt principles they may be compared to one who embellishes a latrine.... Hence, I collected together what is of value in their histories.[20]

Contrary to Khalidi's reading, the relationship that emerges between *siyāsa* and law in this passage is not one of conflict, but one in which good politics protects laws; yet the two are independent of each other such that even bad laws could be protected by good politics and thus could bring prosperity and longevity to the rule. Ṭurṭūshī continues:

It may therefore be said that an infidel ruler who complies with the requirements of conventional policy lasts longer and is stronger than a believing ruler who in his own person is just and obedient to a prophetic policy of justice ... for you ought to know that a single *dirham*, taken from the subjects in a negligent and foolish manner, even though justly, corrupts their hearts more than ten *dirhams* taken from them in accordance with a policy seen to be well regulated and of a familiar pattern, even though unjustly.[21]

We can glean from passages such as this that Ṭurṭūshī had three, not two, fields of governance in mind, even if he does not explicitly state so. One is the actual laws, which govern the essence of all relationships and which he considers to be the most important element of all. The second field is politics, the management and prudent application of those laws. Good politics includes virtues such as justice and consensus. The non-Muslim states protect their arbitrary and inferior laws with good politics, which is like "one who embellishes a latrine!" The third field is the ruler's shrewd management of the perceptions and loyalties of the subjects, a field moderns should immediately recognize as propaganda, public relations, or "spincraft." These practices may be unjust, but when applied well, they will keep the subjects satisfied and in place. Effective rulers, most of all despots and tyrants, are typically masters of this field.

Ṭurṭūshī urges the Muslim prince not only to apply divine laws, but also to master the second field of prudence and the third field of propaganda. He does not much reflect on the possibly troubled relationship between these fields, on whether divine laws could be compromised at

[20] Ṭurṭūshī, *Sirāj al-Mulūk*, 50–1, qtd. in Khalidi, 193–4.
[21] Ibid., 194.

the expense of prudence or propaganda, or whether justice is a goal or merely a tool to achieve stability and control. He is a creature of his age and, as Khalidi rightly notes, sees Persian-style hierarchy and stratification as the ideal of politics and statecraft. He was obsessed with order at any cost and hence with the issue of rank and station, like most writers of mirrors for princes at the time. Islamic egalitarianism and political significance of the Community do not seem to trouble his imagination in the least. Yet his prescription of politics cannot be called "secular." Khalidi's characterization of Ṭurṭūshī's work is misleading in suggesting that there is a contradiction between *siyāsa* and Sharīʿa in Ṭurṭūshī's mind. Ṭurṭūshī seems to have suggested in these passages simply a *distinction* between *siyāsa* and *legal ordinances*, not *contradiction* between *siyāsa* and the Sharīʿa. This confusion is even more surprising given Ṭurṭūshī's explicit pronouncements to the contrary. Despite his appreciation of their politics of "justice, sound policy, consensus and equity in obedience to these ordinances," he could not be clearer about his disapproval of the man-made *laws*. The key to understanding Ṭurṭūshī's prescriptions is the recognition that to him even politics is taught by the Sharīʿa. Ṭurṭūshī's most central distinction, Khalidi observes, is

> between divine or prophetic (*ilāhī*; *nabawī*) justice and conventional (*iṣṭilāḥī*) justice. The first is the sum total of prophetic teachings; the second approximates to conventional policy (*siyāsa iṣṭilāḥiyya*).... The first type of justice is ideally represented in a ruler gathering around him religious scholars, described by Ṭurṭūshī as the "proofs of God," without whose counsel the ruler should not act in any matter. As regards conventional policy, the arrival of Muhammadan *Sharīʿa* confirmed certain policies and cancelled others.[22]

The first type of justice, represented by the legal ordinances and taught by the ulama, who are the "proofs of God," is the direct expression of the Sharīʿa, whereas the second type – the conventional justice represented by *siyāsa* – is guided and restricted by the Sharīʿa. These are not two distinct options but two aspects of justice, and both are regulated by the Sharīʿa. Ṭurṭūshī's claim that a politically wise infidel ruler is better than a pious but politically incompetent one is little more than rhetorical reinforcement of the importance of attending to conventional policy and not merely applying laws without prudence. None of this can be taken to mean that Ṭurṭūshī endorsed the supplanting of the Sharīʿa by secular laws or politics. All evidence from Ṭurṭūshī's biography suggests

[22] Khalidi, 194.

a staunchly orthodox, pietistic, even ascetic commitment to the Sharīʿa. Indeed, Ṭurṭūshī was a critic of his illustrious contemporary, Ghazālī, due to the latter's writing of *Iḥyā'*, in which he slighted *fiqh* in favor of Sufism.[23]

Precisely because Ṭurṭūshī's propositions cannot be explained by secular motivations, his distinction between law (*fiqh*) and policy (*siyāsa*) and his appreciation of just *siyāsa* acquire new significance. Ṭurṭūshī, in fact, was not alone. In the early fifth/eleventh century, Māwardī, the Shāfiʿī chief justice of Baghdad and the author of the most influential treatise on Islamic government, used the same term *siyāsa* to refer to the this-worldly part the job of the *khalīfa* or the *imām*, which he described as "ḥirāsat al-dīn wa siyāsat al-dunya," that is, protection of religion and *siyāsa* of this world. Because the caliphate itself is a religious office (i.e., required by and in service of *dīn*), Māwardī's separation of *dīn* from *siyāsa* is meant to emphasize that the caliph uses worldly means to protect the norms of *dīn* itself, as well as the goals of the polity set by *dīn* through *siyāsa*. Here, just like in Ziyād's use of it in the Umayyad period, *siyāsa* could only mean administration, good management, and wise rule – and, clearly, Māwardī sees it as part of the normative field of Islam. Māwardī too was the author of a few important treatises on statecraft; in them, he bases his insights into human societies and governance explicitly on Persian and Hellenist political thought as well as anecdotal Islamic wisdom, but the basic framework remains at odds with his work on the caliphate.[24] Before we understand why the pro-*siyāsa* ulama embraced this dual personality, let us look at the arguments antagonistic to *siyāsa*.

Siyāsa as Evil

Around the fifth/eleventh century, *siyāsa* seems to have increasingly taken on negative connotations. One of these meanings was "discretionary

[23] He was a renowned Mālikī jurist, traditionist, ascetic, and exegete; he was born in al-Andalus but lived in the Islamic east, and was clearly informed in Persian political heritage. His biographers inform us that he arrived in Alexandria toward the end of the fifth/eleventh century and set up a *madrasa* for the teaching of the Mālikī law; and he pleaded with the vizier to cease the imposition of Fatimid laws on the Sunnis. See Y. Lev, *State and Society in Fatimid Egypt* (Brill, 1991) 138–40. Ṭurṭūshī was one of the teachers of Ibn Tūmart, the Ashʿarī warrior, self-proclaimed Mahdi and the founder of the Almohad (al-Muwaḥḥidūn) movement. Al-Ghazālī's student al-Qāḍī Ibn al-ʿArabī met him in Jerusalem and admired his erudition and asceticism (al-Qāḍī Ibn al-ʿArabī, *Riḥla*, 80).

[24] See later.

punishment beyond the stipulation of the *Sharīʿa*."[25] This is demonstrated clearly in the case of Nūr al-Dīn Maḥmūd b. Zankī (r. 541–68/1146–73), known for his piety and strict adherence to the Shāfiʿī school of law and for raising the banner of *jihād* against the crusaders. David Ayalon reports a Mamluk-period historian's praise of the pious ruler:

> When Nūr al-Dīn annexed Mosul to his kingdom, he ordered its governor to do everything according to the Sharīʿa. The same source states that Nūr al-Dīn never implemented the *siyāsa*. This caused resentment in Mosul, and people there said to Kemishtakīn that the number of criminals, robbers and evil doers had increased, and the only way to overcome that plague was to execute the culprits. They asked him to write to Nūr al-Dīn and explain the situation, but he did not dare to do so. At last Shaykh ʿUmar al-Mulla, Nūr al-Dīn's trusted representative in Mosul, took courage and wrote his master telling him that in view of the dangerous situation, a certain kind of *siyāsa* has to be employed, for only severe punishments like execution could be effective in that kind of situation. To strengthen his argument, al-Mulla asked categorically: "if a person is robbed in the desert [in the open country?] who will give witness on his behalf?" When Nūr al-Dīn received the letter he turned it and wrote on its back that God knows better than man and he made for him a perfect Sharīʿa. Had He thought that the Sharīʿa needed addition, He would have included that addition in the Sharīʿa anyway.[26]

Nūr al-Dīn is praised by the ulama for his insistence on observing formal judicial procedures of *fiqh* despite complaints about their ineffectiveness in securing peace. He deemed them an inalienable part of the Sharīʿa and believed the Sharīʿa (as concretized in *fiqh*) to be in no need of emendations.[27]

Crusades seem to have effected a brief rapprochement and convergence of attitudes between the ulama and the ruling class, which historians have distinctly noted during the reign of the two Muslim heroes against the Crusaders, Nūr al-Dīn and Saladin. Both sultans are depicted

[25] Bernard Lewis goes on to even suggest that "*siyāsa*, at that time and in that place, does not mean politics at all. It means punishment," but later, perhaps correcting himself, continues that "there is of course a connection between politics and punishment, but the two terms are not as yet synonymous. *Siyāsa*, in later medieval Islam, more commonly means punishment than politics, more specifically discretionary punishment administered at the will of the ruler in contrast to legal punishment prescribed in accordance with the holy law of Islam" (Lewis, *Political*, 44).

[26] D. Ayalon, "The Great Yāsa of Chingiz Khan: A Reexamination (Part C2). Al-Maqrīzī's Passage on the Yāsa under the Mamluks," *SI* 38 (1973), 124–5.

[27] The well-known historian of the Ayyūbid age, Abū al-Ḥasan ʿAlī ʿIzz al-dīn Ibn al-Athīr (d. 630/1233), too, uses the term *siyāsa* to mean primarily discretionary punishment, and extols Nūr al-Dīn as "a very religious, very just and good-hearted person" who, presumably unlike other rulers of Ibn al-Athīr's time, "did not punish people solely on the basis of suspicions and accusations" – namely, on the basis of *siyāsa* (Ayalon, C2, 124).

as the embodiment of the Sunni orthodoxy of the age and as defenders of Islam against external enemies and, therefore, as rulers whom one could serve without demur. "Twelfth- and thirteenth-century ulama," Yaacov Lev observes, "expected the rulers to defend Islam as a territorial and political entity (*dār al-Islām*) and as a social organism (*ummah*) and to adhere to the principles of Sunni Islam."[28] Yet despite his personal commitment to the *legal madhhabs*, the political concepts and legitimacy of the dynasty Saladin created had little relationship to the Sharīʿa or to the caliphate, and his dynasty consisted of a number of lesser sultans under a greater sultan, on the pattern of the decentralized and loosely connected Central Asian model.[29] This shows that with the symbolic caliphate in place, even a pious and jurisprudentially correct ruler was not expected to abide by any Islamic model of politics or legitimacy; one simply did not exist.

Beyond the question of the legitimacy and constitution of the actual state (apart from the caliphate, that is), in which even the juristic tradition did not see the Sharīʿa as relevant, there raged a lively controversy about the efficacy of the Sharīʿa in the domain of public law and order which the mainstream jurists did see as its exclusive prerogative. It was in this domain that it was pitted by the state-centered writers against *siyāsa*. Many seem to have accepted that the Sharīʿa was incapable of dealing with the problems of the real world and that *siyāsa*, equated with extra-Sharīʿa punishments, was justified by its utility alone.[30] However, the opponents of *siyāsa* did not simply oppose extrajudicial punishments, but all extra-*fiqhi* policy and nonformal procedures by which crimes could be investigated or culpability established. There was a distinct awareness on both sides of the existence of "administrative justice," which prevented crime more effectively because of a more

[28] Y. Lev, "Symbiotic Relations: Ulama and the Mamluk Sultans," *Mamluk Studies Review* 1 (2009): 10.

[29] S. Humphreys, *From Saladin to the Mongols: the Ayyubids of Damascus, 1193–1260* (SUNY Press, 1977), 365–70.

[30] That many pro-*siyāsa* writers understood and advocated politics as independent of or even opposed to the Sharīʿa is true, but the extent of such writers seems to be exaggerated by modern scholars. In addition to Ṭurṭūshī, Khalidi places Idrīsi (d. c. 560/1165), Ibn al-ʿIbri (d. 1286), Ibn al-Athīr, Ibn Ṭiqṭaqa (d. ca. 709/1309), Ibn al-Fuwāti (d. 723/1323), and Ibn Khaldūn in the *siyāsa* tradition. Of these, Ṭurṭūshī and Ibn al-Athīr's positions have already been noted. Ibn Khaldūn, Gibb has cogently shown, did not privilege *siyāsa* over the Sharīʿa (Gibb, *Studies*, 174). Ibn Ṭiqṭaqa, a Shīʿī historian in the Mongol entourage, appears to be one author who privileged Mongol-style politics as a model, but he cannot be counted among the ulama (Khalidi, 195).

relaxed, rational, or utilitarian system of evidence than *fiqh*; hence the reference in the letter to Nūr al-Dīn to being robbed in the desert, where the two formal witnesses required by the classical jurisprudence would not be available. The equation of *siyāsa* with corporal punishment appears to be its opponents' way to deprecate *siyāsa* altogether. This is evident in the writings of the Mamluk-period Shāfiʿī jurist, al-Maqrīzī (d. 845/1442), also a scholar of *ḥadīth* and historian, who wrote most derisively of *siyāsa*: "Siyāsa ... is a Satanic word the origin of which most people of our time do not know and which they utter negligently and indifferently, saying: this matter is not included in the domain of the Sharīʿa and constitutes part of the siyāsa judgment. They deem it a light matter while before God it is an enormity."[31]

It appears therefore that rulers often had to choose between following the Sharīʿa, as represented by the ulama, and effectively maintaining peace and order. The case of Nūr al-Dīn and Saladin is important only as the exception that proves the rule. Most rulers, as Ibn al-Athīr points out, availed themselves of policies that the jurists did not deem legitimate under the Sharīʿa yet were considered necessary by the rulers for maintaining peace, suppressing disorder, and punishing criminals who could not be punished under the Sharīʿa.

The ulama like Māwardī and Ṭurṭūshī, who did not see *siyāsa* as a contradiction or even limitation of the Sharīʿa, were a minority (neither could be explained away as a "sell-out" – which is not to say there were not many among the ulama motivated by less noble concerns in their support of politics). And although the ulama rarely conceded that the Sharīʿa was anything but what they elaborated, thus leaving the rulers to either conform like Nūr al-Dīn or be condemned in the socioreligious sphere as being outside the bounds of the Sharīʿa, the rulers also at least occasionally seem to have contested the ulama's claim. Ibn Taghrībirdī reports an incident in which a Jewish merchant was unsatisfied with the *qāḍī*'s judgment and contested the trial as having not been in conformity

[31] Ayalon, C2, 109. Maqrīzī is known for his odd opinion that *siyāsa* was nothing but a corruption of the Mongol military code of law, *yāsa*. However, David Ayalon has established that Maqrīzī was well aware of the classical usage of the term in the Islamic context, but he did suggest, and correctly if with some exaggeration, that in his time *siyāsa* has come to refer to the Mongol *yāsa*, which these Mamluk rulers are obsessed with. This corruption and its implications incensed Maqrīzī. Ayalon further notes that it was the great Ibn Khaldun, who flourished half a century before Maqrīzī, who seems to have deliberately conflated the two entirely distinct terms, and translated *al-yāsa al-kabīra* of Gengiz Khan as *al-siyāsa al-kabīra*; although it appears that he did so consciously, it is not clear why (ibid., 118).

with the Sharīʿa. He complained to the Sultan, who asked the *qāḍī* for an explanation. The *qāḍī* said, "What I did is in conformity with the *sharʿ*," upon which the Sultan said something to this effect: "*Siyāsa* is in conformity with the *sharʿ*, while you have judged for some personal end."[32] Ṭurṭūshī would not have disagreed. Incidentally, the Sultan's contention here – that justice is require by the Sharīʿa even if procedurally it goes beyond the formal rules (or imperfect implementation) of *fiqh* – seems to be closer to the original meaning of *siyāsa* down to at least as late as the fourth/tenth century, as suggested earlier, which took *siyāsa* as policy beyond the words of – but in accordance with – the spirit of the Sharīʿa.

One of most important bulwarks against this pro-*siyāsa* tendency was Ghazālī, who believed *siyāsa* to be nothing but the legal ordinances known to the jurists. He writes:

> Men are overwhelmed by undisciplined desires leading to mutual rivalries, hence there is a need for a Sultan to manage them [*yasūsuhum*], and the Sultan needs a law by which to administer [*iḥtāja al-sulṭān ilā qānūn yasūsuhum bihi*]. A *faqīh* is the scholar of the law of politics [*al-faqīh huwa al-ʿālim bi qānūn al-siyāsa]* and the way to mediate between men if they disagree owing to their undisciplined interests. Thus, a *faqīh* is the teacher and guide of the Sultan in ways of administering and controlling men.[33]

Ghazālī seems not to doubt that *siyāsa* is necessary for religion to prosper, but his contention is that it is nothing beyond the law. There is no consideration that cannot be tied down by the stipulations of law and, hence, known first and foremost by the jurists; it is inconceivable that justice could be known outside of the *specific* commandments of revelation.

Both sides among the ulama seemed agreed on the primacy of the Sharīʿa; the question, therefore, had to do with whether the Sharīʿa could be identified with the jurists' enterprise (*fiqh*) or whether there was room left within the Sharīʿa but outside of *fiqh*. The *siyāsa* advocates' naïve optimism toward rational policy as a way to safeguard and implement the divine law was no match for the theoretical sophistication of the opposing and prevalent position. Their recognition of the virtue of prudence and wise policy making beyond the words of revelation was commonsensical, but was not backed by any coherent theory grounded in the Sharīʿa discourse. The real objection that underlay the anti-*siyāsa* stance was theoretical, even theological, and not just the tendency of unbridled

[32] Ibn Taghrībirdi in *Ḥawadith al-Duhūr*, cited in Ayalon, C2, 141.
[33] *Iḥyāʾ*, 1:30.

siyāsa to transgress into tyranny.[34] With rare exceptions, the abuse and tyranny of the rulers continued anyway; outlawing *siyāsa* from the Sharīʿa scarcely helped in that respect. Alienating rulers from the sources of legitimacy, one may argue, may have pushed them further toward unbridled recourse to power. The real concern for the ulama seems to have been to safeguard religious authority. That is, on what basis could the political actions and commands of the rulers be authorized such that it would become religiously normative for the subjects to obey or cooperate? In a society where the sole criterion for normativity of an action is its echo in the afterlife, calculations of interest, benefit, and harm, however rampant, had no real normative basis. The creation of such political authority required religiously authorizing rational ethical judgments. Yet who could authorize such extratextual judgments? In Imāmī Shīʿism, that authority would have been the *imām*. For Sunni Islam, however, it had been the Community. Just as the Shīʿī *imām* went in occultation sometime during the third/ninth century, so did perhaps the Community for the Sunnis. The net result was the same: a fundamental illegitimacy of political life; the authority the Qur'an had granted to the *ulu'l-amr* had to be denied them in the mainstream of classical Islam.

THE CALIPHATE DISCOURSE

The third relevant discourse of the classical period, the one which directly addressed the problem of the caliphate, was the work almost exclusively of the Sunni theologians of Baghdad during fourth/tenth and fifth/eleventh centuries. The replacement of the Community-centered vision with its Sunna-centered variant, which involved surrendering the rights of the community in the political sphere, was a gradual change that started as early as the late second century in the views of juristic traditionalists like Abū Yūsuf and climaxed in Aḥmad b. Ḥanbal's political quietism. It had not, however, yet been formally theorized.[35] The dynastic legitimacy of the

[34] Sibṭ Ibn al-Jawzi, reports a case in 613/1216 in the presence of Al-Ẓāhir Ghāzi, Saladin's son, when a judge, *Qāḍī* Ibn Shaddād, judged against a woman who had slandered someone and said, "She should be lashed with the whip in accordance with the Sharīʿa and her tongue cut off in accordance with *siyāsa*." Ibn al-Jawzi then intervened, "the Sharīʿa is *siyāsa* perfected. To punish her above and beyond the Sharīʿa would be to do her a violent injustice" (Khalidi, 195).

[35] Aḥmad b. Ḥanbal's own opinions on the matter of obedience to unjust caliph/imam are, as usual, divergent (Dumayjī, 537–40), although Cook argues that his practical attitude was quietism (Cook, *Commanding*, 101–13). The three earlier canonical *imāms* of *fiqh*, namely Abū Ḥanīfa, Mālik, and al-Shāfiʿī are all reported to have had "activist"

Abbasid caliphs was at first silently accepted, but, after the Miḥna, with the official endorsement of the traditionalist creed, the traditionalists, in particular the Ḥanbalīs, were only too happy to support a caliphate that surrendered to their religious vision. After the loss of effective Abbasid power to a series of Shīʿī military adventurers, the traditionalists naturally became the caliphate's biggest advocates and supporters. Yet the loss of the Community-centered vision and *shūrā* had not been theoretically justified as the norm of Islamic political thought.[36] Throughout the fourth/tenth and fifth/eleventh centuries, a number of attitudes toward the early history were possible among the Sunnis.

Sunni political thought began to consolidate as the *kalām* tradition took off in the fourth/tenth century, when al-Ashʿarī and his followers took up the banner of defending the traditionalist orthodoxy that was represented by Ibn Ḥanbal and vindicated by his triumph in the Miḥna. The rise of Shīʿī dynasties that ruled over a Sunni majority and their open support for Shīʿī political theology spurred Sunni *kalām* scholars to consolidate and defend Sunni orthodoxy and to provide a theoretical basis for the Sunni caliphate. The challenge for Sunni theologians now was to theorize the caliphate while attempting to defend the historical legitimacy of the early caliphate against attacks by the Shīʿa and the Khārijīs on the one hand and the Sunni compromise that required a limited caliphate on the other. Equally momentous foes were the Muʿtazila, who had backed and fueled the Miḥna, and who continued to pose a substantial intellectual threat, the response to which had been Sunni *kalām*'s raison d'être. Their fall from grace after the Miḥna had not spelled their intellectual demise; that was to be accomplished by the Ashʿarīs. The Muʿtazilī rationalist theology was both the main target as well as the source of the intellectual toolset of Sunni *kalām*.

These theologians wrote over the course of several of centuries and witnessed the Abbasid caliphate reduced to little more than a symbol. Without denying their individual contributions, we can detect a

opinions – in the sense that they permitted *khurūj* (rebellion) against an unjust ruler – although the question of what makes a ruler unjust and deprives him of legitimacy is far from straightforward (Dumayjī, 534–7).

[36] One may argue that the selective acceptance or fabrication of politically oriented *ḥadīth* reports among the traditionalists remains one way in which justification for quietism was being provided. That might be true, but the uses of these reports were so multifarious that without becoming part of a systematic theorization, in itself the collectivity of *ḥadīth* reports did not provide a clear political program. See, for collections of pro- and counter-obedience traditions, Abou El Fadl, 112–31; Dumayjī, 500–48.

continuing thread of concerns and presumptions alongside changing priorities in their theorization of the caliphate as they responded to their changing predicament. Whereas the aforementioned political and intellectual conditions provided this discourse its context, limits, questions, and direction, the theological, epistemological, and political theories that emerged in response cannot be taken as "logical" or predictable developments of these conditions, and hence must be examined in their own right.

The dramatic conversion of the master Muʿtazilī debater Abū 'l-Ḥasan al-Ashʿarī (d. 324/936) to the traditionalist position in the year 300/913 catalyzed the Sunni intellectual counter-assault against the Muʿtazila and the Shīʿa. The fourth/tenth century thereafter saw increasing systematization of Sunni *kalām*, which came to identify al-Ashʿarī as its eponym. Because the key issue in Muslim theological disputes had been political legitimacy, these Sunni theologians customarily included a chapter on the issue of caliphate (interchangeable with "imamate")[37] in theological treatises.

One of the first significant Ashʿarī texts to discuss the caliphate at length is *Al-Tamhīd fī al-radd ʿalā al-mulḥida al-muʿaṭṭila wa al-rāfiḍa wa al-khawārij wa al-muʿtazila* (*The Preliminary in the Refutation of the Deviant Deniers* [of God's attributes], *the Rafiḍīs* [the Shīʿa], *the Khārijīs, and the Muʿtazila*) by the Mālikī al-Qāḍī Abū Bakr al-Bāqillānī (d. 403/1013).[38] As its very title suggests, it was a theological polemic directed against the most prominent threats to Sunni orthodoxy. Another one is the theological treatise of ʿAbd 'l-Qāhir Ṭāhir al-Baghdādī (d. 429/1037), *Uṣūl al-dīn* (*The Principles of Religion*), better organized than Bāqillānī's but otherwise less original, and hence perhaps a better representative of the accepted Ashʿarī doctrine. In the history of Sunni political thought, the work of Abū 'l-Ḥasan b. al-Ḥabīb al-Māwardī (d. 450/1058) is considered a landmark. His influential *al-Aḥkām al-sulṭāniyya* (*Ordinances of Government*) has long been considered by subsequent scholars an authoritative, and for some, *the*

[37] Sunni treatises on this issue typically preferred the term "*imām*/imamate" over "caliph/caliphate" to refer to the ideal ruler of the Community, possibility following the Shīʿa, or simply because it (*imām*, lit. leader) might have been used to clarify the confusion around the multivalent term *khalīfa*.

[38] Abū Bakr Muḥammad b. al-Ṭayyib Ibn al-Bāqillānī, born in Basra, spent most of adult life in Baghdad, and is considered the main systemizer of Ashʿarism (*EI*^{2}, s.v. "al-Bāqillānī"). See also, Y. Ibish, *The Political Doctrine of Al-Bāqillānī* (Beirut: American University of Beirut, 1966).

authoritative, expression of the classical Sunni theory of caliphate. Yet many scholars, traditional as well as modern, have decried it on various grounds. Māwardī differs from the earlier authors in this tradition in important ways. Before Māwardī, the issue of imamate had been discussed in the works of *kalām*; his treatise is not a theological treatise but a new legal genre altogether, in which issues previously discussed in theology (nature, election, and role of the *imām*) were united with those in jurisprudence for the first time. Abū al-Maʿālī al-Juwaynī's (d. 478/1085) *Ghiyāth al-umam* is primarily a theological discussion that corresponds to only the first two chapters of Māwardī's work. Māwardī's legal discussions on administration mostly did not concern other writers in the caliphate tradition. Juwaynī stands out in the Ashʿarī tradition for his realist streak, which was, nonetheless, overturned by his disciple, Abū Ḥāmid al-Ghazālī (d. 505/1111). Ghazālī was one of the most influential thinkers of classical Islam, and his political thought, just as his other writings, both reflected the ironies of his age and left a deep imprint on it. His discussion of caliphate in *Faḍā'iḥ al-bāṭiniyya* (also known as *al-Mustaẓhirī*), then in *Al-Iqtiṣād fī 'l-iʿtiqād*, and finally in *Iḥyā'* had a lasting influence on the caliphate tradition.

Before presenting an outline of this discourse, a note on the placement of the caliphate discourse between theology and law is in order. Issues such as the permissibility of rebellion against an oppressive ruler, obligation on the community of installing an *imām*, and the limits of the powers of the *imām* are all practical questions and hence were naturally discussed in legal discourses. Yet disputes about imamate had always been treated first and foremost as theological issues, because legal treatment of an issue takes for granted certain fundamentals and cannot come into place if theology (or a theory of government) has not made room for it. Premises such as the following had to be established by the Sunnis before the law of caliphate could be written: whether the knowledge of legal obligations derives from the Qur'an and the Sunna or infallible *imāms* or caliphs; whether it is the *imāms* who need to be bound by the law or the law that stands in need of the *imām*'s interpretation or blessing for its validity; whether it is the entire Muslim Community or a particular person or group that inheres the infallibility, charisma, and mission of the Prophet; and so on. It is obvious how theological settlement of any of these issues could profoundly affect the law. Logical causation, however, rarely drives historical development. It was only after the Miḥna, when the caliphate's self-view accorded with that of the ulama, that the latter's wholehearted endorsement of the former could be expected. Regardless of the reason, the fact remains that the juristic discourse was silent about imamate until theology had sorted it out.[39]

In the following, I summarize the development of the Ashʿarī caliphate doctrine from Bāqillānī, through Baghdādī, Māwardī, and Juwaynī, and then to Ghazālī. To guide my comparison, I have used Baghdādī's original headings, which capture well the main debates that defined this tradition across the centuries.[40]

1. *The necessity of the imamate.* Most likely it was the Khārijī insurgency that had made this point a matter of debate. With the exception of the Khārijīs and some of the Baghdādī Muʿtazila,[41] all sects agreed on the necessity of installing an *imām*. Most of the Muʿtazila considered the imamate necessary by reason, whereas most of the Sunnis considered it necessary by *sharʿī* commandment only. For the Baghdādī Muʿtazila, the imamate was only a rational necessity, whereas the Basran Muʿtazila, with the exception of al-Jāḥiẓ, seem to have considered reason as well as revelation the provenance of the obligation. Bāqillānī is silent on this issue, but the reason is likely to be omission rather than disagreement with the general Sunni opinion.[42] Al-Ashʿarī, Baghdādī, Juwaynī, and Ghazālī all insist that the imamate is an obligation by revelation, not reason.[43] Māwardī mentions both opinions, but contrary to the common interpretation, remains noncommittal on the source of this obligation.[44] Juwaynī adds that it is an obligation only if it is possible, otherwise a lay (non-Qurayshī) ruler or the ulama should grab hold of the reins of government.[45]

39 By the time of Ghazālī, the custom of including a chapter on the issue of the imamate in the treatise on creed was so prevalent that he found it irresistible despite disliking it (*Iqtiṣād*, 127).

40 These headings are listed in Lambton, *State*, 77.

41 Some Muʿtazila, like al-Aṣamm (d. ca. 225/840) and Hisham al-Fuwaṭī (d. before 218/833) could contemplate doing without an *imām* in times of peace and when people desisted from harming each other (Dumayjī, 45; Lambton, *State*, 77–8). Dumayjī states that al-Qāḍī ʿAbd al-Jabbār in *al-Mughnī* agrees with the Sunnis on this, probably representing a later Muʿtazilī development (Dumayjī, 46).

42 Lambton suggests that Bāqillānī did not consider the imamate an obligation, see Lambton, *State*, 77. Omission is not sufficient evidence, however, for attributing such a radical departure to Bāqillānī.

43 Baghdādī writes, "Al-Ashʿari argued that the imamate is itself an ordinance of the revealed Law, and that though it can be demonstrated by reason that subordination to it is admissible, the necessity of it is known only by the authority of the Revelation" (ibid., 78).

44 Ibid., 86, states that Māwardī states his own view after listing the two opinions, but in fact he does not (*Aḥkām*, 30).

45 W. Hallaq, "Caliphs, Jurists, and the Saljūqs in the Political Thought of Juwaynī," *MW* 74.1 (1984): 33.

At first blush, the dichotomy between obligation by reason and revelation seems superfluous and not motivated by any immediate concerns, but precisely because of this, it serves as an indication of the intellectual apparatus underlying the entire discourse.

2. *The circumstance of appointment.* This point is designed to counter the Shīʿī claim of having an invisible *imām* – the Sunnis, Baghdādī maintains, require an *imām* who is visible.[46]

3. *The number of imāms at any given time.* Bāqillānī stipulated that there be only one *imām* of the *umma* at any given time, whereas al-Ashʿarī, Baghdādī, and others held that more than one *imām* is possible if separated by a sea – an obvious concession to the Spanish Umayyads.[47] Māwardī, Juwaynī, and Ghazālī rejected the possibility of coexistence of more than one *imām*, but when they wrote, they had in mind the threat of the Fatimid counter-caliphate.[48]

4. *The race and tribe of the imām.* Al-Ashʿarī, Baghdādī, Māwardī, Abū Yaʿlā, and Ghazālī all agree on the requirement of Qurayshī descent. Bāqillānī has contradictory opinions on this; in *al-Tamhīd*, he writes that neither reason nor revelation requires the Qurayshī descent, but in *al-Inṣāf*, he clearly upholds it.[49]

Later, Juwaynī argued to dilute this requirement, not as a matter of principle, but as concession to reality. Clearly, the Saljuqs as the protectors of Sunni Islam could now conceivably occupy this role, which could not have been imagined for the Shīʿī Buyids. Ghazālī, Juwaynī's disciple, however, disagreed and forcefully argued for the necessity of this condition.

5. *The qualifications for the imām.* The requirements for the *imām* for all of the Sunnis were, with some variations: (1) Qurayshī descent, discussed previously; (2) the qualifications of a *mujtahid* in knowledge – Bāqillānī had required the qualifications only of a *qāḍī*, a rank lower than *mujtahid*; (3) the probity (*ʿadāla*) of an acceptable witness before a judge; (4) judgment and capacity to command in peace and war. Notably however, Baghdādī adds to this the ability to know the ranks and classes (*marātib*) of his subjects as well as the ability to keep them in their

[46] Lambton, *State*, 78.

[47] It is noteworthy that the Mālikī Bāqillānī did not accept the legitimacy of more than one *imām* at one time, despite the fact that the Spanish Umayyads had been the patrons of the Mālikīs.

[48] For the opinions of Juwaynī, al-Isfarāʾīnī and Ashʿari on the issue, see Hallaq, 35; for Māwardi, see Lambton, *State*, 90.

[49] Dumayjī, 275.

proper ranks, a clear concession to the increasing stratification and considerations of hierarchy in the classical age; Lambton attributes this to Baghdādī's Persian upbringing.[50]

Māwardī famously accepts the imamate of one overpowered and confined (*ḥajr*) by someone who is not openly rebellious and disobedient – an unveiled concession to the Buyid control of Baghdad, but also a veiled warning to the Buyids, and possibly the Saljuqs, to watch their limits.[51]

Juwaynī adds to Baghdādī's list physical fitness (as does Māwardī), but more important, independent power and self-sufficiency (*istiqlāl* and *kifāya*),[52] which is more than the capacity required by most in (4) – Juwaynī here means actual power, in conscious contrast to Māwardī's potentially overpowered caliph.

6. *Impeccability.* This qualification of the *imām* was a major bone of contention with the Shī'a; that is perhaps why Baghdādī mentions it under a separate heading. He rejects, like Bāqillānī, the Shī'ī requirement of infallibility (*'iṣma*). Bāqillānī, and later Juwaynī, recommended that the electors should look for the best possible candidate (*al-afḍal*). If that is not possible, a less excellent (*al-mafḍūl*) candidate may be elected and may not be replaced if a better one is found afterward.[53] Baghdādī drops this issue altogether.

7. *The means whereby the imām is established in office.* Along with the issue of the source of obligation of the imamate, this issue is the most revealing with regard to the nature of this discourse. Most authors agree that the imamate is established by:

1. Election (*ikhtiyār*) by one or more electors,[54] followed by a contract (*bay'a*).
2. Testamentary designation by the previous *imām* (*'ahd*).
3. Brute force (*ghalba*). This appears, especially starting with Juwaynī, as another independent way of (self-) appointment of the *imām*.

[50] Lambton, *State*, 80n34; he was brought up in Nishapur and Isfara'īn (77).

[51] *Aḥkām*, 58.

[52] Hallaq, 34.

[53] Lambton suggests that al-Bāqillānī is likely to have picked up the *al-afḍal* requirement from the Zaydī Shī'a. For Bāqillānī, see Lambton, *State*, 74; for Juwaynī, see Hallaq, "Caliphs," 35.

[54] The electors are commonly termed as *ahl al-ḥall wa 'l-'aqd* (those who untie and tie); Māwardī replaces this term with simply *ahl al-ikhriyār* (the electors). Baghdādī cites various opinions on the requirement of moral probity (*'adāla*) for the electors, with which Māwardī agrees, but he does not consider election by a *fāsiq* (impious) invalid.

In the early phase of the caliphate discourse, there existed significant disagreement about whether testamentary designation is an independent means of appointing an *imām*. The Muʿtazila consider it invalid altogether.[55] The Mālikī Bāqillānī, the Ḥanbalī Abū Yaʿlā, and others consider it valid only if followed by *bayʿa* by the electors, thus effectively reducing its value to mere nomination.[56] Baghdādī considered designation legitimate but without explicitly specifying whether the confirmation by the electors is necessary. He does state, however, that if the designated person is fit for the imamate, it is an obligation upon the Community to accept it – as in the case of Abū Bakr's designation of ʿUmar – which would mean that the electors' confirmation is unnecessary if the designated *imām* is suited for the office (he does not tell us who makes that decision).[57] Māwardī was the first not only to claim a consensus on the issue, but also to consider designation a method of appointment independent of confirmation by the electors.[58]

Baghdādī reports that al-Ashʿarī accepted election and contract by one qualified elector "just as a marriage can be validly contracted by a single guardian of legal probity,"[59] whereas some Muʿtazila and one Zaydī scholar required at least two electors to make the contract, invoking once again the analogy of marriage. Al-Qalānisī, an Ashʿarī contemporary of Baghdādī, held that "the contract of the imamate is validly made by the ulama of the Community who are present at the residence of the *imām*, irrespective of their number."[60] Such method of election obviously leads to the possibility of multiple simultaneous elections. Baghdādī in such cases suggests redoing the contract;[61] others suggest lottery as a method. Māwardī, using analogy of marriage contract once again, considers the chronologically first one to be valid, and if the two are exactly simultaneous, then he too deems them invalid.[62]

8. The appointment of imām after the death of the Prophet.

[55] For instance, the Muʿtazilī al-Qāḍī ʿAbd al-Jabbār in *al-Mughnī* cited in Dumayjī, 188.

[56] For Bāqillānī's view, see Lambton, *State*, 73–4. Lambton does not fully distinguish the subtle difference between designation as an independent method or merely nomination, however. For a more careful discussion, see Kūnākātā, 25; for Abū Yaʿlā, see Ibid., 32–3.

[57] Lambton, *State*, 82.

[58] *Aḥkām*, 43–4; Kūnākātā, 25.

[59] Lambton, *State*, 81.

[60] Ibid.

[61] Ibid., 82.

[62] *Aḥkām*, 37–8.

9. *Inheritance and testament in regard to the imamate (*naṣṣ*).* The appointment of Abū Bakr after the Prophet and the election of the three subsequent caliphs are the critical historical points around which most controversies regarding the imamate revolved. The Sunni political theology rejected the Shīʿī doctrine on two main points: a normative one, that is, the obligation upon God of appointing an infallible *imām*; and a corresponding historical one, that is, the historical claim of the Prophetic testament (*naṣṣ*) to appoint ʿAlī as the next *imām*.

The Early Phase: Bāqillānī and Baghdādī

Bāqillānī lived through the rise of the Shīʿī Buyid mercenaries, who had placed the Abbasid caliph under virtual house arrest – a situation that we may expect to have been traumatic for the Sunnis. His work, however, seems to be concerned with the theological rather than political implications of Buyid ascendancy. Bāqillānī considers the function of the *imām* to execute the Sharīʿa; he was the *wakīl* of the Community, that is, a representative who acted on the Community's behalf.[63] In this respect, the *imām* was to be guided by the Qur'an, the tradition of the Prophet, and the early caliphs, all of which were elaborated and protected by Sunni scholars. If he strayed from the Sharīʿa, it was the duty of the Community to correct him, and if he transgressed certain boundaries, he was to be deposed.

These early Ashʿarīs were not invested in practical politics; it was the example of the election of Abū Bakr and ʿUmar that informed these theories rather than the contemporary Abbasids. Their focus was polemics against the Shīʿa in defense of the Sunni vision of the Rightly Guided caliphate and the continuity and general redemption of the history of the Community. Bāqillānī and Baghdādī, for instance, are consistent about the lofty qualifications required of the *imām* and, if he strayed from the path of justice or the Sharīʿa, they do not hesitate to suggest he be simply deposed. If the *imām* loses his freedom to rule, as was the case during this time, his imamate was no longer deemed valid: There was no reason to retain the fiction of the imamate if he lost effective power. The fact that the Community would then live without an *imām*, as was the case in their own time, did not much concern them. They had done their homework in history and in theology, but contemporary politics was simply not their concern.

[63] Lambton, *State*, 76.

That they were not interested in real politics is also suggested by their lack of attention to any legal means to depose the *imām*. Legal checks and balances to round off their emphasis on the caliph's obligation to the Sharīʿa were of no concern to them. In emphasizing the centrality of the Community, they were concerned primarily with responding effectively to the Shīʿī requirement of the impeccability of the *imāms*. The logic went something like this: Even though, unlike the Shīʿī *imām*, the Sunni caliph was not infallible, the Community on the whole was, and the Community's feedback and authority – in theory – could guard the Sunni *imām* against serious error and heresy.[64]

Another already noticeable feature of this discourse is its pervasive formalism: Historical coincidences are recruited as universal models for political behavior, and questions of power, over which contenders had massacred men and destroyed cities in not so distant past (these authors could easily recall the dispute of succession between al-Ma'mūn and al-Amīn)[65] are dealt with nonchalantly like theoretical riddles: If two *imāms* were simultaneously contracted, for instance, some recommended drawing lots to decide between them. Similarly, the juristic analogy of marriage contract to the *bayʿa* of a ruler was constantly invoked with no attention to the inconvenient detail that, while in a marriage contract, the two interested parties were required to give their consent. In the case of an *imām*'s appointment, in which not two persons but presumably the welfare of the entire Community rested, the Community – presumably the source of the caliph's authority – was altogether neglected. In the case of marriage, to press this analogy further, the means to dissolve the contract was clear on the part of both the parties.[66] There was no discussion, however, as Lambton frequently points out, about how to dissolve the imamate contract and to depose the *imām* if his conduct went awry. The mechanism to obtain the will of the Community – whose *wakīl* (representative) the *imām* presumably was, in Bāqillānī's view – was entirely ignored. Depending on the authority in question, as few as one, two, or four electors were sufficient to contract the *bayʿa*; some suggested that however many happened to be present at the residence of the deceased imam would suffice. Of the two aspects of the appointment, election (*ikhtiyār*) was virtually ignored, and only the ritual of contract

64 Ibid., 77, 80.
65 Cooperson, *Al Ma'mun*, 39–56.
66 Namely, directly effective divorce, *ṭalāq*, on the man's part, and mediated divorce, *khulʿ*, on the woman's part.

(*bay'a*) was emphasized. In modern times, this would be analogous to British political thinkers ignoring the entire political process and focusing exclusively on the formalities of the inauguration ceremony of the British queen.

Finally, although the establishment of the imamate/caliphate was deemed an obligation, it is noteworthy there was no function that Bāqillānī, or Baghdādī, assigned to the *imām* without which the religious life of the Community could not continue. The *imām*, in other words, was neither indispensable nor the source of legitimacy of the Community's religious life, but only its protector, organizer, and representative, without whom the Community could continue, albeit imperfectly. Baghdādī's justification for the necessity of the *imām* makes this clear: "It is essential for the Muslims to have an *imām* to execute their ordinances, enforce legal penalties, direct their armies, marry off their widows and divide the revenues amongst them."[67] These were functions that any "lay" ruler could perform. All these requirements are known by reason, even if their particular form in Islamic societies is determined by revelation. This is obviously not the caliphate- (or imamate-) centered vision of Islam. It is rather close to the view shared by Abū Yūsuf and Ibn Ḥanbal.

Māwardī: Concessions to Reality

Māwardī's *al-Aḥkām al-sulṭāniyya* has received much attention, but close readings of Māwardī's entire oeuvre have been rare in Western scholarship.[68] Owing particularly to his notorious concession to legitimize a usurper, his was, as Gibb noted, "[s]o far from being an objective exposition of an established theory ... in reality an apologia or adaptation inspired and shaped by the circumstance of his own times.... He took the first steps on the downward slope which was to lead to the collapse of the whole theory."[69] Within a generation the political thought of Juwaynī and Ghazālī had moved "further along the path

[67] Ibid., 77.

[68] Some important exceptions are: H. Mikhail, *Politics and Revelation: Mawardi and After* (Edinburgh U. Press, 1995); N. Hurvitz, *Competing Texts: The Relationship between al-Māwardī's and Abū Ya'lā's al-Aḥkām al-Sulṭāniyya* (Islamic Legal Studies Program, Harvard Law School, Occasional Publications 8, 2007) In Arabic scholarship, important contributions have been made by Riḍwān al-Sayyid, who has edited Māwardī's three works on the subject, all published by Beirut: Dār al-Kitāb al-'Arabī; see in particular his introduction to Māwardī, *Tashīl al-naẓar wa ta'jīl al-ẓafar* (Dār al-'Ulūm al-'Arabīyya, 1987).

[69] Gibb, *Studies*, 142.

of compromise," and this "shows almost startlingly the rate at which the Ashʿarī doctrine was collapsing."[70] The apologia, which began in al-Ashʿarī, in these three authors, "ends up divorcing the imamate from the Sharīʿa" and leads to "the complete negation of the rule of law."[71] Most modern commentators agree that Māwardī's *al-Aḥkām al-sulṭāniyya* was an attempt to legitimize the status quo and legalize the illegal. However, later scholars have criticized Gibb's dismay and censure of Māwardī for, as Crone puts it, "what could be more common in history than the recognition of usurpers?" Māwardī, in Crone's view, helped save the law and its authority.[72] At least in the short term, it is difficult to substantiate either claim, for the law was neither being threatened (hence it didn't need to be saved) nor did it collapse after Māwardī. If anything, the Muslim society, having lost politics, became increasingly dependent on law. If, however, we are concerned with the constitutional legality of government, Gibb's outrage seems to be more justified. What Māwardī did accomplish, in Crone's view, was merely to codify what had long been practiced. Even so, the act of codifying practice is far from an insignificant choice.

The work of the "Ashʿarized"[73] Ḥanbalī al-Qāḍī Abū Yaʿlā al-Farrā' (d. 458/1066), also titled *al-Aḥkām al-sultāniyya*, provides the best contrast to Māwardī's contribution. Abū Yaʿlā's work is usually considered, albeit unfairly, an unimaginative copy of Māwardī's treatise.[74] It is likely that Abū Yaʿlā's work was written later, but the differences between the two works are significant and attributable to a different ideological outlook. Whoever wrote first, it is likely that each was aware of the other's positions. Abū Yaʿlā and Māwardī, writing little over a generation after Bāqillānī, differ from each other in the following important ways:

1. Like Bāqillānī, Abū Yaʿlā requires the *imām* to be the best of men in knowledge and piety if possible – this last requirement (*afḍaliyya*) being one that Māwardī does not require.

[70] Ibid.

[71] Ibid., 143.

[72] Crone, *God's Rule*, 233.

[73] Laoust, *Essai*, 78.

[74] See editor's introduction, *Aḥkām*, 9–11. Laoust's suggestion that "both similarities and differences may be explained by the fact that the two men belonged to the entourage of Ibn al-Muslima but that one was Shāfiʿī and the other Ḥanbalite" appears correct, so long as we keep in mind that it was not their jurisprudence but their theological visions that informed their view of the caliphate (*EI*², s.v. "Ibn al-Farrā'").

2. Imamate, to him, is not established *except by the consent of the majority of the people*; an opinion that Māwardī rejects out of hand (but he does not mention the source of this opinion);
3. Even going beyond Bāqillānī, Abū Yaʿlā does not consider appointment by designation sufficient in itself until the *ahl al-ḥall wa'l-ʿaqd* (lit., the untiers and tiers) approve it. The untiers and tiers are considered in Abū Yaʿlā to be the representatives of the people. Māwardī is the first one to consider their agreement immaterial.

These differences are not accidental. Abū Yaʿlā is consistently more "idealistic" and closer to the earlier Sunni views expressed by Bāqillānī, for he consistently maintains the early ideal of caliph as the representative of the Community.[75] Māwardī seems to be systematically insulating the imamate from the will of the Community or the whims of the caliph-makers – namely, the sultans. In contrast with Bāqillānī, whose concern was responding to the Shīʿī and Muʿtazilī theological attacks against the Sunnis, Māwardī was concerned with the defense of the living Abbasid caliph against the possibility of becoming irrelevant or extinct at the hands of the Buyids or whoever assumed military control next (i.e., the Saljuqs; the decline of the Buyids at the hands of the Saljuqs must have seemed a real possibility by the time Māwardī wrote his work).

Māwardī, it would seem, reenacted the caliphate-centered vision of Islam but did so at a time when the caliphal power had been severely reduced. In this vision, the caliph was seen as chosen by God to be the center of the divine mission on earth, and the Muslim Community merely his extension. As if theoretical claims could compensate for the loss of power and relevance in reality, Māwardī opens his *al-Aḥkām al-sulṭāniyya* thus:

> God Almighty has *appointed* [*nadaba*] for the *umma* a leader by whom He [God] has *followed up the prophethood* [*khalafa bihi al-nubuwwa*], protected the creed [*milla*] and entrusted to him the conduct of policy [*siyāsa*], so that affairs may be managed upon the prescribed way [*dīn mashrūʿ*] and consensus may obtain on the course to pursue. The *imamate* is, therefore, the *foundation* [*aṣl*] upon which the principles of the creed [*qawāʿid al-milla*] are established and whence originate [*ṣadarat ʿanhu*] all the particular offices. It is therefore incumbent to privilege the decrees of [the imamate] over any of the decrees of the ruler [*ḥukm sulṭāni*], and to mention its opinion over any other religious opinion.[76]

[75] Kūnākātā, 33.
[76] *Aḥkām*, 27.

In his *Aḥkām*, Māwardī declared the title "God's caliph" to be illicit, although, although, in his *Tashīl al-naẓar*, written in the statecraft genre, he approvingly employs the title, in keeping with the different sets of sensibilities and limits that attended that discourse.[77] Yet rhetorically, Māwardī gave the caliph all the symbolic sanctity he could short of equating him with a Shīʿī *imām*. In arguing against the Shīʿī concept of imamate, in which the imamate is a part of creed (*uṣūl*), the Sunnis had been generally cautious to make a distinction and consider the caliphate an obligation, but one at the level of branch (*farʿ*), not foundation (*aṣl*).[78] By calling the imamate the "foundation," Māwardī is dangerously nearing the Shīʿī position, but for reasons that are entirely pragmatic.

Three aspects of Māwardī's caliphate theory stand out as distinct from what his predecessors and contemporaries wrote on the subject: (i) He moves the discourse of caliphate from theology to jurisprudence; (ii) he ritualizes the imamate by allowing the separation of caliphal authority from effective power to govern; and (iii) the Community plays no role in his theory.

The reasons for Māwardī's choices are not hard to guess. Māwardī's interest is to wed theory to reality and sustain the caliphate as much as possible, and so he makes the formal aspect of the appointment an easy-to-carry-out ritual. That his political program looks odd and unrealistic is not because it is divorced from practice but precisely because he was trying to wed theory to practice without challenging either too much. Māwardī's "ritualization" of the office of caliphate and preference for an easily manageable *bayʿa* as against the involvement of the representatives of the Community are understandable, for it does not matter if a symbolic caliph has an effective *bayʿa* or allegiance of the Community or not. Besides, the will of the Community had become increasingly difficult to imagine let alone express given territorial and ideological fragmentation.

If there was a theoretical way to resurrect the political role of the Community and avoid the slippery slope perpetual illegitimacy, Māwardī, like all others in the tradition, did not pursue it. The question remains why. It might be that Māwardī had not entirely given up the hope of the revival of the caliphate altogether, and wrote under the assumption that the caliphate could regain control under normal circumstances while all the time making concessions for the present "state of emergency." What

[77] See Chapter 6, on Māwardī's contradicting opinions on the subject.
[78] Al-Ījī, *al-Mawāqif*, quoted in Khan, 23–4.

mattered was that the caliph's office was continued, sanctified, and considered off-limits to any military adventurers.

Riḍwān al-Sayyid has argued that the difference between Māwardī and Abū Yaʿlā stemmed from the fact that Māwardī was able to foresee that the caliphate could never reclaim the power and authority it commanded in the past, and hence he tried to simply safeguard it as an institution. His real intention was not to revive a caliphate-centered vision of Islam but to save the caliphate as a symbol of continuity, legitimacy, and unity of the Community. Abū Yaʿlā, on the other hand, an heir to the Ḥanbalī legacy that had once seen the consequences of an overblown caliphate in the Miḥna of Aḥmad b. Ḥanbal, was not willing to concede the caliph this symbolic power after the caliphate had conceded the socioreligious sphere to the Sunni ulama.[79] This explanation is difficult to accept because when Māwardī wrote the end of the Buyids was in sight, and what the Sunni Saljuqs were to do with the caliph was not yet clear. Regardless, attempting to appreciate the possible motives of Māwardī's concessions need not keep us from evaluating their nature and impact. It was not his infusion of the caliphate with increased religious authority that proved to be the most significant legacy of his thought, but rather the concomitant disappearance of the Community from his political equation. If his theory were to be embraced, there would remain nothing to balance the caliph's authority in theory and nothing to balance the sultan's power in practice. To place such inordinate authority in an empty symbol was to ensure that neither the ulama (the actual source of authority) nor the rulers (the actual source of power) would ever countenance the realization of such a political vision.

Politics is the art of the possible; to put a set of ideals to work inevitably requires compromise. To call Māwardī's political vision pragmatic, expedient, and a compromise, as most modern scholars have done, is to say nothing more than that Māwardī tried to put ideals to work and, in the process, reinterpreted and adjusted them. What is significant is not that he legitimized the usurpation of power – that was an insignificant element of his work anyway – but *how* he did so and how he altered the conception of the caliphate. If the subsequent direction of the tradition is any indication, it seems that by further undermining the role of the Community and detaching normative political thinking from the realm of actual political power, Māwardī contributed to the political desiccation of Islamic thought.

[79] Sayyid, *Jamāʿa*, 55.

Juwaynī: An Attempt to Embrace Power

Māwardī's treatise must have had an impact, for his contemporaries' and successors' writing on the topic had to contend with his opinions. However, the political circumstances that had most concerned Māwardī were to change almost immediately after his writing of *Aḥkām*. The distinguished jurist and theologian Imām al-Ḥaramayn ʿAbd al-Mālik b. ʿAbd Allāh Abū al-Maʿālī al-Juwaynī (d. 478/1085),[80] the next significant writer in the tradition – an Ashʿarī who unlike Māwardī had no qualms about his Ashʿarism – was associated with the great Persian vizier of the Saljuqs, Niẓām al-Mulk. He severely criticized Māwardī at a number of levels in order to make room for his daring proposal that, at least in an emergency situation, a non-Qurayshī like Niẓām al-Mulk or a capable Saljuq sultan could legitimately hold the imamate.[81] He also criticizes Māwardī for not noting all the disagreements about issues surrounding the caliphate, for not being attentive to the nature of the evidence proffered for them, and for differentiating between conclusions based on definitive proofs (*qaṭʿī*) from opinions based on speculative evidence (*ẓannī* or *maẓnūn*).[82] In his *Ghiyāth al-umam*, Juwaynī goes beyond Māwardī in his concession to the reality and proposes yet another modification in the caliphate theory. Given his connection with the new political elite and the changed circumstances, these suggestions are far from unexpected. Juwaynī agreed with Māwardī on the issue of the necessity of the "power state," but criticized him for not going far enough in supporting the sultanate and for suggesting excessive measures to protect an ineffectual symbol of the caliphate. True, Juwaynī seems to be saying, the caliphate is significant because of its historicity, noble lineage, and traditional representation of the inherited Sunni consensus – but that reverence had been granted it for two reasons: its protection of unity of the Community and society (prevention of civil war and other internal strife) and its fighting of the enemy (defense of the house of Islam). The new power-sultans, to him, fulfilled both of these requirements.[83]

[80] Born in Nishapur, Khurāsān, forced out due to a Ḥanafī-Muʿtazilī vizier's animosity, returned at Niẓām al-Mulk behest, who appointed him the head of the Niẓāmiyya *madrasa* (Hallaq, "Caliphs," 27–8).

[81] Hallaq, "Caliphs," 29, ventures that there are good reasons to think that Niẓām al-Mulk entertained the idea of abolishing the caliphate altogether.

[82] Hallaq, "Caliphs," 30–1.

[83] Sayyid, *Jamāʿa*, 56–7.

Juwaynī thus opened up the possibility of "imamate by force," or more accurately, the transfer of the title of imamate to the military rulers, the Saljuqs, the uncouth defenders of Sunni Islam.[84] These new rulers and defenders of Sunni Islam, although far from the ideal candidates for the caliphate, could still fulfill the main requirement of power being used in largely the right direction, however unruly it might have been. He argued against the necessity of Qurayshī lineage for the imamate:[85]

> If there is in an era someone who possesses sufficiency and strength but does not reach independence in his mastery of knowledge, and has dominated by means of his numerous [troops] and helpers and endorsed by the loyalty of powerful people, then he is the ruler and under his power are the affairs of wealth, military and other offices, but it is incumbent upon him to not finalize any matter without the consultation of the ulama.[86]

Juwaynī now is willing to imagine religious life, not only in the absence of an *imām*, but even without any ruler – and in that case, the "affairs become entrusted to the ulama – and it is incumbent upon the people of all different classes (*ṭabaqāt*) to turn to the ulama."[87] Juwaynī had the foresight, Wael Hallaq suggests, to anticipate the decline and even extinction of the caliphate, and wished to create room in the Sharīʿa for such a situation to remain legitimate and comprehensible.

The most important of Juwaynī's contentions on the whole was that the caliphate could not be legitimized without power – that it was not merely a symbolic, ritual office but the locus of actual power, and if the caliph did not have power, he was no caliph at all. In one respect, he followed in Māwardī's footsteps, namely, by putting the caliphate theory to work as a political program and not only for theological polemics.

Hallaq observes that whereas Māwardī had emphasized the "sacrosanctity of the imam," Juwaynī "detached the imamate altogether from the domain of prophecy and sacred objects," thus demoting the *imām* "to a temporal functionary, though still responsible for the well-being of the religion."[88] Hallaq concludes that Juwaynī not only broke with the classical theory, which had held the *imām* as being the only supreme spiritual and temporal leader of the community, but also attempted to inject power (sultanate) and Sharīʿa-mindedness (ulama) as two organic elements into

[84] Juwaynī might have had in mind their Persian vizier Niẓam al-Mulk, the de facto ruler.
[85] Hallaq, "Caliphs," 34.
[86] *Ghiyāthī*, 392; Kūnākātā, 35.
[87] *Ghiyāthī*, 391; Kūnākātā, 36.
[88] Hallaq, "Caliphs," 30.

the body of the government.[89] Yet this is unwarranted; it is more accurate to say that the religious sanctification of the caliphate in the Sunni discourse had been Māwardī's contribution, which Juwaynī rejects. Like the rest of the contributors to the tradition, he suggests deposition of an incapable *imām* without suggesting any mechanisms. He requires the *imām* to be capable of the highest *ijtihād* in knowledge, but if that is to not to be had, consulting with the ulama frequently is suggested. The functions he assigns to the *imām* include the religious ones, such as "the promotion of pious attitudes ... [and] fighting of apostasy" as well as support of all Sunni schools in law but only Ashʿarism in theology, whereas the temporal functions include *jihād* against the enemy, administration, appointment of *qāḍīs*, and most importantly, applying the Sharīʿa. Like Māwardī, he diminishes the significance and involvement of the "untiers and tiers," or the Community, and considers the *imām*'s choice of his heir apparent (testamentary designation, *ʿahd*) irrevocable by them.[90] In fact, like Māwardī, he allows the *imām* to choose a succession of heirs, thus theoretically strengthening the assumption that the *imām* is the owner of the office, rather than a representative of the Community. The *imām* may also "delegate absolute authority and power to officials to act on his behalf concerning all matters of state" – obviously referring to the Saljuqs dependence on Niẓām al-Mulk.[91] Hallaq's conclusion might be an overstatement of Juwaynī's break with the Ashʿarī political tradition. First, Juwaynī did not "inject" sultanate into a well-thought-out theory of government, but simply dropped the Qurayshī lineage requirement from the conditions of imamate in order to make it attainable to his patrons. Second, Juwaynī's admonition to the ruler about paying heed to the ulama is hardly making them an "organic" part of his theory – although admittedly he mentions them in an advisory capacity whereas Māwardī does not. And although the role of the ulama does improve in Juwaynī as compared to Māwardī, the role of the Community does not.

Hallaq's suggestion that "by bringing the sultan's power into this institution as an organic part of it (and not merely as a subordinate entity, as Māwardī viewed it) Juwaynī was breaking ground for a new theory which was to be further elaborated by his disciple Ghazālī"[92] is rendered even more problematic by the fact that Ghazālī fundamentally

[89] Ibid., 41.
[90] Ibid., 34–7.
[91] Ibid., 37.
[92] Ibid., 40.

disagreed with his teacher about the relative significance of power and ritual authority. The assumption that Ghazālī was the first to relate the imamate to the question of political power (which is a non-issue anyway; before Māwardī's exception, the *imām*'s power had always been assumed), which Hallaq bases on Lambton's view, who in turn had based it on Binder's study,[93] has been cogently rejected by Carol Hillenbrand's thorough study of Ghazālī.[94]

Ghazālī: Caliphate as Ritual and Government as Necessary Evil

None of the aforementioned contributors to the Ashʿarī caliphate discourse capture the dilemmas and contradictions of the political and social conditions of the age as clearly and poignantly as Abū Ḥāmid al-Ghazālī (d. 505/1111). Juwaynī, his teacher, was also a towering figure in classical theology and law, but the impact of his pragmatic political concessions to the Saljuqs seems to have been meager both in practice and in subsequent thinking, and his realistic strain seems to have been quickly forgotten. It was partly so because Ghazālī, his disciple of surpassing merit and influence, overturned many of Juwaynī's propositions. If Juwaynī had foreseen the eventual extinction of the caliphate and attempted to provide an alternative to it, Ghazālī too seems to have shared that foresight, but his reaction was the exact opposite: the most desperate attempt yet to rescue the symbol, however empty, of the caliphate.

Ghazālī accepts Juwaynī's emphasis on power but turns it upside down. Juwaynī had emphasized the dimension of power and effectiveness rather than religious symbolism and continuity in the concept of imamate by merging it with sultanate and deemphasizing, for pragmatic reasons, and without altogether eliminating, the Qurayshī-descent requirement. Ghazālī, to the contrary, emphasized the absolute necessity of the Qurayshī descent, going even beyond Māwardī in underscoring the sanctity and religious significance of the Abbasid caliphate. Like Māwardī, he embraced the element of power but invested it in the institution of sultanate – which to him was categorically different from the imamate. Ghazālī charged the possessor of effective power, *shawka*, with

93 Lambton, *State*, 115; L. Binder, "al-Ghazālī's theory of government," *MW* 45 (1955), 233–40.

94 C. Hillenbrand, "Islamic Orthodoxy or Realpolitik? Al-Ghazālī's Views on Government," *IRAN* 26 (1988), 81–94.

political and administrative responsibility to govern the Muslim lands and also with the responsibility to appoint an Abbasid caliph who could then grant him formal legitimacy. The usurper that had been accepted only grudgingly and conditionally in Māwardī had become naturalized in Juwaynī and Ghazālī, although only in the name of necessity.

Ghazālī's political thought is dominated by fear of civil war (*fitna*) and corruption (*fasād*), concern for a workable relationship between the caliph and the sultan, and the threat to Sunni Islam posed by the rise of the Fāṭimid Bāṭinīs in Egypt. Scholars like Leonard Binder, Henri Laoust, and, following them, Lambton ascribed to Ghazālī a "tripartite" or "mixed" concept of the caliphate, in which

> [t]he imamate still stood for the whole of Islamic government, but it had been separated into three main elements, the imam, the sultan, and the ulama, each corresponding to some aspect of the authority behind Islamic government and each performing a function required by that authority.... It is in this point, in relating the imamate to the question of political power, that al-Ghazālī's originality lies. Earlier writers had virtually ignored the problem.[95]

There is, however, little evidence for such a schematic trinitarian interpretation of Ghazālī's political thought. Carol Hillenbrand's exhaustive study of all of Ghazālī's political writings, with attention to their context and objectives, instead finds "an unusually strong element of compromise in al-Ghazālī's ideas," which Ghazālī recognizes and defends through the analogy that "eating carrion is prohibited but that starvation is worse."[96] In reality, Hillenbrand suggests, Ghazālī does little more than offer another compromise under changed circumstances: Because, unlike Juwaynī, he had no disciplined strongman like Niẓām al-Mulk to hinge his hopes on and there remained neither a strong candidate for the caliphate nor for the sultanate, and because the political threats (the Fāṭimid "anti-caliphate" in Egypt and their missionaries) were only getting worse, he suggested a combination of men to do the job: symbolic caliphal authority bolstered by the strong, if unruly – even loathsome – Saljuq Sultans.[97]

95 Ibid.

96 Hillenbrand, 90.

97 Ibid., for the threat of Ismaʿīlīs in Ghazālī's time, 82, for the lack of strong men in politics, 84. Ghazālī presents his seemingly bizarre argument about the necessity of an *imām* – that he is merely a symbol, and that without an *imām* the entire legal life of the Community, from marriages to business contracts, will be rendered invalid – in *Mustaẓhiri* and then repeats it in *Iqtiṣād* (Ibid., 82–83, 88).

Ghazālī's most significant contribution to political theory perhaps was his piercing self-reflection. He recognized that political choices in his time were far from glorious: Reduced to eating carrion or starving to death, his political program consisted in choosing carrion over death. On the whole remaining faithful to the Ashʿarī political tradition, he too introduced his own peculiar flavor to it: a sense of helpless piety and strong cynicism toward power and politics. He wrote:

> There are those who hold that the imamate is dead, lacking as it does the required qualifications. But no substitute can be found for it. What then? Are we to give up obeying the law? Shall we dismiss the *qāḍīs*, declare all authority to be valueless, cease marrying and pronounce the acts of those in high places to be invalid at all points, leaving the population to live in "sinfulness"? Or shall we continue, as we are, recognizing that the imamate really exists and that all acts of the administration are valid, given the circumstances of the case and the necessities of the actual movement? The concessions made by us are not spontaneous, but *necessity makes lawful what is forbidden*. We know *it is not lawful to feed on a dead animal: still, it would be worse to die of hunger*. Of those that contend that the caliphate is dead for ever and irreplaceable, we should like to ask: *which is to be preferred, anarchy and the stoppage of social life for lack of a properly constituted authority, or acknowledgement of the existing power, whatever it be*? Of these two alternatives, the jurist cannot but choose the latter. (emphasis added)[98]

In the following passage, in one of his last and most influential writings, *Iḥya ulūm al-dīn*, Ghazālī sums up his cynical view of politics in its most mature form: "In short, we consider attributes and conditions in sultans with a view to [deriving] the optimum advantages. If we decree that public functions [*wilāya*] are now invalid, the interests of the common weal would also be invalid. *Why lose one's capital by seeking* [to gain interest]? *No indeed, sovereignty nowadays is possible only through force* [shawka]."[99]

In the context of the Ashʿarī political tradition, two of Ghazālī's contributions stand out: first, the radical doctrine of the caliphate as being the source of legitimacy of religious life, which no Sunni theologian had before argued;[100] and second, total disappearance of the Community

[98] Lambton, *State,* 110–11.

[99] Hillenbrand, 90; *Iḥyā'*, 2:178–9.

[100] Hillenbrand argues that Ghazālī's political program was to insist on the indispensability of the Abbāsid caliph al-Mustaẓhir against the backdrop of an unstable Saljuq sultanate and the Fatimid threat in Egypt, thus attempting "to accommodate the political *status quo* into his own system of beliefs on Islamic government," and characterizes it as "pious dishonesty" (idem, 85–6). Yet she suggests that Ghazālī might have actually believed the rather extreme and unique position in Sunni history that the legitimacy of the Islamic life would come to an end without an *imām*, for he repeated it even later

from the political sphere, for now even the symbolic authority of the caliphate was bestowed by the man in power. We conclude, hence, that in terms of their political thought, Ghazālī or Juwaynī broke no significant grounds any more than Māwardī – they remained faithful to the Ashʿarī tradition and its basic concerns and presuppositions. They differed from their predecessors in that they had clear, immediate concerns, which is not to say they sought to go past ritualism and enable political thinking, but rather that their ritualism had different goals.

CALIPHATE, REASON, AND REVELATION

The one premise that is common to all Ashʿarī expositions is the contention that the source of the obligation of caliphate is revelation, not reason. The later and more developed Ashʿarīs like Juwaynī and Ghazālī have been the most emphatic on this point. An example may help illustrate the practical implications of this contention. To say that a practice is an obligation by revelation and not accessible to reason means that it is analogous in Islamic law, for instance, to the prescribed ritual prayer, which cannot be known by reason alone; nor can any of its details of performance.[101] They are to be performed as a ritual – exactly as prescribed. And although the main purpose of the prayers is spiritual connection with God, legally speaking, the validity of their performance is judged based on certain observable and objective factors. If a necessary condition of these prayers, such as ritual ablution, is absent, they are considered invalid altogether and must be repeated. Legally, therefore, a performance of the five obligatory prayers is either valid or invalid, based on whether certain rituals have been performed correctly. On the spiritual plane, which is what truly matters, such performance may be only partially accepted or not accepted at all, depending on the level of spiritual concentration and the right feeling of love for and obedience to the divine.

In contrast, earning money for one's family is a rational as well as revelational obligation in the Sharīʿa. All human beings know the necessity of working to earn a living and feed their families; God's law only

in his life when he was free of any political obligations to defend the caliphate. On the third-/ninth-century Sunni view of the legitimacy of life without a just ruler, see Muḥāsibī, *K. al-Kasb*, ed. Nūr Saʿīd (Beirut: Dār al-Fikr al-Lubnānī, 1992), 71–2.

101 See Ibn Rushd, *The Distinguished Jurist's Primer*, 1:3, where he discusses *wuḍū'* (ablution) as falling between *ṣalāh* (regular prayers), which is a clear ritual worship (*ʿibāda*) that he defines as "not subject to rationalization and intended only for the pleasure of Allāh," and a kind of worship that is also rational such as washing off dirt.

emphasizes it, encourages it, promises reward for it, and circumscribes certain undesirable ways of accomplishing it. Yet even without revelation, human reason knows the necessity of the basic act. Because earning a living is a rational function, its validity is indicated wholly by its efficacy. It has to put food on the table: No amount of "symbolic" pretense of being employed, for instance, will be of any use unless that job brings some form of income.

A further difference might be suggested. A rational obligation is divisible – it admits of division, partial attainment, and compromise – whereas a ritual is not. One may work part time and make less, but as far as the legal judgment is concerned, there can be no half-performance of the ritual prayers; it is either valid or invalid. To say that the imamate is primarily or exclusively a revelational obligation, therefore, is tantamount to saying that it is like the performance of ritual prayers. It has certain formal requirements, such as the prerequisite qualities of the *imām*, and certain means of appointment, such as *bayʿa* by a certain number of electors who fulfill certain criteria, and so forth.

To understand the role of reason versus revelation in Ghazālī's view, let us turn to one concise but comprehensive discussion of the issue in his *Iqtiṣād*. He writes:

> It is not permissible to think that the obligation [*wujūb*] of [the imamate] is based on reason, for we have explained that that [any] obligation must be based on the *sharʿ* [alone]. Except if obligation is understood as an act in which there is benefit and in its neglect some harm; if so, [the reason] then does not deny the obligation [understood as such] of installing an *imām* due to its benefits and the avoidance of the harms of this world. However, we shall demonstrate its obligation by the definitive proof of *sharʿ* [*al-burhān al-qaṭʿī al-sharʿī*] and shall not merely rely in this regard on the consensus [*ijmāʿ*] of the *umma*, but point out the basis [*mustanad*] of this consensus, viz., the good ordering [*niẓām*] of religion is an objective of the lawgiver [the Prophet] without any doubt, and the good ordering of religion cannot be attained except by an imam who is obeyed.[102]

Ghazālī's foregoing passage suggests that there are two types of obligation: rational and revelational. Only a revelational obligation, that is, known by the *sharʿ*, can have soteriological consequences. Oddly, however, the proof that Ghazālī goes on to proffer for the imamate appears rational despite his insistence on characterizing it as revelational. The reason might be that he bases his justification on the consensus of the Community, but, perhaps anticipating the problem of proving such a

[102] *Iqtiṣād*, 127

consensus, he moves quickly to a rational proof in the form of a syllogism. Yet the "rational" proof that he offers as the basis of the consensus has problems of its own. His explication of the logic of the claimed consensus introduces the more difficult problem that one of its premises, namely, the good ordering of religion based on an obeyed *imām*, did not apply to the *imām* in Ghazālī's time. This logic, in fact, undermined the very claim it was supposed to bolster: Because the *imām* possesses no power, he is not capable of securing the good ordering that is the raison d'être of imamate, and hence his imamate is no longer valid.

Ghazālī goes on consider some objections to his position, for instance, the existing *imām*'s lack of knowledge, justice, and "other such qualities." If the *imām* lacks these rather important qualities, a reasonable jurist is forced to accept the imamate because "eating carrion is prohibited, but death is worse." [103] It is not clear whether "other such qualities" include the quality that is constitutive of the imamate, namely, power to secure "the good ordering" of this world. If Ghazālī is willing to let the imamate stand without actual power (in the manner of the Shīʿī *imām*), which indeed appears to be the case, then the entire rational proof, which is brought forth as basis for the consensus, falls. If, on the other hand, Ghazālī still demands political power on the part of the *imām*, then this discussion would apply to the Saljuq ruler (who has power, but no normative legitimacy), not the Abbasid caliph. However, in *Iqtiṣād* as well as his earlier work, *al-Mustaẓhirī*, to which he refers in *Iqtiṣād* approvingly, he leaves no doubt that Ghazālī's discussion is directed toward the Abbasid caliph and not the Saljuq sultan.[104] And although the idea of a symbolic merger of the two, along with the ulama to complete the trinity, might seem attractive in the imagination of later scholars, Ghazālī must have been well aware, as Hillenbrand points out, of the volatile and erratic relationship between the uncouth men of sword and the hapless caliph to posit any unitive institution or "constitution." He does recommend a mutually symbiotic relationship, and recognizing the weakness of his case for a powerless *imām*, compensates with the threat, or appeal, that without the Abbasid caliph all socioreligious life of the Community would cease to be legitimate.

Only in the context of these theological contentions does the symbolic imamate advocated by the Ashʿarī writers, in particular Māwardī and Ghazālī, begin to make sense. The Sharīʿa, in Ghazālī's view, required

[103] *Iqtiṣād*, 130.
[104] *Iqtiṣād*, 120.

an *imām* from whose person all political offices and social relationships sought their legitimacy; ideally, this person of the *imām* also wielded power and control, but if that was not to be had, his symbolic authority was still necessary. This does not mean that Ghazālī denied the rational need for an effective government – quite the contrary. Yet the institution of the caliphate/imamate required by revelation was different in that it remained an obligation even if it did not furnish its rational benefit. This fits well with the Ashʿarī theological insistence that God's commandments need to have no purpose, and that He may oblige humans to perform acts that are rationally unjustified or even downright impossible. Nor could reason pass judgment on acts being good or evil. Reason in the Ashʿarī view could, of course, distinguish the beneficial from the harmful. Hence, reason could undergird interest politics but not normative political action. In following reason's political judgments outside of explicit scriptural command, no matter how beneficial or just such an act might appear, there could be no benefit in the afterlife. In an ethic in which all actions were to be directed toward the afterlife and eternal bliss, political thinking and engagement were thus at best futile.

THE DISAPPEARANCE OF THE COMMUNITY

The increasing disappearance of the Community from the political equation even in theory is a distinct development in Ashʿarī political thought, which is brought about by the Ashʿarī polemical engagement with their Shīʿī opponents. Bāqillānī had seen the *imām* as a representative or an agent (*wakīl*) of the Community who could be theoretically deposed. Māwardī and Ghazālī had already abandoned that notion and embraced the idea of the sanctity of the caliphate. Two centuries later, the concept of imamate in the writings of the influential Ashʿarī-Sunni theologian, ʿAḍūḍ al-Dīn al-Ījī (d. 756/1355), a follower of Ghazālī, is significantly closer to the Shīʿī view of the imamate than the early Sunni one. In his *Kitāb al-mawāqif*, Ījī enumerates and refutes Shīʿī arguments.[105] The first Shīʿī objection is as follows:

> The imamate is God's and the Prophet' s lieutenancy, and so the validity of the office cannot be established by the decision of others, i.e., the electors (*ahl al-bayʿa*); if it were so, then the imam would be their caliph, not God's and the Prophet's.

[105] Cited in Kerr, *Islamic Reform*, 34–5.

Ījī replies:

> The elector's choice of the Imam is itself an indication of the lieutenancy of God and the Prophet, who set him up as a sign of their judgment in favor of that lieutenancy, as is the case with the signs of other ordinances. The explanation according to our view is that the *bay'a* is *not what validates the Imamate*, in the sense you referred to, but rather it is a sign bringing the Imamate to light, as is the case with analogy [*qiyās*] and consensus [*ijmā'*] which indicate [but do not create] the ordinances of the *Sharī'a*.

The second objection is:

> The electors have no authority [lit., disposal] over other persons, and therefore their action and their choice cannot have any binding force over others. They do not themselves enjoy authority over the Muslims, so how can they invest someone else with such authority?

And the answer:

> If their action and choice is a procedure established by God and His Prophet as an indication of their judgment in favor of the Imamate of whomever the electors decide to recognize, then the objection falls. For their *bay'a* becomes a decisive proof for the Muslims and must be followed. Your position is also refuted by the example of the witness and the judge. They must be followed because the Lawgiver made their words an indication of divine judgment which must be followed, even though they have no authority over the object of the testimony and of the judicial verdict.

Commenting on this dialog, Malcolm Kerr rightly observes: "This is a decisive rejection of the contract theory; the *ahl al-bay'a* are considered mere functionaries, not interested parties."[106] What is noteworthy in this polemic is the extent to which the Ash'arī theologians concede the basic premises of their Shī'ī interlocutors. Rather than arguing for the right of the Community to elect one of them as their representative, Ījī simply concedes that the Sunni *imām* is chosen directly by God; but instead of the Shī'ī method of the *naṣṣ* of an infallible *imām*, God guides the electors to the already divinely chosen *imām*. Now, the will of the Community is utterly irrelevant, as is any institutional or political mechanism to obtain and safeguard the right of the Community to choose. The contractors, *ahl al-bay'a*, are simply an instrument of God (in a theological sense), not representatives of the Community, even in theory. To use the earlier

[106] Kerr, 34–5, who rightly sees this as tension between law and theology: "the Shī'ite objection, then, distorts the issue by lifting it entirely out of the realm of law and into that of theology, rendering meaningless any notion of human rights and duties conceived on their own level."

theorists' favorite analogy, marriage may be said by Muslims to be a match made in heaven theologically, but the will of the married parties have a real, legal effect in Islamic law, and the parties could undo the heavenly match if they so choose. The subtle change of rhetoric in Ījī is not semantic hairsplitting at all. Rather, it means the difference between Islamic marriage, a legal relationship, and Catholic marriage, indissoluble because it is truly a match made in heaven in a theological sense. Ījī thus brings theological fatalism to bear on a legal and political dispute to deadly effect. The Community's will no longer is, for political purposes, an instrument or the best approximation of God's will. God's will is done regardless of whom the electors choose as caliph and what the Community wills.

Faced with immitigable domination of the imperial caliphate and failed rebellions, the socioreligious leaders of the Community had relinquished its political claims already, in what I have called the traditionalist's Sunna-centered view of political authority in the early-Abbasid era. This compromise was theorized and normalized, however, only with the consolidation of the caliphate discourse, especially in its most influential forms as elaborated by Māwardī and Ghazālī. As a result, the Community lost its political relevance in theory as well. In the early Community-centered vision, the Community had possessed the symbolic authority over the mission of Islam and could grant it to the caliph; in the caliphate-centered vision, that intermediate step was unnecessary. Yet for the ulama in the classical age, including the pro-*siyāsa* ones, the Community seems to have had no effective currency. It is this vacuum that pre-Islamic imperial traditions naturally filled; it was not that the ulama became "secularized" in any meaningful sense, but rather that the agency of the Community disappeared, and the ruler had to be justified and legitimated by the facts of power and necessity.

This absence, I propose, is the one responsible for the paradoxes modern scholars have observed in the ulama's attitudes toward the legitimacy of the government and the limits of its power. What looks like absolutism is the remnants of a Community-centered vision, in which the Community's role to constrain the religiously bound state is expected. Yet when that role is lost, rather than acknowledging and reviving it, the ulama end up creating fictions. The situation is analogous to refusing to replace the worn-out brakes of an automobile and instead prohibiting the driver from going too fast – in reality, any speed without good brakes is too fast. This is why the medieval state begins to look absolutist if one looks at the formal doctrine (because the brakes – i.e., the

"Community" – are missing), and illegitimate if one looks at its real operation (because the driver is inevitably going too fast).

The medieval military state required no theoretical legitimacy because, although justifying itself through its claim to protect Islam, its law, and community, it sought no moral vision (of Islam or otherwise) beyond itself. So long as the empty symbol of the caliphate was in place, there were no *constitutional* terms the ulama could offer to bilaterally bind the rulers by way of granting legitimacy (by, for instance, legitimizing principled *siyāsa*) in return for accountability and regulation of accession to power.

In reality, the caliphate increasingly became largely irrelevant in the classical age, and the real tug-of-war was between the power of the rulers and the authority of the ulama. The real impact of the classical caliphate discourse was not in that it was ever institutionalized – it wasn't meant to be – but that it embodied ideals, visions, and boundaries of normative thought. Although the bar is set at an impossible height in the proper caliphate theory, it is complemented by "mirrors for princes," in which the rulers are advised to be pious, just, and politically shrewd (even if they can never be legitimate). The trade-off, however, was that it protected the religious doctrine from the ambitions of military rulers. Furthermore, the caliphate discourse maintained and justified the status quo and assured the ulama that nothing in their theoretical constructs or practical conduct was amiss – that it was lack of righteousness of the rulers and people in general (*fasād al-zamān*) that was responsible for their political upheavals, and nothing could be done about it.

The Community, deemed in theory to be the site of legitimacy, was never addressed in either of these genres of political discourse as an *agent*. There was nothing the Community could do to change its plight besides waiting for a savior or an apocalypse; and this is precisely what it did for the most part.

Although the loss of political community and sensibility is ubiquitous in the legal culture of the classical period, perhaps few anecdotes bring out its implications as dramatically as the following one. It concerns the chief judge of Cairo, the great Shafiʿī jurist, an emblem of piety and speaking truth to power, ʿIzz al-Dīn b. ʿAbd al-Salām al-Sulamī (*ca*. 577/1181–660/1262),[107] who would witness later in his life the demise of the Ayyubids

[107] Tāj al-Dīn al-Subkī, *Ṭabaqāt al-shāfiʿiyya al-kubrā*, M. M. al-Ṭanāḥī and ʿA. M. al-Ḥilw (n.p., *Hijr li'l-Ṭabāʿa wa'l-Nashr wa'l-Tawzīʿ*, 1413), 8:209; S. R. Ali, *Izz al-Din al-Sulami: His Life and Works* (New Delhi: Kitab Bhavan, n.d.; first published, 1898), 37.

and the rise of the Mamluks (military slaves) as kings. When al-Sāliḥ Ayyūb b. Kāmil Najm al-Dīn (d. 647), the grandson of Saladin who had ruled over Syria as a governor, acceded amidst internecine warfare to the throne of the Ayyubid dynasty, he brought along to Cairo the slave army he had built during his governorship and distributed governmental offices among them.[108] The biographer Subkī tells us that as a pious, daring, and learned chief judge, ʿIzz al-Dīn,[109] in keeping with the rules of the Shāfiʿī *madhhab*, refused to accept the legitimacy of these Mamluks as governmental officials, which included the commander of the army, and to ratify any contracts they made, which caused great angst and annoyance. When the Sultan interfered, he abandoned his post and prepared to leave town. The Sultan, moved, summoned him and apologized, and finally the *qāḍī*'s verdict was carried out: The Mamluks were publicly auctioned and freed before resuming their posts. After some analysis, a modern historian tells us that even though the details of this story are most likely adornment, it is plausible in its outline.[110] Yet regardless of its historicity, the point of the anecdote is to express the piety and uprightness of a hero, which was expressed, remarkably, by his *unrelenting legal formalism*. To the gradual takeover of the government by imported slaves who were completely detached from the Community and whose instrument of governance was primarily violence, the most heroic scholarly objection was that this violated a minor legal rule that could be fixed by a theatrical act! The great jurist did not, or perhaps could not, produce any "political" critique of this alarming state of affairs. This anecdote is a testament to the state of mind that reduced a historic *political* tragedy to a matter of *legal* trifle.

The predicament that the late A. K. S. Lambton perceptively captures as the loss of "the universal aims of Islam ... in the face of problems which had been raised by the fragmentation of the Islamic world" I have contended can be best understood as the mainstream classical ulama's deliberate flight from politics. The relationship between Islam and politics in the classical age can neither be described as a formal divorce nor a honeymoon, but rather a tenuous and unstable separation of spheres

[108] S. Humphreys, *From Saladin to the Mongols* (SUNY, 1977), 250–300.

[109] ʿIzz al-Dīn had been appointed as the preacher (*khaṭīb*) of the Umayyad Mosque in 637/1239 by the Ayyubid Sultan of Damascus, al-Sāliḥ Ismāʿīl, but when he criticized the Sultan for alliance with and concessions to the crusaders against his Ayyubid cousin in Cairo (namely, the chief Sultan, al-Sulṭān al-Muʿaẓẓam, al-Saliḥ Ayyūb), he had to leave Egypt in 638/1240, where he was received in honor and appointed *khaṭīb* of the main mosque of Cairo and soon the Chief Judge by the Sultan (Ali, *Izz al-Din*, 11–13).

[110] Ibid., 95.

of religious authority from political power that was neither justified in theory nor wholeheartedly accepted.

In order to understand why the classical tradition chose the settlement it did, we need to look into conceptions of reason, agency, and their distribution in the political community that informed the discourse of *kalām* in which the caliphate theory was shaped.

3

Reason and Community in the Classical Period

> There is consensus among [our companions] that the appointment of a caliph is an obligation and that this obligation is [established] by revelation, not reason.
>
> Nawawī (d. 676/1277)

> If revelation and reason contradict each other, reason takes precedence.
>
> Rāzī (d. 606/1209)

The last chapter addressed how the three main discursive sites of Islamic political thought – the caliphate discourse, jurisprudence, and statecraft literature, all of which had their antecedents in the first three centuries of Islam – responded to the political and social transformations of the fourth/tenth century. In these discourses, I have identified some peculiar features of classical Islamic political thought, in particular, the ritualization of the caliphate (the source of its obligation being revelation and not reason) and the exclusion of the Community (*umma*) from even theoretical constructions of political legitimacy. This contrasts sharply with the Community-centered vision that had characterized the first century and a half of Islam. Both of these new features, the reason-revelation debate and the role of the Community, it is worth noting, are in essence theological. This chapter seeks to go behind the scenes, so to say, to investigate the intellectual motivations behind and consequences of these intellectual attitudes toward reason/revelation and the Community.

The political and social changes, such as the political fragmentation that resulted from the demise of the Abbasid caliphate; the rise of the ulama as the veritable socioreligious guides of society and, in a more ambivalent way, of the rulers; and the conversion of most of the inhabitants of Islamic lands to Islam, all provide undeniable potential explanations for the kinds of transformations we observe in political thought. However, discursive traditions, as I have argued, even as they respond to their sociopolitical world do so on their own terms. Sociopolitical circumstances, therefore, can only provide the context but never determinative, causal explanation for discursive transformations. Thus, an intellectual history of these significant and peculiar transformations in Islamic political attitude toward reason, revelation, and Community is warranted, even indispensible, in understanding the overall trajectory of Islamic political thought.

Furthermore, these admittedly sociopolitically contingent attitudes of the classical period became inscribed in Islamic legal, theological, and even spiritual discourses as authoritative doctrines. Discursive traditions, being "living organisms," continue to respond to changes, adding in each generation layers of meanings to inherited concepts of language or even radically changing the terms. Yet history does tend to paint layers produced in some periods thicker than those produced in others (Why is it, for instance, that we all know Aristotle and Plato but not their predecessors or successors?), and thus some periods and thinkers acquire greater formative weight than others; the "classical" period of Islamic thought has been so called for good reason. The orthodoxies that consolidated at the hands of the thinkers of the fourth/tenth through sixth/twelfth centuries have had an abiding imprint on subsequent Islamic thought in their respective traditions, providing compelling solutions for subsequent generations of thinkers. This intellectual momentum continued to inform and indeed shape (without, however, determining) the possibilities of Muslim political thought for centuries to come, even after the passing of the circumstances that brought that political thought into existence.

The influential seventh-/thirteenth-century Shāfiʿī jurist al-Nawawī's summation of the Ashʿarī argument about the basis of the obligation of caliphate serves as an apt starting point for our inquiry:

> There is consensus among [our companions, Shāfiʿī-Ashʿarīs] that the appointment of a caliph is an obligation and that this obligation is [established] by revelation, not reason. Some have disagreed, like al-Aṣamm [a Muʿtazilī] and some of the Khārijites who say that the appointment of a caliph is not an obligation altogether, while some of the Muʿtazila who disagree say that it is an obligation, but by reason, not by revelation. Both of these latter opinions are false. Al-Aṣamm's opinion is based on the argument that the Companions stayed without a caliph until the day of Saqīfa and after ʿUmar's death until the *shūrā* was complete.

But this is no argument because they did not agree on abjuring or neglecting the appointment; rather they strove to appoint a caliph. The latter opinion [that of the Muʿtazilites] is evidently false, for reason has no role in obligating or prohibiting, nor in judging things to be good or bad – for it does so merely as a result of custom.[1]

The insistence that human reason has no ethical capacity is not evidence of out and out antirationalism, but of a complex, even paradoxical, relationship with reason that should be understood against the "principle of interpretation" (*qānūn al-ta'wīl*) that came to define later Ashʿarism and that appears to unequivocally endorse reason over revelation: "If revelation and reason contradict each other, reason takes precedence over revelation. This is based on three premises: one, reason is what, in the first place, leads one to revelation and to ignore reason would be to cut off the very basis of revelation; two, revelation never imparts definitive knowledge ...; three, reason imparts definitive knowledge."[2] This clear formulation of the *qānūn* is the work of Rāzī, but the same principle had been intimated in a less emphatic form by Ghazālī. To understand why the Ashʿarīs insisted on keeping reason out of the realm of normativity despite their apparent claim of reason's superiority over revelation and the implications it had on their political thinking, let us turn to the history of *kalām* and its relationship to reason.

SUNNI KALĀM

The theological speculation that came to be labeled as *kalām* first emerged toward the close of the first century as Muslims attempted to defend Islam in the context of the religious and philosophical traditions of the Near East. "Of the three formative agents of Islamic theology," Schacht observed, "one is politics, another religious piety, and the third Christian polemics."[3] Identifying phases of the reception of *kalām* in Islam, the French Islamicist Louis Gardet suggests that in the first phase, under the Umayyads, it was applied to a "heretical" trend and captured the rationalist discourse of the Murji'a, Qadariyya, and Jabbāriyya (or Jabriyya,

[1] Ibn Ḥajar, *Fatḥ al-bārī* (Dār al-Maʿrifa, 1379), 13:208. This last statement, that what reason deems to be good or evil is merely a result of custom, appears to be a reflection of Ghazālī's 'psychological' explanation of ethics.

[2] See discussion later in the chapter.

[3] Schacht, "Theology and Law," in *Theology and Law in Islam*, ed. Gustave von Grunebaum (Harrassowitz, 1971), 18.

or Jahmiyya). In the second phase, the more politically inclined legacy of the Qadariyya was taken over and doctrinally developed by the Muʿtazila beginning in the second/eighth century.[4] The Muʿtazila flourished under the Abbasid caliph al-Ma'mūn and his successors, but after their key role in the unsuccessful inquisition of the traditionalists, they gradually lost political as well as intellectual ground. In the third phase, from the fourth/tenth century onward, there appear Sunni versions of *kalām* in the form of Ashʿarism in Baghdad and Māturīdism in the East.[5]

The distinct formation of a Sunni caliphate discourse, it has been noted, was the work of these scholars of Sunni *kalām*, and its salient features, including its attitude toward the roles of reason and Community in politics, were mostly rooted in the particular intellectual challenges of *kalām*, although the role of the new sociopolitical arrangements is not negligible either. A. K. Reinhart, for instance, has argued that Muʿtazilism had emerged in the second/eighth century but came to represent by the fourth/tenth century an "archaic form of Muslim thought carrying forward earlier ideas formed in a missionary, that is to say, a minoritarian context." After the third/ninth and fourth/tenth centuries' mass conversions to Islam, there occurs a "shift of the religious paradigm." Muslims were now a majority and were no longer mostly Arabs, yet they were also less confident as a result of political fragmentation. Religious authority now rested securely in the hands of the ulama, who were often insecurely dependent on the rulers. "Their Islam is both imperious and insecure – it needs no further confirmation nor does it tolerate extra-Revelational authority. Their God is a Persian Shah, not an Arab king." The contrast Reinhart presents here could be further sharpened if it is recalled that the early Muslims did not liken their rulers to their God, but thought of him as one of them. Reinhart further brings out the difference he sees between the early rationalist and the later voluntarist (Ashʿarī) theologians: "One trusted the world, and trusted innate human ability to assess human acts, the other did not."[6] Although Reinhart's basic insight is persuasive, I go on in the following to qualify and nuance his account by pointing out a

[4] S. Stroumsa, "The Beginnings of the Muʿtazila Reconsidered," *JSAI* 13 (1990): 265–93, argues that political reasons do not explain the rise of the Muʿtazila, for they had diverse political positions; the only uniting factor was a movement of religious revival. It appears to me that the Qadariyya, like the rest of the factions, become depoliticized about the same time as the traditionalists and the Imāmī-Shīʿa – that is, in the early-Abbasid period following the failed revolt of al-Nafs al-Zakiyya; the Muʿtazila thus emerge as their theologized version.

[5] *EI*², s.v. "Kalām."

[6] Reinhart, 178–9.

few factors in this intellectual struggle over Islam that do not easily fit into his scheme: (1) the role of the traditionalists who rejected *kalām* altogether from early on and, beginning in the fifth/eleventh century (when Reinhart's inquiry admittedly ends), the development of new social and intellectual trends and forces. These were: (2) partial reconciliation of the later Ashʿarīs with their Muʿtazilī opponents beginning in the fifth/eleventh century. (3) The growing influence of the Muslim Neoplatonist Aristotelians, the *falāsifa*, and their embrace of Islamic religious doctrine, or at least its rhetoric, made them a far more serious challenge (aggravated by the ascendancy of Bāṭinī-Shīʿism in Egypt) to Sunni *kalām* generally than Muʿtazilism had been. (4) Finally, the emergence of the intimately related tendencies of esotericism (mystical Sufism as well as Ismāʿīlī Bāṭinism) and elitism (both mystical and social) shaped the social context as well as the intellectual outlook of Sunni theologians and political thinkers.

To return to the realm of ideas, the bone of contention between the traditionalists and the Muʿtazila during the second/eighth and third/ninth centuries had been the interpretation of certain divine attributes in the Qur'an.[7] Al-Ashʿarī's conversion to Aḥmad b. Ḥanbal's position had not been grounded in a clear alternative to Muʿtazilī *kalām*, but rather in the premise that there existed no irreconcilable conflict between the traditionalist position and the foundational assumptions of *kalām*.[8] Al-Ashʿarī and his early followers found themselves trapped between two unflinching parties: the Muʿtazila, who accused them of anthropomorphism, and the traditionalist Ḥanbalīs, who accused them of following the Muʿtazila in reducing God to a theoretical abstraction without any attributes. Both sides accused them of inconsistency.

The lure of rational consistency proved irresistible, and increasingly they leaned toward their rationalist interlocutors.[9] As early as the first

[7] The traditionalists, in particular the anti-*kalām* wing, called themselves *ahl al-ithbāt*, affirmers of God's attributes "without asking how" [*bilā kayf*], and were denigrated by their detractors as Ḥashwiyya or Mujassima, that is, anthropomorphists (J. van Ess, s.v. "Tashbīh wa-Tanzīh," in *EI*[2]).

[8] S. Vasalou, *Moral Agents and Their Deserts: The Character of Muʿtazilite Ethics* (Princeton University Press, 2008), 4. This belief had been shared by most Ashʿarīs after him, with the exception perhaps of Rāzī, who expressed serious doubts about it. See A. Maḥmūd, *Mawqif Ibn Taymiyya min al-Ashāʿira* (Dār al-Rushd, 1415), 515.

[9] Vasalou, 4. M. Watt writes that after conversion, some of al-Ashʿari's writings are based on interpretations of the scripture and in such cases differ scarcely from the content and style of the traditionalists; however, when his opponents used a rational argument, he did not hesitate to use a similar argument. Once, however, the possibility of rational

generation Ashʿarīs like al-Ḥasan al-Ṭabarī (d. ca. 380/990), the distaste for the traditionalist literalism that led in its coarse forms to anthropomorphism is apparent. Yet the Ashʿarīs were also not willing to strip God entirely of attributes (*taʿṭīl*) and hence personality, thus reflecting the ambivalence of the founder, al-Ashʿarī himself.[10] Starting with Bāqillānī, credited as having been the first systematic theologian who established Ashʿarism as a school, rational rather than revelational arguments become predominant.[11] Yet on the issue of divine attributes, Bāqillānī's position is close to the traditionalists' in important respects,[12] and he is at pains to show his commitment to the legacy of Aḥmad b. Ḥanbal.[13] Bāqillānī's opposition to the Muʿtazila had been complete and uncompromising, and in that he was in step with al-Ashʿarī. On the key issue of theodicy, he had embraced al-Ashʿarī's total voluntarism.[14]

The fifth/eleventh century, the century of the so-called Sunni revival, saw a number of key social and intellectual transformations, including the spread and stabilization of Ashʿarism in numbers as well as in the traditional domains of scholarship.[15] Thus far primarily a tradition of theology, its proponents were not known to be skilled in traditional Islamic sciences, namely jurisprudence and *ḥadīth*. With the emergence of loyal Ashʿarīs like al-Bayhaqī (d. 458/1066) in the domains of *ḥadīth* and Shāfiʿī jurisprudence and al-Qushayrī (d. 465/1074)[16] in Sufism, Ashʿarism began to be stabilized as a school. Furthermore, a notable contribution of Sufi writers like Qushayrī to Ashʿarism was increased inclination toward elitism and esotericism in the spiritual and social domain.

arguments was established, at least among his followers, it was possible for the later Ashaʿarīs "to develop this side of his method until in later centuries theology became thoroughly intellectualist. This, however, was far removed from the temper of al-Ashʿarī himself" (*EI*², s.v. "al-Ashʿarī"). See also, Maḥmūd, 557.

10 Maḥmūd, 518ff.

11 Maḥmūd, 556.

12 Such as in affirming that God's having two hands in the Qur'an cannot be reduced by interpreting "hand" as simply power (Bāqillānī, *Tamhīd*, 259; Maḥmūd, 539).

13 Ibn Taymiyya informs us that Bāqillānī would at times sign his name as "Muḥammad b. al-Ṭayyib al-Ḥanbali," identifying himself as a Ḥanbalī, as would al-Ashʿarī himself (*Dar'(S)*, 1:270).

14 J. N. Bell, *Love Theory in Later Ḥanbalī Islam* (SUNY Press, 1979), 56–7, on Bāqillānī's equation of God's love with His will; 62–3 for his denial of causality.

15 M. Subḥī, *al-Ashāʿira*, 93, quoted in Maḥmūd, 586.

16 ʿAbd al-Qāsim al-Qushayrī was a Sufi author and staunch Ashʿarī from Khurāsān who wrote his *Risāla* in defense of al-Ashʿarī as well as the influential *Risāla fī al-taṣawwuf* (Knysh, 130–2). He was perhaps the first to expound the fiction that all great men of Sufism have been Ashʿarīs (Maḥmūd, 599–609).

Intellectually, the first major turning point in the Ash'arī tradition was the work of Juwaynī, whose most significant contribution was a partial rapprochement with the Mu'tazila. His thorough acquaintance with Mut'azilism, it seems, urged him to seek greater consistency in the doctrines of his own school. Because the Mu'tazila in their original form were less of a threat (outside of Shī'ism, that is), Juwaynī did not shy away from acknowledging their cogency and consistency in key issues. In a way, the Ash'arīs had come full circle with respect to the Mu'tazilī doctrines, based on whose methodology and against whose positions they had begun as a school.[17] Perhaps part of the reason for this softening was that by the fifth/eleventh century, the Mu'tazilī threat had been all but replaced by a greater one, the *falāsifa*.[18] In particular, Fārābī (d. 339/950) and Ibn Sīnā (428/1037) had worked out a synthesis of Neoplatonist and Aristotelian ideas, which posed a formidable threat to Sunni tradition. For Ghazālī and after, it was no longer the Mu'tazila but the *falāsifa* and the Ismā'īlī Bāṭinīs[19] that became the main interlocutors and adversaries. In addition to drawing the Ash'arī tradition nearer to *falsafa*, Ghazālī also reasserted Qushayrī's influence of *taṣawwuf* in both *fiqh* and *kalām*. The next major intervention in the Ash'arī tradition was to continue in the direction of reason and *falsafa* at the expense of traditional reliance on revelation. Fakhr al-Dīn al-Rāzī (d. 606/1209), a more thoroughgoing philosopher than Ghazālī, completed the philosophical turn that had begun in Juwaynī and Ghazālī.[20] Rāzī's overall contribution to the Ash'arī tradition is best summed up in the following comment in Ayman Shehadeh's recent study of Rāzī's ethics:

> The gap separating the two traditions [that is, *kalām* and *falsafa*] was initially so wide that many notions central to one tradition of ethical theory were completely alien to the other, in which they would normally be dismissed *in toto*, without

[17] For instance, in the matter of human capacity to act (*istiṭā'a* or *qudra*), Juwaynī refutes al-Ash'arī's doctrine that the power to act is simultaneous with the act itself (idem, *al-Burhān*, 1:277; Maḥmūd, 612f, 620).

[18] A. al-Nashshār, *Manāhij al-Baḥth 'inda Mufakkirī al-Islam*, 4th ed. (Dar al-Ma'ārif, 1978), argues that in Juwaynī we find the first attempt to incorporate Aristotelian logic into *uṣūl al-fiqh*.

[19] Bāṭiniyya, lit., esotericists, a name given to the Ismā'īlī Shī'a, emphasizing their emphasis on *bāṭin*, the "inward" meaning behind the literal wording of the scripture; (*EI*^{2}, s.v. "Bāṭiniyya").

[20] Unlike Ghazālī, his state-sponsored intellectual life and works were much less imbued with pietistic exhortations, F. Griffel, "On Fakhr al-Dīn al-Rāzī's Life and the Patronage He Received," *JIS* 18.3 (2007): 313–44. On Rāzī's tremendous influence on legal theory (*uṣūl al-fiqh*) in Shāfi'ī and Mālikī schools, see Jackson, 8.

engagement in any proper dialogue. Yet there then emerged signs of increasing, and more positive, interaction between *kalām* and *falsafa*, culminating in the efforts of al-Ghazālī, who was both a severe critic of the *falāsifa* and deeply influenced by them in many respects. A century later, Fakhr al-Din al-Rāzī was to open the gates widely, allowing a more liberal exchange of ideas, a 'synthesis' even, between *kalām* and *falsafa*.[21]

FALSAFA, EPISTEMOLOGY, AND POLITICAL ORGANIZATION

To understand the significance of Sunni *kalām*'s rapprochement with *falsafa* and its surreptitious influence on Sunni political thought, we need to begin with an often-ignored part of the story of the intellectual struggle starting in the third/ninth century. At the heart of the validity of *kalām* there had been debates between the traditionalists, the Muʿtazilīs, and the *falāsifa* about the nature and role of *ʿaql* (reason/intellect) and its limits before and after revelation. It affected such basic questions as whether there exists a particular line of speculative reasoning that is necessary to establish the existence of God and whether natural human reason available to the common believers possesses what is needed to do so. More importantly, how intelligence was thought to be distributed within the human community directly bore upon the questions of political agency and social organization. The first philosopher of the Arabs, Abū Yūsuf Yaʿqūb al-Kindī (d. ca. 256/870), already theorized intellect (*ʿaql*), in terms of Neoplatonic realism, as "the First Intellect" – as God's first creation and through which all other things came into being.[22] The first systematic *faylasūf* was al-Fārābī (d. ca. 339/950),[23] who expounded on Aristotle and directly countered the range of Muslim opinions on the issue. Next came the most important figure among the *falāsifa*, 'al-Shaykh al-Ra'īs' Abū ʿAlī Ibn Sīnā (d. 428/1037), who further developed Fārābī's view of the intellect. In the words of Amélie Marie Goichon, the *falāsifa* espoused, owing to Neoplatonist inspiration, an "emanationist theory of creation" whereas "[t]he Qur'an, like the Old and New Testaments, explains creation by a free act of will on the part of God." The Neoplatonist cosmology, in contrast, is necessitarian: "For Ibn Sīnā, by way of Plotinus, the necessary Being is such in all its modes – and thus as creator – and

21 A. Shihadeh, *The Teleological Ethics of Fakhr al-Dīn al-Rāzī* (Brill, 2006), 1.
22 F. Klein-Frank, "Al-Kindi," in O. Leaman and S. H. Nasr, *History of Islamic Philosophy* (Routledge, 2001), 165.
23 *EI*[2], s.v. "al-Fārābī, Abū Naṣr."

being overflows from it."[24] Ibn Sīnā's merit, his modern advocates hold, was precisely his "recognition of the compatibility between the [religious] metaphysics of contingency ... and the metaphysics of necessity, in which the followers of Aristotle had enshrined the idea that the goal of science is understanding as to why and how things must be as they are."[25] Ibn Sīnā's attempt of reconciliation, however impressive and seductive even to such celebrated Sunni theologians as Ghazālī, was on the whole rejected.

The *falāsifa*'s cosmologically grounded epistemological scheme (in a necessitarian system, cosmology, that is, the structure of the universe, was directly related to the process of knowing) had direct implications for the nature and possibilities of human thought as well as collective organization. Modern historians have argued that the Aristotelian epistemology had been fundamentally at odds with the Biblical – and, on the same account, Islamic – worldview in which the universe was created by an act of free will by the transcendental, "personal" God.[26] The Hellenic view is immanentistic, in that "nature is conceived in organismic terms, fraught with purpose and finality and open to investigation by analytic or *deductive* modes of reasoning capable of delivering *knowledge that is certain or absolute*."[27] The concept of a transcendental God who created the world freely, in contrast, presupposes an "external relations" doctrine, which entails "a nominalist epistemology, and a natural philosophy of empirical mode ... emphasizing the conditional nature of all knowledge based on observation of a created and radically contingent world which could well have been other than it is."[28] Yet this incommensurability did not deter medieval Christian theologians, any more than it did Muslim theologians a few centuries later, from attempting to synthesize the two concepts of God and knowledge. Augustine, writes Francis Oakley, "attempted to close the way to any further Christian flirtation with the Greek notion of the eternity of the world," yet he conceded to the Neoplatonists and some of his Christian predecessors "that the creative act was indeed an intelligent one guided by forms, archetypes, or ideas of the Platonic mold, but ideas now situated in the divine mind itself as a sort of creative blueprint."

[24] Ibid.

[25] L. E. Goodman, *Avicenna* (Routledge, 1992), ix.

[26] For the use of the adjective "personal" for God in Islam, see L. Gardet's discussion of it in *EI*^{2}, s.v. "Allāh," 1:409.

[27] F. Oakley, *Natural Law, Laws of Nature, Natural Rights* (Continuum International Pub., 2005), 30; emphasis mine.

[28] Ibid.

This "extraordinary accommodation," however, which secured for "the doctrine of the divine ideas an enduring place in later Christian philosophy ... was a victory for delicate philosophical and theological diplomacy rather than the achievement of any truly stable synthesis."[29]

The Sunni traditionalists at least as early as Aḥmad b. Ḥanbal already rejected the philosophers' view of the intellect and knowledge, which must have appeared as one of the imported heresies of the Greeks, and held resolutely that "intellect is an instinct [*gharīza*], wisdom is recognition, and true knowledge [*al-ʿilm*] is revelation."[30] Al-Ḥārith b. Asad al-Muḥāsibī (d. 243/857),[31] a *ḥadīth* scholar and a spiritually and intellectually inclined contemporary of Aḥmad b. Ḥanbal, defended the traditionalist opinion that intellect "is an instinct [*gharīza*] through which knowledge [*maʿrifa*] is acquired"[32] against the Muʿtazilī view that intellect is knowledge (*maʿrifa*)[33] and the philosophers' view that it is an essence (*jawhar*). Two centuries later, seeing that some Ashʿarīs (like Bāqillānī and Māwardī) had preferred the Muʿtazilī opinion, Juwaynī complained that his contemporary Sunni theologians no longer understood the significance of this issue and that Muḥāsibī's opinion had been the only correct one.[34]

The way these groups understood epistemology had direct implications for their sociopolitical vision. The relationship between epistemology and political thought in the third/ninth and fourth/tenth centuries, a problem seldom treated in modern scholarship notes al-Sayyid, was the subject of intense intellectual struggle "about the vision of the society, the means of governing and constraining it, and the sources of authority in it." "All parties," including the traditionalists, "accepted that the governing constraint and authority for the society is intellect, but differed about "the what-ness of intellect [*mā'iyat al-ʿaql* or *māhiyat al-ʿaql*]." The *falāsifa* insisted that

> the intellect is an essence, not part of the cognitive or physiological foundation of the human being, but an element bestowed from above in order to direct the human person and facilitate his life, and when life leaves the body, intellect returns to its world. And just like the intellect with respect to a human person

[29] Ibid., 46–7.

[30] Ibn Taymiyya, *al-Musawwada fi uṣūl al-fiqh*, cited in Sayyid, *al-Jamāʿa*, 241.

[31] For a list of Muḥāsibī's works, see F. Najjar, *Al-ʿAql* (Fahmi Najjar, 2004), 59–60; for Muḥāsibī's spiritual biography and impact, see Knysh, 43–8.

[32] Najjar, *ʿAql*, 61; Muḥāsibī, *Mā'iyat al-ʿaql* (JK), 1.

[33] See Sayyid's introduction to Māwardī, *Tashīl al-naẓar*, 37.

[34] Najjar, 62.

is both an (external) essence and a function, its relationship to the society is the same, in the sense that the society is governed and constrained in its private and public life by the intellectual elite whom the Active Intellect has endowed with the right to govern in the matters of spirituality [*sulūk*], economy, education and culture. On the political level, the implication of this view is that the ruler is the *ʿaql* of the society – which, accordingly, does not derive from within it but is given to it from above by the verdict of nature. Human society is comprised of instincts, tendencies, and base desires which if left to themselves would clash with each other until they perish, thus leading to near or complete annihilation of the society. Hence the necessity of the constraining and governing social intellect embodied in the ruler.[35]

In contrast, the traditionalists' view is that the intellect is an instinct, an integral part of the human person whose function is to constrain and direct from within, and is reflected in the view that the society inherently and internally directs and organizes itself.[36] This was obviously commensurate with the traditionalists' Community-centered view of political life.

The question is to what extent the *falāsifa*'s epistemology and socio-political vision influenced Sunni *kalām*. Although this encounter has been recognized widely as having had a profoundly formative influence on *kalām*, its extent and nature have been widely debated. On the one hand, Sunni theologians had to defend their orthodoxy at the apex of which was the qur'anic concept of God, but on the other, the attraction of *falsafa* proved irresistible. It is in the context of reconciling revelation with the rational system of the *falāsifa* that we can best understand the development of *qānūn al-ta'wīl*.

THE PRINCIPLE OF INTERPRETATION (QĀNŪN AL-TA'WĪL)

In Sunni *kalām*, the *qānūn* appears to have been first formulated by Ghazālī. In his treatise titled *Qānūn al-ta'wīl*, Ghazālī wrote, "Rational demonstration [*burhān al-ʿaql*] in essence cannot be wrong, for reason can never lead to falsehood. If it is deemed possible for reason to lead to falsehood, its establishment of [the truthfulness of] revelation is called into question."[37] For Ghazālī, the *qānūn* has a simple, "minimalist" function: If one could demonstrate beyond doubt (i.e., establish *burhān*)

[35] Sayyid, *Jamāʿa*, 242–3.
[36] Ibid.
[37] Ghazālī, *Qānūn al-ta'wīl*, translated in Y. Michot, "Mamlūk Theologian," I, 157.

a certain proposition, revelation could not be interpreted in such way as to contradict it. Some of Ghazālī's disciples such as al-Qāḍī ʿIyāḍ also wrote on the subject, but it found its most systematic and dispassionate expression in Rāzī. Rāzī's formulation of the *qānūn*, defended at length in his treatise *Asās al-taqdīs*, is as follows:

> *Faṣl Thirty Two. What if rational proofs oppose the evident meaning of revelation?* Know that if definitive rational proofs lead to a conclusion and we find some revelational evidence that seems to oppose it, one of four possibilities exist: (i) We accept both as true, which would lead to a contradiction, which is impossible; (ii) we reject both, which is also impossible; (iii) we accept the evident meaning of revelation while rejecting the evident conclusion of reason, which is invalid, because it is impossible for us to know the soundness of the evident meanings of revelation except if we already know, by means of rational proofs, the existence of the Creator and His attributes, the nature of the evidence of the miracles that establish the truth of the Apostle of God, may peace be upon him, and the actual occurrence of miracles at the hands of Muḥammad, upon him be peace. If we were to accept the invalidity of rational proofs, reason itself would be invalidated and its conclusions could no longer be accepted. And if that were to happen, revelational evidence itself could no longer be valid. Thus, it has been established that to invalidate reason in order to save revelation leads to invalidating both reason as well as revelation, which is false.
>
> Now that the four [sic.; he probably means three] types have been invalidated, we have no choice but to conclude the validity of definitive rational arguments by holding that revelational arguments are either incorrect or are correct but their true meaning [*al-murād*] is different from their appearance.
>
> Now if we deem metaphorical interpretation [*ta'wīl*] valid, then we engage out of reverence the details of those metaphors; while if we deem it invalid, we leave the true knowledge [of revelational arguments] to God Almighty.
>
> This is the governing principle [*al-qānūn al-kullī*] that must be followed in all equivocal matters. [38]

This can be called a "maximalist" view of the *qānūn*: Revelation was to generally lose its authority against any proposition that reason could "establish." All later *kalām* theologians, perhaps not as daring as Rāzī, had a field of varying sizes – various limits of tolerance so to say – beyond which revelation was to be metaphorically reinterpreted (*ta'wīl*) in a wholesale fashion. The potency of the *qānūn* can be fully appreciated if it is realized that many of the later Ashʿarīs reject altogether – as Rāzī does – the possibility of certitude in any proposition based on revelation, hence they hold that arguments based on reason are the only source

[38] Rāzī, *Asās al-taqdīs* (Maṭbaʿa Muṣṭafā al-Bābi al-Ḥilbī, 1935), 172–3; Maḥmūd, 857.

of certitude and always in principle supersede revelation. In *Nihāyat al-ʿuqūl*, Rāzī writes that "Proof by revelation in foundational matters [*masā'il uṣūliyya*]" – and the significance of this qualification will become clear presently – "is never possible because such proof is based on speculative premises [*muqaddimāt ẓanniyya*] and on refutation of all possible rational objections. And refutation of objections does not yield certain knowledge [*al-ʿilm*], because it is possible that in the same matter [being argued by revelation] there is a contradicting rational argument that opposes what the Qur'an [truly] implies but it did not occur to the interpreter."[39] On the other hand, in case of reason, Rāzī appears quite confident: "This [provisional nature of revelational arguments] stands in contrast to the rational arguments, which consist of premises whose sufficiency does not rely on our lack of knowledge of their invalidity."[40]

The Purpose of the Principle

At first blush, the principle of interpretation seems to represent near-complete triumph of reason in Sunni *kalām*, and it appears that the *mutakallimūn*, in particular in their most developed form such as in Rāzī, are little different from the *falāsifa*, for whom revelation was intended only for the commoners and the intellectually challenged – the real truth was as revealed by *falsafa*. Yet the *mutakallimūn* – who were, after all, faithful Muslims who saw themselves as the defenders of Sunni Islam – could not live with that either. Even though its internal logic is universally applicable, the *qānūn* was meant to justify their denial of certain qur'anic attributes of God that sounded anthropomorphist or contradicted their theodicy. Early Muslim authorities (*salaf*), and following them the anti-*kalām* traditionalists and the early Ashʿarīs, had accepted these attributes as such with the doctrinal caveat of *bilā kayf* (without inquiring about modality). However, later *mutakallimūn* could not accept this attitude. For many, the justification for emphasizing metaphorical interpretation was the desire to safeguard *tanzīh* (God's transcendence or de-anthropomorphism). The critics of *kalām* did not find this explanation sufficient, and criticisms were heaped from both sides, from the *falāsifa* as well as the traditionalists, for this inconsistency and arbitrariness.

This need for *qānūn* arose from the fact that the rational path that was necessary to establish God's existence, and the truthfulness of revelation

[39] Quoted by Ibn Taymiyya in *Dar'(S)*, 1:21, 5:331.
[40] Ibid.

required limiting what revelation could say or, at least, mean. Now, it is understandable immediately that revelation could not, for instance, claim that the God who has sent this revelation does not exist. However, what else revelation could say now depended on whether it agreed with the rational system.[41] The system that had been recruited to defend revelation, in other words, had silenced, or at least severely limited, revelation itself. The *falāsifa*, for their part, had upped the stakes significantly; one was either with them or an ignorant, superstitious fool (and, the worst insult, a commoner). Firstly, they preached the unity of all philosophical truth – it was not a particular system of reasoning that the prorevelation folks had to contend against, but against rational, apodictic truth. Particularly in the hands of Fārābī and Ibn Sīnā, all true philosophers, most of all Aristotle and Plato, were presented as mutually agreed; any real disagreement between the great masters of philosophy would have weakened the case for it. Secondly, the theistic *falāsifa*, in particular Ibn Sīnā, insisted on the compatibility of Greek philosophy with monotheism. The great Greek masters of philosophy, in their view, had been all monotheists – a contention that both justified philosophy and reassured Muslim theologians.[42]

The price of the apparent philosophical coherence proved not to be marginal. The threat this approach posed to scripture in the medieval intellectual milieu cannot be easily appreciated by the inhabitants of a skeptical modern world running dangerously low on apodictic truths. In the Neoplatonist-Aristotelianism of the *falāsifa*, there existed a plethora of such indisputable truths, ranging from metaphysical realities to the structure of the material world. Intellect (*ʿaql*), as noted earlier, was seen as an essence that received truths from the Active Intellect – which was inexorably tied to the First Intellect in a necessitarian cosmos. The truths it received, if grasped properly, were absolute truths. Error, of course, was possible, but it was also avoidable and could hardly be imagined in the agreement of the greatest masters. The truths that these masters arrived at had to be absolute, and it reflected the very structure of the cosmos. This view of intellect was fundamentally at odds, as noted earlier, with the traditionalist view of intellect as a human faculty (*gharīza*): an instrument, like seeing or hearing, that may provide correct data to the extent of its limited reach, but whose propositions have no absoluteness. Its propositions resulted from empirical human encounter with a

[41] M. Fakhry, "Muslim Proofs for the Existence of God," *MW* 47 (1957): 133–45.
[42] M. Fakhry, *Al-Fārābī* (Oneworld, 2002), 35–8.

contingent, created universe that could have been created differently by divine omnipotence. In the *falāsifa*'s best conciliatory attempts with the Abrahamic tradition, the most that could be conceded (as Ibn Sīnā did) was that the prophets were such true philosophers with added facility in imagining and rhetorically conveying effective myths to the masses. In the Avicennan attempt at synthesis, Hellenistic metaphysics remained the organizing principle and revelation was unabashedly reduced to useful myths – noble lies – designed to elicit proper conduct on the part of the common masses, who were incapable of grasping philosophical truth. God, accordingly, became an abstract principle rather than a being with attributes and will. Sunni theologians did not accept the *falāsifa*'s concept of God – Ghazālī declared the Avicennan view of God tantamount to disbelief – but they could not find a way to entirely abjure it either.[43]

Furthermore, the theologians underestimated the difficulty of establishing rational propositions that could be shown to be apodictic and indisputable. Reasoners could, and did, disagree on precisely what could be established through indisputable rational proof. The attempts to mark a line between the cases when the apparent meaning of scripture could be trusted and when the *qānūn* would have to be invoked proved far from convincing. In his famous treatise *Incoherence of the Philosophers*, Ghazālī deemed philosophers like Ibn Sīnā heretical disbelievers because of three principles: their doctrine of the eternity of the world, their denial of God's knowledge of particulars, and their denial of bodily resurrection after death.[44] All of these principles contradicted the qur'anic concept of God so fundamentally that the difference could not be simply interpreted away. However, if Ghazālī was willing to reinterpret clear qur'anic verses – for instance, those that implied God's love, settling on the throne, or human free will – on the basis of rational objections, Ghazālī's philosophical critics argued that their principles too were firmly established by reason. If the great theologian were to fairly apply his own *qānūn al-ta'wīl*, there is no reason why the parts of the Qur'an that contradicted

[43] See the later discussion of Ghazālī's works, in particular his indebtedness for an Avicennan view of God in works like *Mishkāt*.

[44] M. Marmura, *The Incoherence of the Philosophers*, xx; Griffel, *Al-Ghazālī's Philosophical Theology* (Oxford University Press, 2009), 7. Frank Griffel argues that although Ghazālī declared Ibn Sīnā an apostate for denying God's knowledge of particulars and two other specific doctrines, this limited rejection along with larger embrace of the Avicennan system in fact "opened the Muslim theological discourse to the many other important positions held by the *falāsifa*," and Ghazālī remained fundamentally indebted to Ibn Sīnā for his philosophical system.

these doctrines should not be interpreted away as well. Ghazālī was in fact too sharp not to have anticipated this objection, and in his *Tahāfut* offers justification for his selective application of the *qānūn al-ta'wīl* – that justification, once again, was found wanting by the *falāsifa* as well as the traditionalists.[45]

Reason before Revelation, and After

For our purpose, it is the implications and not cogency or rational justification of the *qānūn* that are relevant. The most important conceptual problem for the theologians was how the privileging of reason could be deployed to defend the authority of revelation, which is what they had set out to do. The response was to insist on a crucial distinction between the capacity of reason in matters prior to revelation and those after it. Recall that Rāzī indicates quite clearly that the *qānūn* applies only in the case of "foundational matters" (*masā'il uṣūliyya*), namely, the theological or theoretical questions necessary to establish the truthfulness of revelation.

We notice the concern to limit reason in postrevelation (i.e., real) life as early as al-Ash'arī and Bāqillānī, whose rationalist inclinations were rather limited and amounted to interpreting metaphorically only a few divine attributes. They charge reason with establishing the existence of God, but then, in a canonical point of opposition to the Mu'tazila, find reason utterly incapable of arriving on its own at ethical truths or the distinction between the good and evil nature of acts. Indeed, they find reason incapable of even recognizing a true messenger of God from a pretender (because it cannot tell a good from a bad message on its own), and hence rest the entirety of belief on the production of a true miracle by a prophet.[46] (This also created a problem, because miracle is a violation of natural causality, and they denied causality to save God's omnipotence; a solution, however, was found in the concept of *'āda*, divine custom.[47]) In theology, in any case, the later Ash'arīs increasingly leaned toward reason at the expense of the literal meaning of revelation, but the stronger they leaned toward rationalism in theology, the more distinct a line they needed beyond which reason had no

45 Griffel, *Philosophical*, 214f.

46 F. Griffel, "Al-Ghazālī's Concept of Prophecy," *Arabic Sciences and Philosophy* 14 (2004): 101–2.

47 Jackson, *Islamic Law*, 30–1; Gibb, *Studies*, 172.

authority, or else, they wisely feared, their own system would demolish faith in revelation.

The distinction between rational/foundational and revelational/religious domains of reasoning has caught the attention of recent scholarship, although its implications have not. Arguing for Ibn Tūmart's (d. 524/1130) intellectual connection with the Niẓāmiyya *madrasa* of Juwaynī and Ghazālī, Frank Griffel writes:

> The strict methodological distinction between the rational sciences [*ʿulūm ʿaqliyya*] and the religious sciences [*ʿulūm dīniyya*], and among the latter is *fiqh*, or between the *maʿqūl* [rational] and the *manqūl* [revealed] is more likely to go back to al-Ghazālī in his influential textbook on the methods of jurisprudence. In al-Ghazālī, just as in Ibn Tūmart, a rationalist position in the rational sciences leads to strict methodological restrictions for the use of reason (*ʿaql*) in the religious sciences.[48]

Griffel reasons, however, that this irony owed itself to the fact that an investigation of the limits of reason leads "both thinkers to acknowledge that there is a surplus of information on the side of revelation which reason cannot produce. The truth of this surplus knowledge must be accepted once the truthfulness (*ṣidq*) of the messenger has been established."[49] However, the existence of surplus knowledge does not explain the distinction between theological and religious/jurisprudential domains. For if the issue is simply the surplus of knowledge on revelation's side, the attitude toward law and theology should be the same: Revelation prevails in matters that reason cannot know. Why embrace this odd epistemology that regards reason to be more capable of speculating about unseen matters with certitude than about the normative status of the matters of the empirical world? This distinction, in fact, is necessary to deal with the consequences of the *qānūn*, which in turn is the necessary outcome of the torn philosophical worldview of later *kalām*: It sought to establish theological matters in an Aristotelian-Avicennan thought-world while also justifying revelation's dominance in practical religious life. Revelational claims in theoretical matters disturb that edifice, as does the application of unaided reason in postrevelation (religious, legal, ethical, political) life.

[48] F. Griffel, "Ibn Tūmart's Rational Proof for God's Existence and Unity, and His Connection to the Niẓāmiyya *Madrasa* in Baghdad," in P. Cressier, M. Fierro, and L. Molina (eds.), *Los Almohades: problemas y perspectivas* (Consejo Superior de Investigationes Científicas, 2005), 2:804–5.

[49] Ibid.

LOSING FAITH IN REASON

In the following, I document what I contend were the intellectual and psychological consequences of the settlement reflected in the *qānūn*. An intellectual and personal crisis of sorts is palpable already in masters of philosophized *kalām* like Juwaynī. In his earlier writings, Juwaynī had inclined increasingly toward the Muʿtazila on the issue of divine attributes (much diversity was still possible within the Ashʿarī school so long as one adhered to the school's position on staple issues).[50] Later, however, Juwaynī is reported to have relinquished his confidence in reason and acknowledged that his efforts to rationally pin down God's attributes had been frustrated. In *al-Niẓāmiyya*, the last of his works, Juwaynī claims to have reverted to the "*madhhab* of the *salaf*," which he describes as *tafwīḍ* (leaving the meanings of revelation in matters of divine attributes to God, implying their unknowability).[51] Among other things, Juwaynī's opinion also seems to have changed regarding the intellectual capacity and perspicacity of early Muslims (*salaf*). In an earlier book, *al-Kāfiya fī 'l-jadal*, he had written: "[The *salaf*] realized that there will be after them those whom God will choose for excellence in endeavor, greater understanding, perspicacity and intelligence … they therefore did not engage in depth (with contentious issues) and remained brief and satisfied with allusions."[52] In a later work, however, he makes a different plea: "[The *salaf*] forbade indulging in ambiguities and hair-splitting of confusing issues … sophistry in responses to questions, focusing rather on encouraging people towards piety, benevolence, not harming others, and being obedient to God according to one's capacity.… They were the most intelligent of people and best in speech."[53]

The notes of Juwaynī's terminal regret preserved by his students are even more dramatic, and perhaps not without some embellishment: "Be my witness that I have retracted every opinion that opposes the Sunna, and I die upon that which the old women of Nishapur die upon!" And: "Had I anticipated my affairs, I would not have indulged in *kalām*."[54]

[50] Juwaynī even challenged the Muʿtazila that they could not produce a proof of denial of God's being a body (*jism*) as effective as his (Al-Juwaynī, *al-Shāmil*, 414; Maḥmūd, 615).

[51] Juwaynī, *Niẓāmiyya*, 21, 32–4; Maḥmūd, 618.

[52] Juwaynī, *al-Kāfiya fī'l-jadal*, 346–7, quoted in Maḥmūd, 630.

[53] Juwaynī, *al-Ghiyāthī*, 190–1.

[54] Dhahabī, *Siyar aʿlām al-nubalā'*, 18:463, 474; Subkī, *Ṭabaqāt al-shāfiʿiyya*, 5:191; Maḥmūd, 2:157.

Another one is yet more revealing: "I have read fifty thousand (works) in fifty thousand (topics), then I left the people of Islam with their Islam and their exoteric sciences and dived into the deep ocean and into what the people of Islam have forbidden – all in search for the truth – and I used to run in the past from *taqlīd*. But now I have returned to the truth: you must hold fast to the religion of the old women."[55] Juwaynī's early fascination with reason and *kalām* followed by a distinct sense of loss of confidence in reason is noticeable both in his writings and private confessions.

Ghazālī's has both fascinated and puzzled his readers by the brilliance of his spiritual and intellectual insight and his complex attitude toward the main religious tendencies of his time. In particular, his attitude toward and debt to Avicennan philosophy has been long debated. Some of his interpreters ignore or deny his philosophical and esoteric writings.[56] Others, such as Richard Frank, have focused on his philosophical writings and his debt to Ibn Sīnā, and consider him essentially an Avicennan whose traditional Ashʿarī and pietistic Sufi commitments need either to be rejected or deemed merely a cover for his true doctrines.[57] The most comprehensive recent study of Ghazālī, by Frank Griffel, builds on Richard Frank's work, addresses the many objections raised against it, and concludes that Ghazālī indeed was fundamentally indebted to Avicennan cosmology but was able to reconcile his Ashʿarī commitments with it.[58] Impressive as Griffel's meticulous study is, it is not persuasive in its claim

[55] Ibid. Subkī, a staunch Ashʿarī apologist, attempts to explain these statements in a way so as to avoid the implications against Ashʿarī *kalām*, but does not question their authenticity.

[56] This traditional attitude is shared by many modern scholars; chiefly M. Watt, *Al-Ghazālī: The Muslim Intellectual* (ABC International Group, 2002); M. Marmura, "Ghazālī and Ashʿarism Revisited," *Arabic Sciences and Philosophy* 12 (2002): 101; H. Lazarus-Yafeh, *Studies in al-Ghazzālī* (Magnes Press, 1975); A. Dallal, "Ghazālī and the Perils of Interpretation," *JAOS* 122.4 (2002): 773–87. Griffel, *Philosophical*, attempts a thorough refutation of these views.

[57] Richard Frank, for instance, concludes that Ghazālī's theology was "superficial" and "incomplete"; that he disguised his true beliefs, was increasingly critical of the Ashʿarī school, consistently deplored "the theoretical worthlessness of ordinary *kalām*," and finally, was greatly influenced by Avicennan Neoplatonist cosmology, idem, *Al-Ghazāli and the Ashʿarī School* (Duke University Press, 1994), 98–9. Ahmad Dallal's in-depth review of Frank's work shows that a closer reading of Ghazālī renders many, but not all, of Frank's claims unwarranted (Dallal, "Ghazālī,").

[58] Griffel argues that Ghazālī had accepted the influence of Avicennan philosophy in those domains where the Ashʿarī doctrine had been silent – even if that importation has contradicted the general spirit of the orthodox doctrine (Griffel, "Al-Ghazālī's Concept of Prophecy").

of having arrived at the singular coherent framework that explains all of Ghazālī's works and commitments. I have argued elsewhere that such a framework, as many of Ghazālī's medieval and modern interpreters have insisted, simply did not exist. In order to claim having ultimately found the key to all of Ghazālī, Griffel is forced to ignore or deny too many crucial features of Ghazālī's oeuvre: his thoroughgoing elitism and esotericism as a means to justify teaching different doctrines to different levels of people; contradictions in his works in various phases of his life that cannot be explained away even as esotericism (Griffel rejects Ghazālī's own confessional story of some kind of conversion); his frequent expressions of disillusionment not so much with *kalām* but with reason itself; and finally, his turn to experiential, mystical knowledge: *ʿilm al-mukāshafa* (science of divine disclosure).[59]

Ghazālī's skepticism toward *kalām* is rooted not in some philosophical system as higher theology, but – as Ghazālī contends time and again – the limitation of human reason itself. When his writings are taken seriously in the light of his intellectual dilemmas, it seems that Ghazālī persistently doubted the effectiveness of *kalām* while all the time embracing its inevitability. In *Iḥyāʾ*, his most important and mature work, he writes:

> One should do one's utmost to protect oneself from hearing anything of disputation [*jadal*] and *kalām*.... Compare the belief [*ʿaqīda*] of the people of piety and righteousness among the commoners with the belief of a *kalām* scholar or one who engages in [scholarly] disputations, and you will find that the belief of the commoner in its stability is like a lofty mountain which is not shaken by any earthquake or thunder, while the belief of the *mutakallim* who guards his belief with the categories of disputations is like a thread hanging loose in the wind which the breeze bends now in one direction now in another. The only exception [to this weakening of faith] is someone who hears from a *mutakallim* a proof of an article of faith and then holds fast to that proof without argument [*taqlīdan*] just as he holds fast to that article of faith without argument. [60]

This passage is followed immediately by a lengthy discussion of the benefits and harms of *kalām*. After an impassioned argument that *kalām* is nothing but a natural response to the increasingly demanding intellectual opposition to the truth in his time, nothing but the employment of legitimate reason to defend the articles of faith, Ghazālī moves on to another surprising series of confessions. He writes:

[59] Anjum, "Cultural."
[60] *Iḥyāʾ*, 1:127.

> [In the use of *kalām*] there is benefit and there is harm, and it is prohibited in a time or place in which it is harmful. Its harm is that it raises doubts and shakes beliefs, dislodging them from certitude and firmness. That is what occurs in the beginning, and the restitution of [the earlier state of certitude] is ever doubtful, and it is different for different people. This is the harm of *kalām* for the people of the True Creed [of Ahl al-Sunna]. There is an additional harm in it for heretical innovators, which is to reassure them in their innovative heresies and install them firmly in their hearts, for *kalām* incites them and sharpens their appetite to insist on these heresies.
>
> As for its benefit: it might be supposed [by some] that its benefit is the unveiling of the ultimate truths and the knowledge of their exact nature. Alas, *kalām* does not deliver this noble promise. It may be that confusion and misguidance in it are greater than any unveiling or attainment of knowledge. If you heard this from a *ḥadīth* scholar [*muḥaddith*] or a Ḥashwī [the *kalām* and *falsafa* scholars' derogatory term for those who rejected *kalām*], you might think that people are simply enemies of what they do not know. But hear this from someone who has known *kalām* by experience and after having known its reality and having been completely submerged into it, has detested it ... and has finally reached *the conclusion that the path to the realities of knowledge are shut from this direction.* By my life, *kalām* is not below unveiling, defining or explaining a matter or two, but rarely does it help in case of clear matters that are almost better understood before delving into the arguments of *kalām*!
>
> But its benefit is only one: guarding of the creed that we have previously elaborated for the common people and protecting it against the heretics' skepticism by various types of disputations. For the commoner is shaken by the disputation of a heretic even if it is invalid; while confronting the invalid with the invalid repels it.[61]

Note that in the same discourse, *kalām* is deemed necessary to defend faith against its newfangled intellectual adversaries but simultaneously treacherous and untrustworthy – indeed, a hotbed of doubts and heresies. If the sole purpose of *kalām* is to defend the faith of the commoner, it is not only superfluous but harmful, for it only incites doubts. The contradiction is inescapable, but it cannot be explained by the idea of diachronic development in Ghazālī's thought, for just before these statements in *Iḥyā'*, Ghazālī has treated us with a defense of Ashʿarī *kalām* and its theological positions:

> And the line of moderation [*iqtiṣād*] between this libertarianism [*inḥilāl*] [of the Muʿtazila and the *falāsifa*] and the rigidity of the Ḥanbalīs [*jumūd al-ḥanābila*] is thin and obscure; no one attains it except by God's grace, those who know these matters by divine light, not by tradition [*bi nūr ilāhi lā bi 'l-samāʿ*]. Then, after the secrets of these matters have been unveiled to them, they look at the words of

[61] *Iḥyā'*, 1:130–1.

the scripture, and whatever agrees with what they have observed with the light of certainty, they approve, and whatever disagrees with it, they interpret metaphorically [*fa mā wāqafa mā shāhadūhu bi nūr al-yaqīn, qarrarūhu wa mā khālafa awwalūhu*].[62]

Thus, the Ashʿarī *kalām* is not the final answer to the problem of true knowledge – but it is the best answer in the *objective*, *public* realm. We are forced at this point to take seriously the observation by many scholars that Ghazālī's interaction with Bāṭinī esotericism had been influential, even formative, for him, although the nature and extent of that influence have been disputed.[63] According to Josef van Ess, Ghazālī recruited Aristotelian syllogism in order to fortify theological speculation against error in response to the Bāṭinī claim that only an infallible *imām* could avert error. Sufism was only a cure for "those who were not gifted for speculation." [64] Not without some validity, this explanation is untenable in one respect, which is that Ghazālī's own intellectual journey follows the same course of frustration and turn to Sufism; it was not just the ungifted and the feeble minded who needed that outlet: It was the result of the fact that reason (including *falsafa*) was fundamentally incapable of furnishing certitude about ultimate divine truths.

Ghazālī's view is unapologetically esoteric and mystical in the sense that mystical experience does not merely add delightful certitude to one's rational assent to scriptural teachings; rather, it furnishes qualitatively different knowledge not found in any books[65]:

[The esoteric knowledge, *ʿilm al-mukāshafa*] is the light that appears in the heart when it is purified and purged of its blameworthy attributes, and by virtue of that knowledge many matters of which one used to hear only the names and know only the general meaning open up to him.... This knowledge is not written in books nor those whom God has granted some of it may speak to anyone of it except with others like them by way of reminder and with secrecy – such is the esoteric knowledge.[66]

[62] *Iḥyā'*, 1: 139.

[63] M. Hodgson, *Venture of Islam: Conscience and History in a World Civilization*. 3 vols. (University of Chicago Press, 1974), 2:183–92; Watt, *Muslim Intellectual*, 82–6; F. Mitha, *Al-Ghazālī and the Ismailis: A Debate on Reason and Authority in Medieval Islam* (I. B. Tauris, 2002), 99.

[64] J. van Ess, "Scepticism in Islamic Religious Thought," in C. Mālik (ed.), *God and Men in Contemporary Islamic Thought* (Beirut, 1972), 95–7.

[65] For a distinction between mystical and nonmystical Sufism, see O. Anjum, "Sufism without Mysticism?"

[66] *Iḥyā'*, 1:20–1; Maḥmūd, 2:178.

For Ghazālī, the path to faith and knowledge beyond reason was *mukāshafa* (mystical experience). However, in the move from reason to *mukāshafa* as the defense or proof of the right doctrines, a new dilemma emerges. Once the subjectivity of the ultimate source of knowledge and certitude is acknowledged, how could the truth be separated from false doctrines such that heresies are combated, orthodoxy upheld, and the chaos of subjectivity averted? As a Sunni theologian, Ghazālī was eminently interested in that endeavor, and hence, despite his disparagement of *kalām*, he never abjured it.

The age-old solutions to the problem of esoteric chaos has been hierarchy, election, and elitism. In this respect Ghazālī's encounter with the Bāṭinīs was formative and gave him a taste for Neoplatonist doctrines as well as a new depth of esoteric elitism. In his *Mīzān al-ʿamal*, written most likely after his main tract against the Bāṭinīs, *al-Mustaẓhirī*,[67] the spiritual stratification and difference between private and public knowledge that are the hallmark of the Bāṭinī doctrine (and later of mystical Sufis) are explicitly defended. To the quandary of his seemingly multiple commitments that must have baffled his students and admirers, Ghazālī responded that every master (*kāmil*) has three schools (*madhhabs*): first, what a man inherits from his teachers and parents; second, what one teaches to his students in accordance to their varying levels; and third, "what a man believes privately between himself and God Almighty and no one else but God knows about it; and he does not mention it except to those who share the knowledge that one has, or has reached such a level that that knowledge could be received and understood by him."[68]

Note also that the third level, that between "perfect men" and God, is "private" because of the immaturity or incapacity of the commoner to grasp the true beliefs of the philosopher-scholar. Ghazālī does not shy away in his *Iḥyāʾ* from using the word *bāṭin* – the linchpin of the Bāṭinī doctrine – to characterize this highest form of knowing: "This knowledge

[67] G. Hourani, "A Revised Chronology of al-Ghazālī's Writings," *JAOS* 104.2 (1984): 294–5; Mitha, 100–101.

[68] Ghazālī, *Mīzān al-ʿamal*, ed. Sulayman Dunya (Dār al-Maʿārif, 1964), 405–9. Griffel, *Philosophical*, 359n45, misunderstands this passage of Ghazālī and concludes that here he actually rejects esotericism. For a detailed refutation, see O. Anjum, "Cultural Memory." The conventional reading of the passage by several traditional and modern scholars, that Ghazālī indeed not only favored but espoused the three-*madhhab* opinion, is correct. This reading calls into question Griffel's basic thesis that Ghazālī had worked out a coherent system harmonizing Avicennan philosophy and Ashʿarism and hence did not need esotericism.

[acquired by *ʿilm al-mukāshafa* of the unseen realities of faith] is not written in books nor those whom God has granted some of it may speak to anyone of it except with others like them by way of reminder and with secrecy – such is the esoteric knowledge [*ʿilm al-bāṭin*]."[69] Of the various mystical works Ghazālī wrote in the period after *Iḥyāʾ* and before his final retreat to his birth town of Ṭūs, one work, *Mishkāt al-anwār*,[70] further elaborates his mystical doctrine, employs explicitly Neoplatonist vocabulary, and interprets qurʾanic verses as well as the purpose of the spiritual endeavor in a clearly Neoplatonist way: The men nearest to God are not those like the *salaf* adorned with the qur'anic virtues of piety, fear, patience, struggle, and worship, but rather those who deem God as acting through celestial spheres or even further removed from acting than that.[71] A similar debt to Avicennan doctrine in a different work, *Maʿārij al-quds*, prompted Fazlur Rahman to comment that Ghazālī is profoundly incoherent because he excommunicates philosophers like Ibn Sīnā in some of his writings, "[b]ut then follows the chapter on the 'characteristics of prophecy,' which is almost word to word borrowed from Avicenna."[72] Ghazālī's detractors, in particular Ibn Rushd (Averroes), not surprisingly berated him for "hypocritically rejecting, or pretending to reject, on certain occasions what the *Mishkāt* and other works of Ghazālī espoused."[73]

It is difficult, in the light of the foregoing, to disagree with the conclusion reached by Watt, Hodgson, and Mitha that Ghazālī's encounter with the Ismāʿīlī/Taʿlīmī doctrine was to have deep influence on him, and that he incorporated Neoplatonist elements and esotericism from such encounters into the Ashʿarī tradition. It is instructive, argues Mitha, that "Al-Ghazālī's turning towards Sufism was to begin in earnest very soon after he had written the *K. al-Mustaẓhirī*," – a treatise that he wrote to show the errors of the Taʿlīmī doctrine and bolster al-Mustaẓhir as the rightful caliph and *imām*.[74] The problem of any mystical doctrine is to justify its claims that cannot be defended by objective reason, and elitism

[69] *Iḥyā'*, 1:20–1; Maḥmūd, 2:178.

[70] Griffel, *Philosophical*, 9, points out the centrality of *Mishkāt* in prompting scholars in the twentieth century to reconsider Ghazālī's traditional self-presentation and suggests that it was written after *Iḥyāʾ* (ibid., 264–6).

[71] Ghazālī, *Mishkāt*, 27; Anjum, "Cultural."

[72] Rahman, *Prophecy in Islam*, 98, quoted in Griffel, *Prophecy*, 138.

[73] H. Davidson, *Alfarabi, Avicenna, and Averroes on Intellect* (Oxford University Press, 1992), 130.

[74] Mitha, 99–100.

is its way to solve the problem of authority. In the case of Ghazālī, as for the Bāṭinites, esotericism and elitism served precisely those ends.

The disillusionment with reason and turn to mysticism found in *Iḥyā'* and the *Mishkāt* both intensified and took on a different color in Ghazālī's very last work, *Iljām al-ʿawāmm ʿan ʿilm al-kalām* (*Restraining the Commoners against the Science of Kalām*), an alternative manuscript title for the same text being *Risāla fī madhāhib ahl al-salaf* (*Epistle on the Teachings of the Salaf*).[75] The message of *Iljām* is plain: All commoners, including the scholars of Islam, must avoid engaging in *kalām* and its search for rational proof of God and revelation, restrict themselves to the arguments provided in the Qur'an, and follow the path of the *salaf*, who were to restrain the commoners from such questions. The commoners for him include all scholars of Islam, including those of *kalām*; the only exceptions to this prohibition are those

> who have exclusively devoted themselves to the learning of diving in the oceans of inner knowledge [*maʿrifa*], spending all their lives in that pursuit, turning away from this world and its desires ... abiding by all the prescriptions and etiquettes of the Sharīʿa, emptying their hearts from all else but God the Most High, in rejection and scorn not only for this world but even for the hereafter and the Highest Paradise.... Such are the divers in the ocean of inner knowledge. And even these, with all this, are in grave danger which destroys nine out of ten of them.[76]

It is peculiar here that even a scholar of *kalām* is not supposed to engage in interpretation of reports about God's attributes, leaving us to wonder what else on earth one might do as a *mutakallim*. The only group that has at best a 10-percent chance of properly interpreting these references consists of those who not only abandon this world but also care little about the next, and who devote themselves exclusively to God. The *falāsifa*, incidentally, are entirely absent from this treatise. Much of the case in *Iljām*, it is clear from the title, is set primarily against the other Ashʿarīs, especially those who would impose the obligation of speculative reasoning and metaphorical interpretation on commoners. In a pedagogical dialectic with the Ashʿarīs, who might have found his dismantling of the Ashʿarī tradition troubling, the *mutakallim* objector asks: What if the commoner would not incline toward the creed except by rational evidence? Ghazālī responds that only the evidence given in the Qur'ān may be given to the commoner. What is harmful and indeed a *bidʿa*

[75] Griffel, *Philosophical*, 266.
[76] Ghazālī, *Iljām* (Dār al-Kitāb al-ʿArabī), 49–50.

(a blameworthy innovation) is what the *mutakallims* have undertaken beyond presenting the qur'anic arguments.[77]

In a fasion that is hardly any different from the *ḥadīth* group, Ghazālī then proceeds to destroy the only defense he had himself provided for *kalām* in *Iḥyā'*, namely, the changed times since the early pristine age and the need for using new rational tools against the newfangled heresies. He states that *kalām* is not merely unnecessary but harmful hair-splitting, which the early *salaf* (the Companions) did not develop or even hint at. This silence, he insists, was not because they were incapable of doing so or because they avoided all theoretical or abstract matters – for they did indeed engage in abstract matters in the domain of law – but because they truly found this type of argumentation about theological matters harmful. Indeed, Ghazālī writes, they needed theological arguments against the Jews and Christians, but they preferred using "straight Qur'ānic arguments followed by the sword and the arrow" rather than develop or engage in *kalām*. Furthermore, rational defense misguides two for each one that it may guide, whereas the way of the *salaf* was to stop at the evidence given by the Qur'an and then move to "the whip and the sword" for those who did not feel convinced.[78] One can hear in these far more measured words the echoes of his teacher's disillusionment with reason itself.[79]

Ghazālī's solution to the problem of faith and certitude was not reason but direct experience, hedged against unbridled subjectivist claims by his resort to esotericism and elitism. As far as reason was concerned, the dominant paradigm for Ghazālī, at least before turning completely away from it in his last work (*Iljām*), seems to have been an example he often uses in explaining his political doctrine: to eat carrion is prohibited in Sharīʿa, but to commit suicide is worse, hence we must eat the carrion. Reason, before *Iljām*, appears to be just like politics, that is, the carrion that the Muslim theologian must eat, whereas in *Iljām*, it is a

[77] Ibid., 57, 59–60.

[78] Ibid., 61.

[79] Griffel, *Philosophical*, 266–7, argues that *Iljām* "is the work of a rationalist theologian, exploring how the rationalism of the religious elite can be taught to the ordinary people without causing any damage" to their afterlife or proper practice. I remain unconvinced, however. For one, Griffel gives Ghazālī's definition of the commoners as "all those people who have not studied rationalist theology (*kalām*) and who would be unable to present arguments as to why the anthropomorphic descriptions of God in revelation cannot literally be true." However, Ghazālī's definition reproduced here explicitly includes the scholars of *kalām* among the commoners, and the description of the only exception matches that of the mystics, not theologians or philosophers.

veritable poison that must be avoided at all costs except by those whose subjectivities have already utterly surrendered to God.

The next great Ashʿarī theologian, Rāzī, brilliant and inquisitive, and driven by curiosity to a range of intellectual pursuits from *kalām* to *falsafa* and even magic, began as a rational optimist but exhibited in his final years a deeply conflicted attitude toward all rational enterprise.[80] Like Ghazālī, Rāzī's doctrine is deeply elitist. He too divided men into the commoners (*al-ʿawāmm*) and the elite, but his stratification appears more intellectual than spiritual. He writes in his *Tafsīr*:

> The Qur'an consists of address to the commoners and the elite all at once, and the nature of commoners is averse to excessive effort in grasping truths of things, so if one of them hears affirmation of an existent that has no body or direction, nor can it be pointed to, they think that this amounts to non-existence and negation, so they then fall into denial (or accuse such a person of denial of God's attributes) – hence it is better for them to be addressed in words that signify something in accordance with what they can imagine or their estimative faculties can grasp – and in it there is an element of clear truth.[81]

Also:

> [A prophet] should prohibit them from investigating these defiles [of the true nature of divinity and such] and from wading into these subtleties, except for one who is highly intelligent and accomplished, since, by his profound intelligence, he will comprehend the realities of things. [82]

Not only can ordinary intellects not understand the divine nature accessible to the highly intelligent philosophers, but such commoners needs myths confirming human capacity, free will, the existence of good and evil acts, and causality in order to act ethically: "[The prophet] also shows to them man's being a producer [of acts] and an agent, capable of both acting and omitting and of both good and evil; and he does that to the maximum extent. For were he to present them pure determinism, they would abandon it and not pay any attention to it."[83] God informs the commoners of his nature and attributes by using some anthropomorphic language because that is the only way they can grasp the truth. This is not to say that those who ponder God's words more deeply and in proper context

80 Whereas some scholars have denied the attribution of Rāzī's work on magic and astrology, *al-Sirr al-maktūm fī asrār al-nujūm*, Al-Zarkan confirms its attribution to Rāzī, and Ayman Shihadeh includes it in the list of his writings (Shihadeh, *Teleological*, 267).

81 Rāzī, *Tafsir*, 7:172; Maḥmūd, 2:207.

82 Shihadeh's translation of Rāzī's *al-Maṭālib* in idem, *Teleological*, 145–7.

83 Ibid.

are bound to understand more, or that one ought to realize limitations of human experience and language in interpreting the divine message. Rather, these realities are not beyond human grasp but simply beyond the grasp of the commoners, and the elite who know these realities are those capable of appreciating *falsafa*. Once the apodictic truths have been established about God and his nature, the elite can then interpret away the words of the Qur'an metaphorically, hence the *qānūn al-ta'wīl*.

Ayman Shehadeh argues that Rāzī's later writings show an unmistakable reversal of his most fundamental earlier positions. Al-Zarkān examines these contradictions and finally prefers to explain them as a diachronic development in Rāzī's thought.[84] However, in contrast with his forceful formulation of the *qānūn*, his later writings express sentiments that recall the confessions of Juwaynī. In his final Waṣiyya (Testament), Rāzī wrote: "I have acquainted myself of the ways of *kalām* and methods of the philosophers, and I have not seen in them usefulness that compares with the usefulness that I have found in the Qur'an."[85]

Many specific examples can be adduced to substantiate this general attitude. Rāzī generally held in the majority of his works and formulated in the *qānūn* that traditional proofs (*adilla naqliyya*) can never lead to definitive knowledge and certitude in any matter, hence they cannot be used to argue in theology.[86] In *Nihāyat al-ʿuqūl*, however, he makes a surprising U-turn. On the issue of God's hearing (*samʿ*) and seeing (*baṣar*), two of the seven attributes that the Ashʿarīs confirm without *ta'wīl* (metaphorical interpretation) or *taʿṭīl* (denial) – because, the Ashʿarī view holds, these can be rationally demonstrated – Rāzī shows skepticism about the "rational" proofs and says that the only right way to argue for these attributes for God is by the scripture (*nuṣūṣ al-samʿ*). Anticipating the objection that he himself has consistently argued, that "in these creedal matters that require definitude it is impermissible to argue with the apparent meaning of [qurʾanic] verses," he responds: "We have not mentioned this objection here because of our belief that it cannot be answered, indeed, *the answer to it is the consensus of the* umma *on the permissibility of adhering to*

[84] Muḥammad Ṣāliḥ al-Zarkān, *Fakhr al-Din al-Rāzī wa ārā'uh al-kalāmiyya wa'l-falsafiyya* (Dār al-Fikr), 573. He acknowledges, however, his intention to avoid positing contradictions (616). Maḥmūd questions al-Zarkan's conclusion and argues that al-Zarkan's own research is sufficient to establish the presence of fundamental inconsistencies in Rāzī's commitments in all parts of his career (Maḥmūd, 677).

[85] Rāzī, *Al-Waṣiyya fī ʿuyūn al-anbā'*, 466; Maḥmūd, 697.

[86] Rāzī, *Asās al-taqdīs*, 172–82; idem, *al-Muḥaṣṣal* and *al-Maḥṣūl fī uṣūl al-fiqh* qtd. in Maḥmūd, 695.

the texts of the Book and the Sunna in these matters of definitude."[87] In his *Tafsīr*, he writes in the same vein, "It has been thus established that the certitude of the *mutakallimūn* that divine love cannot mean but His intention to reward is not sustainable, for they have no definitive proof of it; all that can be said is that, other than God's will, no other attribute can be rationally established and hence must be denied, but we have shown in our book *Nihāyat al-ʿuqūl* that this is a weak and invalid argument."[88] In *al-Maṭālib al-ʿāliya*, he ends his chapter on rational arguments for the existence of God with the following comments:

We end this chapter with an ending of great benefit, and that is that the arguments that wise men [*ḥukamā'*, philosophers] and the *mutakallimūn* have mentioned, even if they are perfect [*kāmila*] and strong, [pale in comparison to] the arguments mentioned in the Qur'an which to me are closer to the truth and soundness. For complex arguments, due to their very complexity, open doors of doubts and multiplicity of questions, while the end-result of the way that occurs in the Qur'an is only one, which is prohibition of digging deep and warning against opening the door of hearsay, and basing one's understanding and reasoning upon the myriad of proofs provided by the higher [heavenly] and lower [earthly] worlds. Whoever abjures prejudice [for philosophy] and experiences what I have will know that the truth is what I have just mentioned.[89]

In *Dhamm al-ladhdhāt*, the last of his works, Rāzī writes even more dramatically:

Know that after deep penetration into these defiles, and delving deeply (*taʿammuq*) in exploring the secrets of these matters, I have found that the most correct and advantageous [method] (*al-ṣawāb al-aṣlaḥ*) in this regard {of proving the existence of God and His attributes} to be the method of the holy Qur'an (*ṭarīqat al-Qur'ān*), the Noble Criterion (*Furqān*), which {consists in} the abandonment of delving deeply and inferring the existence of the Lord of the Worlds from the divisions of bodies in the heavens and the earth and {rather} proclaiming the greatness [of God] to the maximum extent (*al-mubālagha fī al-taʿẓīm*) *without wading into details.* [90]

It is notable that Rāzī seems to resign to what he considers the a priori and nonargumentative – and hence nonrational – nature of the qur'anic discourse, which he describes as being limited to "greatly stress[ing] the

[87] Rāzī, *Nihāyat al-ʿuqūl*, 160, quoted in Maḥmūd, 690.
[88] Rāzī, *al-Tafsīr al-kabīr* (Dār al-kutub al-ʿIlmiyya, n.d.), 14:132.
[89] Ibid., 198.
[90] Rāzī, *Dhamm al-ladhdhāt*, in Shihadeh, 263–5; trans. Ibid., 187 (emphasis added). The translation given is Shihadeh's except some modification, enclosed in braces, that I felt were necessary to clarify the passage.

greatness" of God without "digging deeply," which indicates that he does not see the Qur'an as providing sufficient rational arguments for the existence of God or prophethood. Shihadeh concludes that al-Rāzī's last work on ethics "underscores a pronounced moral and epistemological pessimism in the later stage of his career.... al-Rāzī appears to propose an alternative soteriology, which emphasizes spiritual discipline and guidance through the Qur'an."[91] This brief survey of the confessions of the greatest Ashʿarī theologians highlights the common contention that the way to certitude, faith, and bliss is in abjuring rational argument; Ghazālī romanticizes the unreasoned belief of the commoner or the mystic – despite his low opinion of the commoner elsewhere; Juwaynī longs for the faith of the old women of Nishapur; and Rāzī construes the Qur'an to be asking its readers to abandon *taʿammuq*, deep thinking. Clearly it is reason itself and not any flaw of *kalām* or its particular way of reasoning that is blamed by our theologians.

Admittedly, I have not exhausted what could be learned about the views of these theologians on reason. There has been a long-standing debate among Western scholars on where Ghazālī really stood and whether he contributed to the demise of reason, science, and philosophy in Islam. That is not a debate I have touched on, although my exposition in the foregoing has provided a way to better understand the issue by showing that attitudes toward reason in different domains of knowledge and practice may be quite independent of – even contradictory to – each other. Like all intellectual systems, medieval philosophy employed, even valorized, certain types and lines of reasoning but also limited certain other kinds. Being a thoroughly elitist and hierarchical system of thought, it undermined, even abhorred, the commonsense and practical reasoning of ordinary people. Ghazālī, it is now fairly established, embraced philosophical reasoning through much of his career as a tool for understanding metaphysical truths and attaining certainty, even as he criticized and qualified it.

When it comes to reason in empirical and mathematical science that did not touch on metaphysics or ethics, Ghazālī was an enthusiastic

[91] Ibid., 155–6; cf. Shihadeh, "The Mystic and the Sceptic in Fakhr al-Dīn al-Rāzī," in A. Shihadeh (ed.), *Sufism and Theology* (Edinburgh University Press, 2007), in which he notes the similarity between Ghazālī's turn to Sufism and Rāzī's, but then curiously remarks, "does al-Rāzī's turn towards Sufism signal a major defeat for the tradition of *kalām*, as Ibn Taymiyya would have it? Not entirely. This turn should be seen, first and foremost, as yet another sign of increasing eclecticism in the mainstream of the major traditions during this period" (118). The evidence presented previously suggests otherwise.

advocate. The metaphysical denial of causality or occasionalism had no direct bearing on one's belief in empirical scientific enterprise.[92]

The capacity of reason that the Ashʿarī theologians altogether rejected was ethics. Ethical subjectivism had of course been a staple doctrine of Ashʿarism against their old rationalist foes, the Muʿtazila. Yet the reasons Ghazālī and Rāzī had for endorsing this aspect of the Ashʿarī doctrine may have been their own. Safeguarding the supremacy of God's law remained for Ghazālī a nonnegotiable commitment throughout. (Recall that he was, after all, an accomplished jurist from the beginning of his career, and the ultimate saints in his very last work, *Iljām*, are fully Sharīʿa-compliant.) The ethical subjectivism of the early Ashʿarīs primarily had theological motivations, because their rivals, the Muʿtazila, far from threatening the law, had been its committed defenders. For Ghazālī, however, the stakes were different. In both the Bāṭinī esotericism and the *falāsifa*'s rational system that claimed independence from or superiority to revelation, the Sharīʿa norms were no longer the authoritative way to God and could be accepted at best as useful exercises for the commoners. The more our theologians embraced aspects of the *falāsifa*'s cosmology and psychology (in the prerevelation domain, that is), the greater the need there was to safeguard the normative basis of the Sharīʿa (in postrevelation domain) from the claims of reason by asserting a clear distinction between the two domains.

Aside from law and theology, our theologians had acquired yet another kind of attitude toward reason in the psychological or emotional realm. These doubts in reason constitute more than what can be captured as their denial of the ethical capacity of reason; they seemed to have implanted in our theologians an abiding mistrust of reason. If reason is not a friend of revelation in the theological domain, its harms can be limited by circumscribing it in the postrevelation life, but ultimately it is a bargain, not trusting friendship.

The typical loyal Sunni Ashʿarīs (important exceptions aside), who were also primarily jurists of Shāfiʿī or Mālikī legal schools, took to heart Ghazālī's advice in *Iḥyā'*. They considered the Ashʿarī masters' arguments and doctrines a matter of faith – just like the teachings of the Qur'an and

[92] Ghazālī, *Munqidh*, ed. K. ʿIyād and J. Ṣalība (Dār al-Andalus, 1967), 79–85, strongly endorses Greek (foreign) sciences other than metaphysics, in particular logic, physical sciences, mathematics, and even politics. About politics, he makes the odd claim that all of its precepts are derived from the teachings of earlier prophets, and hence must be acceptable.

the Prophet: They were to be believed in and transmitted, rather than critically examined or developed. Because they were only faintly familiar with the philosophical tradition themselves, while dealing with theological issues they accepted on faith the authority of the great Ashʿarīs like Rāzī and Ghazālī, who had for all purposes definitively refuted and vanquished the deviant Muʿtazila, the heretical *falāsifa*, and the narrow-minded traditionalists. Tāj al-Dīn al-Subkī, a Shāfiʿī jurist and a staunch Ashʿarī, while attacking philosophers like Ibn Sīnā, Fārābī, and al-Ṭūsi, who had mixed *falsafa* with *kalām*, anticipates the objection that his heroes of *kalām*, Ghazālī and Rāzī, could be equally charged with this "mixing." He writes:

> If you say: the Proof of Islam al-Ghazālī and the Imām Fakhr al-Dīn al-Rāzī too have delved in the sciences of philosophy, drawn nearer to it and mixed it with the *kalām* of the *mutakallimūn* – so why do you not reproach them too? … I say [in response]: These two are eminent *imāms*, and neither of them delved into these sciences except that [by virtue of it] they became definitive authorities in religion, [to the extent that] they are the stars of the knowledge of *kalām* on the path of *Ahl al-Sunna wa 'l-Jamāʿa*, the Companions and their Successors. Beware of hearing anything different than that – for if you do, you would have made a clear error. For these two *imāms* are great without doubt, and it was their rightful place to have brought victory to the believers and strength to this religion by repelling the vanities and fallacies of those liars [that is, the *falāsifa* and the Muʿtazila]. For there is no blame on someone who has reached the esteemed status of these two to look into the philosophical books – but indeed [for such luminaries] it becomes a virtue to be rewarded.[93]

Subkī further notes that Ghazālī (d. 505) was the reviver (*mujaddid*) of the Muslim faith at the end of the fifth/eleventh century, whereas Rāzī (d. 606) was the reviver of faith at the end of the sixth/twelfth century.[94]

The story of the *qānūn* I have presented here straddles together three relationships that are central to my account: that between reason and revelation, *kalām* and *falsafa*, and *kalām* and politics. The foundations of the classical caliphate theory, namely a ritualistic understanding of the caliphate and depoliticization of the Community, were underpinned by theological cynicism toward reason in postrevelational life on the one hand and elitism on the other, both of which deepened as the Sunni *kalām* doctrine matured in the classical period. Both elitism and cynicism toward reason militated against the other option, that of resurrecting and

[93] Tāj al-Dīn Subkī, *K. al-muʿīd al-niʿam*, 78–8; Maḥmūd, 672–3.

[94] A. Shihadeh, "From al-Ghazālī to al-Rāzī: 6th/12th Century Developments in Muslim Philosophical Theology," *Arabic Sciences and Philosophy* 15 (2005): 141–79.

reimagining a Community-centered vision of Islam. A politically vibrant society requires grounding political practice and theory in the normative apparatus of society, which the sociopolitical trends of the classical period had made difficult to attain and the intellectual commitments of the age had rendered impossible to imagine.

PART II

THE TAYMIYYAN INTERVENTION

Chapter 4

Ibn Taymiyya's World

> [M]ost of the great statements of political philosophy have been put forward in times of crisis; that is, when political phenomena are less effectively integrated by institutional forms.[1]

> Place yourself ... at the center of a man's philosophic vision and you [will] understand at once all the different things it makes him write or say. But keep outside, use your post-mortem method, try to build the philosophy up out of the single phrases, taking first one and then another and seeking to make them fit, and of course you fail. You crawl over the thing like a myopic ant over a building, tumbling into every microscopic crack or fissure, finding nothing but inconsistencies, and never suspecting that a center exists.[2]

The classical age and its intellectual syntheses were deeply disrupted in the sixth/twelfth and seventh/thirteenth centuries as the crusaders from the west and, much more devastatingly, the Mongols from the northeast shook the Muslim societies, shattering and rearranging their polities. This led to new emphases in Muslim thought ranging from ultraconservative and apocalyptic to self-critical. In a milieu of intense crisis and soul-searching, Ibn Taymiyya sought to profoundly reform Islamic society and politics.

Born in 661/1263 in the northern Syrian city of Ḥarrān five years after the destruction of Baghdad by the Mongols, Ibn Taymiyya lived more than two centuries after Ghazālī and one after Rāzī, in one of the most tumultuous periods of premodern Islamic history. The terror

[1] Wolin, *Politics*, 9.
[2] W. James, *A Pluralistic Universe* (Longman, Greens and Co., 1909), 263.

and apparent invincibility of the Mongols, their killing of the Abbasid caliph, destruction of the center of the Islamic world, Baghdad, and the annexation of the entire eastern half of the Islamic world were traumatic beyond comprehension. The world seemed to be nearing its end, and many interpreted these events in apocalyptic terms.[3] Ibn Taymiyya's impression of this tragedy was likely intensified as his own family was forced to flee from its native town, Ḥarrān, to escape the Mongol army that was then pushing northward into upper Syria. Even in Damascus, where Ibn Taymiyya's family took up residence, the Mongol threat continued to be felt for many years, and indeed, on four separate occasions, they launched direct attacks against the city. On at least three of these occasions, Ibn Taymiyya played a direct personal role by not only being involved as a soldier, but also using the full force of his charisma to help rally the local population as well as the scared and fleeing rulers and ulama to defend the city against the invaders.

The political and social upheavals were far from merely a product of the ulama's imagination. Besides the Mongols, there were wars, internal violence, famines, plagues and economic upheavals, which were of course not strange to the medieval world; "what was different [in the Mamluk period] was the perception that they now occurred in combination and with devastating affect [*sic.*] on Muslim society [and] led to a pervasive sense that the past was better than the present and that all things contemporary paled in comparison with the glories of the earlier history of Islam."[4] The historical works of later-Mamluk-period historians like al-Maqrīzī, Ibn Taghrī Birdī and Ibn Ḥajar al-ʿAsqalānī are rife with "a pessimistic criticism of the present and regret 'for the good old days'."[5] In addition to these disasters that seemed to reflect divine displeasure, the failure of the wielders of power and religious authority seemed obvious:

> Internally, the Mamluk state was extremely chaotic. The first half of the era, known as the Baḥrī period, lasted from 1260 to 1382. Over the course of little more than a century, the Sultunate had changed hands 24 times. The second half of the period was dominated by the violent rise of the Circassian Mamluks who saw the Sultanate change 27 times between 1382 and 1517. With each

[3] As Richard Bulliet has reminded us in his *Islam: View from the Edge*, 6–10, to those away from the center (of orthodoxy as well as geography), the fate of Islam might not have looked quite as gloomy.

[4] K. Jaques, *Authority, Conflict and the Transmission of Diversity in Medieval Islamic Law* (Brill, 2006), 1.

[5] W. Popper, *Egypt and Syria under the Circassian Sultans: 1382–1468 A.D. Systematic Notes to Ibn Taghrī Birdī's Chronicles of Egypt* (University of California Press, 1955), 8.

change of Sultan there would follow purges of political authority at all levels of administration. By the middle of the 9th/15th century these purges became extremely violent with mass executions and mutilations as new leaders sought to consolidate their control.[6]

The ulama, Mamluk historians inform us, were often "intimately involved" in the violent political games, "[s]iding with different contenders to the throne, [and they] frequently suffered punishments for falling in with defeated groups, losing wealth and suffering torture and sometimes even death."[7]

Many leading influential jurists, like the prodigious Shāfiʿī jurist and *muḥaddith* of Damascus, Muḥyi al-Dīn al-Nawawī (d. 676/1277), had turned, in a self-critical vein, to their own profession as being a part of the problem. In the midst of the Mongol invasion, Nawawī wrote that legal standards had declined because of the incompetence of the contemporary jurists, in particular their "truly disqualifying lack of [historical and contextual] knowledge" in contrast with the *ḥadīth* scholars' meticulous attention to the same.[8] Perhaps it was in response to this that the *ṭabaqāt* (biographical) literature among the jurists emerged during the next few centuries.[9] What is interesting for our purpose is that Nawawī's diagnosis of the problem consisted of a technicality, a minutia, and the response, if we are to accept Jacques' thesis, was the development of a technical genre of biographical literature. Furthermore, Nawawī's presumption of the critical significance of jurists (*fuqahā'*) and their unquestionable position of religious and social leadership within the Muslim society are also noteworthy. Jurists, according to Nawawī, have "the exclusive right and ability to interpret the texts of revelation so that Muslims, common people and rulers alike, might know what God wants them to do in all walks of life."[10]

Another type of response, even more common, was represented by the Shāfiʿī Ibn Kathīr (d. 774/1373), an admirer and disciple of Ibn Taymiyya. Ibn Kathīr fundamentally understood the decline of the lands of Islam in apocalyptic terms. He blamed not only the corruption and infighting of the Muslim princes, but complained "even the jurists in Baghdad and

[6] Jaques, 19.
[7] Ibid. See also, Chamberlain, *Knowledge*, 94–6; C. Petry, *The Civilian Elite of Cairo in the Later Middle Ages* (Princeton University Press, 1981), 206–9; Johansen, "A Perfect Law," 260.
[8] Jaques, 10.
[9] Ibid.
[10] Ibid., 2.

Damascus were more concerned with their internal struggles for power than they were for the plight of the Muslim community." When Baghdad was attacked and tens of thousands of Muslims were massacred by the Mongols, the leaders of the Muslims, including "court officials, ... judges, Sufis, members of the noble houses as well as commoners" fled the city or collaborated with the invaders, while the Caliph "occupied himself with the concubines."[11] The significance of the Mongol onslaught served for Ibn Kathīr to highlight the "decline of moral conditions and the failure of the scholars to act as guides for the community."[12] The Muslim community was facing what the Israelites had faced according to the Qur'an: a divine censure of apocalyptic proportions, because just as the Israelites "had rebelled and killed many of the prophets and scholars (ulama)," so had Muslims treated the righteous among the ulama. It is not unlikely that Ibn Taymiyya's persecution and eventual death in prison were a vivid demonstration of precisely this crisis in Ibn Kathīr's mind. For Ibn Kathīr, his own time coincided with the end of time. He thought that "the Mongol attacks began a period of eschatological turmoil, and unless the community returns to obeying revelation and listens to those with knowledge (*ʿilm*), God will unleash apocalyptic destruction that will ultimately lead to the day of resurrection."[13]

Resentment against the ulama for their responsibility for the state of the *umma* seems to have had wide currency among the populace and popular preachers. David Cook in his *Studies in Muslim Apocalyptic* observes that the failure of the ulama to guide the Community and set aside their own interests is a common theme in apocalyptic literature.[14] The association of scholars with the rulers is also condemned – an attitude that became common since at least the beginning of the classical age. This criticism had been popularized by widely esteemed scholars like Ghazālī, and traditions attributed to the Prophet had long circulated to that effect. One such report has it: "The ulama are the guardians of Messengers ... [they are] faithful as long as they do not intermingle with the Sultan and (do not) have intercourse with the world. When they do so, they have betrayed the Messenger, and so be wary of them."[15]

[11] Ibid., 5.
[12] Ibid., 6.
[13] Ibid., 6–7.
[14] D. Cook, *Studies in Muslim Apocalyptic* (Darwin Press, 2003), 250–1; Jacques, 8.
[15] Jaques, 7, quoting an eighth-/fourteenth-century preacher al-Daylamī, *Irshād al-qulūb fi'l-mawāʿiẓ wa'l-ḥikam*; D. Cook, *Apocalyptic*, 248.

RATIONAL-REVELATIONAL CRITICISM AS THE RESPONSE TO THE CRISIS

Ibn Taymiyya's recognition that his world was in crisis was not unique,[16] but his understanding of it was, as was his approach to the solution. His diagnosis was neither of a technical nature like Nawawī's nor apocalyptic like that of most preachers and scholars. Rather, it was a total critique of the contemporary Muslim society, starting with its intellectual apparatus and social and political institutions. His criticism was directed at all segments of society, but in particular at the ulama and the rulers. He criticized the ulama not for associating with the rulers, but for failing to guide them properly while maintaining their integrity; not for lack of markers of piety, but for lack of proper balance; not for technical deficiencies that could be fixed by adding a new subfield to their curricula, but for a fundamental mismatch between the abstractions and formulations of their legal and theological systems and the spirit of the scripture they claimed to represent.

Although the Mongol onslaught and the general sociopolitical upheavals of his age are undeniable aspects of the context in which to understand Ibn Taymiyya's writing, he contended that the spiritual and intellectual corruption of the *umma* is far worse than its military defeats. Chastising, for instance, the proponents of the Neoplatonist Sufi doctrine of *waḥdat al-wujūd*, such as the Mercian theosophist Sufi Ibn ʿArabī (d. 637/1240), the antinomian Sufi Ibn Sabʿīn (d. 669/1270),[17] and their contemporary admirers for their antinomian and anti-*Sharīʿa* tendencies, he writes:

> Opposing (by word and deed) these [proponents of *waḥdat al-wujūd*] is the greatest of religious obligations, for they have corrupted intellects and creeds of the people, including shaykhs [Sufis], scholars and rulers ... their harm is greater in religion than harm of the one who corrupts the worldly affairs of the Muslims but leaves their religion untouched such as the bandit or the Mongols who take away people's wealth but leave alone their religion.[18]

Despite a strong practical and activist bent that characterized his life and thought, he prioritized the reform of theology and theory over that of

[16] Jacques, 3.

[17] Ibn Sabʿīn, an Andalusian antinomian and pantheistic Sufi, founder of the Sabʿīniyya order. During his incarceration in Alexandria, Ibn Taymiyya debated and refuted Ibn Sabʿīn's followers; this also motivated his composition of *al-Radd ʿalā al-manṭiqiyyīn* (Leaman and Nasr, *History*, 347–9).

[18] MF, 2:132; Maḥmūd, 870.

jurisprudence. Accordingly, although he considered jurisprudence and *ḥadīth* criticism to be the most genuine and organic of the Islamic sciences, his own proclivity toward theoretical sciences (*uṣūl*) is explicit. Engagement with purely rational sciences is indispensable in order to undo the influence of the corrupting intellectual trends, be they foreign or indigenous: "Were it not for that the propagators of such heresies have become dominant and spread in great numbers and become in the eyes of people respected leaders ... to the extent that they are deemed superior to the prophets ... we would have felt no need to show the falsity of these claims. But alas, error has no limit."[19]

This preference is thrown into sharp relief in a conversation recorded by a disciple of his, Al-Ḥāfidh Muḥammad b. ʿAlī al-Bazzār (d. 749/1350). Bazzār poses the problem in these words: "He, God be pleased with him, wrote profusely in the matters of *uṣūl* (principles or theory) as opposed to the other sciences, so I inquired about that, beseeching him to write a text in jurisprudence (*fiqh*) that would include his preferred opinions, so that it may become a reference for jurisprudential verdicts." Ibn Taymiyya's response, he informs us, was something like this:

> The sciences of the branches (that is, *fiqh*) are an easy matter, and [there is no harm] if a Muslim subscribes to one of the scholars who are followed, so long as it is not done despite the knowledge of that scholar's error. As for the fundamental principles of religion (*uṣūl al-dīn*), I saw the people of heretical innovation, misguidance and desire, such as the philosophized (*mutafalsifa*), the Bāṭinīs, the anti-religious (*malāḥida*), the advocates of *waḥdat al-wujūd*, the atheists (*dahriyya*), the Qadariyya (who denied God's power over human destiny), the Nuṣayrīs, the Jahmiyya, the Ḥulūlīs (monists), *muʿaṭṭila* (deniers of divine attributes), the *mujassima* (anthropomorphists), the *mushabbiha* (those who liken God to His creatures), the Rāwandīs,[20] the Kullābīs, the Sulaymīs, and others who possess heretical ideas become lost in error. It became clear to me that many of them intend to belie the sacred *Sharīʿa* of Muḥammad and the majority of them have led people to doubt the very foundations of their religion – such that rarely do I meet or see someone who adopts their opinions in lieu of adhering to the Book and the Sunna who has not thereby secretly reneged from his faith (*tazandaqa*) or lost certitude in his religion and creed....

[19] MF, 2:357–8; Maḥmūd, 291.

[20] To the medieval ulama, the third-/ninth-century theologian Ibn al-Rāwandi was the arch-heretic. A philosophical freethinker of medieval Islam, he has been judged as merely a nonconformist by some modern scholars, like M. Fakhry and van Ess, and a radical freethinker and outright disbeliever by others. For the second viewpoint, see S. Stroumsa, *Freethinkers of Medieval Islam: Ibn al-Rāwandi, Abū Bakr al-Rāzī, and their Impact on Islamic Thought* (Brill, 1999).

When I saw this, it became clear to me that it is incumbent upon everyone who can repel their doubts and lies and refute their arguments and errors, to do so, in the service of the right creed (*milla ḥanafiyya*) and the correct path.[21]

Ibn Taymiyya's "heretics" cannot be, and perhaps are not intended to be, mapped each to a historical group of people who had systematic doctrines that went by those labels. For instance, he applies the term *mutafalsifa* to those he disparages as following the ideas of Neoplatonist philosophers, often half-heartedly, either because of their lack of understanding or lack of courage to subscribe fully to the philosophical conclusions that defy scripture. Most of the other heretical tendencies listed here share, in his view, this problem of the half-hearted influence of *falsafa*; hence, they are all, in a sense, philosophized (*mutafalsifa*) but rarely were proper philosophers (*falāsifa*). This is not to say Ibn Taymiyya had a soft spot for proper philosophers, but he deems them more consistent within their own scheme, and hence more properly outside the pale of orthodoxy and even Islam.

Based on Ibn Taymiyya's response to a question from his fellow traditionalists (*ahl al-ḥadīth*) about whether they are the only "saved sect" in Islam, George Makdisi succinctly sums up Ibn Taymiyya's "mental map" of orthodoxy:

Ibn Taymiyya's conception of the Muslim community may be described by a series of concentric circles whose common center is marked by the Qur'an and tradition [Sunna]. Around this common center the various schools of theology are located, each of them arranged according to the degree of its 'orthodoxy'. The sole criterion of orthodoxy is the scripture supported by the *consensus of the Muslim community*.

In the first circle, inside all the others, the one which encloses the common center, we find the *salaf* [the early Muslims]. Then come the *ahl al-sunna wa 'l-ḥadīth*, who are follower of the Qur'an and the Tradition [*ḥadīth*] of the Prophet. Next come the Sufis. And after them the *ahl al-kalām*, proponents of rationalist theology. These latter are divided into two groups: the *ahl al-ithbāt* [lit. affirmers], and the *ahl an-nafy* [lit. deniers], also called *aṣ-ṣifātiyya* and *an-nufāt*, respectively. The former is composed of those rationalist theologians (*mutakallimūn*) who accept the divine attributes; the latter refers to the theologians who deny the attributes of God. The former [i.e., affirmers] are divided into three groups: the Ashʿariyya, the Kullābiyya, and the Karrāmiyya, while the second [deniers] are represented by the Muʿtazila. Next come the philosophers, the Khawārij and, finally, the Rāfiḍa [Imāmī Shīʿa] who are farthest removed from the *salaf*. Only the Jahmiyya [a theoretical category; historically extinct] are outside the community,

[21] Al-Bazzār, *al-Aʿlām al-ʿaliyya fī manāqib Ibn Taymiyya*, ed. Z. al-Shāwīsh (al-Maktab al-Islāmi, 1400), 35–7.

but they must be well-informed Jahmiyya, for there are some among the common people who are dupes of the theorists and consequently must not be condemned because of their ignorance.[22]

Given the inclination of the traditionalist Sunnis (his camp) to use the well-known reports about "the saved sect" (*al-firqa al-nājiya*) to justify the exclusivity of their own claim, the complexity of Ibn Taymiyya's response is noteworthy.

To continue with Ibn Taymiyya's response to al-Bazzār:

By God, I have not seen anyone writing in this manner and claiming high place but aiding the destruction of the foundations of Islam by his discourse. The reason for that is neglecting the clear and open truth and what the noble messengers have brought from God and following the ways of philosophy that they have claimed to be wisdom (*ḥikamiyyāt*) and rational truths (*ʿaqliyyāt*), but in truth it is nothing but ignorance and error. Such a person's adherence to [this philosophy] overwhelms him as to cover up his sound reason until he is blinded and unable to differentiate between truth and falsehood.... These are the considerations that made it incumbent upon me to direct my foremost concerns to the sciences of principles (*uṣūl*) and made me attend to their statements and respond to them with what God the Exalted has bestowed upon me of answers, be they from reason or revelation.[23]

Naturally, the more conservative traditionalists did not appreciate his deep involvement with reason and philosophical questions or his nuanced approach to questions of doctrine, and considered him to have been poisoned by philosophy. Al-Dhahabī (d. 748/1348) writes:

[Some] groups, among the imams of the traditionalists, those of them who knew the Qur'an by heart and their jurists, loved the Shaykh and revered him. They however did not like his deep involvement (*tawaghghul*) with the *kalām* theologians and the philosophers, [preferring that he avoided it] just as it had been avoided by the earlier imams of traditionalists, like al-Shāfiʿī, Aḥmad [b. Ḥanbal], Ishāq [b. Rāhawayh], Abū ʿUbayd [al-Qasim b. Sallām] and their like. Likewise, many scholars, among the jurists, the traditionalists and the virtuous, hated his dedication (*tafarrud*) to some odd questions which the Ancients (*salaf*) had disapproved of.[24]

Ibn Taymiyya's commitment to reason was no light matter, however. In contrast with Ghazālī's claim that the *salaf* detested rational argument and proceeded from scriptural dogma to the sword and the whip as means

22 Makdisi, "Ḥanbalī Islam," 257–8 (italics and comments within the square brackets are mine).

23 Bazzār, *Aʿlām*, 37.

24 Ibn Rajab, *Dhayl*, 2:394; Michot, "Mamluk Theologian," I, 166n39.

to persuade, Ibn Taymiyya expanded much effort in refuting this impression. The *salaf*, according to him, not only permitted rational argument in refutation of erroneous ideas, but indeed engaged in such endeavors themselves. They had disapproved only of the invalid ways of argument and the premises of *kalām* but not of responding to the errant ideas by means of valid arguments based on reason as well as revelation. Later Sunnis – both the traditionalists (*ahl al-ḥadīth*) and the theologians – had misunderstood the way of the *salaf*. The theologians had erred not by engaging in rational argument, but by doing so with insufficient knowledge of both the position they defended and the one they refuted. The traditionalists had claimed that the *salaf* avoided rational engagement altogether because rational engagement was prohibited in itself, whereas the masters of *kalām*, like Juwaynī and Ghazālī, lacking firsthand and in-depth knowledge of the *salaf*'s teachings, had taken the traditionalist claim on its face value and had ascribed the revered *salaf*'s supposed anti-rationalism to their excessive piety and exaggerated fear of reason.[25]

Toward his fellow traditionalists, he directs the argument that to refute rational objections to revelation is like providing medicine to one who is sick, and to such a person, sound and necessary nutrition – namely revelational knowledge – brings no benefit because his body, his rational apparatus, has been corrupted. To keep repeating an argument based on revelation before someone who thinks that reason definitively affirms its contrary is going to bring only harm, for such conduct will make an intellectually sick person believe that revelation is flawed.[26] Nevertheless, while seeking to strike a balance between those who defended rational theology and those who rejected it, Ibn Taymiyya reserved his fiercer criticism for the *mutakallimūn*, for, in his view anyway, the simplistic anti-rationalism of the traditionalists had done less harm compared to the intellectual and spiritual havoc wreaked by flawed rational discourse.

A Nonlegalistic Jurist, an Anti-*kalām* Theologian

He was a Ḥanbalī by heritage and initial training, and thus his commitment to the *ḥadīth* of the Prophet followed by "the way of the *salaf*" was nothing new. But his engagement with the range of intellectual trends and problems of the age along with a critical historical awareness of early Islamic history gave him a vantage point of his own. Furthermore, his

25 *Dar'(S)*, 7:149f.
26 *Dar'(S)*, 1:44.

commitment to the Qur'an was also extraordinary[27] and his approach to *ḥadīth* far more nuanced than that of his fellow traditionalists.[28] These foundations explain his independent mind and chastening of many prominent Ḥanbalīs, occasional disagreement with the revered Aḥmad b. Ḥanbal himself,[29] his defense of many non-Ḥanbalīs, in particular the Ashʿarīs, against their indiscriminate condemnation by his fellow Ḥanbalīs, his insistence, even against traditionalist resistance, to engage in rational argument, and his myriad reform attempts in legal theory and practice. To say that he had transcended the Ḥanbalī school and entered the realm of independent *ijtihād*, as it is often said, does not quite capture it.[30] His influence went far beyond Ḥanbalism. Every aspect of the classical Islamic tradition, it is no exaggeration to suggest, was either transformed or profoundly challenged by his intervention.[31]

Modern scholars have frequently asserted numerous influences on Ibn Taymiyya. Goldziher suggested that he was fundamentally influenced by the great Andalusian Ẓāhirī theologian and jurist, Ibn Ḥazm (d. 465/1064)[32] and Laoust that his fiercely independent and egalitarian thought (in particular his political thought and alleged rejection of the idea of the caliphate) was indebted to Khārijī influence. More recently, Michot, perhaps the most perceptive and sustained modern reader of Ibn Taymiyya's philosophical

[27] W. Saleh, "Ibn Taymiyya and the Rise of Radical Hermeneutics: An Analysis of *An Introduction to the Foundations of Qur'ānic Exegesis*," in Rapoport and Ahmad, where Saleh considers Ibn Taymiyya's a major intervention and a turning point in the history of exegesis.

[28] His commitment to *ḥadīth* is not simplistic as that of many fellow traditionalists, but holistic, as being one of many ways of determining the Sunna, aware of the need to ferret out the "raw" material of *ḥadīth* through both isnād and content criticism. His generous appreciation of the early Mālikite school, despite the latter's critical attitude toward isolated *ḥadīth* in favor of anonymous but less corruptible "Sunna" in the form of Medinan practice (*ʿamal*), borders on undermining Ḥanbalism and exceeds any praise by him of the Ḥanbalīs as a group that I have come across (MF, 20:294).

[29] Cook, *Commanding*, 157.

[30] For a recent, brief but insightful, appraisal of his legal scholarship, see Y. Rapoport, "Ibn Taymiyya's Radical Legal Thought: Rationalism, Pluralism and the Primacy of Intention," in Rapoport and Ahmed, *Ibn Taymiyya and His Times*, 191–221.

[31] He criticized many Ḥanbalī masters both in theology and law (A. H. Matroudi, *The Hanbali School of Law and Ibn Taymiyyah: Conflict or Conciliation?* [Routledge, 2006], 92–108).

[32] Among the more able scholars on the subject was Goldziher, who thought Ibn Taymiyya to have been under the influence primarily of the scholar he worked on, Ibn Hazm. To a lesser degree, he was thought by Goldziher to have been under the influence of al-Ghazālī, although he was considered poles apart from the latter because of his opposition to Sufism, proclivity for literalism, and general exclusivism and intolerance as compared to Ghazālī's more embracing inclusivism (Rosenthal, 245n84).

thought, has nonetheless insisted that Ibn Taymiyya was indebted in some fundamental way to Ibn Sīnā.[33] But for a thinker who was as widely read and engaged as Ibn Taymiyya, the simple claim of influence loses any analytical utility unless the influence can be shown to be persistent and systemic, a test that none of the preceding suggestions passes. The sheer number of issues, both in theology and law, in which Ibn Taymiyya took an unpopular and at times entirely unique position is a testament to his fierce intellectual independence. Some modern scholars even characterize him as "philosopher of the first order,"[34] one concluding that:

> Ibn Taymiyya's stance towards all of the Islamic intellectual trends, be it *kalām*, philosophy, or Sufism, was that of (critical) acceptance and refutation; a superficial reading of his vehement attacks against each of these trends at first suggests that he categorically rejected them all, but a careful and surgical investigation demonstrates invariably that Ibn Taymiyya benefited intellectually to the maximum possible extent from each of these.[35]

If we are to recognize resemblance in content and direction, the scholars whose tradition Ibn Taymiyya continues are the philosophized Ashʿarites like Ghazālī and Rāzī; this may sound odd given his fierce critiques of these two. Intellectually, however, there is no better way to describe less space between the two words his project than as a continuation of the project they left behind, of harmonizing reason and revelation to provide a stable foundation for belief and action. In contrast with Ghazālī and Rāzī, however, whose synthetic impulse had taken them to the ends of the available philosophical systems of their day and back, his deconstructive project took this end as its point of departure. He was far from being a system builder; in this lay his greatest strength as well as the limit of all his thought. As Wael Hallaq has observed in his study of Ibn Taymiyya's refutation of Greek syllogism, he had a knack for recognizing the essence of an argument, the foundational premise that animated a discourse, and then he persistently attacked it from all possible angles without being distracted by myriad subsidiary issues hiding it or centuries of imposing authority underpinning it.[36]

He was also, it is less often recognized, an exceptional student of early Islamic history and conflicts and had an uncanny ability – exceptional even in his day of prodigious memorizers – to draw on an astounding variety of references from not only the opinions of the *salaf*, but also the

[33] Michot, "Mamlūk Theologian," I, 156–7.
[34] ʿAbd al-akīm al-Ajhar, *Ibn Taymiyya wa isti'nāf al-qawl al-falsafi fi'l Islām* (al-Markaz al-Thaqāfi al-ʿArabī, 2004), 24.
[35] Ibid., 235.
[36] Hallaq, *Ibn Taymiyya*, xiv.

myriad "heterodox" sects of Islamic history, thus making his points by adeptly pitting his foes against each other. In contrast with most scholars of his age, Laoust notes, he "went directly to the primary sources themselves which he read and studied carefully."[37] Accordingly, even as he rejected the methodological presuppositions of *kalām*, he devoted himself to a serious study of it and had a surpassing mastery over it.[38]

One result of Ibn Taymiyya's wide intellectual and practical engagement and independence of thinking was his rejection of blind following (*taqlīd*). But *taqlīd*, in his view, was not an issue particular to Islamic jurisprudence (*fiqh*) as often understood, nor was the jurisprudential *taqlīd* the most serious threat to the well-being of Muslims. Rather, *taqlīd* is a psychological human proclivity whose worst consequences manifested themselves among intellectuals rather than the commoners. In legal matters, he does not reject the justified following of a trusted juristic authority by an unqualified or less qualified person. Legal *taqlīd* was blameworthy when qualified scholars refused to see the truth of the argument of an opponent or another school out of ego, prejudice for an authority, or school loyalty. However, in a society where communal life and personal identities were so entrenched in legal loyalties, even this moderate critique of *taqlīd* as an institution had profound and disruptive repercussions.[39]

But the *taqlīd* that Ibn Taymiyya criticized most vehemently was that of those who prided themselves in intellectual speculation, namely the philosophized (*mutafalsifa*, which was his derogatory designation for those who blindly followed the trendy philosophical opinions without understanding them) and *kalām* scholars. Blind following of established authority was to him the reason why many Muslim scholars had put

[37] Laoust, *Essai*, 93–100.

[38] Laoust, *Essai*, 89–93; see also, idem, *EI*[2], s.v., "*Ibn Taimīya*."

[39] His views on *taqlīd* are spread throughout his writings and are quite complex. The absolutely prohibited *taqlīd* is to deny the truth of God or a true prophet for custom or partisanship (in matters of creed), or for anyone to follow another despite contradicting clear evidence from the Qur'an or the Sunna (MF, 20:15; 19:260). In legal matters, it is permissible for a nonexpert and even a scholar (*mujtahid*) if he lacks the opportunity or capacity to judge various opinions on his own (19:261). The majority of scholars of Islam correctly hold, in his view, that both *taqlīd* and *ijtihād* are permissible generally, each becoming permissible or impermissible based on factors of capacity, effort, and intention (20:204). Where Ibn Taymiyya differs with a rival trend, *madhhabism*, that had arisen since the consolidation of schools in sixth/twelfth century is the strict discipline of belonging to a single legal school in all matters and systemic rejection of any contrary evidence (33:128). His strongest censure of *taqlīd* (legal or otherwise) is when it becomes blind following of a human authority against clear evidence from revelation (22:248–9).

masters like Ghazālī and Rāzī on a pedestal of unquestionable orthodoxy in *kalām*, the likes of Ibn ʿArabī in Sufism, and Greek philosophers like Aristotle and Plato in philosophy. He included in blameworthy *taqlīd* even blind following of the *salaf*, in particular the four Sunni Imams of jurisprudence, of whom he otherwise thought quite highly. This type of following leads the followers to endorse inherited opinions without fully investigating them and even when they find inconsistencies or errors to explain them away as being the result of some higher wisdom rather than honestly acknowledging them. He writes:

> You will find that the followers of Aristotle follow his teachings in logic, physics and theology, even as many of them arrive by their own reasoning at the opposite of his position. But because of their reverent opinion of the philosopher, they do not dare express their opposition or attribute the contradiction to their own lack of comprehension of the problem.... Indeed, this attitude is found even among the followers of the great imams of jurisprudence and of imams of piety and worship, such as the companions of Abū Ḥanīfa, al-Shāfiʿī, Mālik, Aḥmad and others. They would at times notice something that they deem invalid in the teachings [of their imams], but they fall short of expressing their opposition, believing that their imam is greater in perfection of reason, knowledge and religion than them, while knowing full well that no imam is infallible and quite likely to make mistakes.[40]

With this understanding of human psychology, which makes people impressed more with authority than reason, Ibn Taymiyya sought to engage with and dislodge the masters of a discourse rather than criticize their less independent followers, who would have made much easier targets. Commenting on this method, he writes:

> I have been amazed by what I have observed in this regard. Rarely do I come across a rational argument by a sect that opposes revelation and whose invalidity has become clear to me but that I also find that some of the masters of that sect have already acknowledged the invalidity of that argument and elaborated on it. That is so because God has created His servants upon the *fiṭra* (natural constitution), and sound intellects are naturally inclined (*mafṭūra*) to recognizing the truth (*maʿrifat al-ḥaqq*) were it not for certain obstacles.

Human nature and proper reason are capable of recognizing the truth, or at least certain truths, were it not for irrational obstacles such as excessive reverence of authorities and lack of confidence, courage, or integrity to recognize and express dissent. To persuade the many blind followers of his time, he had to dismantle the authorities of the past, "for the majority

[40] *Dar'(S)*, 1:151–5.

of these groups, despite their claims to rational independence, are blind followers of their masters. When they see that their highest authorities mutually disagree and acknowledge the truth, their knots of blind following are loosened."[41]

There is yet another reason to engage with the present and past heresies; often they are not devoid of all truth, but only of proper balance. One persistent theme in Ibn Taymiyya's writings is that of the golden mean – that truth is the middle path that is often missed by partisans who only see part of it. "Though the content of his doctrinal system was derived essentially from the Qur'an and the Sunna," observes Swartz in his commentary on Ibn Taymiyya's *al-ʿAqīda al-Wāsiṭiyya*, "the spirit and direction of his thought were to a large degree shaped by the concept of *wasaṭ*, the happy or golden mean."[42] This does not mean, Swartz explains, that to Ibn Taymiyya truth always lies between two opposing extremes. Rather,

> the concept of *wasaṭ* carries with it the conviction that truth is a whole or totality. Defined in these terms, then, *wasaṭ* means that doctrinal error or heresy results when one element of the truth is elevated to the level of the whole, so that the integrity and dialectical tension that ought to exist between the parts of the whole are destroyed. Heresy, then, is not so much outright falsehood or error as it is a partial and fragmented truth.[43]

Rather than rejectionist or intolerant, his was a refined understanding of the human intellectual enterprise reflected in his serious engagement with even those positions in Islamic history that had been long condemned as misguided.

Personal Charisma and Activism

If one browses through the biographies of medieval scholars, the image of the typical scholar is that of a schoolman, a jurist, a theologian, a conservative figure who served the authorities as a civil servant, or fled in pious evasion. The typical member of the civilian elite to which the ulama belonged was not an activist, a warrior, or a popular reformer. Ibn Taymiyya was different.[44]

41 Ibid., 1:376–7.

42 Swartz, 115–6.

43 Ibid., 95–6.

44 See H. Q. Murad, "Ibn Taymiyya on Trial: A Narrative Account of his *Miḥan*," *Islamic Studies* 18 (1979): 1–32; S. Jackson, "Ibn Taymiyyah on Trial in Damascus," *Journal of Semitic Studies* (1994): 41–85.

The first thing that set him apart from his contemporaries, much more palpable than his intellectual ingenuity, was his extraordinary personality and persona, heroic piety, asceticism, reformist activism, and single-minded all-out defense of what he believed to be the truth. His rivals among the ulama charged him with heresy and tried to have him executed and succeeded in having him exiled more than once, even while acknowledging these virtues. Donald Little, in his provocatively titled article, "Did Ibn Taymiyya Have a Screw Loose?" observed that Ibn Taymiyya "must have been an exceptional person to evoke such universal respect."[45] Even his adversaries, numerous as they were, betrayed a sense of reverence for his learning, piety, and asceticism. Ibn Makhlūf (d. 718/1318), the Mālikī chief *qāḍī* of Egypt, who had been largely responsible for Ibn Taymiyya's early trials and tribulations in Egypt, reportedly conceded that "[t]here is no one more righteous than Ibn Taymiyya; we should abandon our struggle against him."[46] Taqī al-Dīn al-Subkī (d. 756/1355), an indefatigable defender of Ashʿarism, is reported to have confided the following to al-Dhahabī:

> As for what you say in regard al-Shaykh Taqī al-Dīn [Ibn Taymiyya], I am convinced of the great scope, the ocean-like fullness and vastness of his knowledge of the transmitted and intellectual sciences, his extreme intelligence, his exertions and his attainments, all of which surpass description. I have always held this opinion. Personally, my admiration is even greater for the asceticism, piety and religiosity with which God has endowed him, for his selfless championship of the truth, his adherence to the path of our forebears, his pursuit of perfection, the wonder of his example, unrivalled in our time and in times past.[47]

These statements are all the more weighty because al-Dhahabī was far from an uncritical admirer of Ibn Taymiyya and al-Subkī was Ibn Taymiyya's avowed intellectual foe.[48] His biographers consistently mention his detachment from "his worldly surroundings," his "complete absorption in his religious cause," and his "indifference to the various forms of punishment which might be inflicted upon him."[49] He famously

[45] D. Little, "Did Ibn Taymiyya Have a Screw Loose?" *SI* 41 (1975): 99.

[46] Ibid.

[47] Ibid., 99–100.

[48] C. Bori, *Ibn Taymiyya: una vita esemplare. Analisi delle fonti classiche della sua biografia* (Supplemento no. 1 alle Rivista degli Studi orientali, vol. LXXVI. Istituti editoriali e polignatici internazionali, 2003), 142–8 and 191–4; and summarized in idem, "A New Source for the Biography of Ibn Taymiyya," *BSOAS* 67 (2004): 321–48, 327.

[49] Little, "Did Ibn Taymiyya," 106.

said when given the news of his house arrest, "What can my enemies do to me? My Garden is in my heart; wherever I go, it goes with me. My imprisonment is solitary (worship of God)! My death is martyrdom! My banishment is a journey (across God's earth – reference to a Qur'anic verse)!"[50]

Similarly revealing and intense are his most influential disciple Ibn Qayyim al-Jawziyya's discussion of his spiritual insights and devotion.[51] What his doting admirers like Ibn al-Qayyim took to be his remarkable godliness, resolve, and willpower were seen by his foes as marks of his "pride, impetuosity, obstinacy, intolerance, and tactlessness."[52] His contemporaries, nonetheless, consistently tell us of his incredible clemency toward his detractors, including those jurists and judges who had campaigned to have him executed.[53]

He was a relentless activist who engaged in social reform, even vigilante dispensation of justice and moral policing, which he did with his group of devoted fellow scholars and students. He was also exceptionally well informed about his political and social world.[54] Swartz aptly sums up Ibn Taymiyya's exceptional breadth of practical as well as theoretical knowledge: "It is not going too far to say that Ibn Taymiyya was one of the best informed men of his time. Though he was a staunch defender of Sunni traditionalism, this firm attachment did not prevent his thought from being influenced in important ways by the rationalist theologians, philosophers and sectarian thinkers."[55]

Whereas Ibn Taymiyya doubtless shared with Ghazālī the project of the reform of Muslim thought and spirituality, his attitude toward reason and politics is as far as it could be from Ghazālī's attitude of "eating carrion." Instead, one finds Ibn Taymiyya persistently and optimistically engaged with the political, intellectual, and spiritual problems of the day

[50] Ibid.

[51] See Anjum, "Sufism."

[52] Little, "Did Ibn Taymiyya," 107.

[53] His last epistle from the prison where he died declares his forgiveness for all his enemies and goes on to say, "If a man could be thanked for his evil deeds, I would have thanked all those responsible for [my trial and imprisonment]" (MF, 28:55).

[54] As noted earlier, Ibn Taymiyya's leading part in defending Syria against the Mongols won him great fame and influence in Syria and generally. Ibn Taymiyya provided legal basis for fighting against them and charged that they were conspiring with the crusaders against Muslims (Ibn Kathīr, *Al-Bidāya wa'l-nihāya*, ed. 'Alī Shīrī [Dār Iḥyā' al-Turāth al-'Arabī, 1408/1988], 14:24). Recent studies, incidentally, confirm this charge: R. Amitai-Preiss, "Mongol, Imperial Ideology and the Ilkhānid War," in *The Mongol Empire and Its Legacy*, ed. idem (Brill, 1999), 58–60.

[55] Swartz, 95.

with the conviction that they can be resolved or reformed in the light of reason and revelation.[56] The flip side of his activist scholarship is reflected in the sharp and quick tone of his writings, laced with declarations of deviation and misguidance of his opponents. Even when engaged in involved deconstruction of a most recondite discourse, he did not lose sight of his role as a preacher, a teacher, and a spiritual guide, supremely concerned to alert his readers of the error of these doctrines and their consequences.

IBN TAYMIYYA AND ASHʿARISM: CONSTRUCTION AND CRITICISM

Truth often being a complex balancing act, adherence to it was seen by Ibn Taymiyya as a relative matter rather than a sharp dichotomy. His stance toward Ashʿarism was a manifestation of this general attitude: "The discourses of [the Ashʿarīs] contain sound arguments and that are in agreement with the Sunna, the Community and *ḥadīth*, and they are in fact to be counted from amongst the *Ahl al-Sunna wa'l-Jamāʿa* relative to the likes of the Muʿtazila, the Rāfiḍīs and others."[57] He frequently acknowledged the merits of the Ashʿarīs and defended them against their more vitriolic opponents from both among the traditionalists and rationalists.[58] The great Ḥanbalī Sufi Abū Ismāʿīl al-Anṣārī al-Harawī (d. 481/1089), the author of *Dhamm al-kalām* (Censure of *kalām*), had vehemently censured the Ashʿarīs as being no better than the hated opponents of Sunna, the Jahmiyya, and the Muʿtazila. Defending the Ashʿarīs against this charge, Ibn Taymiyya wrote that al-Harawī "has exaggerated his censure of the Ashʿarīs, for in fact they are the closest of the groups to the Sunna."[59] He acknowledged their contribution in defending the truth (Sunni orthodoxy). He mentions in particular the role of the vizier Niẓām al-Mulk and scholars in his entourage like Juwaynī and Ghazālī who in the wake of the Rāfiḍī and Qarmaṭī threats ... established the Sunna, refuted their heresies, and for that the Community duly reveres and honors them."[60] Saladin, a staunch Ashʿarī, is praised as the champion of the

[56] Jon Hoover's *Ibn Taymiyya's Theodicy of Perpetual Optimism* (Brill, 2007) points out Ibn Taymiyya's optimism in the domain of divine justice. I seek to point out the political optimism that characterized his entire intellectual and practical career.
[57] Ibn Taymiyya, *Naqḍ al-taʾsīs*, 2:87, quoted in Maḥmūd, 727.
[58] MF, 6:55; See also, MF, 12:32–3; *Dar'(S)*, 6:292; and *Manṭiqiyyīn*, 142–3.
[59] MF, 8:230.
[60] MF, 4:18.

Sunna because of his defeat of the Fāṭimids in Egypt.[61] Furthermore, he writes: "There is not one among the [the early Ashʿarī masters] who has not made much appreciated contribution deserving of divine reward in refuting the heretics and enemies of religion and support of religion and the people of the Sunna in a way that is not hidden from anyone who known of them and speaks of them with knowledge, truth and fairness."[62] He writes that the Ashʿarīs "sometimes erred and exaggerated in their reaction to the Muʿtazila, but that can be likened to an army that fights the enemy and in the process commits mistakes and transgressions."[63] Indeed, in a remarkably fair and nonpartisan vein, he comments that some of the early Ashʿarīs were closer to the original position of Aḥmad b. Ḥanbal and the *salaf* than some of the Ḥanbalīs who had engaged in *kalām*, "such as Ibn ʿAqīl, Ṣadaqa b. al-Husain, Ibn al-Jawzī and others."[64] His praise of Bāqillānī is particularly generous, and he considers him the ablest of *kalām* scholars among the early Ashʿarīs and second only to al-Ashʿarī himself in his closeness to the early Muslims' positions.[65] Yet, despite their best intentions to defend the Sunni orthodoxy by using the intellectual arguments of *kalām*, they inadvertently accepted the fundamental premises of their opponents, the Muʿtazila, while rejecting their corollaries in subsidiary issues:

> But this principle [namely, the denial of divine temporality], which they had accepted from the Muʿtazila, confused them. Being learned and intelligent scholars, they needed to respond to it and [in that attempt, they] accepted its premises and corollaries, and that led them to positions which the leaders of religion and knowledge disapproved, and people became divided into extremes regarding them.... Moderation, however, is always the best course.[66]

Against the allegation, reported by al-Sijzī that "al-Ashʿarī had embraced the Muʿtazilī school for [the first] forty years [of his life], then he repented, but [in fact] he reverted only on subsidiary issues (*furūʿ*) and stayed on the [Muʿtazilī] fundamentals (*uṣūl*),"[67] Ibn Taymiyya is at pains to argue that, after his conversion, al-Ashʿarī indeed conformed to all of the traditionalist positions and sincerely sought to refute all the positions of the Muʿtazila,

[61] MF, 3:281.
[62] *Dar'(S)*, 2:102.
[63] *Minhāj*, 1:313.
[64] *Dar'(S)*, 1:270.
[65] *Dar'(S)*, 5:98.
[66] *Dar'(S)*, 2:101–2.
[67] In *Dar'(S)*, 7:236, Ibn Taymiyya reports this opinion as cited the Shāfiʿī Abū Nasr al-Sijzī's (d. 444) *al-Ibāna*, who in turn reports it from a Mālikī jurist Abū Saʿīd al-Barqī.

fundamental or subsidiary, that he understood as having been rejected by the traditionalist imams.[68] His evaluation of the Ashʿarī school is significantly more nuanced, in fact, than even the early Orientalists' who were sympathetic to Ashʿarism, such as Goldziher, who criticized al-Ashʿarī for having capitulated to Aḥmad b. Ḥanbal's doctrine, and insisted that "one must not credit him with something which belongs to the Ashʿarīs of the fifth/eleventh century if one is to remain within the real world."[69]

Turning now to substantive issues in Ibn Taymiyya's critique of Ashʿarī *kalām*, let us recall that the latter had been a response to two major problems that were posed to the traditionalists by various rationalist theologians: the problem of the nature of divine being and attributes and that of human responsibility. The Ashʿarīs had resolved the problem of theodicy by privileging God's omnipotence over justice (thus embracing an extreme form of voluntarism against Muʿtazilī intellectualism), and thus having to undermine human free will and, by corollary, ethical capacity or responsibility (although, as shown later in the chapter, given the primacy of law in Islam, this doctrine was never straightforward, varied overtime, and was often limited to theological polemics). The specific Ashʿarī doctrines that Ibn Taymiyya criticized lay primarily in the domains of theology and ethics[70] and had implications in the domain of law and politics: (1) the problem of the obligation of *naẓar*, rational speculation about God, upon every believer.[71] (2) The method of "temporality of bodies" (*ṭarīq ḥudūth al-ajsām*) as the means to prove the existence of a Creator. (3) Negation (or metaphorical interpretation) of some of the divine attributes affirmed in scripture, namely other than the seven attributes that, according to the Ashʿarīs, could be rationally known. These were: life (*ḥayāt*), power (*qudra*), will (*irāda*), knowledge (*ʿilm*), sight (*baṣar*), hearing (*samʿ*), and speech (*kalām*).[72] The first four (life, power, will, knowledge) are taken to be attributes known by reason, while the last three (sight, hearing, speech) are considered to be accessible only through revelation (*samʿiyyāt*). (4) Primacy of reason over revelation in case when a contradiction is perceived, namely the *qānūn* discussed

[68] *Dar'(S),* 7:236–8; Maḥmūd, 836.
[69] Makdisi, "Ḥanbalī Islam," 224.
[70] Mahmūd, 803.
[71] Ibn Taymiyya, *Dar'(S),* 8:348–358, notes that Juwaynī, Ghazālī, Rāzī, and the Ḥanbalīs Abū Yaʿlā al-Farrāʾ and Ibn ʿAqīl all first held to the obligation of *naẓar* and then later retracted their opinions.
[72] *EI*², s.v., "Allāh" (L. Gardet). For Ghazālī's presentation and defense of these in a summary form, see *Iḥyāʾ*, 1:121–3.

earlier. (5) Extreme emphasis on predestination and voluntarism so as to effectively (but not consistently) deny human agency in the moral world and causality in the natural world.[73] (6) The impossibility of rational knowledge of ethics, or, in extreme form, the denial of even the ontological reality of ethics.[74]

A Theology of Active Obedience and Disciplined Love

Two concerns appear to be paramount in all of Ibn Taymiyya's theological and philosophical writings: the imperative of knowing and loving God and acting righteously (in accordance with the law and reason) as a direct result of it. Henri Laoust aptly emphasizes the second of these commitments: "It thus appears that Ibn Taymiyya's entire theology tends towards one sole aim: that of giving a foundation to his ethics and, consequently, to all his juridical and social philosophy."[75] To secure this end, Ibn Taymiyya, notes Fazlur Rahman, "bluntly points out the discord that exists at the bottom between the Sunni orthodox theological formulas and the presuppositions of the law."[76] Ibn Taymiyya writes,

> You will find many jurists involved in self-contradiction. Thus, when they think along with the theologians who affirm the sole Power of God by saying that the (human) power and efficacy (does not precede) the act (but is created by God) together with the act, they agree with this. But when they think in terms of law, they have to affirm a preceding (and free) human power which is the foundation of the Command and the Prohibition.[77]

To separate God's goodness from the fact of human evil, the difference between divine will (*irāda*) and love (*maḥabba*), not recognized by the Ashʿarīs, is of cardinal significance for Ibn Taymiyya. The Ashʿarīs denied it because (1) given His Omnipotence and lack of any personal interest (*gharaḍ*), they considered it impossible that God loved something but did not will it; (2) attributing love to God is to attribute a weakness (inclination and need of the beloved) not suitable to God; (3) love required some similarity (*munāsaba*) between the lover and the beloved (in holding

[73] *Minhāj*, 1:94–5.
[74] MF, 8:231.
[75] Laoust, *Essai*, 177.
[76] Rahman, *Islam*, 114.
[77] Ibid. Zysow, 103, similarly notes that "orthodox theologians" (i.e., Māturīdīs and Ashʿarīs) negated human free will but, when faced with issues of practical legal theory, had no qualms about accepting the Muʿtazilī-sounding legal doctrine; some even dislike importation of theological contentions into legal theory (121).

this, the Ashʿarīs were reiterating the ancient Near Eastern doctrine on the nature of love), which could not be posited between God and His creation; and finally, (4) love, in its usual sense in the Qur'an and *ḥadīth* literature, is tied to particular acts and states of a beloved servant, which would require that God love a person at one instant when she or he acted righteously and cease to love when the same person sinned. This would entail a change in God, which is impossible. If, however, God's love mentioned in the Qur'an is interpreted as the unchanging divine will to predeterministically reward or punish a particular servant (regardless of his/her state at any particular moment), all of the aforementioned problems can be resolved and the metaphor of divine love can be seen as consonant with the omniscience and timelessness of God.[78]

Al-Ashʿarī's attempt to harmonize his extreme voluntarism (emphasis on God's omnipotence) at the expense of divine justice and human responsibility, along with the traditional insistence on not ascribing evil to God, led him to subscribe to and develop an earlier Muʿtazilī doctrine of *kasb*. According to the doctrine of *kasb*, God created both human action and the power to act at the time of action, yet humans acquire the action and thus become the site of the action. In Ibn Taymiyya's view, this doctrine lacked cogency as well as coherence (in this critique he was simply agreeing with Juwaynī and many others), and upon closer examination it gets reduced to the *jabr* (fatalism) of the type the Jahmiyya had posited.[79] Of course, the Ashʿarīs rejected Jahmism, Ibn Taymiyya argued, but only superficially, "only in choice of words, thus putting forth something that escapes understanding."[80] Later, the more philosophically astute Ashʿarīs, in particular Rāzī, altogether abandoned the doctrine of *kasb* and endorsed unequivocally the doctrine of *jabr* and saw no reason not to extend it to the domain of legal theory; indeed, in his mystical writings, Rāzī draws from it the obvious conclusion of moral indifference.[81]

[78] See Bell, *Theory of Love*, for denial of God's love: Bāqillānī (56–7), Juwaynī (58–9), Ghazālī (206).

[79] MF, 8:339–40 (*Iḥtijāj*).

[80] *Minhāj* 1:326; MF, 8:230.

[81] Thus Rāzī, "It is thus established that ... the human choice is pre-determined, and there is nothing in existence except jabr" (*al-Mabāḥith al-mashriqiyya*); "The existence of the action of a servant depends on the motive (*dāʿiya*) that God creates, and when that motive is found, the action must result, and, therefore, predeterminism (*jabr*) is a necessity" (*al-Maḥṣūl fī uṣūl al-fiqh*), and in his mystical writings, Rāzī takes *jabr* to its logical result of moral indifference: "The mystic knower must have no concern with the acts of the creation, nor does he feel displeasure upon seeing evil being done, for he knows God's secret in predestination (*qadar*)" (*Sharḥ al-ishārāt*; all qtd. in Maḥmūd, 686).

Pointing to a qur'anic verse, namely that "God does not burden someone who does not have capacity,"[82] Ibn Taymiyya rejects *jabr* and insists that "a servant is indeed the doer of his acts."[83]

It is to rescue ethical and religious responsibility from the antinomy latent in the doctrine of *jabr* that Ibn Taymiyya distinguished between two aspects of divine oneness (*tawhīd*): oneness of God's Lordship (*rubūbiyya*), which emphasized God's power and providence, and the even nobler aspect of oneness, oneness of divinity (*ulūhiyya*), which emphasized God's right to be loved and obeyed and human responsibility and capacity to do so.[84] Thus, the doctrine of human responsibility and assertion of God's power became simultaneously built into the very idea of God's oneness. How and whether Ibn Taymiyya himself resolves this problem is beyond the purview of the present study.[85] His statement of creed written for the common Muslims of al-Wāsiṭ best summarizes his view in an uncomplicated way: "Men are actors in the genuine sense of that term; however, God is the creator of their actions (as stated in the Qur'an). Men are the ones who believe or disbelieve, who live piously or impiously, who pray and fast. Men have power (*qudra*) over their deeds and will them (*irāda*), while God, on the other hand, is the creator of their power and their will."[86]

Ibn Taymiyya is careful to separate the issue of God's omnipotence from that of human ethical knowledge. His insistence on the possibility of what we may call natural law must not be tied with any kind of necessitarianism or intellectualism.[87] He writes:

[82] *Minhāj*, 1:274; Kūnākātā, 103.

[83] *Minhāj*, 266; Kūnākātā, 104.

[84] MRK, 2:136, 2:116; Kūnākātā, 104, 163ff.

[85] L. Holtzman, "Human Choice, Divine Guidance and the *Fiṭra* Tradition: The Use of Hadīth in Theological Treatises by Ibn Taymiyya and Ibn Qayyim al-Jawziyya," in Rapoport and Ahmed, *Ibn Taymiyya and His Times*.

[86] *Wāsiṭiyya*, 27–8; Swartz, 123.

[87] Incidentally, the medieval Christian theologian and philosopher, William of Ockham (d. *ca*. 1349) has a remarkably similar doctrine in many respects. Natural law is possible but it does not bind God; rather, it becomes possible because of God's willingness, in the realm of his ordained power. A modern commentator writes: "What Ockham did was to ground the natural law, and indeed all ethical values, on the will of God. Natural laws ceased, therefore, to be a 'dictate of reason as to what is right, grounded in the being of God but unalterable even by Him,' and became 'a divine command … right and binding merely because God was the lawgiver.' … The dictates of natural law, the infallibility of right reason, the very fact that it is virtuous to act in accordance with right reason – all of these amount to nothing more than the inscrutable manifestation of divine omnipotence" (Gierke-Maitland, qtd. in F. Oakley, *The Political Thought of Pierre d'Ailly: The Voluntarist Tradition* [Yale University Press, 1964], 171). Oakley continues, "The finality

Some people think that those who believe in the rationality of good and evil thereby deny *qadar* (omnipotence of God) and are bracketed with the Muʿtazila on the issue of divine justice (*taʿdīl wa tajwīr*). This is not correct. The majority of Muslims do not side with the Muʿtazila in this regard; nor do they agree with the Ashʿarīs in their denial of purpose in divine actions or in their negation of causality in nature .... The issue of (rational) knowledge of good and evil is not tied to the issue of divine omnipotence (*qadar*).[88]

God's acts, to Ibn Taymiyya, have a purpose known ultimately only to Him, for God's reason is nothing like human reason, and hence human reason is not in a position to postulate a purpose for divine actions and require him to act according to its dictates:

God's acts cannot be judged on the pattern of human acts, for humans are slaves while God is their Lord. They wrong each other and commit shameful acts; and He has power to stop them, yet He chooses not to do so. This does not impute evil to God, for He may have a higher purpose (*ḥikma*) behind [allowing such evil to occur] or may have some good to bestow on His slaves. This is what the *salaf*, the jurists, and Muslims in general believe; they all affirm that creation as well as the legislative decree of God has a *purpose* [rational to God, but possibly out of the reach of human reason].[89]

The Ashʿarī doctrine "that God neither loves good nor hates evil" is unacceptable, for it is contradictory to the Qur'an, the consensus of the early Muslim community, as well as common sense.[90] To act ethically in accordance with one's reason, even if not specifically commanded in the law, thus becomes more than mere following the command; it becomes a reflection of one's love for God because God loves both what is good and those who do good.

of right reason is contingent upon God's will, for it is only 'by the very fact that the divine will wishes it that right reason dictates what is to be willed'" (Ibid., 189).

88 MF, 8:428–30; Ansari, 8–9.

89 Ansari, 10. He elaborates elsewhere what this higher rational purpose might be. It is a key doctrine of Ibn Taymiyya that God has chosen to create the universe and acts the way he does out of wisdom, which ultimately can be explained as love. He loves good and justice and has chosen to not do evil or injustice. The question of whether God is bound to love is invalid, for love, just like wisdom and might, are attributes of God, and any questioning beyond this is futile and, for Ibn Taymiyya, against reason as well as revelation. It is significant, however, that Ibn Taymiyya places love at the center of God's creative as well as prescriptive commands (Bell, 209–10).

90 Ansari, 11; MF, 8:428–36.

5

Defending Revelation and Liberating Reason

Reconciling reason and revelation was one of the main intellectual projects of Ibn Taymiyya in all of his theoretical engagement. In particular, he was concerned with the refutation of the Ashʿarī hermeneutical principle, *qānūn al-ta'wīl*, which posited the possibility of contradiction between reason and revelation and gave primacy to reason over revelation in theological matters. The main interlocutors of Ibn Taymiyya, therefore, were the Ashʿarīs: As fellow Sunnis, they shared many of his commitments, yet, precisely because they represented the dominant Sunni tendency, they were the chief target of his criticism. His engagement with the Muʿtazilī *kalām* and the *falāsifa* may be considered corollaries of his key concern to challenge and rectify the prevailing orthodoxy.

DAR' TAʿĀRUḌ: IBN TAYMIYYA'S MAGNUM OPUS

Ibn Taymiyya's critiques of *qānūn al-ta'wīl*, the Ashʿarī principle of interpretation, and the epistemological and hermeneutic principles that underlay it are scattered throughout his massive corpus. His persistent engagement with it can be appreciated by his own account that he refuted one of its premises, namely the impossibility of definitive knowledge based on revelation, in his commentary on Rāzī's *Muḥaṣṣal*, and refuted the rest of its clauses some thirty years later in *Dar' taʿāruḍ*.[1]

Ibn Taymiyya's views on the harmony of reason and revelation were first discussed by Henri Laoust, whose comments on this issue were brief but perceptive. He wrote that according to Ibn Taymiyya, "The Law [*Sharīʿa*]

[1] *Dar'(S)*, 1:22.

then is all reason. No opposition between revelation and reason should exist. The authentic scriptural tradition (*naql ṣaḥīḥ*) and proper reason (*ʿaql ṣarīḥ*) are two manifestations of the one and same reality."[2] Another study that took on this problem was an article by Benyamin Abrahamov, who concluded at first that Ibn Taymiyya comes very close to Ibn Rushd in his manner of denying contradiction between reason and revelation, except that whereas Ibn Rushd considered the two domains true but independent of each other, Ibn Taymiyya chose to confine himself to the terms and rational proofs found in revelation, thus subjugating reason utterly to revelation and allowing it no status outside of it.[3] In a later study of Muslim thought, Abrahamov rejected his former conclusion, arguing that "for Ibn Taymiyya there are rational arguments arising from the human intellect independently of revelation, which are valid so long as they do not contradict revelation. Reason is thus an independent source of knowledge of God."[4] Yahya Michot has reached a similar conclusion.[5]

The endeavor of harmonizing reason and revelation in itself was not new among Muslim theologians; it may be said to be the object of all theology. After all, the *qānūn* was merely a way for the *mutakallimūn* to circumvent the contradictions between reason and revelation that had appeared inescapable. But Ibn Taymiyya's was a challenging time in Islamic history to claim harmony of reason and revelation. In the face of the formidable rationalist metaphysical systems that held sway in the medieval period, the traditionalists had no easy options. They could either defend revelation against all intellectual objections or abandon the intellectual scene completely, declaring it prohibited to even set eyes on the books of *kalām*, let alone *falsafa*. The first option was clearly far more difficult and risky, for rational objections against faith in the statements of revelation were too many and too deeply entrenched to allow positing a facile harmony of the two. Not only the die-hard *ahl al-ḥadīth*, but even the typical Ashʿarī followers found it safer to stay clear of reopening

[2] Laoust, *Essai*, 176–7.

[3] B. Abrahamov, "Ibn Taymiyya on the Agreement of Reason with Tradition," *MW* 82:3–4 (1992): 173–256.

[4] B. Abrahamov, *Islamic Theology: Traditionalism and Rationalism* (Edinburgh University Press, 1998), 51; Hoover, 30n37.

[5] Quoted in Hoover, 30n39. Also, Y. Michot, "Vanités Intellectuales ... L'impasse des rationalismes selon *Le Rejet de la contradiction d'Ibn Taymiyya*," in *Oriente Moderno*, 19/80 NS (Rome, 2000), 597–617; N. Heer, "The Priority of Reason in the Interpretation of Scripture: Ibn Taymiyya and the *Mutakallimūn*," in *Literary Heritage of Classical Islam: Arabic and Islamic Studies in the Honor of J. A. Bellamy*, ed. M. Mir (Darwin Press, 1993), 181–95.

questions that had been settled by the great masters. Ghazālī had himself advised the commoners and lesser scholars, in his *Iḥyā'* and more passionately in *Iljām*, against delving in *kalām* if one wished to keep one's "glass of faith" intact. Ibn Taymiyya's way of demonstrating the harmony of reason and revelation denied easy shortcuts, namely the theologians' interpreting away the problematic revelational texts to fit rational judgments as well as the traditionalists' convenient solution of endorsing reason only where it agreed with revelation. Instead, he argued for taking both reason and revelation seriously, each on their own grounds, and attempted to show that they invariably agreed.

Ibn Taymiyya's Letter to a Syrian Prince as a Summary of *Dar'*

Known for their digressive style and lack of didactic markers, Ibn Taymiyya's writings pose many a challenge to the modern reader. What more than compensates for these stylistic infelicities, however, is a certain methodological simplicity made possible by a profound coherence in his entire corpus. Taking our cue from William James and beginning by looking for the center of his vision rather than crawling like a "myopic ant" over the massive edifice of his thought makes the task of understanding *Dar'* manageable.[6] Despite the complexity of the subject matter, the vast range of issues and interlocutors, and the length of the treatise, the coherence of its overarching argument makes the presentation orderly and logical.

Our task of analyzing *Dar'* is further facilitated by what I contend is the author's own summary of his argument in a brief epistle he wrote a few years after the completion of *Dar'*. *Dar'* has been dated to have been authored between AH 712 and 717.[7] The epistle, addressed to a

[6] James, *A Pluralistic*, 263.

[7] The editor Muḥammad Rashād Sālim (see later in the chapter) dates the writing of *Dar'* to somewhere between 712 and 717, the earlier being the more likely case. The first modern edition of *Dar'* was published in an incomplete form as *Bayān muwāfaqat ṣarīḥ al-ma'qūl li-ṣaḥīḥ al-manqūl* (Exposition of the Agreement of Clear Reason with Authentic Revelation) on the margins of an early edition of *Minhāj* in Cairo (Būlāq), 1321/1903. This corresponds to *Dar'*, 1:3–4:295. Another incomplete edition appeared as *Muwāfaqat ṣarīḥ al-ma'qūl li-ṣaḥīḥ al-manqūl*, ed. M. M. 'Abd al-Ḥamīd and M. Ḥāmid al-Fiqī (Maṭba' al-Sunna al-Muhammadiyya, 1370/1951). Another incomplete edition appeared as *Dar'* in Cairo, 1971, edited by Muḥammad Rashād Sālim, which was then completed in a full eleven-volume edition (al-Mamlakah al-'Arabīyah al-Sa'ūdīyah, Jāmi'a al-Imām Muḥammad ibn Sa'ūd al-Islāmīyah, 1979–1981), and then reprinted several times.

Syrian prince Abū 'l-Fidā' (d. 732/1331) who was "the then Governor of Ḥama' … and a well-known historian," is dated between 720/1320 and 726/1326.[8] It was most likely written as a part of Ibn Taymiyya's missionary activism to spread his message as far and wide as possible. Siraj Haque, who first published it in 1952, incorrectly surmised that it was written "on the request of some person, whose name has been suppressed in the manuscript, and was meant to serve him as a letter of introduction to the Sultan." Furthermore, Haque misinterpreted crucial cues as to the purpose of the letter masking its relationship to *Dar'*.[9] The letter effectively states its main purpose in a few statements and concludes abruptly with the ending salutation without suggesting any other intention but religious advice. Haque further mistakes a description for a title, surmising that Ibn Taymiyya refers his reader to his treatise entitled *Maqālāt al-ʿālim [sic.] fī mas'alat ḥudūth al-ʿālam wa-qidamih* (Opinions of the scholar on the issue of the temporality of the world and its eternity). In reality, this segment is merely a reference to *Dar'* in which, Ibn Taymiyya states, he has discussed "opinions of [the philosophers] of the world on the issue of the temporality of the world versus its eternity."[10] Haque dating of the letter, however, seems correct. The content of the letter suggests that Ibn Taymiyya had written *Dar'* already and now was ready to provide an effective summary of its recondite arguments in a few statements, which we may take to be his final and mature position on the matter.

The letter opens with the usual praise for God followed by a brief discourse on the nature of revelation, insistence that the Greeks were devoid of revelational knowledge, and refutation of the *falāsifa*'s claim that the

[8] S. Haque, "A Letter of Ibn Taymiyya to Abū 'l-Fidā'," *Documenta Islamica inedita* (1952): 155–61.

[9] Haque, 155. However, nothing in the letter justifies that it was meant as a letter of introduction; rather, as the letter suggests, the unnamed person seems to have served only to have introduced and praised the Sultan before Ibn Taymiyya. The main thrust of the letter also confirms this conclusion.

[10] No treatise of Ibn Taymiyya by the title Haque suggests is extant or mentioned by his biographers. The text surrounding the segment makes is clearer: *wa-lahum fī 'l-mabādi' kalāmun ṭawīlun qad basaṭnāhu fī 'l-kitāb al-kabīr alladhī dhakarnā fī-hī maqālāt al-ʿālam fī mas'alat ḥudūth al-ʿalam wa qidamih* (and they [the Greek philosophers] have much to say in this matter, which we have explained in the big book in which we have mentioned the opinions of [the scholars of] the world on the issue of the origination of the world or its eternity). The only known lengthy treatise of Ibn Taymiyya that elaborated in great detail on the issue of the creation versus eternity of the world is *Dar'*, which, according to M. Sālim, the editor of the critical eleven-volume edition of *Dar'*, can be dated somewhere between 713/1313 and 717/1317. This also corroborates Haques' suggestion that the latter had originated between 720/1320 and 726/1326.

qur'anic hero Dhu 'l-Qarnayn ("the two-horned one") was the same figure as Alexander the Macedonian, for Alexander was pagan, whereas the qur'anic hero a righteous monotheist. These references appeal, for one, to Abū 'l-Fidā's historical interest and also suggest that Ibn Taymiyya was concerned with the influence on the prince of the propaganda that Aristotle, the First Teacher of philosophy, was a monotheist given that his disciple, Alexander the Great, had been mentioned with praise in the Qur'an as a monotheist. Then there follows a rational defense of the position that only God is eternal, and those who claim the eternity of the world following Aristotle contradict reason as well as revelation. Then Ibn Taymiyya takes up his main point:

Whoever considers definitive rational proofs (*al-adilla al-ʿaqliyya al-yaqīniyya*) with due thoroughness will know that they agree with the teachings of [God's] messengers and prove the necessity of trusting them. Similarly, whoever considers revelational proofs (*al-adilla al-samʿiyya*) with due understanding will know that God has guided His servants in His Book to definitive rational proofs by which can be known the existence of the Creator, the subsistence of His attributes of perfection ... the truthfulness of His messengers ... and that [the messengers] have perfected for God's servants what their unaided intellects were incapable of comprehending.

The means of knowledge are three, sense perception (*ḥiss*), speculative thinking (*naẓar*), and report (*khabar*). The early adherents (*salaf*) of this Community had acquired the knowledge of the ultimate purpose of both types of sciences, rational as well as revelational, and they knew that each of the two entails the other, there being no contradiction between them. God has revealed in His Book that both reason and revelation lead to salvation (*anna kullaⁿ min al-ʿaql wa 'l-samʿ yujībᵘ al-najāt*), thus God informs us of the denizens of the Fire that "they shall say: 'Alas, had we listened or reasoned, we would not be among the companions of the Fire!'" (Q, 68:10) ...

Thus God has implied that reason by itself (*mujarrad al-ʿaql*) leads to salvation, and so does revelation by itself, except that revelation does not benefit without reason, for mere transmission by an informer cannot guide[11] if its truthfulness is not known, and the truthfulness of prophets can be known only by reason.

However, a group of the people of *kalām* has supposed that the guidance of revelation is limited to mere transmission and, realizing that mere transmission of information is of no benefit if the truthfulness of its transmitter is not known, have made the arguments of reason external (and prior) to what the messengers have taught. But the best masters of *kalām* (*ḥudhdhāq al-mutakallimīn*) know well that the Messenger elucidated for the people rational arguments by which is

[11] The editor, Haque, informs us that he has replaced the original *yadull* (guides) with *yudrak* (is comprehended), but upon reading the full sentence, his replacement turns out to be awkward whereas the original reads perfectly well.

known the existence of the Creator, His Oneness, His attributes and the truthfulness of His Messenger...

[The early Muslims knew of the validity and mutual necessity of reason and revelation] but there came from among the *kalām* theologians those who were deficient in their knowledge of the Prophet' s teachings and in what rightly guided reason necessitates, and they conjectured erroneously regarding God's words and deeds in [the context of] the problem of the creation/temporality of the world (*ḥudūth al-ʿālam*). Their conjectures contradicted both the teachings of prophets as well as the requirements of reason. These people, ignorant of the Messenger's teachings [in depth], assumed that they knew them well and found them in contradiction of clear reason. This is the reason for people's confusion in the matter of messengers.

A group[12] among them [tried to explain this contradiction by suggesting] that [messengers] taught only by way of imaginative allegories and have only addressed commoners. Another group opined that their teachings do not state what they intend but rather the opposite of what they really mean, leaving people to have to discover the truth on their own. Then they go on to interpret prophetic teachings metaphorically (by means of *ta'wīl*) to fit what they have (thought up). Yet another group opines that prophetic teachings are equivocal (*mutashābiha*) and their meanings are known to no one, including the messengers themselves, except God.[13]

According to this passage, reason and revelation are not two entirely distinct sources of knowledge, but ones that overlap in some cases and mutually complement each other in other cases. They never contradict because they emanate from the same source. Without rational argument, the truth of revelation cannot be ascertained nor can its content be assessed, and although reason may subsist without revelation and guide human life, it will do so only imperfectly. Unaided reason, furthermore, cannot grasp the unseen truths necessary to perfect and guide human life to the ultimate happiness in this life and the afterlife. In fact, contrary to the *mutakallimūn*'s contention, theological knowledge regarding God and the afterlife is in even greater need of revelation

12 This is a brief list of the interlocutors of *Dar'*, a more complete version of which can be found in *Dar'(S)*, 1:176. The first group is the *falāsifa*, who teach that revelation consists of useful metaphors meant only for the commoners; the second group is a reference to the later Ashʿarīs like Rāzī, who do not consider the scripture entirely useless but profess to interpret it in ways vastly divergent from the literal meaning and sometimes opposite to it; the third reference is to others, including Juwaynī and Rāzī in their disillusioned phase, who argue that the true meanings of scriptural description of the unseen cannot be known to anyone but God. Finally, there are those like Ghazālī who hold that the truth may only be known through *kashf*, mystical revelation available to the elect few, a position that endorses the Ashʿarī conclusions but by using the Sufi method.

13 Haque, 159; for a slightly different translation of a part of this passage, see Hoover, 31.

because those truths are entirely beyond human reason in contrast with the empirical world.

The Main Objectives

Beyond demonstrating the harmony of reason and revelation, the three main objectives of *Dar'* may be identified as follows: to demonstrate the incoherence of the *qānūn*, to expose its consequences, and most significantly, to question the claims of necessity and universality of *kalām* by unsettling its very epistemological foundation and providing an alternative epistemological foundation that is rationally sound as well as in line with revelation.

1. *Incoherence of the Qānūn*

Ibn Taymiyya argues the invalidity of the *qānūn* by using three intertwined strategies: by showing its internal contradictions, its contradiction with revelation, and the incoherence of its epistemological premises. He begins by shifting the focus from the question whether reason or revelation is to be given preference to the more fundamental question of which of the two is definitive *on rational grounds*: "It could be that both arguments [that are said to contradict] are definitive (*qaṭʿī*), or that both are non-definitive (*ẓannī*), or one is definitive while the other is non-definitive." Because definitive knowledge (*ʿilm*) obtains in one of three ways – sensory experience, inferential reason (*naẓar*), and report (*khabar*) from a trustworthy source – revelation and rational inference, epistemologically, are at the same level in their respective domains. Hence, in determining which type of argument is to be given preference, what matters is the relative level of certainty that each argument furnishes, not its source:

> If both rational and revelational proofs are definitive, we do not concede that a contradiction is possible.... However, if [the contradiction is posited when] both are non-definitive (*ẓannī*), then the preferred position is the one that is preponderant. If one of them is definitive while the other is non-definitive, then the definitive one is privileged without question. And if it is judged (*quddira*) that the rational argument is definitive, then it is privileged, not for being rational, but for being definitive.... It is therefore established that to privilege rational over revelational without qualification is an error.... We do not claim that rational arguments are invalid, or that [the rational arguments] by which we know the validity of revelation are invalid, but that it is rationally inadmissible to oppose revelation by reason or privilege reason over it.[14]

[14] *Dar'(S)*, 1:86–7.

It is notable that the process of determining the relative weight of various arguments is a rational one – as reflected in Ibn Taymiyya's choice of words, "*quddira*" – a rational process of weighing and judging. In this respect, Ibn Taymiyya agrees with theologians. Revelation cannot be accessed without first establishing its veracity and then interpreting its meanings by rational means. It might seem here that reason, even in Ibn Taymiyya's scheme, has the upper hand.

However, two of Ibn Taymiyya's key contentions recover the authority and necessity of revelation. The first contention is that natural reason (*ʿaql fiṭrī*) as a faculty is to be distinguished from the judgments of inferential reason or speculation (*maʿqūlāt*). The concept of natural constitution (*fiṭra*) attached to reason gives reason legitimacy, indeed a divine nod, but also serves to limit the scope of rational speculation that might challenge revelation. *Fiṭra* is hard-wired, in Ibn Taymiyya's view, to love what is beneficial and to conclude that there is a Creator and that He is good, and hence to love God. What is beyond the ken of immediate experience and natural reason, however, falls into the category of rational speculation, such as the details of God's nature and attributes, and cannot be known with certainty except by revelation.

The second contention is that revelation already contains the best of rational arguments that appeal to the human *fiṭra* and guidance on how to use reason to interpret it; hence the dichotomy of reason and revelation is false. In the first article of *Darʾ*, Ibn Taymiyya writes: "A *sharʿī* argument could be revelational (*samʿī*) or rational (*ʿaqlī*). Being *sharʿī* for an argument means either that the *sharʿ* has established it and guided to it, or has considered it permissible."[15] This is a critique of the theologians' view of the reason-revelation problem in two ways. Firstly, they had treated revelation as if it consisted only of information or positive assertions about practical or unseen matters, devoid of rational arguments. The *qānūn* embodies their simplistic attitude toward the reason-revelation problem: Before the truth of revelation is ascertained by independent (namely, rational) means, revelation is to be treated like a black box; human reason must establish its truth without looking into it. All matters pertaining to this endeavor have come to be labeled as intellectual or fundamental matters (*masāʾil ʿaqliyya* or *uṣūliyya*). Secondly, once this truth has been established, then, in the postrevelation universe, reason becomes incapacitated, except in interpreting the commands of revelation. The latter is considered to be the domain of transmitted, subsidiary, or practical

[15] *Darʾ(S)*, 1:198–9; Maḥmūd, 320–1.

matters (*masā'il naqliyya, furū'iyya* or *'amaliyya*). Ibn Taymiyya questions these presumptions both in cases before and after the encounter with revelation.

Before one comes to accept the veracity of someone's claim of having received divine revelation, one naturally looks into it. Given that, in Ibn Taymiyya's scheme, in contrast with the Ash'arī view, unaided human reason is capable of knowing not only the existence of God, but also ethical verities, which revelation confirms, rational engagement with the content of revelation becomes one way for the human mind to judge its veracity. He writes in *Nubuwwāt*, "The difference between a (true) prophet and a false claimant ... is to be found in their respective characters and attributes (*ṣifāt*), acts (*af'āl*), commands, teachings about the unseen (*khabar*), and signs (*āyāt*).... Hence one who believes in prophets (generally) does not rely solely upon miracles (*khawāriq*) which might be performed by infidels and the impious, but seeks evidence in the [character of the] one who follows that prophet."[16] A true prophet commands what is known to reason to be good, such as "oneness of God, sincerity towards Him, and forbids worshipping false gods, lying, injustice (*ẓulm*). Therefore, intellects (*'uqūl*) and natural constitutions (*fiṭar*) confirm [a truthful prophet] and other prophets before him. Thus he is confirmed by clear reason (*ṣarīḥ al-ma'qūl*) and authentic revelation (*ṣaḥīḥ al-manqūl*) other than his own."[17] He goes on to ground his affirmation of ethical rationalism in an even more fundamental theological point about divine purpose in which he rejected the Ash'arī view that denied that God had any interests, and hence any purpose, in His acts:

> This discourse on prophethood is a corollary of affirming God's wisdom (*ithbāt al-ḥikma*) which makes God do all that wisdom requires and not do all that is against it. It says: He the Exalted and Glorified is Most Wise, places everything in a place appropriate for it, and it is not permissible for him (*lā yajūzu 'alayhī*) to equate the essence of truth and falsehood, or the just and the unjust, or the knowing and the ignorant, or the reformer and the corrupter.[18]

For the same reasons (divine wisdom and ethical rationalism), after the truth of a particular claim of revelation has been established, reason does not lose its effectiveness in the normative domain. Indeed, revelation itself endorses reason because it requires its adherents not only to obey what it specifically commands, but also to do good generally and gives

[16] *Nubuwwāt*, 24.
[17] Ibid., 216.
[18] Ibid., 374.

general commands to be just and benevolent without specifying all the ways of seeking these goods, and thus prompting the believers to continue to use reason.

Ibn Taymiyya thus rejects the categorical distinction implied in the Ashʿarī system between *uṣūl*, theoretical/theological (in prerevelation time) issues in which reason trumps revelation, and *furūʿ*, practical/legal/religious (in postrevelation time) issues in which revelation reigns supreme and reason plays no independent role. The sequence of pre- and postrevelation reasoning as presupposed by the Ashʿarīs was arbitrary and may be easily reversed, for in reality, the two types of reasoning are concurrent: One may look into and follow the teachings of a religion before having complete faith (hence the distinction between *islām*, submission, and *īmān*, faith[19]), and afterwards one continues to seek faith and conviction through obedience and appreciation of its commands.

Arguing for the unity of epistemology in the two domains, he contends reason and revelation agree and complement each other in both theoretical and practical domains, and, in both domains, each leaves room for the other. He posits the same trichotomy in both domains: there are issues in which only reason can judge, those in which only revelation can judge, and those in which the two complement and confirm each other.

Accordingly, in the practical domain, he writes elsewhere, revelational commandments are of three kinds: (1) those known by revelation alone and altogether not accessible to reason, and these are few, such as God's commandment to Abraham to offer his son in sacrifice or to the believers to not eat pork; (2) those commanded by revelation but completed, implemented, or corroborated by the use of reason, such as the five ritual prayers, whose benefits and some of the details are known by reason, but the basic obligation in its particular form is known by revelation alone; and (3) those whose desirability or benefit is known only by reason.[20] Now, even in the first and third cases, while seeming to judge independently of each other, reason and revelation in fact cooperate and corroborate. For instance, in the first category, Abraham knew that it is most rational to act in accordance with God's commandment. Similarly, an act in the third category, judged by reason to bring benefit or remove harm, automatically becomes endorsed by revelation, because revelation, in its general commandments, requires its adherents to attain human benefit and remove harm.

[19] MF, 7:7f., (*K. al-Īmān*).
[20] MF, 8:433–6; also, Ansari, 12–13.

In the theoretical domain, he gives a similar tripartite classification. God's messengers inform their followers of things that either agree with reason (revelation, in fact, provides the best rational arguments for God) or are acknowledged by reason to be beyond its scope, but never contradicted by its definitive judgments.[21] Finally, as noted earlier, there are truths that must be known by reason in order to establish the authenticity of revelation.

The reason Ibn Taymiyya was able to reject any categorical distinction between practical and theoretical domains is that he differed with the theologians of either kind on the nature of revelation as well as of reason. On the issue of revelation, his contention that rational certitude indeed is possible through revelation was two-pronged; he tried to show that the *qānūn* effectively rendered revelation entirely meaningless – and would not be acceptable even to its advocates (an argument I elaborate on below) – but also provided direct critique of the hermeneutical techniques that the *qānūn* implied.[22] In the process of establishing this position, he was led to review the entire foundation of classical textual hermeneutics and language and proposed an alternative theory of linguistic pragmatics. His hermeneutic theory, however, is beyond the scope of the present study.[23]

2. *Exposing the Consequences of the* Qānūn *as a "Shock Therapy"*

Although nowhere explicitly stated, reading between the lines we may suggest that one of the objectives of *Dar'* is a kind of "shock therapy" for the Sunni theologians and their followers by highlighting that this ill-conceived settlement of reason and revelation in fact led to losing faith both in reason, or revelation, or both. In Article 32 of *Dar'*, Ibn Taymiyya makes the potent argument that the *qānūn* renders revelation utterly ineffectual in imparting any definitive knowledge in any matter whatsoever – a proposition that is dangerously close to the *falāsifa*'s position, which the Ashʿarīs agreed amounted to a heretical rejection of the

[21] MF, 13:136–41; translated in Ansari, 17–19; see also, *Dar'(S)*, 5:297, 7:327; Maḥmūd, 334.

[22] Ibn Taymiyya states that he wrote that in his commentary of the first part of Rāzī's *al-Muhaṣṣal*, only part of which has survived in unpublished form. It is found in his *Naqḍ al-ta'sīs* (A Critique of Rāzī's *al-Ta'sis*), the only study of which I have come across is Maḥmūd, 861f.

[23] M. M. Y. Ali, *Medieval Islamic Pragmatics: Sunni Legal Theorists' Models of Textual Communication* (Routledge-Curzon, 2000).

TABLE 5.1. *Reason and Revelation as Sources of Knowledge in Ethical and Theological Domains*

	Theological Domain (prerevelation)	Ethical/Practical Domain (postrevelation)
Mu'tazila	Reason: Effective Scripture: Dependent/ Ineffective [denial of most divine attributes in scripture through metaphorical interpretation]	Reason: Effective Scripture: Dependent (intellectualism; God bound by rational ethics) [scripture confirms reason]
Ash'arīs	Reason: Effective Scripture: Dependent/ Ineffective [metaphorical interpretation of selected scriptural divine attributes]	Reason: Ineffective Scripture: Effective (strict voluntarism; ethics not rational but God's command) [scripture initiates ethical norms]
Ibn Taymiyya	Reason: Dependent Scripture: Effective [acceptance of all scriptural divine attributes without modality]	Reason: Effective Scripture: Effective [middle position of divine self-obligation] [scripture confirms reason]
Falāsifa	Reason: Effective Scripture: Ineffective [scripture as useful myths, theological truth by reason alone]	Reason: Effective Scripture: Effective [scriptural law useful for commoners]

truth of revelation. The *falāsifa*, who held that metaphysical truths could only be discovered by their method, had also attempted reconciliation with revelation by reducing revelation to morally effective myths that addressed only the commoners. Ibn Sīnā had written, "What is demanded by the *shar'* and creed (*milla*) which have come to us through the tongue of any of the prophets is to address (*khiṭāb*) all the crowd (*al-jumhūr al-kāffa*)."[24] Ibn Rushd wrote, in a similar vein, that the *Sharī'a* intended "simply to teach the masses (*ta'līm al-jamī'*)" and to "take care of the majority (*al-'ināya bi 'l-akthar*)."[25] Ibn Taymiyya did not fail to link the

[24] Michot, "A Mamlūk," I, 169.
[25] Ibid., 170.

consequences of Rāzī's *qānūn* to the bolder Avicennan principle that while "the prophets indeed meant [by their revelation its] outward meanings, even though these outward meanings, as far as the matter itself is concerned, are a lie and opposed to the truth; they wanted to make the crowd understand by means of lies and vain things what is in their [own better] interest (*maṣlaḥa*)."[26]

Ghazālī had similarly repeatedly complained that "[the *falāsifa*] accused the prophets ... of lying in the [public] interest.... They say that the Prophet taught in opposition to what he knew to be true, in the [public] interest (*li 'l-maṣlaḥa*)."[27] He wrote elsewhere that according to the *falāsifa*, "[the Prophet] was not able to state the truth openly because the wits of men were too dull to grasp it."[28] Ibn Taymiyya agreed with Ghazālī's critique and ultimate judgment against the *falāsifa*'s teachings as heretical, but he also agreed with the *falāsifa*'s critique of Ghazālī and the Ashʿarīs, who denied certain qur'anic divine attributes, that their own *qānūn* was nothing but a version of the same phenomenon for which they had denounced the *falāsifa*.

Rāzī's formulation of the *qānūn* in *Nihāyat al-ʿuqūl*, as noted earlier, emphatically posits that reason is the only source of definitive knowledge. Anticipating the objection that this utter incapacity of revelation despite its own claim to convey absolute truth would entail that God had revealed a false discourse, Rāzī distinguishes himself from the *falāsifa*'s view by reaffirming the standard Ashʿarī voluntarism:

> If it is said [in objection]: God would not reveal to the accountable believer [*mukallaf*] a discourse whose apparent meaning is contradictory to reason, for then it would be obligation upon God to inspire that rational [corrective] upon the believer, or else, God would be blamed for misleading His servants, and that is not legitimate. We say in response: this [objection] is based on the principle of good and evil [having independent existence outside of God's commands], and that God can be obligated to do something. But we do not hold that.[29]

But then Rāzī goes on to entertain the objection anyway, and argues that even though there is nothing in his theology that would prohibit God from misleading the believers, in this case, it is not so, because it is the responsibility of the believer to not rely on the apparent meaning and look for the real one, and if he fails to do so, the fault is his, not God's. Then

[26] *Dar'(S)*, 1:9; Michot, "A Mamlūk," I, 158.
[27] Ghazālī, *Qānūn*, 226; Michot, "A Mamlūk," I, 159n32.
[28] *Iqtiṣād*, 120.
[29] Quoted in Ibn Taymiyya, *Dar'(S)*, 5:333.

Rāzī concludes: "The conclusion of what we have mentioned is that it is invalid to adhere to revelational arguments in intellectual matters (*masā'il ʿilmiyya*) … It is permissible to adhere to [revelation] in traditional matters (*masā'il naqliyya*)… as in case of the rulings of *Sharīʿa*."[30]

Of this line of reasoning, Ibn Taymiyya's criticism is devastating. The upshot of Rāzī's insistence that revelation secures certainty only when confirmed by reason amounts to relegating revelation to an utterly superfluous status, even in suprarational matters of the unseen. Now, this critique seems to ignore Rāzī's explicit statement that revelational knowledge *is* effective in suprarational matters. But when Rāzī's limited concession to revelation is closely examined, it turns out to be less than real. In Article 32, Ibn Taymiyya argues that the essence of Rāzī's argument boils down to this:

> [N]one of the intellectual matters (*masā'il ʿilmiyya*) whatsoever can be argued by the Qur'an and Prophetic teachings, and that the information given by God and His Messenger may not be used to confirm anything.… For if someone grants that the knowledge imparted by God or His Messenger … contains that which contradicts definitive reason … it is not possible for him to establish with certainty anything that the Messenger has taught.… Indeed, such a person does not believe in anything that the Messenger has taught simply because he is the Messenger, nor does he obtain knowledge or guidance from revelation. In fact, he does not believe in any of the unseen things that have been taught by the Messenger, because [by definition] he does not know them by his reason.[31]

Put differently, how could revelation, once believed to be misleading in some matters, be trusted at all? Thus Ibn Taymiyya reduces Rāzī's position to that of the *falāsifa*, who were explicit in considering revelation a noble lie.

Ibn Taymiyya's contention must be read in the context of the greatest of Ashʿarī theologians' own troubled retractions and confessions with regard to reason and rational inquiry. It seems calculated to shock his fellow Sunni theologians and their followers who prided themselves on their rational defense of faith and orthodoxy. The great Ashʿarīs like Ghazālī and Rāzī had not been unaware of these gnawing difficulties and had tried to reconcile at times by attempting intellectual compromises, other times by abandoning the intellectual pursuits in favor of fideism (*tafwīḍ* of Juwaynī and Rāzī in his later life), and yet other times, as in the case of Ghazālī, by turning to subjective spiritual experience (*kashf*)

[30] Ibid.
[31] *Dar'(S)*, 5:242–3.

for certitude. The overall effect of this inescapable contradiction between what they believed to be reason and what they understood to be revelation had led to a fundamental mistrust of reason. In this context, Ibn Taymiyya's contribution was one of the most far-reaching attempts in Islamic intellectual history to "exculpate" and rehabilitate reason, paradoxically, by defending revelation.

3. *Critique of the Foundations of* Kalām *and Falsafa*

The third main concern of *Dar'* that claims most of its space as well as intellectual ingenuity is the critique of the very foundations of *kalām*, namely its view of the nature and role of reason. Given, as he writes, that "all intelligent people agree that what we label as rational argument (*dalīl ʿaqlī*) could be true or false (in its conclusion or premises),"[32] the challenge was to account for this obvious subjectivity of reason and mutual disagreements of various philosophers and theologians while maintaining trust in the validity of reason. What kind of reason was trustworthy if the best of philosophers and theologians fundamentally disagreed with each other and, even more ominously, with revelation, while all claiming to invoke reason? This led Ibn Taymiyya to engage in a comprehensive examination of the epistemological foundations of *kalām*, which, he held, had become involved in Greek metaphysics. This in turn led him to challenge the foundations of Aristotelian metaphysics, especially in the form developed by the great Muslim Aristotelians, Fārābī, Ibn Sīnā, and Ibn Rushd. In a move of truly outstanding intellectual courage and stamina, he offered an original critique of syllogism and pioneered a nominalist and empiricist epistemology, challenging the edifice not only of *kalām*, but of centuries of prevailing Hellenistic philosophy. Nothing less than an alternative account of epistemology could rehabilitate trust in reason after its conflicted encounter with revelation.

He had completed aspects of his critique of syllogism before the writing of *Dar'* during his imprisonment in Alexandria around 709/1309 in *al-Radd ʿalā al-manṭiqiyyīn*. An abridgement of *al-Radd* by Jalāl al-Din al-Suyūṭī (d. 911/1505) has been translated recently by Wael Hallaq. Its usefulness is limited by the fact that Suyuṭī had excised all theological and metaphysical discussions of *al-Radd* focusing solely on logic.[33] This means that Hallaq's valuable study – an important contribution in the

[32] *Dar'(S)*, 1:191.
[33] Hallaq, *Ibn Taymiyya*, liv; lviii.

budding field of Taymiyyan studies – does not exhaust what could be learned about Ibn Taymiyya's contribution in *al-Radd*. *Dar'* is perhaps a more developed and philosophically significant work, but its fuller understanding would benefit from focused studies of *al-Radd*. *Dar'* can be seen as the next philosophical step to *al-Radd*, in which Ibn Taymiyya further develops that epistemology by providing positive foundations for it in the qur'anic concept of *fiṭra* and puts it to use in addressing the reason-revelation problem.

Hallaq ably sums up Ibn Taymiyya's reason for engaging in a thoroughgoing refutation of syllogism:

> It is not difficult to understand why Ibn Taymiyya should have chosen to attack the entire system of logic through the theories of definition and syllogistics. Since the beginning of the fourth/tenth century, Arabic logicians had held that the acquisition of knowledge, as well as the principles governing the correct uses of the methods and processes by means of which knowledge is acquired, are the tasks of logic. As there must be some postulates presupposing the acquisition of new knowledge, logic was seen as the sole tool through which sound human knowledge can be derived and augmented. On this view, then, logic stood not merely as a set of tautologies, but equally served as an epistemic system, a theory of knowledge proper. In this theory, it was emphasized that, to avoid an infinite regress, the mind must be seen as proceeding from some *a priori* or pre-existent axiomatic knowledge to new concepts (*taṣawwurāt*) by means of definitions. If we know, for instance, what 'rationality' and 'animality' are, we can form a concept in our minds of 'man,' who is defined as 'a rational animal'. It is through definitions, then, that concepts are formed.... [F]ollowing in the footsteps of Aristotle, Arabic logicians deemed the syllogism as the only argument capable of yielding apodictic knowledge, and thus they considered it the chief, indeed the only, tool which can bring about *taṣdīq* [confirmation] with certitude.[34]

The belief that logic was the only rigorous way to acquire knowledge and evaluate judgments was shared by Ibn Taymiyya's most important interlocutors: Ibn Sīnā, Ghazālī, and Rāzī, and the later *mutakallimūn* generally. The *qānūn* that Ibn Taymiyya sought to dismantle was in fact based on arguments that claimed to be apodictic based on these claims of logic. Ibn Taymiyya's grievance against the exaggerated claims of logicians, Greek or Arab, is summed up in a passage in his *al-Radd*. Responding to the advocates of Greek logic such as Ghazālī and Ibn Rushd, who had argued that logic and syllogisms are prescribed by the Qur'an – Ghazālī having gone to the extent of declaring his mistrust

[34] Ibid., xiv–xv.

of the religious knowledge and learning of scholars who do not study logic[35] – Ibn Taymiyya writes:

> No intelligent man should think that the rational balance (*mīzān*) which God revealed [referred to in the Qur'an, 55:7–8] is Greek logic.... They have further claimed that it is a canonical instrument which, when properly used, can protect the mind from erring in its thought.... [This is invalid, for] when natural intelligence is sound, it measures [things] by means of the rational balance, but if it is dull, logic only renders it more so.... It prolongs the road; renders the clear ambiguous; and causes errors and fallacies. But when they relinquish natural (*fiṭrī*) and rational (*ʿaqlī*) knowledge of particulars in favor of categorical syllogisms – whose concepts, which they have coined, are ill defined and include both truth and falsehood – the result is so erroneous that it stands in contrast to what the balances are meant to be. Such balances become instruments of injustice, not of justice.[36]

Ibn Taymiyya's critique began by rejecting that apodictic knowledge could be obtained by means of syllogism because definitions are arbitrary, conventional, relative, and mental rather than exact verbal parallels of some universal existents. He held, in accordance with the early Sunnis doctrine, that intellect is a faculty (*gharīza*) that empirically senses the external world and creates concepts to express it. The function of human intellect was therefore not to grasp some universal existents and thus derive apodictic knowledge by using syllogism. Yet, later theologians like Ghazālī, despite himself being a nominalist of sorts,[37] endorsed syllogism as a guarantee of apodictic knowledge, thus failing, or refusing, to see the link between the system of definitions and essences that syllogism presupposed and its realist epistemological foundation. Ibn Taymiyya, in contrast, insisted that "what is at stake in adopting a realist theory of universals is no less than an entire metaphysic" and attempted "to show how involved logic is in metaphysics."[38]

Ibn Taymiyya's unrelenting empiricism is a reflection of his clear thinking on the subject – his insistence that there is no necessary connection between the mind and the external world is directly dependent on the

[35] Hallaq, *Ibn Taymiyya*, 100, par. 160, n. 1.

[36] *Manṭiqiyyīn*, translated in Hallaq, *Ibn Taymiyya*, 162–3.

[37] Griffel, *Al-Ghazālī's*, 176–8, argues that Ghazālī advocated a moderate nominalism and was not always consistent in avoiding epistemological realism under Ibn Sīnā' s influence.

[38] For an elaboration of the connection between language, logic, and metaphysics in the thought of the Arabic Aristotelians, see S. B. Abed, *Aristotelian Logic and the Arabic Language in AlFārābī* (SUNY Press, 1991).

concept of an omnipotent, personal God with will, power and knowledge, who could create the world any which way He wished, and the human intellect is only an instrument of observation and interpretation. In Ibn Taymiyya's scheme, the process of ratiocination is a creative and active process in contrast with the realist epistemology of the *falāsifa* and the Greeks, for intellect does not simply detect the absolute reality that is out there, but observes and interprets it subjectively.

Confidence in natural reason or common sense had been an early casualty in the rise of *kalām*. The *mutakallimūn* as early as Bāqillānī had required of every believer speculative reflection (*naẓar*)[39] about the existence of God and the knowledge of the way to prove divine existence. The preferred proof of God's existence in Sunni *kalām* was the method of "the temporality of bodies" (*ṭarīq ḥudūth al-ajsām*), its central premise being that "whatever is not devoid of temporality is temporal/created" (*mā lā yakhlū min al-ḥawādith fa huwa ḥādith*), thus temporality could not be attached to God. For this way of proving God's existence to work, this premise had to have an axiomatic status that even God's revelation could not contradict. If it did, it had to be subjected to *ta'wīl*. To Ibn Taymiyya, limiting what one knew to be God's words by the measure of one's own speculation amounted to an absolutist and unwarranted trust in one's rational capacity.

The reason for this dilemma was, as he addressed at length in *Radd*, that the *mutakallimūn* had wittingly or unwittingly accepted Greek concepts of apodictic knowledge, taking the propositions thus produced to be the absolute and universal judgments of reason.[40] In *Dar'*, Ibn Taymiyya attacked these premises of *kalām* in two complementary ways: by invoking scripture to persuade the believers and rational arguments to refute theologians and philosophers on their own turf.

*Is Theoretical Speculation (*Naẓar*) an Obligation?*

The last two articles of *Dar'*, which occupy more than half of the multivolume tome, are devoted to refuting the necessity of *kalām* in guarding

[39] For Ibn Taymiyya's usual thorough cataloguing of the development of various opinions on the obligation of *naẓar*, see *Dar'(S)*, 8:348–58 and MRK, 2:346–7 (*Fiṭra*). See also, Hoover, 31n52.

[40] In the words of Sherman Jackson, Ibn Taymiyya's problem with the prevalent theological and philosophical thought in the classical Muslim legacy was "that [certain] rationalist forces had succeeded in identifying their particular system of reasoning with reason itself, such that only those who paid homage to the former could lay any legitimate claim to the latter" (*Islam and the Blackamerican* [Oxford University Press, 2005], 10–11).

faith and making a case for its error and redundancy in most (but not all) cases. The arguments seem to echo Ghazālī, Juwaynī, and Rāzī's disenchantment with *kalām*, except that whereas these theologians seemed to have lost hope in the efficacy of reason in attaining proper faith altogether, Ibn Taymiyya attempts to provide a coherent alternative basis for harmonizing reason and revelation.

Interestingly, as Yahya Michot points out, Ibn Taymiyya agrees with Ibn Sīnā and Ibn Rushd in their criticism of *kalām* scholars for imposing on the common believers the arcane propositions they had formulated. For the *falāsifa*, the reason that the masses cannot be required to know the real truth is their intellectual incapacity. Ibn Taymiyya's reasoning was the exact opposite. He held that the truth that is most worthy of being known is as accessible to common believers as to the pompous intellectuals, thus underscoring "the self-sufficiency of the religious rationality manifested in scriptural literality and common faith, and its validity for all, the elite as well as the crowd."[41] Believers could not be required, he insisted, by any political or religious authority to believe in anything but the self-evident meanings of the scriptural texts. In this vein, he criticized the Ashʿarī warrior Muḥammad b. Tūmart (d. 524/1130) and the Muʿtazila (recall their role in the *Miḥna*) for imposing their theological creeds on all Muslims. He contended that all Muslim authorities have "agreed that what is compulsory for a Muslim to believe is what God and His Messenger have made compulsory, nobody else having the right to make compulsory something that neither God nor His Messenger have made compulsory."[42] Rational speculation (*naẓar*) is not necessary for all people in order to establish the existence of a Creator, for that knowledge is readily available to those whose natural reason has not been corrupted. The various claims to being the one correct path to establishing God's existence are unjustified in their exclusivism, even if a given method might be correct in its own right: "Whoever limits the way of knowing (the truth about God) to one particular path (of reasoning) that consists of a particular definition and a particular argument has erred, as has one who holds that another's definition and argument [in this regard] that differs from his own can never be correct."[43]

[41] Michot, "A Mamluk Theologian," I, 171.

[42] Ibid.

[43] *Dar'(S)*, 3:303–4; Maḥmūd, 313. See also Hallaq, *Ibn Taymiyya*, 11, for an elaboration of this "relativity" of ways of arriving at fundamental truths.

Systematic rational speculation in unseen matters is not without its usefulness. In the matter of acquiring knowledge about God, however, its usefulness can be likened to that of medicine, which is needed only by those who suffer from some ailment. Ibn Taymiyya goes on to emphasize the subjectivity and relativity of human ways of attaining knowledge of all types; only divine revelation is above this relativism:

> This knowledge [of God] is necessarily obtained by those of sound constitution (*ahl al-fiṭar al-salīma*), but many need speculative thinking (*naẓar*) in order to acquire it. Therefore, some could acquire this knowledge without *naẓar* while others need it. The same is the case with definitions: in some cases they are needed while in other cases they are not. Similarly relative is the judgment on whether a certain proposition is necessary versus acquired speculatively (*naẓariyyan*), and definitive versus conjectural. Something can be definitively known to a certain person in a certain situation, while in another situation it becomes unknown let alone non-definitive. Similarly, a proposition may be necessary for a person but theoretical for another in a different condition. In contrast, what the Prophet has taught is truth in itself and the difference in people's beliefs and conditions does not change it.[44]

But if the ways of acquiring knowledge are so utterly relative and contingent on human experience, what makes the knowledge of God accessible to all? How could Ibn Taymiyya respond to the theologians' concern to find a rationally irrefutable proof of God's existence, an endeavor that necessitated and justified the enterprise of *kalām*? It is here that we find Ibn Taymiyya's employment of the qur'anic concept of *fiṭra* to develop a theory of human psychology and epistemology that served as an alternative to *kalām*.

FIṬRA AS THE ALTERNATIVE EPISTEMOLOGICAL FOUNDATION

The concept of *fiṭra* appears in the Qur'an and had been long recognized by Muslim scholars: "So set your face to the religion (*dīn*), as a man of pure faith (*ḥanīf*); the constitution (*fiṭra*) on which He has created humankind; that is the right religion but most men know not" (Q, 30:30). The contributions of two fifth-/eleventh-century scholars, Ẓāhirī Ibn Ḥazm (d. 456/1064) of Cordoba and Māwardī are worth mentioning in this regard. Camilla Adang's study presents various exegetical views on the term *fiṭra* and states that some exegetes "saw *fiṭra* as an inborn tendency, a

[44] *Dar'(S)*, 3:303–4.

natural disposition towards monotheism (*tawḥīd*), or even towards Islam itself," although there were also those who interpreted God's creation of human being upon the *fiṭra* as meaning "a healthy physical condition, a state of perfection," or, in a predestinarian vein, in accordance with His plan or destiny.[45] The majority of Muslim thinkers, however – Ibn Ḥazm included – "came to equate *fiṭra* with Islam and, hence, to believe that everyone starts his life as a Muslim. They found corroboration for their interpretation in another passage from the Koran, specifically S. 7:172, in which God makes a covenant with the descendants of Adam, who unanimously and unwaveringly confirm that God is their Lord."[46] Ibn Ḥazm's concern is primarily with the issue of the children of the unbelievers who die before the age of distinction, who he forcefully argues are to be considered believing Muslims who will enter paradise, even though, legally speaking, they are to be considered part of their parents' community.[47] Ibn Ḥazm, like most exegetes, seems to have no epistemological or metaphysical but rather purely legal and contingently theological considerations in mind for his attention to this concept.

Māwardī's understanding of reason or intellect (*ʿaql*) gives us another clue about the conceptual space for *fiṭra* among Muslim thinkers, even though he does not use the term *fiṭra* itself. In *Aʿlām al-nubuwwa* (Signs of Prophethood), he writes:

> [Knowledge is of two types, axiomatic and acquired.] The way to obtain acquired knowledge is theoretical reasoning and argumentation (*al-naẓar wa'l-istidll*), for this knowledge is not axiomatic (*badīhat al-ʿaql*), since it is legitimate in its case to require evidence. Such non-axiomatic knowledge may be acquired by reasoning or revelation. The matters of reasoning are again of two types, those that are known by necessity of reason (*ḍarūrat al-ʿaql*) and those that are known by rational arguments (*dalīl al-ʿaql*). The first type, that known by necessity of reason, are those about which there can be no rational objection, such as Oneness of God, which is a matter of necessary knowledge (*al-tawḥīd fa yūjibu al-ʿilm al-ḍarūri)*, even if its necessity is established by means of arguments of necessary reason (*wa in kāna ʿan istidlāl^in li 'l-wuṣūl ilayhi bi ḍarūrat al-ʿaql*). The second type of knowledge, that known by rational argument, is that the opposite of which might be true, such as the claim of one particular person to be a prophet of God.[48]

What is noteworthy here is the ambiguity in Māwardī's categorization of the human knowledge of the Oneness of God: *It is necessarily known*

[45] C. Adang, "Islam as the Inborn Religion of Mankind: The Concept of *Fitra* in the Works of Ibn Hazm," *Al-Qantara* 21(2000): 393.

[46] Ibid.

[47] Ibid., 408–9.

[48] Māwardī, *Aʿlām*, 3–4.

by reason, yet it is not axiomatic. Māwardī then goes on to establish the existence of God by the classic proof of *ḥudūth al-ʿālam* (temporality of the universe) in a traditional *kalām* style. What makes a non-axiomatic rationally argued statement necessarily true, however, he does not consider.

To later theologians who inhabited an increasingly stratified society, *fiṭra* became a dysfunctional concept beyond the kind of limited legal debates noted earlier, for theological proofs of God's existence and monotheism were no longer deemed available to commoners. In Article 44 of *Dar'*, Ibn Taymiyya reports at length the elitist views of theologians and philosophers on the subject. Abū 'l-Ḥasan al-Ṭabarī al-Kiyā al-Harāsī (d. 504/1110), a student of Juwaynī, mentions that although the Ashʿarī masters have agreed that common believers are to be deemed believers, there is a difference in opinion regarding the nature of their knowledge of God. Some Ashʿarīs have held that commoners do possess that knowledge but are unable to articulate it, whereas others hold that they are to be deemed believers but without possessing the essence (*haqīqa*) of the knowledge of God. Kiyā then goes on to support this latter opinion, arguing that the commoners have only a superficial idea of God, that they can be persuaded either way about God's existence easily, and that it is rational theology that establishes necessary proofs. Such commoners are still considered believers for no act of their own, but because of God's predetermination, "for God has destined for them this destiny [of being believers] but has not destined for them the *ʿilm* (definitive knowledge)."[49] Kiyā argues for the indispensability of the kind of *kalām* theology he was engaged in because, he states, the qur'anic arguments for God's existence lack "domination and incapacitation" – that is, they do not completely silence the opponents and skeptics the way *kalām* does.[50] As we have seen in Ghazālī and Rāzī, the more sophisticated Ashʿarī theologians were to soon lose Kiyā's somewhat naïve confidence in *kalām*.

Ibn Taymiyya likens the philosophers and negationist theologians to the practitioners of Alchemy, who rarely attain their desired object and often get lost in the way or have misgivings about the truth as well as themselves. In an anecdote he relates in *Dar'*, Ibn Taymiyya captures his view of *kalām*'s violation of common sense. The anecdote concerns an eminent contemporary theologian who, like most Sunni theologians,

[49] *Dar'(S)*, 7:360.

[50] This disparagement of scripture, of course, never fails to hit Ibn Taymiyya's raw nerve, provoking in this case a vehement refutation of al-Kiya and his cohort (Ibid.).

denied some of God's scriptural attributes, and hence, in Ibn Taymiyya's language, was inclined toward Jahmism. When the scripturalist teaching of unqualified affirmation (*ithbāt*) of divine attributes (re)appeared among the common people in that region, theologians like him were expected to fiercely oppose this tendency. But he did not. When asked by his companions why he did not respond, he said, "When people hear this [i.e., affirmation of God's attributes without any modalities, *bilā kayf*], they accept it and agree wholeheartedly with it, and it appears to them to be the truth which the Messenger has brought. As for us, if we took a person, educated him, fed him, and cajoled him for thirty years, and thereafter wanted to make what we say go down his throat, it would not go down his throat but painfully." Ibn Taymiyya then goes on to add,

> The truth is indeed as he said. God, the exalted, has set up proofs and signposts of the truth and the light against falsehood and darkness. He gave the pristine nature (*fiṭra*) of His servants the capacity to apprehend realities [of things] (*ḥaqīqa*) and to know them. If, in the hearts, there were no such capacity (*istiʿdād*) to know these realities, neither speculative thinking (*naẓar*) would be possible nor demonstration (*istidlāl*), neither discourse nor language. [He Almighty prepared them], praise to Him, just as He gave physical bodies the capacity to accept nourishment: if there were no such [capacity], it would not be possible to feed them and to make them grow. Just as, in the bodies, there is a faculty that separates between suitable and unsuitable food, likewise, in the hearts, there is a faculty that separates even more between truth and falsehood.[51]

Kalām arguments, even when valid, serve not as nutrition needed by all but as medicine needed by the sick, whose minds are ailing from corruption and doubts:

> They are needed by those who either do not know or turn away from other (easier) ways to these truths.... For some people, the more difficult the path, the more involved in convoluted premises, the more impressed they are by it. Such people have become used to long deliberation over abstruse matters, and if an argument requires few premises or is simple, they are not pleased by it. *For such people, the method of kalām and syllogism may be used in accordance with their habits, not because the required knowledge is dependent exclusively on these means.*[52]

Ibn Taymiyya justifies his own engagement in theological arguments based on the need to refute opponents based on their own premises and method. The problem, in his view, is not that their arguments on God's

[51] *Dar'(S)*, 3:62; Michot, "Mamluk Theologian," II, 350–1.
[52] *Manṭiqiyyīn*, 1:253–4; Maḥmūd, 292 (emphasis added).

existence are altogether invalid, but that the theologians and the philosophers narrow these proofs to one or two arbitrarily and give them a dogmatic status, whereas in fact there are myriad ways to establish the existence of the Creator:

We have explained that many of the thinkers (*nuẓẓār*) follow a particular argument to the desired result and assert that the result cannot be obtained except by this path; but his exclusivity is unwarranted, even if his path is in itself valid. For *the greater the need the people have to know a truth, the easier God makes it for the intellects of the people to know its proofs*. Hence the proofs for the existence of the Creator, his Oneness and the signs and proofs of prophethood are numerous indeed. Similarly numerous are the ways by which the people may reach these truths – and most of these ways are not needed by most of the people.[53]

In light of the aforementioned, the common claim that Ibn Taymiyya deemed *kalām* or philosophical proofs of existence of God essentially invalid cannot be maintained.[54] He in fact chastises those traditionalists who "reject outright all rational argument and believe that they have been manufactured by theologians," as well as those theologians who think "that the Qur'an only avers truths (without rational argument)."[55] Furthermore, intellectual exercises, whereas for some merely a way to seek self-importance, do have a utility of their own, for they train the mind and make it capable of perceiving things quickly, thus sharpening the natural reason. Speculative rational argument about the unseen, if valid and divested of false premises and contradictions with the definitive teachings of revelation, is useful. This would suggest that it is possible for a valid type of systematic rational discourse to exist and help protect the revelational truth against false doctrines, even if Ibn Taymiyya would not put it in these words.

Such a properly rational discourse had already emerged, Ibn Taymiyya held, among early Muslims who were the most intelligent people by the standards of this natural reason, for they were the most successful in serving God actively and intelligently and interacting with revelation most naturally. Their uncorrupted reason made them understand the meanings of the Qur'an and the Prophetic teachings better than anyone after them:

For when the Messenger, God grant him peace, addressed them in order to teach them God's Book and his example (Sunna), he made sure that they knew exactly

[53] Ibid.
[54] Recently, this claim has been repeated by B. Johansen, "A Perfect Law," 262.
[55] MF, 13:136–41; translated in Ansari, 17–19.

what he meant by those words – and thus the Companions' acquaintance of the Qur'an was even greater than their knowledge of its words, and they communicated to the Successors those meanings even more than they communicated its words.[56]

Elsewhere:

It is known that the closer one is to the Sunna and to the method of the prophets, the more correct his discourse in theology (*ilāhiyyāt*) by rational means, just as his discourse is more correct by the standards of revelation – for the proofs of truth mutually agree and reinforce rather than oppose and contradict each other.[57]

Fiṭra and Reason

Fiṭra and reason are related but not synonymous, according to Ibn Taymiyya. Hallaq holds that Ibn Taymiyya reserves the term *ʿaql* for the faculty whose "function it is to conduct inferential operations," whereas *fiṭra* is "the faculty of natural intelligence, or the innate faculty of perception which stands in contrast to the acquired methods of reasoning that bring about perceptions in our minds."[58] Hoover rejects Hallaq's distinction and suggests that *fiṭra* and *ʿaql* in Ibn Taymiyya's usage are "closely linked," but it is hard to pinpoint the exact relationship.[59] Hoover attempts to better define the two concepts and suggests that Ibn Taymiyya's statements on the relationship are vague, sometimes suggesting that *fiṭra* is synonymous with reason; at other times, *fiṭra* appears to be the foundation of reason whereas, at other times, reason seems to be the basis of *fiṭra*.[60] Hoover sums up his view that reason and *fiṭra* are two "functionally equivalent" sources for attaining knowledge of God's existence and the ethical truths.[61] Hoover's misgivings ignore Ibn Taymiyya's general use of language, which is consistent with his theoretical understanding of language as fundamentally "relative" and "pragmatic,"[62] and his dislike for formal and technical definitions of, in particular, scriptural terms like *fiṭra* and *ʿaql*, for such formalization for theoretical neatness might distance the terms from how they have been used in scripture. The question of which comes first, *fiṭra* or *ʿaql*, would have been disregarded

[56] MF, 17:353; Maḥmūd, 295.
[57] *Dar'(S)*, 6:248; Maḥmūd, 305.
[58] Hallaq, 55.
[59] Hoover, 39.
[60] Ibid.
[61] Hoover, 45.
[62] Ali, *Medieval*, 237.

by Ibn Taymiyya as obscure and futile unless the entailments of that question become clear.

It is best therefore to turn to Ibn Taymiyya's own usage and description of the two terms. In Ibn Taymiyya's formulation, *fiṭra* is best understood as God's way to make human reason incline toward truth and righteousness. That natural constitution may be corrupted for a number of reasons, but correct rational argument still can salvage and recover the original human nature. Yet, without the original inclination toward goodness in the *fiṭra*, reason would itself be of no help, just like medicine is of no use to the body if the body lacks basic biological capacity; no amount of language training can make a monkey talk. And if *fiṭra* has not been corrupted, belief in and love of one God would necessarily obtain given the myriad of arguments that reason in its natural environment furnishes. Thus, Hallaq's view that *fiṭra* is distinct from intellect (*ʿaql*) is closer to the mark, except that a more precise way to distinguish Ibn Taymiyya's usage of the terms would be that while intellect is a tool, *fiṭra* is an inclination. When *fiṭra* is corrupted, intellect loses its "true north" and is overwhelmed by desires or confused by doubts. God sends messengers to guide humans and unveil the truth to which their *fiṭra* is already inclined. This the messengers accomplish by two means: by conveying reports of the unseen and accountability and, more significantly for Ibn Taymiyya, by invoking and teaching the rational arguments that would appeal to the intellect and undo the corruption of *fiṭra*. He writes in *al-Radd*, "God Almighty has created his servants on a constitution (*fiṭra*) in which there is the knowledge (*allatī fīhā maʿrifa*) of truth and its affirmation and the knowledge of falsehood and its rejection; the knowledge of that which benefits one and love for it and knowledge of that which harms one and its dislike."[63]

An imprecise reading of statements like this may have led Hallaq to conclude that Ibn Taymiyya's views on *fiṭra* as a basis of the knowledge of God's existence are inconsistent.[64] For, Hallaq suggests, sometimes Ibn Taymiyya presents *fiṭra* as a means or faculty for knowing necessarily from created things that they must have a creator, whereas at other times, he regards *fiṭra* as an inborn knowledge of God requiring no evidence whatsoever. This second view, however, is explicitly rejected by Ibn

[63] MF, 4:32 (*Manṭiq*); Maḥmūd, 325.
[64] Hallaq, "Ibn Taymiyya on the Existence of God," *Acta Orientalia* (Copenhagen) 52 (1991): 49–69; for Hoover's critique of Hallaq, see Hoover, 40–1.

Taymiyya. The phrase "*allatī fīhā maʿrifat al-ḥaqq*" could mean "that which contains the knowledge of the truth," but it could also mean, "in which there is that which leads to the knowledge of the truth." Another important subtle clue in this passage is that Ibn Taymiyya here has used the term *maʿrifa*, which cannot be used for inborn knowledge, for, linguistically, his disciple Ibn Qayyim al-Jawziyya explains, *maʿrifa* is applied only to "acquired knowledge," whereas *ʿilm* is knowledge which may or may not have been acquired.[65]

But we scarcely need to guess what Ibn Taymiyya means, for he explains his concept of *fiṭra* in much greater detail elsewhere while explaining the Prophetic tradition, "Every newborn is born in the state of *fiṭra*":

> Every human being has in his nature the submission to God (*islām*). If this nature is not corrupted by the erroneous beliefs of the family or society, everyone would be able to see the truth of God and submit to it.... *Fiṭrah* is the original nature of the human being, uncorrupted by subsequent beliefs and practices, ready to accept the truth of *Islām*, which is nothing but submitting to God and to none else... The *fiṭrah* is to the truth as the eye is to the sun – everyone who has eyes can see the Sun if there are no veils over them. It is like saying that every human being likes sweets, except if some corruption occurs to his sense of taste and sweetness turns into bitterness in his mouth.
>
> However, the fact that people are born with *fiṭrah* does not mean that a human being is born with the Islamic creed inscribed in his mind. To be sure, when we come out of the wombs of our mothers we know nothing. We are only born with an uncorrupted heart which is able to see the truth of Islam and submit to it.[66]

The most systematic discussion of the concept of *fiṭra* and its extensive defense appears in the final article of *Dar'* (Article 44), which alone spans almost half of the length of this massive treatise. Here Ibn Taymiyya provides a rational explanation for his position:

> It has been shown that in the human constitution (*fiṭra*) there is an urge (*quwwat^{un} yaqtaḍī*, lit. a power that requires) to believe in the truth and intend the beneficial. Now, either confirming the existence of the Creator, his knowledge and belief in him, is the truth or its opposite. The falsity of the latter is known with certainty, hence the former is true: it becomes established that the *fiṭra* has an urge to know the Creator and believe in Him. Also, after believing in Him, either loving Him is beneficial or not loving Him; since the second is known to be invalid, (the first is established) for loving the beneficial is part of the *fiṭra*. Then, either worshipping Him alone without any associating any partners to Him is beneficial and closer to perfection for the people, both in terms of knowledge and intention, or

[65] Hence, the term *maʿrifa* is never applied to God's knowledge, which is invariably referred to as *ʿilm* (*Madārij*, 1:124).

[66] MF, 4:245–7.

associating false gods with Him. The invalidity of the latter is known, hence it is established that the *fiṭra* has an urge for *tawḥīd*.[67]

He also describes *fiṭra* as possessing "an urge (*murajjiḥ*) for the right religion whose basis is the knowledge of the Creator, His love and exclusive submission to Him."[68]

We may now conclude that *fiṭra* is neither used inconsistently by Ibn Taymiyya, nor is it a loose concept "functionally equivalent" to reason, as Hallaq and Hoover have suggested. *Fiṭra* is neither equivalent to intellect, nor primordial propositional knowledge, nor a rational premise or argument. Rather, *fiṭra* is a divinely placed inclination in the human psyche toward all that is good, which provides guidance to intellect, which is a tool and could be used for good or evil. *Fiṭra* separates "right reason" from reason's misguided uses. In reaching the ultimate truths, *fiṭra* and intellect are complementary and interdependent and, therefore, insufficient without each other. This becomes clearer as we see *fiṭra* in action.

Fiṭra and Rational Knowledge of Ethical Truths

As noted earlier, Ibn Taymiyya held, as many authorities in Islamic law and theology had, that ethical truths are, in a qualified way, accessible to unaided human reason.[69] Except that now, when such a proposition could no longer be negligent of the objections that Ashʿarī theologians had raised for centuries, one needed a consistent foundation to claim ethical rationalism that was rationally coherent as well as scripturally grounded. That foundation was *fiṭra*. Its philosophical centrality can be understood best if we appreciate the formidable objections to ethical rationalism (parallel problems were being raised across the Mediterranean in the Christian West) of which Sunni theologians were only too aware, such as how could one square rationality of ethics with God's omnipotence, given

[67] *Dar'(S)*, 8:458–9; Maḥmūd, 325.

[68] Ibid.

[69] The issue of the rational knowledge of good and evil exemplifies Ibn Taymiyya's historically grounded style of metaphysical argument: "On the question of whether good and evil [attribute of acts] are known through reason, there are different views among the Orthodox community (*Ahl al-Sunnah wa 'l-Jamāʿah*), that is, the four schools of jurisprudence as well as others. The Ḥanafīs, and many of the Mālikīs, Shāfiʿīs and Ḥanbalīs believe in their rationality. This is also the view of the Karrāmīs and the Muʿtazila, as well as that of many sects among Muslims, Jews, Christians, Zoroastrians and other religions. On the other hand, many of the followers of al-Shāfiʿī, Mālik, and Ibn Ḥanbal oppose that position, and this is the view of the Ashʿarīs" (MF, 8:428; translated in Ansari, 7).

that now God, in order to be good, was bound to act in accordance with human rational judgments? And, more pertinent to Ibn Taymiyya's system, given that he held to a nominalist epistemology and denied the existence of universals, on what grounds could any universals be defended?

To this second problem, *fiṭra* was Ibn Taymiyya's answer. It provided the psychological foundation necessary for a rationalist epistemology, for it was universally available to all humans without requiring extramental universals. Reason, in this system, enables the mind to grasp, through empirical encounter with the world, the nature of things, their relationship and consequences, whereas *fiṭra*, a divinely placed moral compass in the human heart, turns this knowledge into ethical verities and inclines the human heart to the love of good and, hence, of God.

Scholars are beginning to note Ibn Taymiyya's ethical thought but have not appreciated its remarkably coherent foundation in *fiṭra*. Jon Hoover, for instance, states that Ibn Taymiyya reduces the various ethical terms the Muslim theologians had used – such as *ḥusn* (beauty) and *qubḥ* (ugliness), terms perhaps of the early Muʿtazilī origin, or perfection (*kamāl*) and imperfection (*naqṣ*), terms the *falāsifa* preferred – to "pleasure and pain and the suitable and incompatible."[70] Hoover, however, does not explicate the underlying epistemological system of which this reduction is a part. Accepting the philosophical and theological terminology, he astutely incorporates it into his own system, arguing that "the soul takes pleasure in what is perfection for it, and it suffers pain in the imperfection. So, perfection and imperfection go back to the compatible and the incompatible."[71] His definition of good is agreement with or suitability to the self (*nafs*); the standard, in other words, lies within the self. This contention is entirely consistent with his notion of *fiṭra*. "Souls," he writes more explicitly elsewhere, "are naturally disposed (*majbūla*)[72] to love justice and its supporters and to hate injustice and its supporters; this love, which is in the *fiṭra*, is what it means for [justice] to be good."[73]

[70] Hoover, 34.

[71] MF, 8:309–10 (*Iḥtijāj*).

[72] The term *majbūla*, from the Arabic root *jabala* (to predispose; *jibilla*) is carefully chosen by Ibn Taymiyya here in conscious opposition to *jabr* (compulsion). There are two reasons given elsewhere in *Dar'* for this choice: firstly, the latter word, *jabr*, which the *kalām* theologians used, was not used by the revelation, whereas the former was used by the Prophet. Secondly, *jabr* has connotations of coercion against one's will, which, according to the early Imams, Ibn Taymiyya reports, does not befit God, hence the word used in the Prophetic traditions is more befitting to God (*Dar'(S)*, 1:65–72, 1:254–6, 8:414–27, 8:498–502).

[73] *Manṭiqiyyīn* 423, Hoover 42 n. 101.

The potential clash of ethical rationalism with divine omnipotence is addressed by Ibn Taymiyya on several occasions in his writings. The Baghdādī Muʿtazila, as noted earlier, attributed the ethical value of an act to an essential feature of the act itself, a position known to Western scholars as "rational objectivism" or *intellectualism*.[74] Rejecting the implications of this position that compromised divine omnipotence, the Ashʿarīs adopted the other extreme that Hourani has called "theistic subjectivism," also known as voluntarism.[75] This position implies that: (1) acts have no essential ethical value (*ṣifa dhātiyya*), they acquire it upon divine command, (2) which is not bound by any purpose, and is arbitrary, as demanded by divine omnipotence, and hence, (3) ethical value can only be known by explicit revelation of God, and finally, (4) reward and punishment in afterlife can obtain only on the basis of revelation, not what reason judges to be good or bad.

Ibn Taymiyya charts a middle course between the two groups of theologians, agreeing with the Muʿtazila in that unaided reason has the capacity to know ethical verities, but with the Ashʿarīs regarding the contingency of good and evil on God, thus positing a moderate voluntarism. He reconciled the two positions, namely God's absolute power (voluntarism) and rationality of good and ethics (intellectualism), by means of the *ḥadīth*-based notion of God's self-obligation to act in accordance with the standards of good and evil that He has freely created.[76]

Agreeing with the Ashʿarīs that acts do not have an essential ethical attribute (1), he writes:

> [S]ome thing may be good, loved and profitable in some circumstances and bad, hated and harmful in others. Acts have attributes by which they become good or bad, but these are accidental (*ʿāriḍa*) and must be considered in light of what is suitable (*mulā'im*) or unsuitable (*munāfir*) to the agent.... Some things like eating meat that has not been slaughtered may be bad in some circumstances and good in others.[77]

On divine purpose (2) and ethical epistemology (3), however, he parts ways with the Ashʿarīs and seeks to disengage them from the divine authorship of ethics (1). God acts out of wisdom, inscrutable as it may

[74] G. Hourani, *Islamic Rationalism: The Ethics of ʿAbd al-Jabbār* (Clarendon Press, 1971); also, Hoover, 35n64.

[75] Hourani, *Islamic Rationalism*, 8–14.

[76] MF, 18:136–209 (*Abū Dharr*), where he comments at length on a long *ḥadīth*, recorded in *Muslim*, which begins thus: "God says, 'O my servants, I have prohibited injustice upon myself."

[77] Hoover, 35–6, paraphrasing *Minhāj*, 3:76, 78; MF, 8:310f.

be to the human mind, freely bestows acts with ethical value and makes it accessible to human reason. This was the precise view, notes Sherman Jackson, that the Basran Muʿtazila had held.[78] Ethical value is neither arbitrary nor created by revelation; rather, it is only clarified by revelation to a human nature already inclined toward them:

> [Prophetic commandments] were brought forth to perfect the *fiṭra* and firmly establish it, not to replace it or change it. They command only what agrees with what is right to rational minds which pure hearts accept with receptivity.... The prophets perfected the *fiṭra* and made humankind open their eyes to [their own nature].... Their opponents [on the other hand] corrupt perception and reason just as they obfuscate the proofs of revelation.[79]

God being the source of revelation and intellect both, any fundamental contradiction between the two, if they are properly grasped, is impossible. Thus, on the human side, Ibn Taymiyya leaned more toward the Muʿtazila, whereas on the divine side he was closer to the Ashʿarīs.

On issue (4) of the soteriological value of acts (i.e., punishment or reward in the afterlife), Hoover deems Ibn Taymiyya vague or noncommittal and in disagreement with the Ashʿarīs.[80] This is incorrect, however, for Ibn Taymiyya clearly agrees with the Ashʿarī position and rejects the Muʿtazilī doctrine that reason's judgment can lead to reward or punishment in afterlife.[81] Yet, even here, there is a caveat, because his inclusive definition of the normativity of Islam (the *Sharīʿa*) which, as we have shown, included judgments of reason that revelation has approved: "Being *sharʿī* for an argument means either that the *Sharīʿa* has established it and guided to it or has considered it permissible."[82] Because God has commanded justice and goodness in general, even if a particular act is not explicitly prescribed or prohibited, if its justness or the opposite becomes known to human reason, it becomes part of the *Sharīʿa* and is rewarded or punished in the afterlife.

[78] S. Jackson, *Islam and the Problem of Black Suffering* (Oxford, 2009), 84, explains the teachings of two Muʿtazilite schools on ethical objectivism: "For the Baghdādīs, it was a confirmation of the inherent characteristics of acts themselves; for the Basrians, if was a confirmation of the mental schemas that God had pressed on the human psyche as the normative prism through which uncorrupted humans naturally viewed the world." The Basrans held this rational human ethical knowledge to be grounded "in a primordial psychological schema of norms and values that was a direct result and reflection of God's will."

[79] *Nubuwwāt*, 431–2; Hoover, 44.

[80] Ibid.

[81] *Nubuwwāt* 162–3; MF, 8:435 (*Taḥsīn al-ʿaql*); Ansari, 14–15.

[82] *Dar'(S)*, 1:198.

The implication of the distinction between particular and general commandments of scripture and, hence, the crucial role of *fiṭra* are quite subtle and have been missed by earlier commentators on the subject like Laoust and, following him, Johansen. Johansen, for instance, writes that "according to Ibn Taymiyya [the Qur'an] contains the spirit and the letter of all religious knowledge and from God's revelation not only all major principles of law but also all rules of detail can be deduced."[83] This observation needs to be corrected. If one holds to a voluntarist ethic that deems ethical reason to be ineffectual and, therefore, demands specific indication in the scriptural texts to pass judgment on an act, as the Ashʿarī-Shāfiʿī theory did, then the general ethical commands of the Qur'an exhorting to be just and good are indeed not very meaningful. This Ibn Taymiyya explicitly rejected. Such general ethical commands are in fact not meaningless or "empty"; rather, they are part of the *Sharīʿa* even though they require the use of human reason to determine their implications. Thus, the Qur'an indeed contained all that is good and rational, but, for Ibn Taymiyya, human rational ethical endeavor guided by the spirit of the Qur'an was a necessary part of this guidance. The real impact of this teaching of Ibn Taymiyya's is felt in the domains of legal and, even more distinctly, political thought.

[83] Johansen, "A Perfect Law," 263.

6

Fiṭra, Community, and Islamic Politics

> The establishment of the caliphate is an obligation [upon the Community] and exemption from it may be permitted only on grounds of necessity.[1]
>
> If they had not accepted Abū Bakr's pledge and not given allegiance to ʿUmar, he would never have become an imam, regardless of whether this act of theirs would have been permissible or impermissible.... For imamate (caliphate) is rule (*mulk*) and authority (*sulṭān*), and a ruler does not become ruler by the agreement of one or two or four, except if the agreement of these few will guarantee the agreement of the rest.[2]
>
> –Ibn Taymiyya

The myriad contentions of Ibn Taymiyya's vast corpus, I have argued, were straddled by one underlying contention, the hermeneutic primacy of natural reason (*fiṭra*-guided *ʿaql*), which he insists is always in harmony with authentic revelation. This contention forms the core of an epistemological system that contrasts with the prevailing elitist and esotericist intellectual systems and underpins his critique of classical tradition in both theological and practical domains. This chapter recounts the political implications of this epistemology.

Ibn Taymiyya's concept of *fiṭra* is comparable to, yet distinct from and critical of, Ghazālī's concept of *kashf* (spiritual disclosure) as an epistemological tool. In fact, *fiṭra* can be seen as the universally available *kashf* – its "democratic" version. Ibn Taymiyya is explicitly critical in *Dar'* of the esotericism and elitism implied in the notion of *kashf*. Based

[1] MF, 35:18–20.
[2] *Minhāj*, 1:189–90.

on his confidence in *fiṭra*, Ibn Taymiyya rejected what appeared to him to be a stringent and elitist view that limited knowledge of God to the initiated few and argued that the knowledge of God's existence and goodness is available to the commoners (*ʿāmmat al-khalq*).

The various positions on the matter are brought out clearly by the following example. The great successor of Rāzī in philosophical *kalām*, al-Āmidī, explains his view on the means of attaining knowledge of God in his response to an objector who questions the obligation of theoretical speculation (*naẓar*) in this respect. The objector says that such knowledge may be attained

> through God's voluntary creation of knowledge in the responsible believer, or through someone in whose truthfulness there can be no doubt – such as someone who is supported by truthful miracles [namely, a prophet], or by means of a path of spiritual training (*ṭarīq al-sulūk wa 'l-riyāḍa*), purification of the soul and perfection of its essence, until it becomes connected to the higher (supernatural) world and, thus, becomes acquainted with what is evident and what is hidden without recourse to learning and teaching.

To this, al-Āmidī responds, clearly conceding to Ghazālī and other spiritually leaning Ashʿarīs: "We require the obligation of speculation (*naẓar*) only for those who have not acquired that knowledge by some other means."[3] Thus, Ghazālī's endorsement of *kashf* against *naẓar* had already made a crack in the necessity of *kalām*, which later Ashʿarī theologians had to concede. With Ibn Taymiyya, the crack becomes a floodgate, and the source of true faith and knowledge, *fiṭra*, becomes available to all, thus flattening the stratification of both spiritual (*kashf*) and intellectual (*naẓar*) kinds.

The present chapter is concerned with the implications of this epistemology in the postrevelation domain.

FIṬRA AND THE COMMUNITY'S RECTITUDE

Sunni Islam had been based, of course, on the twin foundations of the rectitude of the Community and the Sunna (hence the name: *Ahl al-Sunna wa-l-Jamāʿa*) and, certainly by Ibn Taymiyya's time, history had vindicated that foundation: Even after the caliphate had faded away, the Community had continued to preserve Islam. At a psychological level, Ibn Taymiyya's doctrine of *fiṭra* reflected this Sunni doctrine. But his appreciation of

[3] Al-Āmidī, *al-Abkār*, quoted in *Dar'(S)*, 7:356.

human *fiṭra* was perhaps even more general, as he frequently invoked the common sense of not only Muslim but also Jewish and Christian believers in their recognition of divine magnificence as being closer to what is rational and proper than what he believed to be the abstruse and at times downright irrational propositions of Muslim theologians and philosophers. He thus claimed to represent and theoretically ground the common sense of the believers. Often, even his adversaries were willing to concede this much. Badr al-Dīn Ibn al-Jamāʿa, a contemporary of Ibn Taymiyya and a loyal Ashʿarī, berated his Ḥanbalī opponents but conceded that their school was "closer to the mind and understanding of the commoner."[4]

Recalling aspects of the early Community-centered vision of Islam, Ibn Taymiyya affirmed the centrality and theological significance of the Community against any claims of imams, caliphs, or sects, for it was the Community that truly inherits the two defining attributes of the Prophet: 'protectedness from error' (*ʿiṣma*)[5] and the responsibility of "commanding right and forbidding wrong." Indeed, in a creative interpretation, Ibn Taymiyya supports the case for protectedness, typically built solely on *ḥadīth* reports, by linking it to the qur'anic mandate of commanding what is right and forbidding what is wrong:

> The consensus of the *umma* is truthful, for the *umma* – and God be praised – does not agree on error, as God characterizes it as such in the Book and the Sunna. God says, "Ye are the best Community brought forth for humankind; ye command right, forbid wrong, and believe in God." [Q, 3:110] The *umma* is characterized as such because they command all that is right and forbid all that is wrong.... If the *umma* held a doctrine in religion which was false, then it could not command right (as indicated in the verse) nor could it forbid wrong in that regard. [Hence, the protectedness of the Community as a whole.][6]

Ibn Taymiyya defends the doctrine of consensus against the possibility that all Muslims could conceivably agree on an error by his contention that even if there is such error, it can persist only temporarily, for "they are protected (*maʿṣūmūn*) [not from agreeing on an error but] from persisting in it."[7] What saves them from persisting in error is the practice of mutual advice, the commanding of right and forbidding of wrong. This way of endorsing the authority of *ijmāʿ* (consensus) has a particular

[4] Ibn Jamāʿa, *Īḍāḥ al-dalīl fī qaṭʿ ḥujaj ahl al-taʿṭīl*, quoted in Maḥmūd, 709.

[5] For a discussion of Ibn Taymiyya's complicated concept of the *ʿiṣma* of the Prophet Muhammad, see S. Ahmed, "Satanic Verses."

[6] MF, 19:176–7 (*Maʿārij*); Kūnākātā, 111.

[7] Zysow, 238, citing Ibn Taymiyya's *al-Musawwada fī uṣūl al-fiqh*.

Taymiyyan color, for now it is a dynamic process. What further set him apart from classical orthodoxy was the similarity of this protectedness of the Community to the protectedness from error of the Prophet himself. As Shahab Ahmed notes, Ibn Taymiyya in a radical departure from classical doctrine "conceived of the *ʿiṣma* (protection) of the Prophets as their Protection, not from committing sin and error, but rather from persisting in them once committed."[8] Explicitly equating the authority and the responsibility of the Community as a whole to those of the prophets, he writes,

God has made [the believers] witnesses unto humankind and given their testimony the status of the testimony of the Messenger ... and if the Lord has made them witnesses, that means that their testimony cannot be false – hence if they testify that God has commanded a thing, he indeed has, and if they testify that God has forbidden a thing, God indeed has. If their testimony had the possibility of being false or mistaken, God would not have made them His witnesses on earth.[9]

This contention comes out clearly in Ibn Taymiyya's distinctive response to the Shīʿī claims of the infallibility of the imams. (Note that because Ibn Taymiyya understands *ʿiṣma* as a dynamic process of correction, it is better rendered as "protectedness" rather than "infallibility.") He challenged the Shīʿī premise that the imam was the site of the continuity of the prophetic mission, and hence the source of legitimacy and infallibility. Responding to the Shīʿī theologian Ibn al-Muṭahhar al-Ḥillī, he wrote:

[The opponent claims that] the imam must be the protector of the *Sharʿ* since the revelation has ceased after the death of the Prophet, peace be upon him, and the absence in the Book and the Sunna of rulings about the details of affairs until the Day of Resurrection, hence the necessity of an imam protected (*maʿṣūm*) from mistakes and errors.... This can be refuted in a number of ways. Firstly, we do not concede that the imam must be the guardian of the *Sharʿ* – but indeed, it is the *umma* that must be the guardian of the *Sharʿ*![10]

He goes on to say:

The *protectedness of the Community suffices and the infallibility of the imam is no longer needed*, and this is what the ulama have mentioned in the wisdom of the protectedness of the Community. They say that when the communities before us (like the Israelites) would alter their religion, God would send a prophet who would show the truth; this Community, whose prophet is the very last one,

[8] Ahmed, "Ibn Taymiyya," 123.

[9] *Minhāj*, 3:272–3; Kūnākātā, 115.

[10] *Minhāj*, 3:270.

stands in its protectedness as a whole in the place of prophethood. Hence it is not possible for one of them to change anything of the religion without God sending forth someone (from among them) who will point out that error – so that the Community will never [continue to] agree on error.[11]

Given that the divine protection of the Community is not a result of any infallible source of orthodoxy in a person or an institution, but rather in the entire Community, actualized through the divinely guided *historical* process of mutual correction, revival, and reform, it is attached to the paramount responsibility of commanding and forbidding. Individuals and groups within the Community will doubtless err and go astray, but the process of commanding and forbidding as a way of mutual correction, no doubt protected by God himself, will guarantee the Community's protectedness. Because the will of the Community can never be reduced to that of any individual or institution, a "theocracy," in any usual sense of the word, is not a possibility within the Taymiyyan vision. Dependent on the moral activism of some groups of the believers, what is guaranteed is a continuous historical process that cannot be reified beyond the already well-known cases of *ijmāʿ*. This has led a modern commentator to the following apt conclusion concerning his political thought: "Ibn Taymiyya's political philosophy shows that, while it is religious, it is far in every way from theocracy; and while it is concerned with the theory of power and coercion, it does not condone or endorse personal dictatorship."[12]

Let us now turn to how Ibn Taymiyya deploys his concept of *fiṭra* and the plentitude of Community-centered "raw material" provided by the early tradition in the practical domains of law and politics.

POLITICAL JUSTICE AGAINST FORMALISM IN JUDICIAL DOCTRINE

The aspect of Islamic law that most directly interacts with government is its actual application, in particular the judiciary (*qaḍā*) and the public enforcement of religious norms (*ḥisba*). For the sake of brevity, I will limit my attention to Ibn Taymiyya's critique of the prevailing formalist judicial doctrines that had emerged in the classical period. Baber Johansen has already noted the distinctively political emphasis of Ibn Taymiyya's juridical doctrines. The predominant classical juristic doctrine, Johansen

[11] *Minhāj*, 3:272–3; Kūnākātā, 115.
[12] Kūnākātā, 117.

notes, of "all four Sunni schools" had displayed "marked epistemological scepticism regarding the *qāḍī*'s ability to distinguish between true and false statements" and had disallowed the use of circumstantial evidence.[13] This "formalistic character of the judicial procedure protect[ed] both the *qāḍī* and the rights of the defendant."[14] This doctrine on the nature and limits of "evidence, proof and procedure underwent important changes during the Mamluk period" at the hands of Ibn Taymiyya who, by "rationalizing the concept of proof and evidence ... gave a new impetus to the doctrine of *siyāsa sharʿiyya*."[15] Johansen bases his study on Ibn Taymiyya's brief political tracts (*Siyāsa* and *Ḥisba*) and the more systematic elaboration of his contentions on judicial reform by his disciple, Ibn Qayyim al-Jawziyya, in *al-Ṭuruq al-ḥukmiyya*.[16] Johansen's conclusion on how Ibn Taymiyya "deviated from the classical *fiqh* doctrine on proof and procedure" can be summed up in two significant propositions: Ibn Taymiyya's critique of formalism and his epistemological optimism, both of which intended to bolster political considerations such as stability, order, and commonsense justice.

In their critique of formalism, the reformists (the term Johansen uses to refer to Ibn Taymiyya and Ibn al-Qayyim) argued that "in order to follow the constraints of systematic reasoning," the formalist jurists had "construct[ed] abstractions that correspond[ed] neither to the life experience of the ordinary Muslim nor to the example of the charismatic members of the early Muslim community."[17] To combat this formalism, the reformists "highlight the model of charismatic figures of the early Muslim community, not in order to justify the legal categories that are the product of legal reasoning and its systematic constraints, but to downplay them." Anti-formalism entailed relaxation of "the legal profession's control over the judiciary," such that "the dispensation of justice" becomes a function to be fulfilled by all authorities, including political

[13] Not all jurists adhered to legal formalism as completely as implied by Johansen's statement. One could speak of a prevalent "classical doctrine," but the exceptions are significant enough. Johansen notes some of these (Johansen, "Signs," 174–5).

[14] Ibid., 179.

[15] Ibid., 170.

[16] Johansen generalizes these changes to a new trend among Mamluk period jurists, including a the Mālikī Ibn Farḥūn (d. 799/1397); it is more precise in my view to attribute this reformism to Ibn Taymiyya's overall critique of classical thought and trace his influence among his disciples like Ibn al-Qayyim. I cannot judge whether Ibn Farḥūn, who as a Mālikī must have been naturally receptive to this critique of formalism, was directly influenced by Ibn Taymiyya, but it appears likely.

[17] Ibid., 186.

authorities, which means that "judgments can be based not only on *fiqh* norms but also on political considerations and state interest." [18] Johansen notes a trade-off in the reformists' agenda, for "the goal of the new doctrine is not to guarantee the rights of the defendant, but to protect the public interest and the ability of the political authorities to control disturbances and lawlessness."[19] Johansen's observation presumes an opposition between justice and efficiency in Ibn Taymiyya's mind and explains his emphasis on commonsense justice as merely a means to governmental efficiency, hinting that bolstering the Mamluk state as well as some other personal or group interest may have been the agenda of the reformists. This is a result of perhaps too narrowly focusing on Ibn Taymiyya's juridical texts to the exclusion of the theological and epistemological system that directly bears on the issue.

Johansen notices, but does not give any explanatory role to, the reformists' own stated reasons for attacking the formalism of the classical schools. The reformists argued, he notes, that "[i]n order to return to a correct understanding of the revealed law ... one must follow the examples of the charismatic members of the early Muslim community, not the normative constructions of later jurists who deviated from these examples."[20] As pro-*ḥadīth* Ḥanbalī Sunnis, the reformists considered deviation from the examples of the early community (*salaf*), in particular those deviations that had in their view violated both justice and scriptural teachings, a sufficient reason for censure and reform. Johansen takes it for granted that Islamic law ought to be treated as secular law and does not make much of the fact that the reformists' critique challenged the formalists on the turf they shared, namely the Qur'an, *ḥadīth*, and teachings of the early Sunni authorities, including the eponyms of the four legal *madhhabs*, in addition to justice and reason (which, Ibn Taymiyya taught, are scriptural values). Ibn Taymiyya chastised *taqlīd* insofar as it led to injustice and inefficiency, made the *Sharīʿa* look ineffectual, and undermined it as the normative basis of the political community.[21]

But surely, even "secular" reasons for opposing *taqlīd* and formalism[22] are not as enigmatic as Johansen's speculation might suggest. In Islamic

[18] Ibid., 180.
[19] Ibid., 180.
[20] Ibid., 186.
[21] *Ṭuruq*, 91–2; Johansen, "Signs," 186.
[22] In this context, the two terms are interchangeable, for the medieval jurists' *taqlīd* of their school doctrines had prevented them from responding to the problem of stifling formalism.

law, the natural conservatism of law was enhanced even further by its non-state, if not antistate, posture since the third/ninth century and led in the classical era to the consolidation of what Sherman Jackson has called the "regime of *taqlīd*." Jackson goes on to observe that "the *terminus ad quem* of *taqlīd* and legal scaffolding is often increased rigidity and farther removal from the practical needs of society."[23] It is little surprise that Ibn Taymiyya's effort to introduce change, despite its earnest intention to safeguard the normative fount of law itself, was an extralegal or metalegal exercise that was bitterly resisted by the legal mainstream.

The other key feature of the reformists' thought, Johansen notes, is that its anti-formalism was grounded in an epistemological optimism. In place of the classical *fiqh*'s "epistemological skepticism" regarding the judge's function, limited to relying on the utterances of the disputants, their doctrine was "characterized by the optimistic conviction that the judge, by relying on signs and indicators, has the ability to determine the truth and to base his judgment on it."[24] Given Ibn Taymiyya's view of *fiṭra* and reason, this epistemological optimism is precisely what we would expect.

Johansen rightly notices that one of the key motives of the reformists appears to be to strengthen the state and ground it in the *Sharīʿa*,[25] but two qualifications should be added to this generalization. Firstly, the state that Ibn Taymiyya sought to strengthen only happened to be the Mamluk state of his time that defended Sunni Islam against the Mongols, but his motives are better understood in the context of his larger case for Islamic politics. Secondly, that reinvigorating the political sphere could or should be attained according to Ibn Taymiyya by sacrificing individual rights for state efficiency seems untenable in the light the his uncompromising commitment to justice, as I show in the discussion that follows.

THE CASE FOR SHARĪʿA POLITICS

Ibn Taymiyya's contentions in the juridical sphere were a reflection of his overall project to reconfigure the contours of normative authority in Islam by bringing political as well as spiritual domains of thought and practice within the guidance of the *Sharīʿa* and limiting the hold of the legal profession over it. This project is summed up in the following

[23] Jackson, *Islamic Law*, 99.
[24] Ibid., 180.
[25] Ibid., 168.

important passage that appears in Ibn Taymiyya's brief tract on public morality, *al-Ḥisba*, and its significance is evident by its full reproduction by Ibn al-Qayyim in his *Ṭuruq*. It states:

Some rulers (*wulāt al-umūr*) have fallen short [in ruling by the demands of rational justice] while others have transgressed in this matter, which has led to their neglect of the rights (*ḥaqq*) of the people and much injustice. The term *sharʿ* [i.e., *Sharīʿa*] no longer corresponds to its original meaning; rather, in these times, it is used in three senses:

[The first meaning is] the revealed *Sharīʿa* (*al-sharʿ al-munazzal*), which consists of the Book and the Sunna (of the Prophet). Adherence to this revealed law is obligatory, and those who refuse to follow it must be fought [as rebels or illegitimate rulers]. This *sharʿ* is inclusive of the roots and the branches of religion (*dīn*), the policy-making of the government officials and of those in charge of finances (*siyāsat al-umarāʾ wa-wulāt al-māl*), the judgment of the rulers or judges (*wa-ḥukm ʾl-ḥākim*), the spiritual enterprise of the Sufi masters,[26] and those in charge of *al-ḥisba*[27] and others. All of these must judge by the revealed *Sharīʿa*.

The second meaning of the *Sharīʿa* is that which is reached through interpretative reasoning. This is the sphere of disagreement (*nizāʿ*) and individual reasoning (*ijtihād*) by the imams (of jurisprudence).[28] Whosever accepts an opinion in which *ijtihād* is legitimate, it becomes established upon him, but the rest of the people have no obligation to agree to it except if it is confirmed by an irrefutable argument from the Book and the Sunna.

The third meaning [that goes under the rubric] of *Sharīʿa* consists of its corrupted form (*al-sharʿ al-mubaddal*), such as [the decisions in the name of the *Sharīʿa*] established by false testimony (*shahādāt al-zūr*). In this category fall judgments by ignorance or injustice.... To rule by this type of ruling [even when given in the name of the *Sharīʿa*] is forbidden and to witness it is forbidden. If the judge knows the [hidden] truth of a matter whose [visible aspect] does not correspond to the truth and still judges by it [formalistically, following evidently false testimony], he acts as an oppressor and a sinner.[29]

The prefatory remark makes it clear that the primary concern that motivates this redefinition of the *Sharīʿa* – or, as Ibn Taymiyya would put it, recovery of its proper original meaning – is the problem of politics (*siyāsa*), which was being threatened by two sides. On the one hand were

[26] Johansen translates the phrase "*mashyakhat al-shuyūkh*" implausibly as "those who control the markets."

[27] Johansen renders this as "fiscal market inspectors," but Ibn al-Qayyim himself explains the office of *ḥisba* as including all those cases not initiated by a plaintiff but that are a matter of enforcement of public policy, including public morality and fiscal practices.

[28] Johansen translates this as "free interpretation," but it clearly refers to matters of detail that are disputed among various Sunni legal *madhhabs*.

[29] Ibn al-Qayyim, *Ṭuruq*, 88–89.

most rulers who neglected the *Sharīʿa* and abused personal discretion to the point of tyranny, and on the other were mainstream jurists who rejected political prudence and considerations of public welfare.[30] His purpose is the inclusion of all of normative life within the *Sharīʿa*. The opening list gives us a sense of the target groups. One group (jurists) overstates its authority whereas other groups accept this parochial claim and, leaving the *Sharīʿa* to the jurists, feel free to claim their own sources of authority (the Sufis in the name of some mystical reality, *ḥaqīqa*, and the political elite in the name of *siyāsa*).

By positing a distinction between the sphere of the *Sharīʿa* in which rulings are based on indisputable proofs from the Qur'an and the Sunna, well-known to all members of the Community and, hence, independent of the juristic enterprise – and the sphere of matters that are disputed – Ibn Taymiyya makes the *Sharīʿa* more inclusive and limits the authority of the jurists to the second sphere. The first type of issues is brought out into the political sphere, leaving the second in the domain of legal *madhhabs*. This inclusivity is not tantamount to the semantic claim of what the label '*Sharīʿa*' should refer to. For although a semantic relaxation is also intended, it primarily allows Ibn Taymiyya to argue for the supremacy of the *Sharīʿa* and gives epistemological unity to all these domains of thought and practice.[31] This contradicted the Ashʿarī doctrine, upheld most stridently by the Shāfiʿī jurists, that no normative judgment could be established beyond the explicit purview of the scriptural texts. At best it could concede that human reason could know its interests, but pursuing those interests, as they argued against the Muʿtazilī doctrine, was indifferent to the *Sharīʿa*. Hence, no religious consequence could obtain from such rational judgments.[32] Thus there could be no "Islamic politics," only Islamic law administered by its experts; politics as such was indifferent to the *Sharīʿa*.

Ibn Taymiyya's inclusion of politics in the purview of the *Sharīʿa* was double-edged: Because these policies and political decisions must obey the *Sharīʿa*, if they do so, they acquire its authority and become part of it. There is a clear analogy in Ibn Taymiyya's mind between the two discourses that competed with *fiqh* for authority, one Sufism and the other politics; one difficult to anchor in texts because of its subjectivity, the

[30] See Chapter 2 for the classical ulama's attitudes toward *siyāsa*.
[31] '*Sharīʿa*' could refer in early centuries to laws as opposed to creed or ethics (see its etymology in Chapter 1).
[32] Jackson, *Islamic Law*, 29–30.

other because of its dependence on human judgment and contingency. Criticizing both the Sufis and the jurists for their exclusivist claims over the truth, Ibn Taymiyya writes:

> Sometimes by "*Sharīʿa*" is meant that which the jurists (*fuqahā'*) of the *Sharīʿa* say on the basis of their own effort of thought, and by the truth (*ḥaqīqa*) is intended what the Sufis find by direct experience. Undoubtedly, both these groups are seekers of truth; sometimes they are right and sometimes wrong while neither of them wish to contravene the Prophet. If the findings of both agree, well and good, otherwise neither of them has an exclusive claim to be followed, except by a clear proof from the *Sharīʿa*.[33]

A similar critique of the legalism of the jurists and the attempt to include Sufism as a legitimate science had been launched two centuries earlier by Ghazālī, albeit by introducing the alternative epistemological basis of subjective mystical experience (*kashf*). But his attitude toward political reason was even less accommodating than the typical Ashʿarī's (including that of his own teacher, Juwaynī). In contrast, for Ibn Taymiyya, a single epistemological basis placed legal, spiritual, and political discourses in analogous relationship to the *Sharīʿa*.

The two-way relationship he envisioned between the *Sharīʿa* and the Sufi discourse is also envisioned with politics. Just politics could be part of the *Sharīʿa*, even if not found in explicit formal rulings of *fiqh*, whereas an oppressive and unfair ruling of *fiqh*, "attributed to [the *Sharīʿa*] by means of forced interpretation (*ta'wīl*),"[34] was not part of it. The *Sharīʿa* is thus understood not just as a body of doctrines and rules, but more as an ideal that diverse groups of reasoners could interpret and through which they could negotiate in a shared "Islamic public sphere" of sorts.

Recall that for Ghazālī, politics was a necessary evil, essentially a burden, even in its best form in the golden age of the *Rāshidūn* Caliphs, which the pious legists (*fuqahā'*) among the Companions kept at bay.[35] For Ibn Taymiyya, "Governance for the one who understands it as a religious obligation by which he seeks nearness to God and carries out his obligations in it to the best of his capacity is among the most meritorious of righteous deeds, to the point that Imam Aḥmad had narrated in his *Musnad* that the Prophet said, 'The dearest of creatures to God is a just imam, and the most despised of creatures to God is an oppressive

[33] Quoted in Rahman, *Islam*, 112–3.
[34] Ibn al-Qayyim, *Ṭuruq* 127; Kūnākātā 148.
[35] *Iḥyā'*, 1:61.

imam.'"[36] In *Siyāsa* he writes, "If the purpose of (possessing) authority and wealth is drawing nearer to God and using it in God's path, then it is success in this world as well as the hereafter."[37] Analogy of wealth with power is a potent argument, for wealth and earning a livelihood, since the early days of Islam, had become established as a legitimate pursuit as a tenet of Sunni orthodoxy despite its potential corrupting influence.[38]

Eulogizing politics would do little if the substance of politics were not appreciated or consistently endorsed. Michael Cook's magisterial history of the duty of commanding right and forbidding wrong in Islam offers much to elucidate Ibn Taymiyya's doctrine in the context of the teachings on the subject across the centuries. Ḥanbalīs, Cook informs us, had always been known for their "populist" bent and their street power, especially in Baghdad, to command right and forbid wrong, usually on ritual and social matters such as encouraging correct performance of prayers and prohibiting musical instruments and drinking of wine. However, before Ibn Taymiyya, the "political" content of this duty in the minds of the Ḥanbalīs was insignificant – not that the rulers were not subjected to moral criticism, but that the issues were mostly religious and social. Ibn Taymiyya's attitude contrasted sharply with "the traditional Ḥanbalī queasiness over the exercise of political power." While Aḥmad b. Ḥanbal is reported to have disliked or considered illicit any office of the state,[39] "Ibn Taymiyya's political thought conveys no such sense that power is inherently contaminated and contaminating."[40] He preached cooperation with government in matters of justice and piety and by offering advice and warning. Rejecting the idea that power was inherently "contaminated and contaminating," he was at pains to distinguish "good" from "bad" association with power; it is this vacuous pietism, he believed, that had led to the disappearance of moral considerations from the political sphere. Cook sums up Ibn Taymiyya's positive yet discriminating attitude toward political authority as given in a passage in *Siyāsa*:

People, he tells us, fall into three groups with respect to their attitudes towards political power [the actual terms used by Ibn Taymiyya here are *sulṭān* (authority,

[36] MF, 28:65 (*Ḥisba*).
[37] MF, 28:394 (*Siyāsa*).
[38] For the debate in early Sunni doctrine (in third-/ninth-century Baghdad), see Sayyid, *Jamāʿa*, 246–9.
[39] On Aḥmad b. Ḥanbal's dislike of state offices, see Ibn Abī Yaʿlā, *Ṭabaqāt*, cited in Cook, *Commanding*, 156; on the Damascene Ḥanbalīs' emphasis on distance from power, including holding official judgeship positions, see Cook, *Commanding*, 145–8.
[40] Cook, *Commanding*, 156–7.

government, king) and *siyāsa* (politics)]. The first group holds, in effect, that there can be no such thing as political morality;[41] so it opts for politics without morality. The second shares the premise, but opts for morality without politics. The third group is, of course, the one that gets it right, avoiding the extreme positions of the other two by rejecting their shared premise. The group that concerns us here is the second, moralistic group. Their moralism, he tells us, comes in two – very different – styles. The first might be labeled quietist moralism. The quietist moralist, for all his uncompromising righteousness, is characterised by a certain timidity or meanness of spirit. This failing can lead him to neglect a duty the omission of which is worse than the commission of many prohibited acts; it can equally lead him to forbid the performance of a duty [of political nature] where this is tantamount to turning people aside from the way of God. The second style can be labeled activist moralism. The activist moralist believes it to be his duty to take a stand against political injustice and to do so by recourse to arms; thus he ends up fighting against Muslims in the manner of the Khārijites. The distinction runs parallel to one that Ibn Taymiyya makes in his tract on forbidding wrong between those who fall short in the performance of the duty and those who go too far. Now it costs Ibn Taymiyya nothing to take a firm stance against the Khārijites. But in condemning the quietist variety of moralism, he was dissociating himself from something perilously close to the attitude of the founder of his school.[42]

This "political morality" of Ibn Taymiyya, Cook observes, was different from earlier Ḥanbalīs in two ways: (1) his "utilitarianism" and (2) his connection of the performance of this duty to the authorities. Elaborating on Ibn Taymiyya's "utilitarianism," Cook draws on Laoust's discussion of the issue and observes that although "[n]one of this should be taken to imply the absolute sovereignty of utility ... the utilitarian idiom of costs and benefits, with its brushing aside of moral absolutes, is a striking feature of his political thought."[43] Ibn Taymiyya writes in *Siyāsa*, for instance: "The obligation is to attain and complete what is good and remove or reduce harm; if there is a contradiction in this regard, then procuring the greater of two goods, while possibly losing the lesser one, or avoiding the greater of two harms, while possibly tolerating the lesser one, is the essence of the *sharʿ*."[44]

Cook underestimates, however, the internal coherence of Ibn Taymiyya's political thought and, despite his appreciation for something unusual in Ibn Taymiyya's attention to utility and political activism, casually

41 The original being "*al-siyāsa al-dīniyya*" or "*al-siyāsa al-sharʿiyya*."
42 Cook, *Commanding*, 157, paraphrasing MF, 28:293–5 (*Siyāsa*).
43 Ibid., 154.
44 MF, 28:396 (*Siyāsa*).

characterizes it as "haphazard" and "brisk Islamic utilitarianism."[45] To the contrary, it seems to me that there is a consistent appreciation in Ibn Taymiyya's thought of the fact that politics is the art of the possible – as a modern political theorist puts it (in a very different context), "The man who treats everything as a matter of principle cannot be happy with politics."[46] "Thus in making an appointment to a public office," the ruler's duty in Ibn Taymiyya's view, as reported by Cook, "is to appoint the best man available (*al-aṣlaḥ al-mawjūd*); and provided that, in the absence of the right man for the job, he appoints the best man he can, he is a just ruler even if some undesirable consequences ensue. In short, the ruler has a job to do, and he has nothing to be ashamed of provided he does it to the best of his abilities. More than that, all forms of political authority have the blessing of the holy law (*Sharīʿa*) and all public offices are religious offices (*manāṣib dīniyya*)."[47] Given that in politics one must make compromises to attain any benefit, Ibn Taymiyya's teaching is that a ruler or anyone in a political office "will not be held accountable for what is beyond his capacity."[48]

Justice – the Ultimate Political Virtue

A reader familiar with medieval Sunni literature is likely to be struck by the remarkable emphasis Ibn Taymiyya places on justice (*ʿadl*). It is the guiding virtue for Ibn Taymiyya in law, ethics, and, most of all, politics. Politics, Ibn Taymiyya seems to have realized, is especially in need of it because the utilitarian mode of reasoning that politics requires is often beyond the reach of prefabricated formulae or specific scriptural texts. In *Minhāj*, he writes, "Ruling by justice is an absolute obligation in all occasions upon everyone and with respect to everyone." "Ruling" here includes judging and deciding in any capacity. To the disconcerted Sunni theologian-jurist who was too aware of the threat of such claims of justice against scriptural dicta, Ibn Taymiyya is prepared with a response: "Ruling by what God has revealed unto Muḥammad, upon him be peace, *is but justice in a particular form* – indeed it is the most perfect and best type of justice and ruling by it an obligation upon the Prophet himself

[45] Cook, *Commanding*, 154, 156.
[46] Crick, 136.
[47] Cook, *Commanding*, 156.
[48] MF, 28:396 (*Siyāsa*).

as well as upon those who follow him."[49] Yet, there is need for justice beyond the words of the scriptural texts:

> Similarly [justice is an obligation] in transactions such as trade (*mubaya'āt*), renting (*ijārāt*) and representation (*wikālāt*) … justice in these matters could be *that which is obvious to everyone just as payment to the seller, or it could be what is obscure (to commonsense) and is settled by some divine laws, such as the law of Islam.* For the generality of what the Book and the Sunna have prohibited comes back to establishing justice and prohibiting injustice – be it obvious or obscure.… This includes matters in which the Muslims have mutually disagreed because of their obscurity and subtlety, and the basic principle in such matters is that no transactions that people need should be outlawed for them except what the Book and the Sunna have outlawed.[50]

Justice is the spirit of the specific laws of the *Sharī'a*, and even when the words of the *Sharī'a* are absent, policies that seek justice must regulate that space. The nature of this justice is unspecified, hence the wide scope allowed to *fiṭra*-guided practical reason. Ibn al-Qayyim echoes his teacher's doctrine and states explicitly that what is called *siyāsa* (politics) and outlawed typically by the formalist jurists is part of the *Sharī'a* if it is just:

> Just politics (*al-siyāsa al-'ādila*) is part and parcel of [the *Sharī'a*] and a branch from its branches. One who truly comprehends the objectives (*maqāṣid*) of the *Sharī'a*, its rulings and their proper contexts, will never need any politics other than it. Politics is of two kinds: unjust politics (consisting of oppressive or wrongful policies), which the *Sharī'a* prohibits, and just politics, which takes the rights of the weak from the unjust and the transgressing and hence is part of the *Sharī'a*; some know this and others don't.[51]

Indeed, "By whatever means justice is established, that is part of the religion."[52] Nor must the partisans of politics assume that the *Sharī'a* contradicts or limits just policies; indeed, the two are identical: "We name it politics only following your terminology, for *it is in reality nothing but the justice of God and His Messenger, which is manifested through these signs and tokens.*"[53] Both jurists frequently repeat and rephrase this contention, appreciating how remarkable and new it was and how likely it was to fall on deaf ears: The *Sharī'a* is not merely a law limited to jurisprudence (*fiqh*) that the ulama preserve and pass on as *madhhab*

[49] *Minhāj*, 1:32.
[50] MF, 28:385–6 (*Siyāsa*); Kūnākātā, 178.
[51] *Ṭuruq*, 10.
[52] Ibid., 11.
[53] Ibid., 18 (emphasis added).

doctrines, but inclusive of just policies of rulers as well as fair judgments of *qāḍīs*. That Ibn Taymiyya and Ibn al-Qayyim fully understood the demands of normative political practice is indicated by their consistent linkage of wisdom, utility, and weighing of harms and benefits to it. Unlike Ghazālī who insisted that politics is nothing beyond the laws of the ulama, and they therefore are the teachers of its laws to rulers,[54] the reformists insist that politics may well be beyond the words, but never the spirit, of the *Sharīʿa*: "Just politics (*al-siyāsa al-ʿādila*) is not limited to the details specified in the *Sharʿ* and is amenable to change based on changing times and places. Except that its general objective is the establishment of justice, and its standard and criterion are the attainment of the welfare of the Community."[55]

In perhaps his most forceful statement on the subject, Ibn Taymiyya famously stated that, politically speaking, justice (which is the epitome of collective piety, or political virtue) is even more important than personal piety, and that God sustains an unbelieving government if it is just but not a believing government if it is unjust:

> Human welfare in matters of this world can be attained more with justice that is accompanied by sins (other than injustice) than with injustice in matters of people's rights even if that does not accompany (any other) sins. That is why it has been said: God establishes a just state (*dawla*), be it unbelieving, but does not establish an unjust state, be it Muslim. It is also said: (the affairs of) this world can last with justice and unbelief but cannot last with injustice and Islam. The Apostle of God, peace and blessings be upon him, has said in the same vein: "No sin is quicker in divine chastisement than usurpation of other's rights (*baghy*) and severance of family ties." The usurper is punished in this very world, even if he might be forgiven in the Hereafter, for justice is the principle (*niẓām*) of everything. Thus, inasmuch as its affairs are based on justice, a state will persist even if its rulers have no share in the Hereafter (due to their lack of faith); and if justice is absent, it will not persist, even if its rulers are rewarded in the Hereafter for their faith.[56]

This set of contentions of Ibn Taymiyya is what makes proper political thought possible. It echoes the dictum we are familiar with in pro-*siyāsa* ulama like Ṭurṭūshī, but now it is fully backed by a scripturally grounded epistemological and ethical system. It implies no secularism but simply that, when it comes to political matters, justice is a rational necessity for any political system to prosper. In contrast, faith in God – the greatest of

54 *Iḥyā'*, 1:30.
55 *Ṭuruq*, 16.
56 MF, 28:146 (*Amr*).

all obligations – is not a rational necessity for a political system to prosper (at least in the short term, for without divine guidance, the intensely spiritual Ibn Taymiyya would remind us, human reason, ever veiled and corrupted by doubt and desire, is unlikely to adhere to just ways). The crucial contention is that justice is the axis on which God has established the creation – in other words, the social world is predictable, governed by rationally accessible laws, which reason even without revelation can discern through experience and reflection. But if just politics is accessible to even non-Muslim statesmen and philosophers, what makes this politics Islamic? What, in other words, is *al-siyāsa al-sharʿiyya*? The answer lies more in the function or vision of politics and government than its details.

Commanding and Forbidding as the Foundation of the State

Between the rise of Sunna-centered depoliticization and Ibn Taymiyya's intervention, nearly every significant move in Islamic intellectual tradition had militated against the possibility of normative politics, ranging from the theological denial of ethical reason and even causality, the antipolitical bent of legal doctrine, to esotericism and stratification in spiritual and social domains.[57] If Ibn Taymiyya wished to revive political ethics within the *Sharīʿa*, he needed armor heavy enough to break through centuries of antipolitical calculus. It is no wonder, therefore, that he politicized the central qur'anic mission assigned to the Community, namely commanding right and forbidding wrong, by asserting that all political offices in Islam are nothing but an institutionalization of this one function. In his treatise on the office of public morality or censor (*Ḥisba*), he wrote:

> The summation of religion and the entirety of the [governmental] offices are but command and prohibition: the command that God has sent His messenger with is the commanding of right and the prohibition which God had sent His messenger with is the prohibition of wrong ... this is an obligation upon all capable Muslims of a communal nature (*ʿalā 'l-kifāya*). If not carried out by someone, it becomes an individual obligation (*ʿalā 'l-ʿayn*) upon someone who is capable of it.... The condition of obligation is capability, and [commanding and forbidding] is an obligation upon every person in proportion to his capability.[58]

[57] I discuss the role of mysticism in absorbing and reproducing apolitical social existence through its elitism, hierarchy, and unquestioned obedience in O. Anjum, "Mystical Authority and Governmentality in Medieval Islam," in *Sufism and Society: Arrangements of the Mystical in the Muslim World, 1200–1800 C.E.*, eds. John J. Curry and Erik S. Ohlander (Routledge, 2011).

[58] MF, 28:65–6 (*Ḥisba*).

He went on to elaborate:

> The sole objective of the entirety of the Islamic governmental offices (*al-wilāyāt al-islāmiyya*) is commanding right and forbidding wrong, be it the ministry of defense, such as the deputyship of the Sultan, or smaller offices such as the ministry of police, ministry of justice, ministry of finance – which is the ministry of records – and the ministry of public morality (*ḥisba*).[59]

Ibn Taymiyya's unusual emphasis on commanding and forbidding, one scholar observes, is akin to the Muʿtazilī inclusion of commanding and forbidding as part of the creed.[60] But it is not so much redefining creed as rethinking politics that commanded his interest. Equating all governmental authorities and offices with the function of commanding and forbidding makes it the *raison d'être* of the state. Thus, all the offices of a government that takes up this responsibility as its normative purpose become firmly rooted in the Qur'an. From the perspective of political thought, this was the most important but least appreciated of Ibn Taymiyya's contributions. Even less understood are the implications of defining government through the qur'anic arch-obligation that had been given as the mission of the entire Community of believers. It is because of this equation that politics, serving in any capacity, becomes a bona fide virtue. If carried out justly, it is rewarded by God and is one of the ways to get closer to God.

Ibn Taymiyya was not the first, of course, to link the practice of commanding and forbidding with government. Within the Ḥanbalī tradition, notes Cook, this linkage was unusual. But beyond Ḥanbalism, the practice had long been associated with the governmental institution of *ḥisba*. We find the Shāfiʿī Māwardī complain in *Aḥkām* of the neglect of the ulama in his time of this obligation in the context of *ḥisba*. Another instance of this link can be seen in the case of the Ashʿarī Ibn Tūmart (d. *ca.* 524/1130), the founder of the Almohad state, whose theologically motivated movement imposed its creed on the populace. This instance was explicitly chastised by Ibn Taymiyya, for a government in his view does not have a right to impose on Muslims by way of belief what is not definitively proven in the *Sharīʿa*, the proper venue for such issues being debates among scholars.

The adoption of the practice by the medieval state, one scholar notes in the context of North African mahdist movements, meant that "the precept

[59] Ibid.
[60] Kūnākātā, 113.

is no longer the engine of social reform but acts as a mere reminder of prohibitions on wine, gambling, or musical instruments, suggesting that the *ḥisba* loses its radical character when it is exercised or, rather, appropriated by the powerful."[61] The same, Yaacov Lev remarks, can be argued for the Mamluk state and its adoption *of al-amr bi-l-maʿrūf* as a political manifesto.[62] Such a sabotage of the "civic" potential of commanding and forbidding may be seen as expected and natural, as demonstrated by the record of the modern Saudi-Wahhabi state that often explicitly invokes Ibn Taymiyya's model in justification of such practices. But if ideas have their own significance and logic beyond their historical manifestations or co-optations, Ibn Taymiyya's views need to be investigated on their own. It is only when we appreciate Ibn Taymiyya's view of government and its relation to the Community can we see the political potential of this doctrine.

The Nature of Political Authority

An immediately distinctive feature of Ibn Taymiyya's political writings (reflected also in his dealings with the Mamluk kings) is that the ruler is treated as a common Muslim, one of many officials administering the affairs of the Community, neither deemed a tyrant nor expected to be a near-infallible embodiment of perfection and piety. Far from being absolute in any way, political authority is not even seen as embodied in one office, but rather diffused throughout governmental offices. In essence, political authority and the corresponding responsibility are not different from authority within the society, ranging from the authority of a schoolteacher over his students and a judge over litigants to the military commander over his troops or the Sultan over his subjects. The difference in power from one member of the community to the other is a matter of degree, but all are essentially engaged in a common task: "Whoever is incapable of endorsing religion by means of authority and struggle must do of good what he can."[63]

The qualifications required of a ruler are another good indication of one's view of the office. In Ibn Taymiyya's scheme, governmental offices – the Sultan being no different – require the realistic minimum: the

[61] M. Garcia-Arenal, *Messianism and Puritanical Reform*, trans. Martin Beagles (Brill, 2006), 176.
[62] Lev, 12.
[63] MF, 28:396 (*Siyāsa*).

competence and the probity to do the job required. These two are not only rational but, as usual, supported by Ibn Taymiyya through a qur'anic reference: "The best of those you employ (*ista'jarta*) is the one who is strong (*qawiyy*) and trustworthy (*amīn*)" (Q, 28:26). Note that this verse, cited frequently by Ibn Taymiyya in this regard, was not mentioned by any of the writers of Caliphate theory or statecraft literature in this context before. Ibn Taymiyya's use of it is significant in another way. It emphasizes the concept of the "employment" of rulers; this idea is also reinforced in *Siyāsa* where Ibn Taymiyya relates a report in which the first Umayyad Caliph is addressed by a Companion of the Prophet as *ajīr* – an employee.[64] But even more explicitly, he writes elsewhere, "[The rulers] are the representatives (*wukalā'*) of people over themselves as one of the two parties [in a common cause or contract]."[65]

Ibn Taymiyya's *Siyāsa* further stands out among all the writings on the caliphate as well as statecraft literature in that consultation, *shūrā*, plays a significant role and is emphasized as an important need for the ruler – "a ruler cannot dispense with consultation."[66] It is not simply a personal virtue of the perfect ruler but a necessity for the ruler because he is now essentially no different from others and needs to be advised and corrected by his subjects. No matter how great in knowledge and wisdom, no one can ever be always right. It is the Community, not the ruler, who has been protected from persisting in error, and that protection is because of the mechanism of mutual advice, commanding, and forbidding. But because the ruler has a greater share of power and responsibility, his responsibility to consult others is greater.

The contrast between his view of the ruler and the classical view of the Sultan cannot be overstated. It comes out clearly in Ibn Taymiyya's polemics against the Imāmī Shīʿa. The context of the view presented here is significant, for it means that Ibn Taymiyya's view of the ruler's role was uniform between theological polemics (concerned with the ideal caliph or imām, in which exaggeration was harmless and freely employed) and practical statecraft (directed at the medieval Sultans). He wrote:

> The statement of the Rāfiḍīs [Imāmī Shīʿa] that "among the functions of the imam is to perfect the ruled, [if the imam is not perfect in himself, as the Sunnis claim,]

[64] Although the report mentioned in *Siyāsa* suggests the ruler is an employee of God, given Ibn Taymiyya's Community-centered vision, the only way to know God's will is the will of the Community, hence the distinction in this context is not that significant.

[65] MF, 28:251–2 (*Siyāsa*).

[66] MF, 28:386 (*Siyāsa*).

then how it can be expected of him to perfect (*takmīl*) others," can be answered in many ways:

> Firstly, we do not concede that the imam perfects them or that they perfect the imam; instead, *the imam and the ruled (raʿiyya) cooperate in goodness and piety but not in sin or transgression* (Q, 5:2).
>
> Secondly, both of God's creatures, the ruler and the ruled, are completed (*istikmāl*) by each other just like those who debate with each other in knowledge, advise each other in reaching opinions, cooperate and participate in the benefit of their world and their hereafter – it is for the Creator alone to be above this.
>
> Thirdly, even students correct and remind their teachers at times, and the teacher benefits from them even though he is the one who has taught them the majority of the principles (of a given science) – the same is true of industry and other professions.[67]

This response to Shīʿī polemics was similar to that given by early Ashʿarīs, like Baqillanī, but different from the theoretical powers claimed for the caliph by later theologians from Māwardī to Ījī.[68] But Ibn Taymiyya goes further than Bāqillānī and Abū Yaʿlā in his Community-centered emphasis, elaborating the relationship between the ruler and the ruled through the qur'anic precept of cooperation (*taʿāwun*). Rather than the unbridgeable separation of the rulers and the ruled that had so pervasively characterized medieval societies, this emphasis brings to mind the early Medinan model of cooperation and mutual advice that had for long adorned pious literature but rarely seemed relevant to real political life.

The Role of the Ulama

Among the classical caliphate writers, Juwaynī comes closest to Ibn Taymiyya in his realistic attempt to deal with power and advise the ruler to consult with the ulama. In Ibn Taymiyya's vision, however, the political players and their roles are different. The ulama are not the sole advisors of the rulers. Rather, all three facets of the triangle – the ruler, the Community, and the ulama – offer mutual advice and criticism to each other and cooperate for the common good. Furthermore, even though the significance of the ulama is beyond doubt, as a professional group, they do not have any categorical privilege over others. The ruler himself must exercise *ijtihād* in matters that he can, for

67 *Minhāj*, 4:215; Kūnākātā, 130 (emphasis added).
68 See Chapter 3 in this volume; Lambton, *State*, 77–8.

both the rulers and the ulama must seek obedience of God and His messenger in all his words and deeds, and follow God's Book, and whenever it is possible in unclear matters to know the teachings of the Book and the Sunna, that is an obligation; and if that is not possible due to paucity of time or incapacity of the seeker or difficulty in preferring one argument over another, it is legitimate for him to follow (*taqlīd*) someone with whose piety and knowledge he is satisfied.[69]

Ibn Taymiyya seeks to mitigate the exclusive authority of the ulama over the *Sharīʿa* and writes in *Siyāsa*, addressing specifically the lay rulers: "If a commoner (*al-ʿāmmiyy*) is capable of reasoning independently (literally, do *ijtihād*) in some matter, it is permissible for him to do so. For independent reasoning (*ijtihād*) is a faculty which accepts division and specialization. What matters is the capacity or lack thereof; a man may be capable in some matters but incapable in others."[70] On another occasion, he writes, "Everyone's independent reasoning is [valid] to the best of his capacity."[71] Thus, unlike the classical view as voiced by al-Nawawī, the jurists have no *categorical* superiority over other members of the Community in interpreting the *Sharīʿa*. The exclusive authority of the experts in religious matters is curtailed to those matters in which there is need for expert knowledge and room for difference in opinion. The ulama "who seek to dominate others on the basis of their expertise in religion" are in the wrong.[72]

Shifting the Focus from the Ruler to the Sharīʿa

Having consolidated after the caliphs had already effectively lost power, classical Sunni polemical response, as I have demonstrated, had focused on forms and rituals of the caliphate. For the same reason, it had been centered on the person of the ruler, neglecting the substantive issue of how he ruled. Ibn Taymiyya breaks from the classical tradition in another crucial way by shifting the focus of legitimacy of the state from the person of the ruler to the substance of government. As seen in his judicial doctrine, he systematically preferred the substantive over the formal.[73]

[69] MF, 28:388 (*Siyāsa*).

[70] MF, 5:203–4.

[71] MF, 20:212.

[72] Invoking the verse "The abode of the hereafter have We made for those who desire neither domination in earth nor corruption" (Q, 28:83), he concludes that all those who desire domination over others with or without desire to exploit them, be they rulers or scholars, are in error (MF, 28:393 [*Siyāsa*]).

[73] It is going too far perhaps to suggest, as at least one scholar has, that Ibn Taymiyya was the first to do this in Islamic tradition (Heck, *Construction*, 194). In fact, as we

This feature is consistent throughout his corpus and shows clearly, for instance, in his polemics against the Shīʿī claim of the need for an infallible imam. Ibn Taymiyya, as noted earlier, responded in formal terms as well by centering the Community rather than the imam as the source of "protectedness," but he offered a further, even more forceful rejoinder by going beyond theology and shifting the focus to properly political considerations. He contended that the caliphate/imamate is primarily a form of government, and as such is inseparable from power; the claim of legitimacy of an imam or lack thereof is relevant only if he is a ruler. A figure under house arrest or in occultation, no matter how saintly or deserving, could simply not be an imam. If submitting to the government of a powerless or invisible person were incumbent in God's religion, it would amount to God's curse rather than mercy (for such a person would be incapable of bringing peace and justice to society), and such a religion would be absurd. This argument not only disarms the Shīʿī claims, but rejects a crucial element of the mainline classical Sunni development.

An even clearer manifestation of Ibn Taymiyya's emphasis on the substance of rule rather than the person or ritual qualifications of the ruler is his bold critique of the well-entrenched juristic tradition on the law of rebellion. It should be noted that unlike the scholars of *kalām* and *falsafa*, he considered the early jurists the true scholars of Islam, whose discourse, unlike *kalām*, was an organic part of Islam, and hence, despite disagreement, his tone is cautious. Giving a nuanced historical account of the development of the doctrine among the Sunni jurists, which placed the person of the imam rather than the *Sharīʿa* at the center of their doctrines, he wrote:

> The earlier [jurists] have done three things that require caution and correction. First, [their legalization of] fighting against anyone who rebels against any ruler, even if the rebel is similar to him or the same as the ruler in the extent of his following of the *Sharīʿa* and the Sunna, [arguing that] that leads to division, division being breakdown of order (*fitna*) [which is prohibited]. Second, their equation between those [who rebel against the ruler] and those who rebel against some or all of the rulings of Islam. Third, their equation between those and the Khawārij… That is why you find [the jurists who conflate these issues] getting mixed up in the vain ambitions of kings and rulers and commanding [on account of their religious authority] to join them against their enemies in fighting.[74]

have seen earlier, the grievances of the early Community-centered ulama like Mālik, Abū Ḥanīfa, and others who had rebelled with Ibn al-Ashʿath and al-Nafs al-Zakiyya included primarily substantive concerns about how the caliphs ruled (justice, treatment of new Muslims, *shūrā*, fiscal practices, moral decadence, etc.).

[74] MF, 4:450–2.

The first error these jurists made, to put it succinctly, was to legalize a historical event rather than proceed, as proper juristic theory would demand, from the Qur'an and the Sunna. Starting with ʿAlī's treatment of rebels, these jurists not only idealized and legalized ʿAlī's conduct, but also imported the contextual presumptions, such as that because ʿAlī was in the right, so is every ruler, and the way he treated the rebels, so must any ruler, regardless of the adherence of the ruler to the *Sharīʿa* or the cause of the rebels. But the Qur'an and the Prophetic Sunna, Ibn Taymiyya complained, has "no mention of fighting against those who rebel against a ruler, but all such reports are directed against those who rebel against the *Sharīʿa* (*ahl al-ridda wa 'l-ahwā'*)."[75] In an immediate contextual sense, there was no religious ground in his mind for the internecine wars of the Mamluk warlords. Against the backdrop of the ulama routinely getting involved and slaughtered or promoted in petty politics of the *amīrs*, his advice was to judge the rulers by their commitment to the *Sharīʿa* rather than blindly (or self-servingly) following one or the other contender's interests. If a ruler is committed to the *Sharīʿa* and the rebels threaten it, fighting against the rebels is justified. Similarly, if the ruler has neglected the *Sharīʿa* – as the Mongols had even after having nominally embraced Islam – then fighting against him, if possible, is necessary.

Although it is true, as Johansen has suggested, that bolstering the Mamluk state as the bulwark of Sunni Islam against the continuing Mongol menace was a goal in his mind, his positions clearly had a deeper logic than immediate politics. On the matter of rebellion, Ibn Taymiyya subscribed to the traditionalist position that even an oppressive ruler should not be rebelled against so long as he established the *Sharīʿa*.[76] But he was far from being a "quietist" in that he never preached indifference to injustice, but only that the means of censuring such a ruler ought not to be violent rebellion, but rather social criticism, advice, commanding and forbidding, and even political action, such as mobilizing public opinion, as he himself did, against the ruler's unjust conduct or policy. Justice, no doubt, is an indispensable political virtue, but the way to combat injustice could never be rebellion because – and here Ibn Taymiyya relied on what had become the Sunni wisdom on the subject – rebellion and civil war always cause more harm than good. Nor does he teach indifference toward rebellions directed against rulers, but insists that the standard of judging whether to get involved and which party to support must

[75] MF, 4:450–2; 28:486–7.

[76] *Minhāj*, 2:86–7; Khan, 166–9, 178.

be the *Sharīʿa*. His anti-rebellion stance seems to be pro-state, whereas his emphasis on the *Sharīʿa* instead of the ruler as being the principle of loyalty points in the opposite direction.

Khaled Abou El Fadl addresses at length Ibn Taymiyya criticism of classical jurists' doctrine that depoliticized the law of rebellion (that is, decoupled it from the legitimacy or justice of the ruler). Other revisionist jurists in the postclassical period, Abou El Fadl notes, also came to modify the classical rebellion discourse by legalizing certain kinds of rebellion and incorporating the conduct of the ruler as a consideration, but these jurists remained legalistic in their attention to technicality and formality, whereas Ibn Taymiyya took a perspective that Abou El Fadl attributes to the fact that he "was more of a moralist, and less of a jurist than he perhaps realized."[77] This insightful statement captures an important half-truth about Ibn Taymiyya. Politics, properly speaking, is a branch of ethical reasoning. Far from being confused about his juristic acumen, Ibn Taymiyya's seems to have understood the implications of his bold political reform which involved relaxing the claws of juristic formalism that had, in his view, become too distant from the moral foundation of Islam and its Community. Even if a law could be technically updated, that was simply not what he desired. All legal systems value the authority that longevity, accumulation, and development bestow on them, and Islamic legal tradition had invested in idealizing and authorizing its past perhaps too successfully for its own good. But there was a counter-argument even mainstream jurists could often appreciate. The authority of Islamic law came, ultimately, not from the weight of the tradition or the brilliance of its casuistry, but from the divine revelation and the Community that had mediated the divine approval of the Islamic legal enterprise and underpinned the construction of its authority. Without unraveling that edifice entirely, Ibn Taymiyya intended to clear up its unwieldy sprawl in order to recover some of the moral agency of the living Community. That was the role of Islamic politics.

FORMAL DOCTRINE: IBN TAYMIYYA AND THE CALIPHATE

Having considered the theoretical foundations of Ibn Taymiyya's political, ethical, and legal thought, we are in a position to adjudicate between the various available interpretations of his political thought. On the one hand, there are those, from Laoust to Johansen, who focus on his substantive

[77] Abou El Fadl, 278.

approach to politics and political institutions and conclude that he indeed had a remarkably new and distinct concept of Islamic politics, which sprang from his rejection of the classical model of the caliphate. On the other hand, others point out the fatal flaw in this interpretation, namely that Ibn Taymiyya clearly and consistently endorsed the institutions of the caliphate as an obligation. These scholars go on to argue that not only did he embrace the caliphate theory; there is nothing essentially new in Ibn Taymiyya's political thought. Both sides have missed a crucial element of Ibn Taymiyya's political thought but are correct in observing one aspect of it. Reconciling the two approaches is not a matter merely of negotiation, but requires a fundamental rethinking of Ibn Taymiyya's view of politics. Let us turn to putting it all back together.

To the substantive contentions of the substance-centered interpreters of Ibn Taymiyya, the advocates of the "nothing-new" position respond that what explains the matter is simply the genre and the context: *al-Siyāsa al-shar'iyya* is a mirror for princes written by a traditional jurist and not a "legal manual, a book of *fiqh*, where one would look for standard delineations of *aḥkām* ... [r]ather a treatise designed to advise those already in power ... [and hence] more significantly comparable to the genre of advice literature, typically referred to as 'Mirrors for Princes' in which the state structure is a given, and its leading officials should be guided to the best of practices."[78] Mona Hassan goes on to ask rhetorically, "[W]hat would a 'Mirror for Princes' written by a jurist look like?", suggesting that just like the secular statesmen wrote their own pieces of advice, jurists like Māwardī, Ghazālī, and Ibn Taymiyya wrote theirs. It is natural and commonsensical, in this view, that Ibn Taymiyya would use qur'anic verses and the Prophetic traditions to advise the rulers and the Community about political matters in a "mirror" like *al-Siyāsa al-shar'iyya*.[79]

Of course, the jurists could have written practical political advice literature based on the Qur'an and the Sunna just as well, but the historical fact remains that they did not, for reasons I have recounted at length. The raw material of which Ibn Taymiyya's political tracts like *Siyāsa* and *Ḥisba* are constructed is entirely scriptural, but its deployment and construction by Ibn Taymiyya do not resemble any classical discourse. There is some overlap with the preclassical discourse as typified by Abū Yūsuf's *K. al-Kharāj*, which consists of Sunna-centered advice to an established

[78] Hassan, "Modern Interpretations," 347.
[79] Ibid., 349.

imperial caliph and which, therefore, takes the caliph's authority for granted and does not reflect on justification for an Islamic government nor on the role of the Community. But since the classical period, the tempo of political advice literature had changed. The statecraft literature written by jurists like Māwardī, (pseudo-)Ghazālī, and Ṭurṭūshī presupposed a political framework that was essentially indebted to the familiar Near Eastern, in particular Persian, model of kingship and not Islamic scriptural sources or the early Islamic model. In Tarif Khalidi's words, these mirrors treated the Qur'an as one mine among many of political wisdom.[80] Nor did they attempt to harmonize the workings of *fiqh* with politics. Māwardī is one, albeit early and therefore mild, case of what appears to be a multiple-personality disorder: His *Aḥkām* is the textbook example of the formal treatment of Islamic politics, namely the caliphate, whereas his actual political advice in his *Tashīl al-naẓar* draws on a wide array of Islamic and extra-Islamic sources in a framework that looks more like that of the state-centered secretaries like Ibn al-Muqaffaʿ (d. 139/756) or Qudāma b. Jaʿfar (d. 337/948) than his own in *Aḥkām*.[81] To illustrate with one poignant example, in *Aḥkām*, Māwardī deems impermissible calling the caliph *khalīfat Allāh* and insists that it must be *khalīfat rasūl Allāh*.[82] In *Tashīl*, however, he presents a different model of political authority, quoting the Persian emperor Ardshīr b. Bābak's pledge of allegiance with his governors that "religion and kingship are twins" and asserting without reservation that "the king is God's caliph in his lands."[83] Similarly, the difference in the political vision between Ghazālī's theological-juristic writings on the caliphate and the *Naṣīḥat al-mulūk* attributed to him is so significant that scholars like Crone and Hillenbrand have deemed the latter spurious. Whereas its authenticity may be questionable on other grounds, as a phenomenon, a fundamental contradiction between "orthodox" and political advice works by the same author would not be unique to Ghazālī.[84]

[80] On Ṭurṭūshī's "mining" of the Qur'an for such political wisdom within a Persianate political framework, see Khalidi, *Arabic*, 195n31.

[81] Māwardī quotes Ibn al-Muqaffaʿ in *Tashīl*, 38. For Qudāma b. Jaʿfar's vision of the state, see Heck, *Construction*, esp. 195f.

[82] He states explicitly in *Aḥkām* that "The majority of scholars have prohibited [the use of this title] and deemed it a great sin, arguing that succession (*istikhlāf*) is for someone who is deceased, and God is neither absent nor deceased," and then he goes on to cite Abū Bakr's disapproval of the title (*Aḥkām*, 50).

[83] Māwardī, *Tashīl*, 46–7.

[84] Hillenbrand concludes that *Naṣīḥat al-mulūk* (Ghazālī's alleged mirror for princes) is inauthentic because it endorses a Sasanian theory of statecraft with the Sultan as the "shadow of God on earth" imbued with the Sasanian concept of divine effulgence

The difference between the caliphate discourse and political advice literature had been, we must conclude, not merely of genre but of basic vision of state and politics. *Sharīʿa*-based politics was a problematic proposition to the classical ulama – it was their ideological commitment as well as professional interest that the *Sharīʿa* remain confined to *fiqh* (law) and not become extended to *siyāsa* (politics), which relied on the judgment of those in power. Writing practical tracts authorizing *Sharīʿa*-based, legitimate politics for the lay rulers was a bold and potentially dangerous step. Such a treatise could not be written without conceptually expanding the scope of the *Sharīʿa* to include politics, and hence to include the rulers and the Community in the circle of normativity.

Was the Early Caliphate Normative for Ibn Taymiyya?

The most detailed study of Ibn Taymiyya's reflections on the caliphate is Hasan Kūnākātā's, which has the rare distinction of correctly recognizing some of the distinguishing elements of Ibn Taymiyya's vision of the caliphate. It recognizes Ibn Taymiyya's writings about the caliphate but ends up proposing a thesis similar in all practical purposes to Laoust's, namely that Ibn Taymiyya rejected the institution of the caliphate. According to Kūnākātā, Ibn Taymiyya limited the Rightly Guided Caliphate to the first four caliphs based on the Prophetic *ḥadīths* that predict that the proper caliphate will last for thirty years, deemed the proper caliphate to be religiously mandated for the individuals designated by the Prophet, and therefore unique and irreproducible. This unique doctrine, Kūnākātā holds, not only guarded these caliphs against polemics by the Shīʿī detractors, but also removed them from the realm of normativity to be followed, thus freeing up posterity from any normative political model.

Kūnākātā's argument is based on his contention that Ibn Taymiyya precludes any speculation about the legitimacy of the early caliphs by asserting that Abū Bakr, the first caliph, was appointed by the Prophetic designation, *naṣṣ*, and that numerous references in the Prophet's teachings to this effect establish this.[85] Kūnākātā goes on to write:

> Contrary to [the traditional caliphate theory], in Ibn Taymiyya's view the imamate of the Rightly Guided caliphs in Medina was established by a scriptural text

(*farr-e-izadī*), who must be obeyed by virtue of his God-given position. Such a view is different from the concept of the dual government of caliph and sultan and abject pessimism about obtaining anything better than a façade of power for the symbolic caliph in a political world in which military might is all that mattered, which characterizes Ghazālī's authentic writings (Hillenbrand, 92).

[85] Kūnākātā, 75–6.

(*naṣṣ*), and it did not require election (*ikhtiyār*) nor consensus (*ijmā'*), and, in addition, that caliphate came to an end after thirty years and ended with the ending of 'Alī's reign, so there is no point in legislating the imamate based on election, for the caliphate was, for one, established by a text, and two, it ended after the Rightly Guided caliphate.[86]

This claim of Kūnākātā – and hence much of his interpretation built on it – is simply incorrect. Ibn Taymiyya clearly did not believe in *naṣṣ* (scriptural or prophetic commandment) as the basis of Abū Bakr's appointment. Kūnākātā seems to have been confused by Ibn Taymiyya's wording:

> Had the Prophet's allusion to Abū Bakr been less than clear, he would have made it clear to them by a definitive statement. But since the Prophet had repeatedly pointed out that Abū Bakr was to be the appointed one and they understood the Prophet's intent ... the Muslims elected him without a pledge (with the Prophet to do so), and the scriptural texts (Qur'an and Sunna) alluded to the correctness of the Muslims' choice.[87]

Ibn Taymiyya goes on to make it even clearer as he writes that this was an even stronger credential for Abū Bakr as well as the judgment of the Muslim Community, for a direct statement by God on a political matter would have been less forceful than indirect allusions confirmed by the Community's own choice. A modern Saudi scholar, al-Dumayjī, confirms this reading, stating that "Ibn Taymiyya's view is that the Prophet did not command the Muslims to appoint Abū Bakr as the caliph, but the Prophet knew from God that the Muslims will elect him because of his merits."[88]

Ibn Taymiyya agreed with the majority of the Sunni ulama about Abū Bakr's caliphate as having been based on election by the Muslims (*ikhtiyār*) and not Prophetic command. And whereas these implicit texts (that speak generally of Abū Bakr's virtue and piety over others), from a religious perspective, are stronger approval of Abū Bakr's caliphate than consensus of the Community, consensus too did occur. In fact, Ibn Taymiyya held that not only that the consensus occurred, but that *Abū Bakr could not have been a caliph had it not occurred, despite all the texts*. The Prophet's thirty-year prophecy of righteous caliphate simply meant that the reign of the first four caliphs was implicitly approved, but the order of the caliphs was not religiously stipulated.

86 Kūnākātā, 82.
87 *Minhāj*, 1:139.
88 Dumayjī, 132.

Finally, Kūnākātā's suggestion that Ibn Taymiyya believed that the Rightly Guided Caliphate provided no model for later Muslims is also contradicted by Ibn Taymiyya's clear statements that the caliphate is an obligation on all Muslims because of the Prophet's clear command to make the early caliphate a normative model.[89] Ibn Taymiyya unequivocally endorses the idea that *khilāfa al-nubuwwa* (literally, the prophetic successorship) is an obligation, and *mulk* (kingship) is unlawful except when forced or otherwise necessitated:

> [T]he question arises whether kingship (*mulk*) is lawful and the Prophetic Caliphate simply preferred, or it [*mulk*] is unlawful and may only be justified in the absence of the knowledge (that it is obligatory) or power to establish the caliphate?
>
> In our view, kingship is essentially unlawful, and the obligation is to set up a Prophetic Caliphate. This is because the Prophet said, "You must follow my practice and the practice of the rightly guided caliphs after me; stick to it and hold it fast. Refrain from innovation, for every innovation is an error." ... This hadīth is therefore a command; it exhorts us to follow by necessity the practice of the Caliphate (of the Prophet), enjoins us to abide by it and warns us against deviation from it. It is a command from him and makes the establishment of the caliphate a definite duty.... Again, the fact that the Prophet expressed his dislike for kingship that will follow the Prophetic Caliphate proves that kingship lacks in something which is compulsory in religion .... Those who justify monarchy argue from the words of the Prophet to Muʿāwiya, "If you attain kingship, be good and kind." But this does not constitute a proof.[90]

In the next passage, Ibn Taymiyya goes on to state that "the establishment of caliphate is an obligatory duty and exemption from it may be permitted only on grounds of necessity."[91] He presents his position characteristically as the middle position between two unseemly extremes: "To insist on it as an individual duty of all Muslims regardless of the circumstances is an extreme position held by the Khawārij and the Muʿtazila.... The opposite extreme is to consider kingship (*mulk*) lawful and to think that the caliphate on the pattern of the Rightly Guided Caliphs is not an obligation at all; this is an incorrect view held conveniently by unjust rulers, libertarians and some Murji'a."[92]

[89] MF, 35:22.
[90] MF, 35:18–20.
[91] Ibid.
[92] Ibid.

Kingship (*Mulk*) versus Caliphate

Ibn Taymiyya states, on the one hand, that 'Prophetic Caliphate'[93] is an obligation on the Community whenever possible, and *mulk* (kingship) is unlawful except when necessary, but also holds, on the other hand, that mixing *mulk* with caliphate does not entirely invalidate the caliphate. He also contends that before the specific *Sharīʿa* given to the Prophet Muḥammad, *mulk* used to be a valid form of government, as exemplified by the earlier Israelite prophets mentioned in the Qur'an, such as Sulaymān (Solomon) and Dawūd (David), who are praised in the Qur'an as mighty prophets as well as righteous kings.[94] To put it differently, in his view, (1) kingship (*mulk*) is distinct from caliphate in some essential way, and (2) that caliphate is an obligation for the followers of Muḥammad, and a more meritorious form of government in general, whereas *mulk* is unlawful in the *Sharīʿa* but had been permissible for the earlier communities before the Prophet Muḥammad.

Because prophets, including the Israelite prophet-kings mentioned in the Qur'an, are the most righteous of humankind, more so than the first four Rightly Guided Caliphs of Islam, the distinction of the Prophetic Caliphate is not a function merely of the personal righteousness of the ruler.[95] The difference between the Prophetic Caliphate and kingship (*mulk*), therefore, must lie in the *institution* or some *formal* credentials stipulated by the *Sharīʿa* (i.e., the specific teachings of the Prophet Muḥammad), rather than *personal virtue*. A ruler, no matter how just and righteous, could not be called a proper Prophetic Caliph unless he fulfills these formal criteria. These formal criteria for Ibn Taymiyya are similar (but not identical) to those that appear in the early, pre-Māwardī formulations of the Sunni-Ashʿarī theory: the Qurayshī genealogy, his election and rule by *shūrā*, and the *status* of the ruler as an elected representative (*wakīl*) and employee (*ajīr*) of the Community.

93 It should be kept in mind that the concern for Ibn Taymiyya is the "Prophetic Caliphate" obligated in the aforementioned *ḥadīth*, not mere caliphate, which could mean merely a successor, and even the prophet-king David is called in the Qur'an a caliph in that general sense.

94 On David and Solomon's piety, see, for instance, Q, 6:84, 17:55, 21:79, 27:15; on their kingship, 27:16, 34:10. In particular, on David's caliphate on this earth, see 38:26: "O David! We did indeed make thee a *khalīfa* on earth: so judge thou between men in truth (and justice)."

95 Ibn Taymiyya reports the consensus of all Muslims that prophets (*anbiyāʾ*) are superior to all other humans, including saints (*awliyāʾ*), in virtue and status before God. Among prophets, some are distinguished as messenger-servants (*rusul ʿabīd*), like Muḥammad, Jesus, and Moses, who are superior to prophet-kings (MF, 13:89 [*Furqān*]).

Yet, to Ibn Taymiyya, the Prophetic Caliphate cannot be not merely a formal position; the caliphate is, first and foremost, a rational (as opposed to ritual) obligation. And because it is so, one ought to obtain its rational benefit to the best one can: "The adulteration of caliphate with kingship is permissible in our *Sharīʿa* ... Muʿāwiya adulterated caliphate with *mulk*, and this does not invalidate his caliphate."[96] Muʿāwiya famously compromised *shūrā* and adopted some royal ways that emphasized personal glory, thus "adulterating" his caliphate with kingship. Summing up Ibn Taymiyya's attitude on the subject, Kūnākātā insightfully observes:

> Hence, the caliphate can be mixed with *mulk* in Ibn Taymiyya's view, while in the view of other Sunni (Ashʿarī) theorizers of imamate, the imamate of a ruler is either valid or invalid, with no middle ground. The valid imamate is that which is established by the *Sharīʿa* means stipulated in *fiqh*. In other words, the standard of the imamate in the view of the *majority of jurists is based on how it was established*, while in Ibn Taymiyya's view the caliphate is realized to the degree that the path of the Rightly Guided Caliphs is followed. It may be concluded that Ibn Taymiyya's view of caliphate is dynamic while the majority of scholars view is static.[97]

Kūnākātā, however, mistakenly attributes the cause of this difference to Ibn Taymiyya's rejection of the normative relevance of the early caliphate: "There is no need to establish the obligation of the imamate based on a unique historical event such as the agreement of the Companions on the imamate of Abū Bakr as the Sunni jurists have done. Ibn Taymiyya's perspective on the imamate is unique in that he sees it as a part of the society which does not differ in essence from the rest of its parts."[98]

Here, Kūnākātā is only half right: True, Ibn Taymiyya would have argued for the necessity of a government on rational grounds, but an equally important contention of his was that the Companions indeed did what was both rationally and revelationally correct, and that particular historical model is critically important because it is privileged by revelation. Kūnākātā incorrectly implies that Ibn Taymiyya considers reason to be the source of government and revelation to be irrelevant. Ibn Taymiyya explicitly considered revelation as well as reason to be the source, with the consequence that revelation adds a "formal" dimension to government, which turns mere government (*mulk*) based on rational necessity into caliphate (formally legitimate government), which is a religious obligation of Muslims to enact, and which makes it superior to

[96] MF, 35:27.
[97] Kūnākātā, 80 (the original is in Arabic; emphasis added).
[98] Kūnākātā, 85.

all other forms of government. Kūnākātā is further mistaken in holding that Ibn Taymiyya is unique in Sunni tradition in asserting reason as the source that obligates government, for classical Sunni thinkers, as we have seen in Māwardī as well as Ghazālī, too believed that government is a rational obligation. The real distinction was that they separated government from imamate, whereas Ibn Taymiyya did not, and hence imamate becomes both rational and revelational obligation.

To recast in Ibn Taymiyya's distinct categorization, an Islamic government is both *Sharʿī*-rational and *Sharʿī*-revelational, for the *Sharīʿa* both directly commands instituting a particular kind of government and rationally requires the protection of interests that in turn require instituting such a government.

The *historical occurrence* of the Rightly Guided Caliphate is not the moment of the founding of the obligation, but a moment of *confirmation* of what reason as well as revelation already requires. That model further provides the best way of attaining this obligation; by the decree of the Prophet, following that model is also an obligation, where fulfilling its formal requirements turns any rationally just government into Prophetic Caliphate. What has been attained through this subtle formulation is that now reason is a valid measure of the effectiveness of government, and *mulk* and caliphate are *commensurate* institutions. They share functions, rationale, and must be evaluated on the same bases. Just as it is absurd to speak of a ruler who has no power to enforce his will and keep order, so it is to speak of a caliph who has no power. Caliphate, in other words, is only a form of *mulk*, albeit a superior form and an obligation on the Community of Islam. An analogy would be marriage; an Islamic marriage (the ritual, the contract, the relationship that ensues) has the same essential functions as a non-Islamic marriage and hence the marriage of non-Muslims is legally acceptable to Muslims, although Muslims have been instructed to perform it in a particular, and presumably superior and God-pleasing, way.

Putting together Ibn Taymiyya's two contentions that the caliph is a ruler who must possess actual power and be just, and that the Prophetic Caliphate requires something in addition, namely, its fulfillment of formal requirements:

Prophetic Caliphate =Substantive Legitimacy (*Sharīʿa*-bound Governance) +

Formal Legitimacy (representation of the Community, Qurayshī lineage, etc.)

In reality, Ibn Taymiyya realized, this is a tall order in his time, and one must make do with what is possible, hence his focus on substantive legitimacy, the first part of the equation. One consequence of Ibn Taymiyya's view is that caliphate or *mulk* are interchangeable when dealing with substantive issues, which explains why in his practical treatise of advice on Islamic politics, *al-Siyāsa al-sharʿiyya*, he uses the generic term *wilāya*. Ibn Taymiyya's argument for government falls into the category of rational-revelational arguments (*dalīl ʿaqlī sharʿī*, as opposed to purely revelational argument, *dalīl samʿī*). He writes:

> It must be known that governing the affairs of the people is the greatest of obligations of religion (*dīn*); in fact religion cannot be established except by it ... because many of the obligations of religion, such as commanding right and forbidding wrong, *jihād* and dispensation of justice, establishment of *Ḥajj* and holidays, protection and support of the oppressed, and establishment of the penal system, cannot be undertaken except by means of power and leadership. It has been said, "The ruler is God's shadow on earth" and that "Sixty years of an oppressive ruler are better than a day without a ruler." Experience has shown this to be true.[99]

As usual, this rational argument is backed up with a purely revelational argument: A Prophetic *ḥadīth* states: "When three of you travel, make one among yourselves a leader."[100]

Limiting the religious authority of the caliph/ruler, in keeping with his Community-centered vision of Islam, is a key concern for Ibn Taymiyya. Unlike Māwardī and Ghazālī who make the caliph the center of legitimacy of the Community's religious life, Ibn Taymiyya considers the Community the real source of legitimacy and the caliphate as one of its needs. In the same vein, unlike some of his Ashʿarī interlocutors, Ibn Taymiyya emphasizes a categorical distinction between the Prophet, who was infallible and divinely guided, and any other ruler. He rejected even the characterization of the Prophet as an imam of his time; the problem of governance is categorically different after the death of the Prophet than during his lifetime. Note that the imamate as one of the functions of the Prophet and the necessity of its continuity for the sake of infallible guidance of the Community even after the Prophet's death were essential

99 MF, 28: 390–1 (*Siyāsa*). Recall also that Ghazālī too invokes a formal syllogistic argument for the obligation of a government, but he does so strictly for the "lay" ruler, whose necessity is known by reason – and hence he invokes no specific scriptural evidence for it. This underscores the point that the lay ruler (*sulṭān*) is categorically different from the caliph, whose necessity is known by revelation alone.

100 MF, 28:64–5, 28:169, 28:390.

features of the Shīʿī doctrine, which the Sunni *kalām* theologians had long wrestled with and at times conceded to, thus accepting a semblance between the imam and the Prophet.[101] Ibn Taymiyya would have none of it, for "Obedience to the Prophet is incumbent even if he has no one with him, if all men reject and belie him; it was incumbent in Mecca before he had any helpers."[102] "His prophethood is sufficient to make his obedience incumbent as opposed to the imam, who becomes an imam only when he has aides who implement his commands."[103]

This distinction could be explained on the basis of the theoretical distinction between descending and ascending authority to which Walter Ullmann has drawn our attention in the context of the medieval West.[104] The Prophet, to Ibn Taymiyya, derives his authority from God and his authority persists regardless of anyone's obedience: His authority is descending. Any post-prophetic ruler, be it a formally legitimate caliph or not, has an ascending claim to authority: He derives his authority from the community he rules and is recognized because he can deliver something they need, namely law, order, and defense. If he does not possess power and authority, he is a false claimant, a pretender, but not an imam or a caliph.

This view could not be more different that the view of caliphate proposed by Māwardī and then Ghazālī. These Sunni theologians had employed a type of reasoning that interpreted historical events, stripped of their context, as materials for normative legal principles. Arguments such as this were common:

The Objector (the Muʿtazilī al-Aṣamm): "There was a period of separation between the Prophet's death and Abū Bakr's appointment, hence it is permissible to not appoint a caliph."

The Ashʿarī response: "No, the Companions were actually trying to appoint one in that period – therefore, it is not permissible."

Let us, for instance, recall Māwardī's presentation of the formal conditions for the appointment of a caliph. These are the opinions that Māwardī lists:[105] (1) One group of scholars says that the legitimate appointment of a caliph requires the contract (*bayʿa*) of "the majority of 'untiers and tiers' from every city, so that the agreement on the caliph may be general

[101] See earlier discussion, in particular on Ijī in Chapter 2.
[102] *Minhāj*, 1:18
[103] *Minhāj*, 1:20.
[104] Ullmann, *A History of Political Thought*, 12–13.
[105] *Aḥkām*, 33–4.

and submission to his imamate by consensus." (2) The number of "untiers and tiers" (i.e., electors) must be at least five, as was the case for Abū Bakr and 'Umar. This is the opinion of the *kalām* scholars and jurists of Basra. (3) The jurists of Kufa say that the number is three, counting two witnesses and one *qāḍī* needed to render effective a marriage contract (!). (4) It needs only one person because ʿAbbās, ʿAlī's uncle, supposedly said to him that if he pledge allegiance to ʿAlī', people will say "the uncle of the Messenger of God, peace be upon him, had pledged allegiance to his cousin," and no one will disagree over that. Therefore, the pledge of one member of "untiers and tiers" is effective.

Of these four opinions, Māwardī rejects out of hand the first one – the only one that could potentially lead to actual substantive confirmation of the caliph's authority and power, threaten the ritual nature of the process, and actually involve the Community in the election. His reason is, as usual, the elevation of a historical anecdote to the level of a formal principle: This did not happen in the case of the appointment of Abū Bakr (in Māwardī's view, at least). Furthermore, in all of these three cases, a particular historical incident, chosen almost arbitrarily, is made into a legal precedence without noting any difference between a historical event in which actors made contingent and commonsensical decisions (i.e., political decisions) and the formal legal (namely, universal) rules they seek to draw from them. This is not an exception but the rule in the classical-period *kalām*-inspired jurisprudence.

The earlier opinion, rejected out of hand by Māwardī, is the closest to what Ibn Taymiyya reports to be the opinion of the *salaf*, the early Muslims, in which common sense plays the dominant role. Ibn Taymiyya, in his refutation of the Shīʿī argument that the Sunnis accept the appointment of the imam by four or such number of "untiers and tiers," rejects the Ashʿarī version, and writes:

The imamate [, in the view of the *salaf*,] is established by the agreement of *ahl al-shawka* (those who possess influence), whose allegiance delivers the objective of imamate. The objective of imamate can be obtained only by power (*qudra*) and authority (*sulṭān*). If someone is given allegiance by means of which he acquires power and authority, he becomes the imam. This is why the leading scholars (*imāms*) of Sunna say that whoever attains power and authority by which he carries out the functions of a government, he is from the *ulu'l amr* which God has commanded to obey so long as they do not command disobedience to God. *For imamate is power (mulk) and authority (sulṭān)*, and a ruler does not become ruler by the agreement of one or two or four, except if the agreement of these few will guarantee the agreement of the rest, and that is what makes him a king.... The ability to make [and enforce] policies might be obtained either by the

> people's [willing] obedience to him, or by his coercive power over them. *When he becomes capable of making policy among them by either his coercive power or their willing obedience, he is the authority that is to be obeyed so long as he commands obedience to God.* This is why Imam Aḥmad [b. Ḥanbal] said … "the principles of Sunna in our view are to hold on to way of the Companions of the Prophet, peace be upon him," until he said, "whosoever is given the caliphate and people have agreed about him and are pleased with him, or the one who has overwhelmed [the rest] with his sword and became a caliph and is named *Amīr al-Mu'minīn*, the dispensation of obligatory charity to him (as to a legitimate ruler) is permissible, be he pious or impious …"
>
> The imam becomes an imam by the allegiance of the people of authority and power (*qudra*) to him. Similarly, ʿUmar became the imam upon Abū Bakr's pledge to him only when they gave their allegiance to him and obeyed him. *If they had not accepted Abū Bakr's pledge and not given allegiance to ʿUmar, he would never have become an imam, regardless of whether this act of theirs would have been [religiously] permissible or impermissible.* For the permissibility or impermissibility is related to acts, as for the essence of rule (*wilāya*) or authority (*sulṭān*), it is strictly a matter of power and ability. *This power might be obtained by means that God and His Messenger love, as the Rightly Guided Caliphs did, or by sinful and disobedient means as oppressive rulers do.*[106]

This attention to power is what makes Ibn Taymiyya's thought essentially *political*. The ruler with whom one must reckon and with whom normative political thinking must be concerned is the one who has effective power. Put differently, the apparatus of theorization about government must be directed at the actual ruler, be he formally and religiously legitimate or illegitimate. Denying Abū Bakr's appointment of ʿUmar might have been religiously illegitimate for the people, but if they did so, ʿUmar simply could not have been a caliph. This is a clear indication of the distinction between formal and substantive legitimacy of government in Ibn Taymiyya's thought. This further indicates that Ibn Taymiyya does not deny the formal criteria that the Sunnis generally held, but is primarily interested in directing the attention of political thought toward reality and away from formalities, symbols, and images to which it had become addicted.

In conclusion, the same Taymiyyan iconoclasm that we observed in his epistemological and legal discourse is found in his treatment of the theory of the caliphate. He rejects the classical formulations of that theory that were grounded in particularities of *kalām* and historical contingencies, but tries to recover the normative guidance found in the *Sharīʿa* texts and the model of the early Muslim Community. To sum up, the following

106 *Minhāj*, 1:189–190 (emphasis added).

are the contentions that made Ibn Taymiyya's treatment of the caliphate distinct.

1. For Ibn Taymiyya, imamate is necessary both by revelation and reason; the two simply do not contradict. Because Ibn Taymiyya's epistemology is the same in pre- and postrevelation domains, whether the obligation of the caliphate belongs in theology, law, or politics does not affect his approach.
2. Because he saw the caliphate as a rational institution, its fulfillment needed to be evaluated on a rational basis; a symbolic caliph without power was no caliph at all, and neither religion nor reason has any basis for such an institution.
3. The caliphate is not an article of faith, contrary to the Shīʿī belief, but an obligatory means to facilitate the life of the Community guided by the *Sharīʿa*.
4. The Sunni tradition had established certain formal requirements for the caliphate to be legitimate on the basis of historical precedent and Prophetic *ḥadīth*; these requirements are clearly endorsed by Ibn Taymiyya. Yet, the *substantive requirements* for the office, namely the management of the Community's affairs by the rules of the *Sharīʿa*, are, in his view, essential (without which the claim of a pretender to power is invalid), whereas without the *formal requirements* the rule is lacking but legally tolerated. That is, rebellion is not allowed against a ruler lacking formal requisites but is valid against one lacking substantive requisites.
5. Ibn Taymiyya's view of Islamic legitimacy, based on the fulfillment of certain rational functions – commitment to the *Sharīʿa* – accepts compromise and gradation. The Prophetic Caliphate is an Islamic government that fulfills both substantive and formal requirements of legitimacy. In the domain of politics, Ibn Taymiyya recognizes the need for an ethic of compromise and accepting the lesser of two evils.

These commitments help explain Ibn Taymiyya's attitude of "principled pragmatism" in his political writings as well as his public life.

7

Conclusion

The first century or so of Islam can rightly be understood as the era of politics. Islam's nascent but triumphant community faced its many challenges with practical reason and missionary zeal. In the qur'anic ideal, the Community of Muslims was the center of this mission and their leader was a representative from their midst, not a king. In the Near Eastern imperial context, this Community-centered vision was remarkably and self-consciously distinct. In the rapidly expanding empire, this ideal quickly gave way to a series of accommodations, without, however, ever fully disappearing. When faced with the loss of the ideal, the pious froze the model of the Prophet and the early community in a Sunna-centered vision of Islam, whereas the rulers of the expansive empire came to approximate a ruler-centered vision of religio-political authority familiar to the ancient Near East. Although this political apparatus soon dissolved, giving rise to a multitude of provincial dynasties by the fourth/tenth century, the civilization it had created adjusted to the new circumstances and thrived, preserved primarily by its ulama, the socioreligious leaders of Islam and keepers of Islamic law. The political thought of early Islam was first inscribed as orthodoxy by these legal minds in the context of intense theological polemics and political insecurities.

After the demise of the central caliphate, the predominant mood in the classical era was to live between memory and desire and accept the poverty of the present. Accepting that politics in reality was always "corrupt and corrupting" was concomitant with an ideal of politics that was so lofty that it could be fulfilled only in the distant past or messianic future. In the present, one lived with piety and law, seeking solace in one's family and religion, doing what God or one's kin and clients required. Compared to its early ideals, to use Samuel Huntington's metaphor, the Community lived a "U-shaped" life: If we plot loyalty versus scale of association, medieval Muslims relied on family, the nearest unit of association, and then identified with the worldwide Community of Muslims, the *umma*; political institutions that occupied the middle played little role in their life.[1] From law and education to commerce and trade, one's interaction with and reliance on government was minuscule; it was a government so small that it makes today's libertarian ideal seem like communism.

The classical intellectual mood, amid cultural efflorescence, intellectual consolidation, expanding horizons, and political tragedies, was predominantly one of synthesis, and the triumphs of this era were in the realm of scholastics and casuistry rather than collective projects such as conquest, administration, or social and political justice. The power of this intellectual and social world was such that it could assimilate waves after waves of invading armies. A typical Muslim scholar of classical Baghdad would have seen engagement with power as disdainful and ephemeral and the new nomadic conquerors as uncivilized, while also reverently cherishing a similar conquest as the Golden Age of Islam. The new invaders paid homage to the sanctity and usefulness of the keepers of Islam's tradition and law, but went about their business of ruling largely untouched by Islamic political ideals. The rulers and the ruled, like the two banks of a river, flowed together but seldom met. In reality, life without political responsibility proved to be a mirage, and the lack of mutual loyalty and shared norms between rulers and society led to constant internal dissention and disorder as well as feuds between petty principalities, leaving them vulnerable to further invasions. The Crusades and, in particular, the Mongol invasion threw into sharp relief the weakness of the classical arrangement. But the centuries-old classical world had lasted long enough to give its ideas and institutions an air of timelessness. The well-oiled intellectual apparatus had gone through enough cycles of thesis, antithesis, and synthesis to explain away any inconsistencies.

Elitism and even disdain for the commoner alongside sanctification of kingship were nothing new in the Near Eastern intellectual traditions. But in the religion of the "Unlettered Prophet" (Q, 7:157), which had been based in Community-centered ideals, action-oriented common sense, and qur'anic egalitarianism, the accommodation to elitism was far from easy.

[1] For this metaphor to describe Muslim societies, including contemporary ones, see S. Huntington, *Who Are We? The Challenges to America's National Identity* (Simon & Shuster, 2004), 16.

It was facilitated, among other factors, by a particular settlement between reason and revelation. Seen as potentially mutually contradictory, a settlement was worked out by dividing intellectual life into two turfs. Reason reigned supreme until it proved revelation's truth in theology, whereas revelation trumped reason in postrevelation life of law, ethics, and politics. This theological settlement engendered cynicism toward common sense and practical reason. The common believer's encounter with scripture, which had earlier on obstructed caliphal absolutism and challenged the caliphal aggrandizement for the first two centuries, now produced no worthwhile action or knowledge: the theologian knew God's nature, the jurist God's will, and the mystic God's secrets. The ruler could often claim God's shadow. The Community was left out in the sun.

Ibn Taymiyya posed a monumental challenge to the dominant classical setup in both intellectual and political domains. In contrast with both the rejectionist and the synthesizing tendencies in Sunnism toward disparate foreign rational systems, Ibn Taymiyya's approach was deconstructionist. In his reopening of the classical reason-revelation settlement, his explicit motive was to defend revelation against those who challenged it in the name of reason. In fact, however, reason stood to benefit equally, if not more, from this reconciliation. Natural human reason, he contended, had far more potential for recognizing truth and justice than classical Sunni theology had conceded. This subversion of elitism was particular suited for *ethico-political* as opposed to *legal* mode of reasoning, calculated to try to revive the political life of the Community.

Ibn Taymiyya's most significant contribution in this regard was his view of the basis of political rule in Islam. In an interpretation that was unprecedented yet appeared obvious, he grounded all political authority in the qur'anic arch-obligation of commanding right and forbidding wrong, an obligation that appears in the Qur'an as the mission of the entire Community. Any government necessarily commands and prohibits based on some standards of good; given that Islamic community is a community of true revelation, to follow *that* truth as the standard of command and prohibition in collective matters becomes a rational as well as revelational requirement.[2] His later interpreters were to ignore the radical implications of this idea and reduce his teachings to the familiar deployment of commanding and forbidding as the prerogative of the state alone. But his teaching, properly contextualized, had an altogether different tenor. If the justification of the state is based on an inalienable mission and prerogative

[2] MF 28:62–3 (*Ḥisba*).

of the Community, the state is justified primarily as a representative of the Community. Furthermore, if political authority is based on the practice of commanding and forbidding, the entire Community now becomes the site of political authority. It is not the Community that owes unqualified obedience and service to the Islamic state, but the state that derives its *raison d'être* from its fulfillment of the Community's mission. This justification of an Islamic state not only legitimizes political authority by offering it a realistic normative alternative to perpetual illegitimacy, but also – and more importantly – *politicizes* the Community. The rulers are neither infallible nor superior to the common believer and stand in need of advice and criticism themselves. Furthermore, the state is to be judged by its adherence to the *Sharīʿa* that the Community, in particular its ulama, uphold, and the *Sharīʿa* – the source of legal as well as political norms – not the ruler, is the ultimate object of loyalty. The ruler and the ruled become seamlessly connected through mutual advice and cooperation. The difference between the capacity and hence authority and responsibility of various members of the Community – the rulers, the ulama, and the commoners – is one of degree rather than essence.

These three (possibly overlapping) kinds of groups – the ulama, the rulers, and the common believers – constitute the agency in Ibn Taymiyya's sociopolitical vision of the Community. The ulama, the most important actors, are conceived of not as a social category or members of a particular legal profession, but as the carriers of the knowledge of the *Sharīʿa* and exemplars of its teachings; scholars of *fiqh*, *ḥadīth*, and spirituality all participated in interpreting the *Sharīʿa*, none having exclusive claim to its authority. The ulama are, in fact, warned against seeking ascendancy over others, as are the rulers (excepting the authority that flows from their roles). The commoners, although dependent on ulama for knowledge and rulers for protection, are not without agency of their own. Vis-à-vis the ulama, they have the right as well as responsibility to choose the righteous ones to follow, demand evidence if they are capable of judging it, and they are not bound to follow one single school or scholar. He famously advocated a liberal doctrine of *ijtihād* and limited the scope of *taqlīd*. Vis-à-vis the rulers, the rights of the commoners are even better protected, for they can reject a command if the ruler decrees a matter touching on religious law and has religious justification for it on the basis of the opinion of a credible scholar or school, but which goes against their own conviction.[3] When it comes to matters on which there

[3] Ibn Taymiyya, *Al-Mustadrak ʿalā Majmūʿ al-Fatāwa*, 3:205.

is legitimate religious disagreement, it would seem, the believer is entirely free to choose.

Accordingly, he divided rulings of the *Sharīʿa* into the core agreed on by the rightly guided Community (Sunnis, that is) and those on which legal schools disagreed. Not unlike Ibn al-Muqaffaʿ, he grounded the legitimacy of the state in its adherence to that agreed-on core. Entirely unlike Ibn al-Muqaffaʿ, however, he did not give the right of legislation in other matters to the caliph, but distributed it within the Community. The ulama get the lion's share, of course, but *ijtihād*, he taught, as had Ghazālī, is a divisible qualification, and professionals and experts in different fields are capable of making independent religious judgment in their own domains.

Political thinking and action require a measure of unity and a shared set of commitments. Johansen puts the matter perhaps too emphatically in saying that according to Ibn Taymiyya, "[i]n a state that commands the good and forbids the evil, the jurist does not have to defend any particular school doctrine."[4] The jurists' loyalty to their own traditions certainly ought not to come in the way of the welfare of the whole. There is no indication, however, that Ibn Taymiyya intended to eliminate the legal schools as they had developed, believing that legal differences of schools did not, in theory, jeopardize that unity. Once the *Sharīʿa* is expanded to include political and ethical considerations by expanding its reach beyond the formalist reasoning limited to specific texts, it becomes possible to create theoretical space for an Islamic political sphere in which authoritative Islamic reasoning could take place on the basis of the more general ethical principles expounded in the Qur'an.

The commonly agreed-on set of doctrines of the *Sharīʿa* that were beyond the purview of *madhhab* disputes provided the shared arena of concern and competence for all Muslims. In this setup, the ruler has a wider canvas for *siyāsa*, but if the Community's freedoms that his theory intimates – but does not elaborate on – are granted, the ruler's powers can be quite limited. But he simply did not think in terms of institutions; his sole concern was deconstruction. In this respect, there was a veritable void in Ibn Taymiyya's political thought. His ideas point in many new directions, but his immediate program made sense only in his medieval world. He could take for granted the ulama's hold over religious authority and the urgent need for the rulers' military support of Islam against foreign threats; his realism and deep involvement with the multitude of

[4] Johansen, "Signs," 186.

reformist contentions did not allow him to ask what seems to us to be the next set of questions emerging from his political ideas. And while his spiritual and legal ideas found a worthy successor, the illustrious Ibn Qayyim al-Jawziyya, his political ideas did not.

In fact, Ibn Taymiyya's thought was not political in any usual sense. He did not devote his best intellectual energies to writing explicitly political theories, imagining sustainable political systems, or self-consciously creating a new science of politics or history as Ibn Khaldūn was to do a generation later. Ibn Taymiyya's explicitly political works make only a modest fraction of his overall oeuvre. Nor did he demonstrate great political tact or ambition in his life – as a man without family or any discernable personal interests, he led a life of celibacy, highly unusual among Muslims – and was an unlikely man to personally understand political "interest" in the usual sense. Perhaps it was his lack of personal interest or ambition that made him identify his interests with those of the Community, and therefore create the possibility of the political by putting the Community at the heart of his concerns. Regardless of his motivations, the common thread through his conceptual innovations can be best described as the reinvigoration of ethico-political thought and action in Islam. That the political would be revived by a deeply religious impulse, we may note incidentally, is not an unfamiliar occurrence in history. In Wolin's view, for instance, what revived the sense of community in the politically moribund Roman Empire was the emergence of Christianity. Despite its otherworldly orientation and a deep unease with the political order, the new religion "put forward a new and powerful ideal of community which recalled men to life of meaningful participation."[5]

Against all odds, the Taymiyyan moment was a radically political one.

I have explored the impact of Ibn Taymiyya's theological and epistemological ideas on his contentions in law, ethics, and politics, but have not explored the historical impact of these ideas. Besides the scope of this study and my own limitation, there are reasons to decouple his contentions, which he made in conversation with the greatest minds of the classical world and hence can be appreciated first and foremost in that context, from the subsequent appropriations of his ideas, which deserve to be studied in their own right. In fact, this decoupling is called for in this case precisely because he had significant impact and elicited such strongly

[5] Wolin, 87–9.

polarized reactions that his own ideas have been at times remarkably disguised by posterity's appropriations. While focusing on the tradition in which Ibn Taymiyya wrote instead of on those who wrote for or against his, I hope I have provided a framework that will enable such new and much needed research in understanding the reception of his ideas through the centuries.

Intellectually, there is no better way to describe Ibn Taymiyya's project than as a continuation of the project the great Ashʿarīs, in particular Ghazālī and Rāzī, had left behind, namely harmonizing reason and revelation to provide a stable foundation for belief and action. In contrast with Ghazālī and Rāzī, however, whose synthetic impulse had taken them to the ends of the available philosophical systems of their day and back, his deconstructive project took this end as its point of departure.

To recall the clarion call of Wael Hallaq, the *Sharīʿa* is all but dead and unresuscitable, except if a legitimate modern polity devotes itself to reviving the legal core of the *Sharīʿa*. I have argued that the interdependence between law and politics that Hallaq deems necessary in reviving Islamic law had, in fact, always been present in Islamic history. Islam furnished a broad vision of life, which was in particular circumstances formulated as, at times forced into, bodies of law. Yet, Gibb has noted perceptively, in practice and outside of the attempts at formulation, "Muslim thought refuses to be bound by the outward formulae."[6] The relative roles of politics and law, of jurists, rulers, and spiritual leaders, and the configurations of law and politics and epistemology and ethics have all been negotiable, although some settlements have lasted longer than others. Limits of law as the predominant mode of normative Islamic thought have become clear at crucial junctures in Islamic history. The overlegalization of Islamic tradition has been opposed at such junctures not just by marginal or syncretic movements, but by mainstream jurists such as Ghazālī, in the name of a spiritual vision, and by traditionalists such as Ibn Taymiyya in an even more forceful way. The possibilities of Islam's authentic negotiation with modernity and the nation-state, however they are conceived (problematizing these constructs, while indispensable, has been beyond the scope of this study), cannot be exhausted unless Islamic history is seen as merely legal history. This recognition prompts us to rethink the familiar debate among medieval Muslim as well as modern scholars about the role of *ijtihād* and *taqlīd*, the two modes of reasoning that have often been understood in strictly legalistic sense. These debates

[6] Gibb, *Studies*, 149.

assume new dimensions if their meta-legal, political dimension is accentuated. Under the rubric of *ijtihād* and *taqlīd* were debated the very epistemological foundations of the law, its goals and relative location vis-à-vis the political and the spiritual domains.

The significance of Ibn Taymiyya's contribution, as it is clear by now, lies not in elaborating robust political institutions, but in making such thinking possible by deconstructing the doctrines and developments that had foreclosed the very possibility of political thinking. At the heart of Ibn Taymiyya's iconoclastic intervention in the Islamic legal and theological tradition was an epistemological optimism grounded in his innovative use of the qur'anic concept of *fiṭra*, which complemented and legitimated human reason and helped bridge the gap between reason and revelation. It is this reworking of *fiṭra* that made possible transgressing the inherited boundaries and imagining once again *al-siyāsa al-sharʿiyya*, Islamic politics.

Bibliography

Primary Source Abbreviations

Aḥkām Māwardī, *al-Aḥkām al-sulṭāniyya*
Dar'(S) Ibn Taymiyya, *Dar' taʿāruḍ al-ʿaql wa 'l-naql*
Iḥyā' Ghazālī, *Iḥyā ʿulūm al-dīn*
Iqtiṣād Ghazālī, *Al-Iqtiṣād fī'l-iʿtiqād*
JK *Al-Jāmiʿ al-kabīr li kutub al-turāth al-ʿarabī wa 'l-Islāmī*. Markaz al-Turāth. An electronic database of classical works in Arabic. Only those titles not available in print to me, and not critical to the present study, have been cited from JK alone.
Manṭiqiyyīn Ibn Taymiyya, *Kitāb al-radd ʿalā al-manṭiqiyyīn*
MF Ibn Taymiyya, *Majmūʿ fatāwa*
Minhāj Ibn Taymiyya, *Minhāj al-sunna*
Milal Sharastānī, *al-Milal wa 'l-niḥal*
MRK Ibn Taymiyya, *Majmūʿat al-rasā'il al-kubra*
Nubuwwāt Ibn Taymiyya, *K. al-nubuwwāt*
Ṭab. Ṭabarī, *Tarīkh*
Ṭuruq Ibn Qayyim al-Jawziyya, *al-Ṭuruq al-ḥukmiyya*

Journal Abbreviations

IJMES: International Journal of Middle East Studies
ILS: Islamic Law and Society
IRAN: Iran: Journal of the British Institute of Persian Studies
JAOS: Journal of the American Oriental Society
JIS: Journal of Islamic Studies
JNES: Journal of Near Eastern Studies
JSAI: Jerusalem Studies in Arabic and Islam
MW: The Muslim World
SI: Studia Islamica
SOAS: Bulletin of the School of Oriental and African Studies

Primary Sources

Abū Yūsuf, al-Qāḍī. *Kitāb al-kharāj.* Cairo: al-Maṭbaʿa al-Salafiyya, 1382.

ʿAsqalānī, Aḥmad Ibn Ḥajar al-. *Fatḥ al-bāri sharḥ ṣaḥīḥ al-Bukhārī.* Beirut: Dār al-Maʿrifa, 1379.

Ghazāl ī, Abū Ḥāmid al-. *Mīzān al-ʿamal.* Edited by Sulayman Dunya. Cairo: Dār al-Maʿārif, 1964.

al-Munqidh min al-ḍalāl. Edited by K. ʿIyāḍ and J. Ṣalība. Beirut: Dār al-Andalus, 1967.

Tahāfut al-falāsifa. The Incoherence of the Philosophers. A parallel English-Arabic translation by M. E. Marmura. Provo, UT: Brigham Young University Press, 1997.

Mishkāt al-anwār. The Niche of Lights. A parallel English-Arabic text translated and edited by David Buchman. Provo, UT: Brigham Young University Press, 1998.

Iḥyāʾ ʿulūm al-dīn. Edited by Sayyid ʿImran. 5 vols. al-Qāhira: Dār al-Ḥadīth, 1425/2004.

Al-Iqtiṣād fī ʾl-iʿtiqād. Edited by ʿAbd Allāh Muḥammad al-Khalīlī. Beirut: Dār al-Kutub al-ʿIlmiyya (Dar al-Kotob Al-ilmiya), 1424/2004.

Ghazālī, Abū Ḥāmid al-. *Iljām al-ʿawāmm ʿan ʿilm al-kalām.* Edited by Muḥammad al-Muʿtaṣim biʾllah al-Baghdādī. Beirut: Dār al-Kitāb al-ʿArabī, n.d.

Ibn ʿAbd al-H ādi. *Al-ʿUqūd al-durriyya fī manāqib Shaykh al-Islām Ibn Taymiyya.* JK.

Ibn al-Athīr, Abū al-Ḥasan ʿAlī. *Al-Kāmil fīʾl-taʾrīkh.* 10 vols. Edited by ʿAbd Allāh al-Qāḍi. Beirut: Dār al-Kutub al-ʿIlmiyya, 1415.

Ibn al-Farrāʾ, al-Qāḍī Abū Yaʿlā. *Al-ʿUdda fī uṣūl al-fiqh.* 3 vols. Edited by Aḥmad b. ʿAli, Beirut: Muʾassasat al-Risāla, 1980.

Ibn Kathīr, Ismāʿīl b. ʿUmar. *Al-Bidāya waʾl-nihāya.* Edited by ʿAlī Shīrī. N.p.: Dār Iḥyāʾ al-Turāth al-ʿArabī, 1408/1988.

Ibn Qayyim al-Jawziyya. *Madārij al-sālikīn fī manāzil iyyāka naʿbudu wa iyyāka nastaʿīn.* 3 vols. Edited by ʿImād ʿAmir. Cairo: Dār al-Ḥadīth, 1416/1996.

Al-Ṭuruq al-ḥukmiyya fī al-siyāsa al-sharʿiyya. Edited by Sayyid ʿImrān. Cairo: Dār al-Ḥadīth, 1423/2002.

Ibn Qutayba al-Dīnwarī (d. 276 AH). *Al-Imāma wa ʾl-siyāsa.* Edited by Khalil al-Manṣūr. Beirut: Dār al-Kutub al-ʿIlmiyya, 1418/1997.

Ibn Rushd. *Bidāyat al-mujtahid wa nihāyat al-muqtaṣid.* Trans. Imran A. K. Niyazee. Reading: Garnet Publishing, 2000.

Ibn Taymiyya. *Darʾ taʿāruḍ al-ʿaql wa ʾl-naql.* Edited by Muḥammad Rashād Sālim. 11 vols. Riyadh: Dār al-Kunūz al-Adabiyya, 1391/1971.

Majmūʿat al-rasāʾil al-kubrā. Vol. 2. Beirut: Dār Iḥyāʾ al-Turāth al-ʿArabī, 1392/1972.

Kitāb al-nubuwwāt. Edited by Muḥammad ʿAbd ʾl-Raḥmān ʿAwaḍ. Beirut: Dār al-Kitāb al-ʿArabī, 1411/1991.

Minhāj al-sunna al-nabawiyya fī naqḍ kalām al-Shīʿa wa ʾl-Qadariyya. Edited by Muḥammad Ayman al-Shabrāwī. 4 vols. (8 parts). Cairo: Dār al-Ḥadīth, 1425/2004.

Kitāb al-radd ʿalā al-manṭiqiyyīn. Beirut: Dār al-Maʿrifa, n.d.

Majmūʿ fatāwā Shaykh al-Islām Aḥmad b. Taymiyya. Edited by ʿAbd al-Raḥmān b. Muḥammad b. Qāsim and Muḥammad b. ʿAbd al-Raḥmān b. Muḥammad. 37 vols. Cairo: Dār al-Raḥma, n.d. (MF includes all of the writings in an earlier collection, *Majmū ʿāt al-rasā'il wa 'l-masā'il*. Edited by Muḥammad Rashīd Riḍa. 5 vols. Cairo: Maṭbaʿat al-Manār, 1341–49/1922–1930.)

Al-Mustadrak ʿalā Majmūʿ al-Fatāwa. Edited by Muḥammad b. ʿAbd al-Raḥm ān. 5 vols. N.p.: n.pub., 1418.

Kardarī, Al-. *Manāqib al-Imām al-Aʿẓam*. Hyderabad: Dā'irat al-Maʿārif, 1321.

Maḥmūd, ʿAbd al-Raḥmān Āl. *Mawqif Ibn Taymiyya min al-Ashāʿira*. Riyadh: Maktabat al-Rushd, n.d.

Maqrīzī Taqī al-Dīn al-. *Khiṭaṭ Maqrīziyya*. Dār al-Ṭabāʿa al-Miṣriyya, n.d.

Māwardī, Abū ' l-Ḥasan b. Ḥabīb al-. *Al-Aḥkām al-Sulṭāniyya*. Edited by Khalid A. al-ʿAlm ī. Beirut: Dār al-Kitāb al-ʿArabī, 1994.

Tashīl al-naẓar wa taʿjīl al-ẓafar fī akhlāq al-malik wa siyāsat al-mulk. Edited by Riḍwān al-Sayyid. Beirut: Dār al-ʿUlūm al-ʿArabiyya, 1987.

Muḥāsibī, al-Ḥārith b. al-Asad Al-. *al-ʿAql wa'l-fahm al-Qur'an*. JK.

Mā'iyat al-ʿaql. JK.

K. al-Kasb. Edited by Nūr Saʿ īd. Beirut: Dār al-Fikr al-Lubnānī, 1992.

Niẓām al-Mulk. *Siyāsat-nāma or Siyar al-mulūk*. Allahabad: Ram Narain Lal Arun Kumar Publishers, 1964.

Rāzī, Fakhr al-Dīn al-. *al-Tafsīr al-kabīr*. Beirut: Dār al-Kutub al-ʿIlmiyya, n.d.

Al-Arbaʿīn fī uṣūl al-dīn. Edited by Aḥmad Ḥijāzī al-Saqā. Cairo: Maktaba al-Kulliyyāt al-Azhariyya, n.d.

Al-Maṭālib al-ʿāliya min al-ʿilm al-ilāhī. Edited by Aḥmad Ḥijāzī al-Saq ā. 9 parts in 5 vols. Beirut: Dār al-Kitāb al-ʿArabī, 1407/1987.

Asās al-taqdīs fī ʿilm al-kalām. Cairo: Maṭbaʿa Muṣṭafā al-Bābī al-Ḥilbī, 1935.

Muḥaṣṣal afkār al-mutaqaddimīn wa 'l-muta'akhkhirīn. Edited by Tāhā ʿAbd 'l-Ra'ūf Saʿd. Cairo: Maktaba al-Kulliyyāt al-Azhariyya, n.d.

Riḍā, al-Sharīf al-. *Nahj al-Balāgha*. Edited by Muḥammad ʿAbduh. Cairo: Dār al-Ḥadīth, 2004.

Shahrastānī, Muḥammad b. ʿAbd al-Karīm al-. *al-Milal wa 'l-niḥal*. 2 vols. Edited by M. S. Kīlānī. Beirut: Dār al-Maʿrifa, 1404.

Shams, Muḥammad ʿAzīz wa ʿAlī b. Muhammad al-ʿImran . *al-Jāmiʿ li sīrat Shaykh al-Islām Ibn Taymiyyah*. Dar ʿĀlam al-Fawā'id, 1420/1999.

Shāṭibī, Abū Isḥāq Ibrāhīm Al-. *al-Iʿtiṣām*. Edited by Maḥmūd Ṭ. Ḥalb ī. Beirut: Dār al-Maʿrifa, 1420/2000.

Subkī, Tāj al-Dīn al-. *Ṭabaqāt al-shāfiʿiyya al-kubrā*. Edited by M. M. al-Ṭanāḥī and ʿA. M. al- Ḥilw. N.p.: Hijr li 'l-Ṭabāʿa wa 'l-Nashr wa 'l-Tawzīʿ, 1413.

Subkī, Tāj al-Dīn. *Ṭabaqāt al-shāfiʿiyya al-kubrā*. Cairo, 1323–4/1905–6.

Ṭabarī, Muḥammad b. Jarīr al-. *Tarīkh al-umam wa 'l-mulūk*, 5 vols. Dār al-Kutub al-ʿIlmiyya, 1407.

Jāmiʿ al-bayān fī ta'wīl al-qur'ān. 24 vols. Mu'assasa al-Risāla, 2000.

Secondary Sources

Abed, Shukri B. *Aristotelian Logic and the Arabic Language in AlFārābī*. SUNY, 1991.

Abou El Fadl, Khaled. *Rebellion and Violence in Islamic Law*. Cambridge University Press, 2001.

Abrahamov, Binyamin. "Ibn Taymiyya on the Agreement of Reason with Tradition." *MW* 82.3–4 (July–October 1992): 256–273.

"A Re-examination of Al-Ashʿarī's Theory of *kasb* According to *Kitāb al-lumaʿ*." *Journal of the Royal Asiatic Society* 2 (1989): 210–21.

Islamic Theology: Traditionalism and Rationalism. Edinburgh University Press, 1998.

AbūSulaymān, ʿAbdulḤamīd A. *Towards an Islamic Theory of International Relations: New Directions for Methodology and Thought*. 2nd rev. ed. The International Institute of Islamic Thought, 1993.

Adang, Camilla. "Islam as the Inborn Religion of Mankind: The Concept of *Fiṭra* in the Works of Ibn Ḥazm." *Al-Qantara* 21 (2000): 391–410.

Afsaruddin, Asma. *Excellence and Precedence: Medieval Islamic Discourse on Legitimate Leadership*. Brill, 2002.

"The Excellences of the Qur'an: Textual Sacrality and the Organization of Early Islamic Society." *JAOS* 122.1 (2002): 1–24.

Ahmed, Shahab. "Ibn Taymiyya and the Satanic Verses." *SI* 87 (1998): 67–124.

Ajhar, 'Abd al-Ḥakīm Al-. *Ibn Taymiyya wa isti'nāf al-qawl al-falsafī fī'l Islām*. Beirut: al-Markaz al-Thaqāfī al-ʿArabī, 2004.

Ali, Mohamed M. Yunis. *Medieval Islamic Pragmatics: Sunni Legal Theorists' Models of Textual Communication*. Routledge-Curzon, 2000.

Ali, Sayyid Rizwan. *Izz al-Din Al-Sulami*. New Delhi: Kitab Bhavan, 1898.

Amitai-Preiss, Reuven. *Mongols and Mamluks: The Mamluk-Ilkhānid War, 1260–1281*. Cambridge University Press, 1995.

Angelika Neuwirth. "Structure and the Emergence of Community." In *The Blackwell Companion to the Qur'an*, edited by Andrew Rippin. Blackwell Publishing, 2006.

Anjum, Ovamir. "Islam as a Discursive Tradition: Talal Asad and His Interlocutors." *Comparative Studies of South Asia, Africa and the Middle East* 27.3 (2007): 656–72.

"Sufism without Mysticism? Ibn Qayyim al-Jawziyya's Objectives in Madārij al-Sālikin." In *A Scholar in the Shadow: Essays in Legal and Theological Thought of Ibn Qayyim al-Jawziyya*, edited by Caterina Bori and Livnat Holtzman. Oriente Moderno 90.1, 2010.

"Cultural Memory of the Pious Ancestors (*Salaf*) in al-Ghazālī." Suppl. to *Numen* (issue on Cultural Memory, edited by Andrew Rippin), Brill, 2011 (forthcoming).

"Mystical Authority and Governmentality in Medieval Islam." In *Sufism and Society: Arrangements of the Mystical in the Muslim World, 1200–1800 C.E.*, edited by John J. Curry and Erik S. Ohlander. Routledge, 2011.

Ansari, Muhammad Abdul-Haqq. *Ibn Taymiyyah Expounds on Islam: Selected Writings of Shaykh Al-Islam Taqi Ad-Din Ibn Taymiyyah on Islamic Faith, Life, and Society*. Imam Muhammad b. Saud University, 2000.

Arabi, Oussama. "Contract Stipulations (*Shurût*) in Islamic Law: The Ottoman Majalla and Ibn Taymiyya." *IJMES* 30.1 (1998): 9–50.
Asad, Talal. *Genealogies of Religion: Discipline and Reasons of Power in Christianity and Islam*. Johns Hopkins University Press, 1993.
'Askar, Abdullah Al-. *Al-Yamāma in the Early Islamic Era*. Garnet Publishing, 2002.
'Aṭwān, Husayn. *Malāmiḥ min al-shūrā fī al-'aṣr al-umawiyy*. Dār al-Jīl, 1991.
Ayalon, David. "The Great Yāsa of Chingiz Khan: A Reexamination (Part C2). Al-Maqrīzī's Passage on the Yāsa under the Mamluks," *SI* 38 (1973): 107–56.
Azmeh, Aziz Al-. *Muslim Kingship: Power and the Sacred in Muslim, Christian and Pagan Polities*. I. B. Tauris, 1997.
Bambrough, Renford. *The Philosophy of Aristotle*. Signet, 1963.
Bell, J. N. *Love Theory in Later Ḥanbalite Islam*. SUNY Press, 1979.
Binder, Leonard. "al-Ghazālī's Theory of Government." *MW* 45 (1955): 233–40.
Blankinship, Khalid Yahya. *The End of the Jihad State : The Reign of Hisham Ibn Abd Al-Malik and the Collapse of the Umayyads*. SUNY Press, 1994.
Bosworth, C. E. "The Heritage of Rulership in Early Islamic Iran and the Search for Dynastic Connections with the Past." *Iranian Studies* 11.1 (1978): 7–34.
Islamic Dynasties. Clark Constable Ltd., 1980.
Bulliet, Richard W. *Islam: The View from the Edge*. Columbia University Press, 1994.
"Islamic Reform or 'Big Crunch'?" *Harvard Middle East and Islamic Review* 8 (2009): 7–18.
Butterworth, Charles E. "Prudence versus Legitimacy: The Persistent Theme in Islamic Political Thought." In *Islamic Resurgence in the Arab World*, edited by Ali E. Hillal Dessouki. Proeger, 1982.
Caterina Bori. *Ibn Taymiyya: una vita esemplare. Analisi delle fonti classiche della sua biografia*. Supplemento no. 1 alle Rivista degli Studi orientali, vol. LXXVI. Istituti editoriali e polignatici internazionali, 2003.
"A New Source for the Biography of Ibn Taymiyya." *BSOAS* 67 (2004): 321–48.
Chamberlain, Michael M. *Knowledge and Social Practice in Medieval Damascus, 1190–1350*. Cambridge University Press, 1994.
"Military Patronage States and the Political Economy of the Frontier, 1000–1250." In *A Companion to the History of the Middle East*, edited by Youssef Choueiri. Blackwell Publishing, 2005.
Cook, David. *Studies in Muslim Apocalyptic*. Darwin Press, 2003.
Cook, Michael A. *Commanding Right and Forbidding Wrong in Islamic Thought*. Cambridge University Press, 2000.
Cooperson, Michael. "Two Abbasid Trials: Aḥmad b. Ḥanbal and Ḥunayn Ibn Isḥāq." *Al-Qanṭara* 22 (2001): 375–93.
Al Ma'mun. Oneworld, 2005.
Coulson, Noel J. *Conflicts and Tensions in Islamic Jurisprudence*. University of Chicago Press, 1969.

A History of Islamic Law. Edinburgh University Press, 1964.

Crone, Patricia. *Slaves on Horses: The Evolution of the Islamic Polity*. Cambridge University Press, 1980.

God's Rule: Six Centuries of Medieval Islamic Political Thought. Columbia University Press, 2004.

Crone, Patricia and Martin Hinds. *God's Caliph: Religious Authority in the First Centuries of Islam*. Cambridge University Press, 1986.

Dallal, Ahmad. "Ghazālī and the Perils of Interpretation." Review of *Al-Ghazālī and the Ashʿarite School*, by Richard M. Frank. *JAOS* 122.4 (2002): 773–87.

Davidson, Herbert Alan. *AlFārābī, Avicenna, and Averroes on Intellect*. Oxford University Press, 1992.

Donner, Fred McGraw. *The Early Islamic Conquests*. Princeton University Press, 1981.

"The Formation of the Islamic State." *JAOS* 106.2 (1986): 283–296.

The History of al-Ṭabarī. Vol. X. SUNY Press, 1993.

Narratives of Islamic Origins: The Beginnings of Islamic Historical Writing. Darwin Press, 1998.

Donohue, John J. *The Buwayhid Dynasty in Iraq 334 H. Islamic History and Civilization*. Brill, 2003.

Dumayjī, ʿAbd Allāh b. ʿUmar b. Sulaymān Al-. *Al-Imāma al-ʿuẓmā ʿind ahl al-sunna wa 'l-jamāʿa*. Dār Ṭība, 1404/1987.

Duri, Abd al-Aziz. "Al-Zuhri: A Study in the Beginning of History Writing in Islam." *BSOAS* 19.1 (1957): 9–10.

The Rise of Historical Writing among the Arabs. Princeton University Press, 1983.

Emon, Anver. *Islamic Natural Law Theories*. Oxford University Press, 2010.

Estelle Whelan. "Forgotten Witness: Evidence for the Early Codification of the Qur'an." *JAOS* 118.1 (1998): 1–14.

Ezzati, A. *Islam and Natural Law*. Saqi Books, 2002.

Fakhry, Majid. "The Classical Arguments for the Existence of God." *MW* 47 (1957): 133–45.

Ethical Theories in Islam. 2nd ed. Brill, 1994.

Al-Fārābī, Founder of Islamic Neoplatonism: His Life, Works, and Influence. Oneworld Publications, 2002.

A History of Islamic Philosophy. 3rd ed. Columbia University Press, 2004.

Garcia-Arenal, Mercedes. *Messianism and Puritanical Reform*, trans. Martin Beagles. Brill, 2006.

Garden, Kenneth. "Al-Ghazālī's Contested Revival: *Iḥyā' ʿulūm al-dīn and Its Critics in Khorasan and the Maghreb*," PhD dissertation, University of Chicago, 2005.

Gibb, H. A. R. *Studies on the Civilization of Islam*. Beacon Press, 1962.

Goldziher, Ignaz. *Muslim Studies*. Aldine Pub. Co. 1973, 1966.

Griffel, Frank. "Al-Ghazālī's Concept of Prophecy: The Introduction of Avicennan Psychology Into Ashʿarite Theology." *Arabic Sciences and Philosophy* 14 (2004): 101–44.

"Taqlīd of the Philosophers. Al-Ghazālī's Initial Accusation in the Tahāfut." In *Insights into Arabic Literature and Islam: Ideas, Concepts, Modes of Portrayal*, edited by Sebastian Günther. Brill, 2005.

"Ibn Tūmart's Rational Proof for God's Existence and Unity, and His Connection to the Niẓāmiyya *Madrasa* in Baghdad." In *Los Almohades: problemas y perspectivas*, edited by Patrice Cressier, Maribel Fierro, and Luis Molina. 2 vols. Consejo Superior de Investigationes Científicas, 2005. Vol. 2.

"On Fakhr al-Din al-Rāzī's Life and the Patronage He Received." *JIS* 18 (2007): 313–44.

Al-Ghazālī's Philosophical Theology. Oxford University Press, 2009.

H. Q. Murad. "Ethico-Religious Ideas of 'Umar II." PhD Dissertation, McGill University, 1981.

Hallaq, Wael B. "Was the Gate of Ijtihād Closed?" *IJMES* 16.1 (1984): 3–41.

"Caliphs, Jurists and the Saljuqs in the Political Thought of Juwayni." *MW* 74.1 (1984): 26–41.

"Ibn Taymiyya on the Existence of God." *Acta Orientalia* (Copenhagen) 52 (1991): 49–69.

Ibn Taymiyya Against the Greek Logicians. Oxford University Press, 1993.

"Was al-Shafi'i the Master Architect of Islamic Jurisprudence?" *IJMES* 25 (1993): 587–605.

"Juristic Authority vs. State Power: The Legal Crises of Modern Islam." *Journal of Law and Religion* 19.2 (2003–4): 243–58.

"Can the Sharī'a be Restored?" In *Islamic Law and the Challenge of Modernity*, edited by Y. Haddad and B. Stowasser. Altamira Press, 2004.

Sharī'a. Cambridge University Press, 2009.

Haque, Serajul. "A Letter of Ibn Taymiyya to Abū 'l-Fidā'." *Documenta Islamica inedita* (1952): 155–61.

Hassan, Mona. "Modern Interpretations and Misinterpretations of a Medieval Scholar: Apprehending the Political Thought of Ibn Taymiyyah." In *Ibn Taymiyya and His Times*, edited by Y. Rapoport and S. Ahmed. Oxford University Press, 2010.

Heck, Paul. *The Construction of Knowledge in Islamic Civilization: Qudāma b. Ja'far and his Kitāb al-Kharāj wa ṣinā'at al-kitāba*. Brill, 2002.

Hess, Andrew C. "The Islamic Civilization and the Legend of Political Failure." *JNES* 44.1 (1985): 27–39.

Hibri, Tayeb El-. "The Reign of the Abbasid Caliph al-Ma'mun (811–833): The Quest for Power and the Crisis of Legitimacy." PhD Dissertation, Columbia University, 1994.

Hillenbrand, Carol. "Islamic Orthodoxy or Realpolitik? Al-Ghazālī's Views on Government." *IRAN* 26 (1988): 81–94.

Hodgson, Marshall G. S. *Rethinking World History: Essays on Europe, Islam, and World History*. Cambridge University Press, 1993.

The Venture of Islam: Conscience and History in a World Civilization. 3 vols. University of Chicago Press, 1974.

Hoover, Jon. *Ibn Taymiyya's Theodicy of Perpetual Optimism*. Brill, 2007.

Hourani, George. *Islamic Rationalism: The Ethics of 'Abd al-Jabbār*. Clarendon Press, 1971.

"Islamic and Non-Islamic Origins of Mu'tazilite Ethical Rationalism." *IJMES* 7 (1976): 59–87.

"A Revised Chronology of al-Ghazālī's Writings." *JAOS* 104.2 (1984): 289–302.

Reason and Tradition in Islamic Ethics. Cambridge University Press, 1985.

Humphreys, R. Stephen. *From Saladin to the Mongols: The Ayyubids of Damascus, 1193–1260*. SUNY Press, 1977.

Huntington, Samuel. *Who Are We?: The Challenges to America's National Identity*. Simon & Shuster, 2004.

Hurvitz, Nimrod. "Who Is the Accused? The Interrogation of Aḥmad Ibn Ḥanbal," *Al-Qanṭara* 22 (2001): 359–73.

Competing Texts: The Relationship between al-Māwardī's and Abū Yaʿlā's al-Aḥkām al-Sulṭāniyya. Occasional Publications 8, Harvard Law School, 2007.

Ibish, Yusuf. *The Political Doctrine of Al-Bāqillānī*. American University of Beirut, 1966.

Jackson, Sherman A. "Ibn Taymiyyah on Trial in Damascus." *Journal of Semitic Studies* (1994): 41–85.

Islamic Law and the State: The Constitutional Jurisprudence of Shihāb Al-Dīn Al-Qarāfī. E.J. Brill, 1996.

"The Alchemy of Domination? Some Ashʿarite Responses to Muʿtazilite Ethics." *IJMES* 31 (1999): 185–201.

The Boundaries of Theological Tolerance in Islam: Abū Ḥāmid al-Ghazālī's Fayṣal al-Tafriqa Bayna al-Islam wa al-Zandaqa. Oxford University Press, 2002.

Islam and the Blackamerican. Oxford University Press, 2005.

Islam and the Problem of Black Suffering. Oxford University Press, 2009.

Jaques, R. Kevin. *Authority, Conflict and the Transmission of Diversity in Medieval Islamic Law*. Brill, 2006.

Jeffery, A. "Ghevond's Text of the Correspondence between ʿUmar II and Leo III." *The Harvard Theological Review* 37.4 (1944): 269–332.

Johansen, Baber. *Contingency in a Sacred Law: Legal and Ethical Norms in the Muslim Fiqh*. Brill, 1998.

"Signs as Evidence: The Doctrine of Ibn Taymiyya (d. 1328) and Ibn Qayyim al-Jawziyya (d. 1351) on Proof." *ILS* 9.2 (2002):168–93.

"A Perfect Law in an Imperfect Society." In *The Law Applied: Contextualizing the Islamic Shariʿa*, edited by Peri Bearman, Wolfhart Heinrichs and Bernard Weiss. I. B. Tauris, 2008.

Julaynid, Muhammad al-Sayyid Al-. *Al-Imām Ibn Taymiyyah wa mawqifuhu min qaḍiyyat al-ta'wīl*. Cairo: al-Hay'a al-ʿĀmma li-Shu'ūn al-Maṭābiʿ al-Amiriyyah, 1973/1393.

Kennedy, Hugh. *The Prophet and the Age of the Caliphates: The Islamic Near East from the Sixth to the Eleventh Century*. Longman, 1986.

Kerr, Malcolm. *Islamic Reform*. University of California Press, 1966.

Khalidi, Tarif. *Arabic Historical Thought in the Classical Period*. Cambridge University Press, 1994.

Khalil, M. H. "Ibn Taymiyya on Reason and Revelation in Ethics." *Journal of Islamic Philosophy* 2 (2006): 103–32.

Khan, Qamar-ud-Din. *Al-Māwardī's Theory of the State*. Lahore: Bazm-i-Iqbal, 1960.

The Political Thought of Ibn Taymiyah. Islamic Research Institute, 1973.

Knysh, Alexander. *Islamic Mysticism: A Short History*. Brill, 2000.
Kūnākātā, Ḥasan. *al-Naẓariyya al-siyāsiyya ʿind Ibn Taymiyya*. Dār al-Akhillā', 1994 (based on a dissertation presented at the University of Cairo, Egypt).
Lambton, Ann K. S. *State and Government in Medieval Islam: An Introduction to the Study of Islamic Political Theory: The Jurists*. Oxford University Press, 1981.
Theory and Practice in Medieval Persian Government. Collected Studies Series. Variorum Reprints, 1980.
"The Dilemma of Government in Islamic Persia: the *Siyāsat-nāma* of Niẓam al-Mulk." *IRAN* 22 (1984): 55–66.
"Concepts of Authority in Persia: Eleventh to Nineteenth Centuries A.D." *IRAN* 26 (1988): 95–103.
Laoust, Henri. *Essai sur les doctrines sociales et politique de Taki-D-Din Ahmad b. Taymiya*. Imprimerie de l'Institute Francais D'Archeologie Oriental, 1939.
Lapidus, Ira M., "The Separation of State and Religion in the Development of Early Islamic Society." *IJMES* 6.4 (1975): 363–85.
"The Golden Age: The Political Concepts of Islam." *The Annals of the American Academy of Political and Social Science*, vol. 524, Political Islam (November 1992): 13–25.
A History of Islamic Societies. 2nd ed. Cambridge University Press, 2002.
Leaman, Oliver and S. H. Nasr. *History of Islamic Philosophy*. Routledge, 2001.
Lenn E. Goodman. *Avicenna*. Routledge, 1992.
Lewis, Bernard. *The Political Language of Islam*. University of Chicago Press, 1988.
Islam in History. 2nd ed. Open Court Publishing Company, 2001.
Little, Donald P. "The Historical and Historiographical Significance of the Detention of Ibn Taymiyya." *IJMES* 4.3 (1973): 311–27.
"Did Ibn Taymiyya Have a Screw Loose?" *SI* 41 (1975): 93–111.
Maḥmūd, ʿAbd al-Raḥmān b. Ṣāliḥ Al-. *Mawqif Shaykh al-Islam min al-Ashāʿira*. Al-Riyāḍ: Dār al-Rushd, 1415.
Makdisi, George. "Ashʿari and the Ashʿarites in Islamic Religious History." *SI* 17 (1962): 37–80.
"Ibn Taymīya: A Sūfī of the Qādiriya Order." *The American Journal of Arabic Studies* 1 (1973): 118–29.
"The Sunni Revival." In *Islamic Civilization, 950–1150*, edited by D. S. Richards. Oxford University Press, 1973.
"Hanbalite Islam." In *Studies on Islam*, edited and translated by Merlin Swartz. Oxford University Press, 1981.
"Authority in the Islamic Community." In *La notion d'autorite au Moyen Age: Islam, Byzance, Occident*, edited by George Makdisi. Presses Universitaire de France, 1982.
"The Guilds of Law in Medieval Legal History." *Zeitschrift fur Geschischte der Arabisch-Islamischen Wissenschaften* Band 1 (1984): 233–52.
Marlow, Louise. *Hierarchy and Egalitarianism in Islamic Thought*. Cambridge University Press, 2002.

Marmura, Michael. "Ghazālī and Ashʿarism Revisited." *Arabic Sciences and Philosophy* 12 (2002): 91–110.

Marsham, Andrew. *Rituals of Islamic Monarchy*. Edinburgh University Press, 2008

Masud, Muhammad Khalid, Brinkley Messick, and David Powers. *Islamic Legal Interpretation: Muftis and their Fatwas*. Harvard University Press, 1996.

Matroudi, Abdul Hakim I Al-. *The Hanbali School of Law and Ibn Taymiyyah: Conflict or Conciliation?* Routledge, 2006.

Mawdūdī. *Khilāfat-o-mulūkiyat*. New Delhi: Maktaba-e-Islāmī Publishers, 2001.

McNeill, William. *The Rise of the West: A History of the Human Community*. University of Chicago Press, 1963.

Melchert, Christopher. *The Formation of the Sunni Schools of Law, 9th–10th Centuries C.E.* Brill, 1997.

Review of *Religion and Politics under the Early Abbasids: The Emergence of the Proto-Sunni Elite*, by M. Q. Zaman. *ILS* 6.2 (1999): 272–75.

Memon, Muhammad Umar. *Ibn Taimīya's Struggle Against Popular Religion: With an Annotated Translations of His Kitāb Iqtiḍā' ṣirāṭ al-mustaqīm mukhālafat aṣḥāb al-jaḥīm*. Mouton, 1976.

Michel, Thomas. "Ibn Taymiyya's Sharḥ on the Futūḥ al-Ghayb of ʿAbd al-Qādir al-Jīlānī." *Hamdard Islamicus* 4.2 (1981): 3–12.

Michot, Yahya J. "Ibn Taymiyya on Astrology: Annotated Translation of Three Fatwas." *JIS* 11.2 (2000): 147–208.

"A Mamlūk Theologian's Commentary on Avicenna's *Risāla Aḍḥawiyya:* Being a Translation of a Part of the *Dar' al-Taʿāruḍ* of Ibn Taymiyya, With Introduction, Annotation, and Appendices." *JIS* 14 (2003): 149–203 (Part I) and 309–63 (Part II).

Muslims under Non-Muslim Rule: Ibn Taymiyya. Interface Publications, 2006.

Mikhail, Hanna. *Politics and Revelation: Māwardī and After*. Edinburgh University Press, 1995.

Mitha, Farouk. *Al-Ghazālī and the Ismailis: A Debate on Reason and Authority in Medieval Islam*. I. B. Tauris, 2002.

Morony, Michael. Review of *God's Caliph*, by Crone and Hinds. *JNES* 48.2 (1989): 135–6.

Mosca, Gaetano. *A Short History of Political Philosophy*. Crowell, 1972.

Mottahedeh, Roy P. and Ridwan al-Sayyid. "The Idea of the Jihad in Islam before the Crusades." In *The Crusades from the Perspective of Byzantium and the Muslim World*, edited by Angeliki E. Laiou and Roy P. Mottahedeh. Dumbarton Oaks, 2001.

Mottahedeh, Roy P. *Loyalty and Leadership in an Early Islamic Society*. Princeton University Press, 1980.

Motzki, Harald. *The Origins of Islamic Jurisprudence: Meccan Fiqh before the Classical Schools*. Trans. Marion H. Katz. E. J. Brill, 2002.

Murad, Hasan Qasim. "Ibn Taymiyya on Trial: A Narrative Account of his Miḥan." *Islamic Studies* 18 (1979): 1–32.

Najjar, Fahmi. *Al-ʿAql: Dirāsah ʿilmiyya muwaththaqa li-mafhūm al-ʿaql ʿinda Shaykh al-Islam Ibn Taymiyya*. Fahmi al-Najjar, 2004.
Nashshar, A. Al-. *Manāhij al-baḥth ʿind mufakkiriy al-Islam*, 4th ed. Dar al-Maʿārif, 1978.
Nawas, John A. "A Re-examination of Three Current Explanations for Al-Ma'mun's Introduction of the Mihna." *IJMES* 26 (1994): 625–9.
"The Miḥna of 218 A.H./833 A.D. Revisited: An Empirical Study." *JAOS* 116.4 (1996): 698–708.
Nizami, Khaliq A. "The Impact of Ibn Taimiyya on South Asia." *JIS* 1(1990): 129–49.
Oakley, Francis. *The Political Thought of Pierre d'Ailly: The Voluntarist Tradition*. Yale University Press, 1964.
Natural Law, Laws of Nature, Natural Rights: Continuity and Discontinuity in Histry of Ideas. Continuum International Publishing, 2005.
Oakshott, Michael. *Rationalism in Politics and Other Essays*. Basic Books Publishing, 1962.
Perho, Irmeli. "Man Chooses His Destiny: Ibn Qayyim al-Jawziyya's View on Predestination." *Islam and Christian-Muslim Relations* 12 (2001): 61–70.
Petry, Carl F. *The Civilian Elite of Cairo in the Later Middle Ages*. Princeton University Press, 1981.
Pocock, J. G. A. *The Machiavellian Moment: Florentine Political Thought and the Atlantic Republican Tradition*. Princeton University Press, 1975.
Popper, William. *Egypt and Syria under the Circassian Sultans: 1382–1468 A.D. Systematic Notes to Ibn Taghrī Birdī's Chronicles of Egypt*. University of California Press, 1955.
Qāḍī, Wadād al-. "The Term 'Khalīfa' in Early Exegetical Literature." *Die Welt Des Islams* 28.1 (1988): 392–411.
"The Earliest 'Nābiṭa' and the Paradigmatic 'Nawābiṭ'." *SI* 78 (1993): 27–61.
Rabīʿ, Muḥammad Maḥmūd. *The Political Theory of Ibn Khaldūn*. E. J. Brill, 1967.
Rahman, Fazlur. *Islam*. University of Chicago Press, 2002 (originally published in 1966).
Islam in the Modern World. Paine Lectures in Religion. Edited by Jitt Rait, 1984.
"The Principle of Shura and the Role of the Ummah in Islam." In *State Politics and Islam*, edited by Mumtaz Ahmad. American Trust Publications, 1986.
Revival and Reform in Islam. Oneworld Publications, 2000 (published posthumously).
Reinhart, A. Kevin. *Before Revelation: The Boundaries of Muslim Moral Thought*. SUNY Press, 1995.
Rippin, Andrew. Review of *God's Caliph*, by Patricia Crone and Martin Hinds. *SOAS* 51.2 (1988): 328–9.
Rosenthal, E. I. J. *Political Thought in Medieval Islam: An Introductory Outline*. Cambridge University Press, 1962 (first printed in 1958).
Rubin, Uri. "Prophets and Caliphs: The Biblical Foundations of the Umayyad Authority." In *Method and Theory in the Study of Islamic Origins*, edited by Herbert Berg. Brill, 2003.

Sadeghi, Behnam and Uwe Bergmann. "The Codex of a Companion of the Prophet and the Qur'ān of the Prophet." *Arabica* 57 (2010): 343–436.

Ṣāwī, Ṣalāḥ al-. *Jamā'at al-muslimīn: mafhūmuhā wa kayfiyyat luzūmihā fī wāqi'inā al-mu'āṣir*. Cairo: Dār al-Ṣafwa, 1413/1992.

Sayed, R. *Die Revolte des Ibn al-Ash'atth und die Koranleser*, Freiburg i.Br. 1977

Sayyid, Ridwan Al-. *Mafāhīm al-jamā'a fī al-Islām: dirāsa fī al-susyūlūjiyya al-tarīkhiyya li 'l-ijtimā' al-'arabī al-islāmī*. Dār al-Tanwīr, 1984.

Al-Umma wa 'l-jamā'a wa 'l-sulṭa. Dār al-Kitāb al-'Arabī, 1984.

Al-Jamā'a wa 'l-mujtama' wa 'l-dawla. Dār al-Kitāb al-'Arabī, 1997.

Schacht, Joseph. *An Introduction to Islamic Law*. Clarendon Press, 1966.

The Origins of Muhammadan Jurisprudence [Electronic Resource]. Corr. ed. Clarendon Press, 1967.

"Pre-Islamic Background and Early Development of Jurisprudence." In *Formation of Islamic Law*, edited by Wael Hallaq. Ashgate Publishing, 2004.

Shahin, Aram. "Arabian Political Thought in the Great Century of Change." PhD Dissertation, University of Chicago, 2009.

Shamsy, Ahmed El. "Rethinking *Taql īd in the Early Shāfi'ī School*." *JAOS* 128.1 (2008): 1–23.

Shihadeh, Ayman. "From al-Ghazālī to al-Rāzī: 6th/12th Century Developments in Muslim Philosophical Theology." *Arabic Sciences and Philosophy* 15 (2005): 141–79.

The Teleological Ethics of Fakhr al-Dīn al-Rāzī. Brill, 2006.

"The Mystic and the Sceptic in Fakhr al-Dīn al-Rāzī." In *Sufism and Theology*, edited by Ayman Shihadeh. Edinburgh University Press, 2007.

Sibley, Mulfrod Quickert. *Political Ideas and Ideologies: A History of Political Thought*. Harpercollins College Div., 1970.

Skinner, Quentin. "Surveying the Foundations: A Retrospect and Reassessment." In *Rethinking the Foundations of Modern Political Thought*. Cambridge University Press, 2006.

Stroumsa, Sarah. "The Beginnings of the Mu'tazila Reconsidered." *JSAI* 13 (1990): 265–93.

Swartz, Merlin L. *Studies on Islam*. Oxford University Press, 1981.

Tilman Nagel, *Rechtleitung und Kalifat*. Selbstverlag des Orientalischen Seminars der Universität, 1975.

Die Festung des Glaubens: Triumph und Scheitern des islamischen Rationalismus im 11. Jahrhundert. C. H. Beck, 1988.

Tsafrir, Nurit. *The History of an Islamic School of Law: The Early Spread of Hanafism*. Islamic Legal Studies Program, 2004.

Ullmann, Walter. *A History of Political Thought: The Middle Ages*. Penguin Books, 1965.

Unger, Roberto Mangabeira. *Knowledge and Politics*. The Free Press, 1984.

Van Ess, Josef. "Ibn Kullab und die Mihna." *Oriens* 18–19 (1965–6): 92–142.

"Scepticism in Islamic Religious Thought." In *God and Men in Contemporary Islamic Thought*, edited by Charles Malik. Syracuse University Press, 1972.

"Political Ideas in Early Islamic Religious Thought." *British Journal of Middle Eastern Studies* 28.2 (2001): 151–64.

Vasalou, Sophia. *Moral Agents and Their Deserts: The Character of Mu'tazilite Ethics*. Princeton University Press, 2008.

Vogel, Frank. *Islamic Law and Legal System: Studies of Saudi Arabia*. Brill, 2000.

Watson, Alan. *Nature of Law*. Edinburgh University Press, 1977.

Watt, W. Montgomery. *The Formative Period of Islamic Thought*. Edinburgh University Press, 1973.

Al-Ghazālī: The Muslim Intellectual. ABC International Group, 2002 (first edition published in 1953 as *The Faith and Practice of Al-Ghazālī*).

Wolin, Sheldon S. *Politics and Vision*, revised and expanded edition. Princeton University Press, 2004 (originally published in 1960).

Yücesoy, Hayrettin. *Messianic Beliefs and Imperial Politics in Medieval Islam: The 'Abbāsid Caliphate in the Early Ninth Century*. University of South Carolina, 2009.

Zaman, Muhammad Qasim. *Religion and Politics under the Early Abbasids: The Emergence of the Proto-Sunni Elite*. Brill, 1997.

Zarkān, Muḥammad Ṣāliḥ al-. *Fakhr al-Dīn al-Rāzī wa ārā'uh al-kalāmiyya wa 'l-falsafiyya*. Dār al-Fikr, n.d.

Index

Titles in the series (continued from page iii):

POPULAR CULTURE IN MEDIEVAL CAIRO *Boaz Shoshan*

EARLY PHILOSOPHICAL SHIISM: THE ISMAILI NEOPLATONISM OF ABŪ YA'QŪB AL-SIJISTĀNI *Paul E. Walker*

INDIAN MERCHANTS IN EURASIAN TRADE, 1600–1750 *Stephen Frederic Dale*

PALESTINIAN PEASANTS AND OTTOMAN OFFICIALS: RURAL ADMINISTRATION AROUND SIXTEENTH-CENTURY JERUSALEM *Amy Singer*

ARABIC HISTORICAL THOUGHT IN THE CLASSICAL PERIOD *Tarif Khalidi*

MONGOLS AND MAMLUKS: THE MAMLUK–ĪLKHĀNID WAR, 1260–1281 *Reuven Amitai-Preiss*

HIERARCHY AND EGALITARIANISM IN ISLAMIC THOUGHT *Louise Marlow*

THE POLITICS OF HOUSEHOLDS IN OTTOMAN EGYPT: THE RISE OF THE QAZDAĞLIS *Jane Hathaway*

COMMODITY AND EXCHANGE IN THE MONGOL EMPIRE: A CULTURAL HISTORY OF ISLAMIC TEXTILES *Thomas T. Allsen*

STATE AND PROVINCIAL SOCIETY IN THE OTTOMAN EMPIRE: MOSUL, 1540–1834 *Dina Rizk Khoury*

THE MAMLUKS IN EGYPTIAN POLITICS AND SOCIEITY *Thomas Philipp and Ulrich Haarmann(eds.)*

THE DELHI SULTANATE: A POLITICAL AND MILITARY HISTORY *Peter Jackson*

EUROPEAN AND ISLAMIC TRADE IN THE EARLY OTTOMAN STATE: THE MERCHANTS OF GENOA AND TURKEY *Kate Fleet*

REINTERPRETING ISLAMIC HISTORIOGRAPHY: HARUN AL-RASHID AND THE NARRATIVE OF THE 'ABBĀSID CALIPHATE *Tayeb El-Hibri*

THE OTTOMAN CITY BETWEEN EAST AND WEST: ALEPPO, IZMIR, AND ISTANBUL *Edhem Eldem, Daniel Goffman, and Bruce Masters*

A MONETARY HISTORY OF THE OTTOMAN EMPIRE *Sevket Pamuk*

THE POLITICS OF TRADE IN SAFAVID IRAN: SILK FOR SILVER, 1600–1730 *Rudolph P. Matthee*

THE IDEA OF IDOLATRY AND THE EMERGENCE OF ISLAM: FROM POLEMIC TO HISTORY *G. R. Hawting*

CLASSICAL ARABIC BIOGRAPHY: THE HEIRS OF THE PROPHETS IN THE AGE OF AL-MA'MŪN *Michael Cooperson*

EMPIRE AND ELITES AFTER THE MUSLIM CONQUEST: THE TRANSFORMATION OF NORTHERN MESOPOTAMIA *Chase F. Robinson*

POVERTY AND CHARITY IN MEDIEVAL ISLAM: MAMLUK EGYPT, 1250–1517 *Adam Sabra*

CHRISTIANS AND JEWS IN THE OTTOMAN ARAB WORLD: THE ROOTS OF SECTARIANISM *Bruce Masters*

CULTURE AND CONQUEST IN MONGOL EURASIA *Thomas T. Allsen*

REVIVAL AND REFORM IN ISLAM: THE LEGACY OF MUHAMMAD AL-SHAWKANI *Bernard Haykel*

TOLERANCE AND COERCION IN ISLAM: INTERFAITH RELATIONS IN THE MUSLIM TRADITION *Yohanan Friedmann*

GUNS FOR THE SULTAN: MILITARY POWER AND THE WEAPONS INDUSTRY IN THE OTTOMAN EMPIRE *Gábor Ágoston*

MARRIAGE, MONEY AND DIVORCE IN MEDIEVAL ISLAMIC SOCIETY *Yossef Rapoport*

THE EMPIRE OF THE QARA KHITAI IN EURASIAN HISTORY: BETWEEN CHINA AND THE ISLAMIC WORLD *Michal Biran*

DOMESTICITY AND POWER IN THE EARLY MUGHAL WORLD *Ruby Lal*

POWER, POLITICS AND RELIGION IN TIMURID IRAN *Beatrice Forbes Manz*

POSTAL SYSTEMS IN THE PRE-MODERN ISLAMIC WORLD *Adam J. Silverstein*

KINGSHIP AND IDEOLOGY IN THE ISLAMIC AND MONGOL WORLDS *Anne F. Broadbridge*

JUSTICE, PUNISHMENT, AND THE MEDIEVAL MUSLIM IMAGINATION *Christian Lange*

THE SHIITES OF LEBANON UNDER OTTOMAN RULE *Stefan Winter*

WOMEN AND SLAVERY IN THE LATE OTTOMAN EMPIRE *Madeline Zilfi*

THE SECOND OTTOMAN EMPIRE, POLITICAL AND SOCIAL TRANSFORMATION IN THE EARLY MODERN WORLD *Baki Tezcan*

NON-MULSIMS IN THE EARLY ISLAMIC EMPIRE: FROM SURRENDER TO COEXISTENCE *Milka Levy-Rubin*

THE LEGENDARY BIOGRAPHIES OF TAMERLANE: ISLAM AND HEROIC APOCRYPHA IN CENTRAL ASIA *Ron Sela*

RITUAL AND PIETY IN MEDIEVAL ISLAMIC LAW *Megan Reid*

THE ORIGINS OF THE SHI'A: IDENTITY, RITUAL, AND SACRED SPACE IN EIGHTH-CENTURY KUFA *Najam Haider*

Milton Keynes UK
Ingram Content Group UK Ltd.
UKHW022025300723
426060UK00032B/971

9 781107 687110